The Lost Tornado

First published in Scotland in 2015 by Jim Divine.

All similarities to actual characters —
living or dead — are purely coincidental.

Cover design: Jim Divine

www.TheLostTornado.com

The Lost Tornado
James Dean Divine

A massive thank you to Trish
my family & friends, for putting up with me.

TO JANICE & ANDY
HOPE YOU ENJOY

ACT ONE

As my brother John and I headed over the grass verge towards the big green door for the last time, I stopped, looked back at the house. Norman's mum, Celia, came out of the kitchen, ran down the two flights of stone stairs in a panic. 'Have you seen Norman?' She was crying, almost hysterical.

'No, why?' I asked, knowing fine well what was going on.

'Everybody's looking for him but there's just no sign.' She whimpered, the blue mascara she slapped onto her lashes framing her bloodshot eyes, was running down her cheeks, merging with the red lipstick she'd smeared all over her face. Made her look like a clown.

'He'll be in David's bedroom,' I said. 'I'm sure I heard David talking to someone earlier.'

She ran off frantically in that direction.

Mrs Mason – Celia's best friend, our foster mum – had made our lives an absolute misery, I was never sure how long we went away for but it always felt like an eternity. It might have been a month, maybe more, maybe less. We'd been sent there while our mum was having twins. Another two kids to add to the original eight. It was always John and me that were fostered out, as we were the eldest boys. At the time John was eight, I was nine. We'd been to some terrible places before. At the last place the last woman forced, and held my face into a plate of mince and onions because I refused to eat it, but this place beat that by a long shot.

Ever since we'd walked through the door of this big depressing house we'd been treated like scum. No sooner had we dropped our bags into the bedroom than we were summoned through to the living room. Mrs Mason sat there with a chair, two towels, a bucket of hot water, some kind of disinfectant and a steel comb.

'Right, you two, over here,' she said.

I sat down on the chair first, knowing what she was going to do;

The Lost Tornado

I'd been through the drill, had the horribly painful metal comb through my hair so often. Her three kids sat on the couch eating sweets, watching us, as if it was some kind of freak show. She poured the stinging chemical onto my head; it burned like hell, she then scraped the damn comb across my scalp, felt like she was creating furrows on my scalp. I stood up to run but she grabbed me, forced me back down.

'If you don't sit still while I get those nits I'll get Lloyd to come in and strap you to that chair.'

I had no idea who or what Lloyd was, but the thought of being strapped into a chair freaked me into submission. I was terrified, a nine-year-old kid being subjected to that kind of humiliation on the first day of a long fostering.

'I don't have nits.' I protested, but she wasn't interested in anything I had to say, a quick skelp across my lug let me know who was in charge.

Every time we were fostered out we were told, 'It'll be different this time. These foster parents really love kids.' It was always the same, they did love kids. Their own! They only happened to hate the ones they were being paid to look after.

John and I were only looking for a bit of happiness until we could return home, we never, ever, had any idea when we'd be going home. Mrs Mason's three were very spoilt. Seemed to have everything they wanted. Donna was ten; Abigail nine, and David was seven. We were warned not to play with or speak to them, if she caught us using any of their toys there'd be Hell to pay. We'd been taken down to register at St. John's school earlier, that was another upheaval, learning to make new friends quickly.

The kids turned out to be OK; they wanted to play with us and did so behind their mum's back.

A week or two later Abigail and I went to her bed to sleep together. Pure innocence on our part, we were snuggling up, happy warm, safe, until … The light went on, Mrs Mason went ballistic.

'What the fuck are you doing in bed with my wee girl?' She

bellowed.

What's the problem here? I thought to myself. It was the first time I'd seen anyone overreact and didn't understand what was happening.

'Abigail is only nine years old, what the fuck do you think you're doing to her, you monster?'

'We were only sleeping together, Mum,' she said. 'We weren't doing anything.'

'Yeah, we were only cuddling,' I said.

'You shut that trap of yours right now or you'll get my belt across your arse.'

I could see a redness in her eyes, the fury was palpable, I did not want to go there.

She put her hands on top of her head, began to wail like a banshee. As she was going through this disturbing scene she glanced over to the corner of the girls' bedroom, noticed that her other daughter's bed was bulkier than usual. She ran over and pulled back the covers. The first scream was trivial compared to her next one. John was lying in bed with her oldest daughter and her youngest son! She grabbed John by the hair, hauled him from the bed, dragged him into the hallway, kicked him up the arse he was sent flying back against the door and into our bedroom. A few seconds later she came back for me, dished out the same treatment. She banged the door shut, shouted through it.

'You two little bastards are out of here tomorrow. I knew it was a mistake agreeing to look after folk from Pilton.'

We walked back to our room in silence, where an uncomfortable, sleepless night was had. We got up for breakfast the next morning, dawdled through to the kitchen. She was at the table nattering with a posh looking woman wearing a flowery dress that seemed too big for her, who was smoking and sipping at her cuppa. As we appeared at the door they stopped talking. Her son, Norman, was hanging about, sucking an ice pole. He looked up, went to the fridge, took two ice poles out, walked towards us, handed them to John. They were snatched from his hand by Mrs Mason. She threw them back into the freezer and pointed at us.

'That's them, Celia,' she said to her friend. 'Little tramps.'

'Yes, they do look a bit scruffy,' the woman said as she sipped her drink, blowing smoke from the side of her mouth. 'I'm not sure I want you to look after my Norman if they are still here, Madge.'

'Don't worry,' she said, 'they won't be here that long. Trust me, as soon as Social Services can get them to somewhere more suitable they'll be out of here like shit off a shovel.' They both laughed.

'Make sure they are,' Celia said. 'I've heard things about these kinds of people.' She put a hand to the side of her face, covering her mouth, hoping we wouldn't hear her, whispered, 'Why do people have all of these children if they can't bring them up properly?'

I walked out of the room feeling utterly worthless.

We spent the whole day locked in our room, isolated from everyone. At eating times the snib on the door would be unlocked and we'd be handed a plate of food, then the door would close immediately. Later that night I heard the door being unlocked. We were ushered to a smaller room along the hallway by a man who I'd never seen before. I wondered if it was Lloyd, who strapped kids to chairs. He smelled of vinegar and wore a maroon cardigan with leather patches on the elbows. He never said a word, closed the door behind us, then I heard the key turn a few times. In the semi-darkness of the new room I could see there was a cot with a baby in it. It must have arrived while we were in quarantine. I looked in and saw a tot in a blue romper suit. As it lay there sleeping, I noted with interest that it was holding a rich tea biscuit in each hand. *They'll be mine later*, I thought, *as long as it stays asleep.*

Hours passed, my stomach was growling at me as I lay tossing and turning in the darkness. I got up as quietly as I could, made my way stealthily over to the cot. The biscuits were in bits, but the biggest chunks were still in the baby's hands, a bit soggy with its sweat but still edible. I reached over to pick up the bits that lay around its head, stuck some into my gob and chewed contentedly. I put some on the unit beside his bed for John to eat when he awoke. I went back for the big prize. As I leaned further into the cot I tried to loosen the baby's grip. As soon as I touched the biscuit, the baby let out an almighty roar. I shit myself, jumped into my bed and under the covers in a single bound.

The hall light went on, a very angry Mrs Mason came in; the man was with her. She had her nightgown on, but he was still dressed the same. She put the light on, John sat bolt upright in his bed. I could see from beneath my covers that he was bewildered, he sat there rubbing his eyes, blinking, looking around. She went over to the baby, picked it up, soothing it. She looked at the biscuits on the unit by the side of his bed, put the baby down and stormed over to John. She grabbed him by the hair, wrenched him from the bed.

'Can you little bastards not take a telling?' She said, hitting John repeatedly over the head with the baby's rattle. He was trying to protect himself, sobbing. I'd had enough. I jumped onto her back, grabbed the stupid rattle from her, threw it at the man and pulled her hair. The shock sent her haywire. She easily threw the two of us off, grabbed the baby and left the room, locking the door behind her. The man was still standing there, looking at us, fidgeting with something in his cardigan pocket. The door quickly opened and he was yanked outside.

'You two are history,' she said, locking the door again. By this time there was a commotion in the hall. It seemed everyone was up and about.

Again, we headed to bed with a flea in our ear.

Next morning, the sun was streaming in through the shutters on the window. I looked over to John's bed, I was glad that he was still sound asleep. We'd both had a rough time, but he was taking it a bit harder than me. All I wanted was for him to be happy. I sat up, looked towards the door; there was a black plastic bin liner lying inside it. I got up, had a rummage. Our clothes were crammed into it. I woke John up, we got dressed, tried the door handle and was relieved that it had been unlocked. We walked through to the kitchen where both women were sitting in their usual positions.

The Lost Tornado

'What do you think you're doing here?' Mrs Mason said.

'Getting something for breakfast?' I said.

'No way!' She said. 'There's somebody coming to pick you little bastards up soon. Get back to your room until you hear a knock at the door. I'll be glad to see the back of you, I hope I never set eyes on either of you again.'

'Well said, Madge,' said Celia.

We walked back to the room, hurt and hungry. There were biscuit crumbs all over the place, but too small to make any difference to the hunger we felt. We sat in silence for ages, John drawing a picture in the condensation on the window. After a little longer an idea popped into my head.

'Come on, John,' I said, 'let's get out of here, have a bit of fun.'

We sneaked out of the room through the window, headed to the play area. A few of the kids were on the swings and around the corner, under the fir tree, Norman, Celia's son, was playing alone in the sandpit.

'Hi, Norman,' I said. 'Fancy playing a game?'

He nodded his wee ginger head about twenty times.

An hour or so later our taxi pulled up outside; I could clearly hear it from behind the great stone wall.

'Right, Johnny boy,' I said, 'let's get out of this hole.' We climbed back into the room, I grabbed the black bin liner with our stuff in, then we scrambled back out of the window and strolled into the house through the front door. In a show of defiance we walked down the hallway, into the kitchen where everyone, including Lloyd, was in a panic.

'Where is he? Where is he?' They said. Norman's mum was breathless with panic and hysteria, I nudged John and we laughed as we headed out of the front door.

We were taking our last steps, heading for the door in the wall, and freedom. I took a detour to the sandpit, lifted the upside down yellow bucket that sat there and winked at Norman, his head was the only part of him sticking above the sand.

'Shhhh,' I whispered. 'You are definitely the best boy I've ever seen at hide and seek.'

He gave me a toothless smile, whispered, 'Mummy no gonnae find me.'

'No way, Norman,' I said. I placed the plastic bucket back over his head and tapped it gently.

I went back to where John stood, we looked back at the building we'd grown to hate. There were frantic silhouettes running all over the house. We both laughed, headed for the door. As we got there the handle turned and the door was opened by a big burly guy with a smile.

'Taxi for Divine?' The driver said, taking the bag from John.

I smiled in utter satisfaction as I slowly pulled the green door shut.

Chapter 1

I was freezing my bollocks off on a shitty night, in a shitty bed in a shitty dorm. Completely understood why they called it a scratcher, the 1940s army issue blanket was itching me up something chronic. I'd been lying awake for the past twenty minutes figuring out what to do about the pish that was threatening to burst me in two. My bladder had reached maximum capacity, I was moving every couple of seconds, trying to find a bit more space in it, there was no way I was going to the bog. For a start, it was a long way away, it was outside, plus there were no lights and, to make matters worse, the ghost could still be out there. I knew that pissing the bed was not an option, but I was rapidly running out of ideas. I lifted my head from beneath the covers, looked around the dark room, illuminated only by the light of a full moon flooding in from the skylight window. Not a movement. All I could see were plumes of condensation coming from the mouths of the gadges lying in the freezing cold beds. I took a deep breath and sat up. I was getting really close to the moment of no return. I put my hand under the cover, inside my green tracky bottoms, held my willie to try to keep the pish in. The pain receded for a minute or two, but then the waves of pressure on my bladder returned with a vengeance. I reckoned I'd got about a minute to evacuate the bed and deliver the payload somewhere.

A memory from earlier in the day came back to me like a film clip or some dream-like vision. I'd overheard Speccy telling one of the kids that he'd stopped pissing the bed, that was why he'd been allowed to come to camp for the first time in ages. He'd been before but the students would not allow him to come back until he'd managed to control his 'negative dreaming body'. 'Fuck knows what they were on about but my old man told me if I pissed the bed again he'd wire the fuckin mattress up tae the mains! That would teach me. It worked though. Not a dribble has passed in the night since.'

I was on the case like an Aberdonian at a pour out.

I made my cautious way across the six big, grey, metal bunk beds to where I thought Speccy was lying. The beds were all locked together, as I stepped onto the first one it made a low range, metal on metal snapping sound, as my weight pushed the metal frame and springs into their lock position. I cursed quietly at those idiots, the students who'd put them up for us. I stood stock still to see if anybody had moved; by then I was gripping my knob as hard as I could to keep the pish as far back as possible in the tube. That dunt seemed to have made it leak a bit, a dark spot on the front of my tracky that told me the situation had moved from red to imminent. Thankfully the noise and clattering made no difference, not a soul had flinched. I got all the way to the last bed before I saw the mass of brown sticky up hair that looked like it hadn't been washed for weeks and finally, thank Christ, found Speccy.

I almost emptied my bladder as I stifled a laugh with my clean hand. The silly twat still had his glasses on. I let go of my willie, pulled it out, there was a bit of sprinkling and spraying as I struggled to pull the wee felly over the tight elastic welt of the tracky. I realised I was shaking, but wasn't sure if it was the fear of the ghost, getting caught, or the freezing air. As I was pissing a big black patch was forming on his blanket, a puddle was forming. I was getting more alarmed as the pish kept coming. It was beginning to make a noise, as if I was peeing on cardboard. I couldn't believe it, his glasses were steaming up. I wanted to piss myself laughing, but I was too busy pissing on him. After what seemed like an hour my pish ran to a dribble, I gave the wee felly a shake then whipped him into my tracky bottoms. I decided to climb down the end of Speccy's kip and make my way back to my bed over the floor rather than risk waking anybody as I clambered across those dodgy beds again.

As I was walking back I could feel dribbles running down my leg getting into the cut I got earlier on from the barbed wire. It was the least of my worries; my priority was getting back under the covers as soon as possible, leaving not one iota of evidence to what I'd done. I trod very carefully because of the slippy lino on the floor.

As I pulled the covers over my head I could feel my heart thumping like a greyhound on a rabbit track, but I was lying there, warm and content. It was only when I was about to nod off that I realised how big a risk I'd actually taken. I checked around the room to make sure that I hadn't been seen. It was still silent. I looked over to Speccy's bed, there was a massive plume of condensation rising from his midriff. I sniggered, put my head back under the covers, drifted off to a nicer place.

'Fuck you aw, it wisnae me, ya poofy bastards.'

I was rudely awakened by shouting.

'So are you suggesting, Alex, that someone other than you did this?' The posh English voice of Graeme, the head student said.

'Aye, I fuckin well am. I told you aw I hadnae pissed the bed for yonks. Do you think I wouldnae have felt it? Do you think I wouldnae have got up and gone to the bog?'

'Maybe you were scared of the ghost,' Graeme said, sneering.

'Fuck you, ya posh twat,' Speccy said, as he walked over to the sink, his towel over his shoulder. He started the tap running and proceeded to take his sodden pyjama bottoms off. He got a handful of cold, soapy water to wash the piss off himself. Graeme was standing next to him, watching.

'What the fuck are you lookin at, ya fuckin homo? Want to see my dick?'

'Come on, Alex, there's no need for that kind of language. The other boys don't want to hear that language. Why don't I let you cool your jets a bit and we'll discuss this after breakfast?'

'Cool my jets? Are you havin a laugh? When have you ever heard of somebody pishing the bed and it's wetter on the ootside than the inside, eh?'

'It's the cold atmosphere in here; obviously it's seeped to the top.'

'Seeped to the top? You ARE jokin? How could it? I sleep fuckin face doon, if it was gaun to seep anywhere it would have seeped ontae the radge beneath ays.'

Graeme walked closer to try to pacify him, attempted to put a caring arm around his shoulder.

'I completely understand your frustration and disappointment, Alex, but everyone makes mistakes.'

'Get off me, ya poof, I fuckin telt ye, it wisnae me.' He got a handful of the cold, soapy water that he'd washed his cock with, threw it at the student; it splashed in his face some went into his mouth.

Graeme spluttered, horrified. 'Right, that's it, you stupid boy, you're out of here as soon as the next bus comes,' he said, wiping the foam from his mouth.

'Big fucks, it's shite anyway,' Speccy said, throwing handfuls of water and eventually a bar of carbolic soap at the departing student.

As I jumped down from the top bunk I noticed faded salty footprints that ended up at my bed. *Shit*, I thought; my socks must've been wet from the pish on Speccy's bed, I'd trailed it over the red lino. I quickly slid back over all the marks in my socks, removing every trace. Thankfully nobody noticed. I stood there shaking my head. I looked around at the shitty room, the torrential rain outside tried to ignore the smell of piss coming from Speccy's bed. I sat on a chair at the table thinking about how I'd ended up here.

'C'mon, get yer stuff ready, the taxi'll be here soon.' Mum was getting four of her brood ready for the Council camp trip. I had only been told that we were going a day in advance. I suspected it would be a crap holiday and didn't want to go, but I had no choice. 'It's go with them or stay with yer granny for a week,' - it was a no-brainer.

'I'll go then! I said as I looked out of the window. From the corner of my eye I spotted this big orange spastic bus, it pulled up to the front door.

'That's the taxi,' Mum shouted.

'No way!' I said in horror, 'that's not a taxi, it's a spazzo bus.'

'Stop using that language, they're disabled and mentally handicapped not spastics. I don't want to hear you using that kind of language again,' Mum said to me.

The Lost Tornado

'OK, it's still not a taxi though.'

'It is, it's your taxi you're goin in it NOW! Get yer stuff together, why is it that you're always the last to get ready? Head full of nonsense, as usual.'

'I've changed my mind, Mum, I'll stay with Granny.'

'Too late, son, other arrangements've been made. Yer goin.'

'I cannae go into a spastic bus, Mum,' I said, almost crying, 'my pals'll see me.'

'I've told you before, stop calling it that,' she said, 'do you want yer faither's hand across yer cheek? Cause if you keep goin on, that's exactly what ye'll get.'

I was mortified. I waited as long as I could before having to get on board. I waited in the stair doorway until the very last possible moment. I could see some of the neighbours hanging about, I hoped they wouldn't see what had come to pick us up.

A big fat guy got out, walked towards the house. 'You're a shy little chap, aint ya?' The driver said, as he saw me hiding behind the stair door.

'Aye,' I said, 'painfully shy.' As I was talking my eyes were scanning in every direction, looking for any sign of movement on the street. I thought I spotted the curtains moving in the house opposite us, it gave me an idea. The fat twat had a big green parka on, one of those that went down to his knees.

'Can I hide under your coat, mister?'

'On you go, squire, as long as you don't make me look fatter than I am,' he said, laughing at his own joke.

I hid under the coat until I got close to the mongo mobile, I then tried to crawl in through the side door so's even the sneakiest curtain twitcher wouldn't see me. I thought I was clear when at the very last second that prick Andrews across the road got a peek at me through his curtains. He pointed at me, killing himself laughing. He then made mong actions, slapping the back of his wrist, sticking his tongue out of the side of his mouth. I was squirming, I knew he'd tell everybody in school about this. It was the end of my street cred.

John, Karen and Susan all sat smiling and waving to Mum and the other kids. I sat at the back of the bus, duffel coat hood up over my head, talking to nobody. After a couple of miles John, Karen and wee Susan were all joining in with *Ging Gang Goolie* and other shitty religious songs with a whole load of student pricks as the bus bounced along towards the countryside. I must've seen a hundred people doing the mong actions as we drove miles through the towns and villages, every one made me slink deeper into that duffel coat. Eventually we got to the farmhouse, I sensed that the good bit of the holiday had passed.

'I want to go home,' I said to the head student as soon as the bus stopped. I saw the muddy road leading up to a big decrepit building. It had been raining all the way up to Kinross, even though we'd stopped for a chippy, which lifted my spirits for about ten minutes, I knew this was going to get worse.

'No way, no can do, kiddo,' he said. 'You'll love it. All the kids love it.' He patted me on the head, winked at me, made a kind of camera shutter noise with the side of his mouth. I knew there was no point in arguing so I grabbed the plastic bag with my clothes in it, walked to the front door, tracky bottoms and trainers already covered in wet slimy mud and cow shit.

When I got to the big front door there was this big Speccy boy holding it open for me.

'Thanks.'

'Yous dinnae look too bad for mongs,' he said.

'We're no mongs, we're normal.'

'What you doin oan a spazzy bus then?'

'Don't know, it turned up at our house for us.'

'How many of you are there? Is that big lassie with the lippy and the red shoes yer sister?' He said, trying to tidy up his hair, straightening his glasses.

'Aye, but keep yer hands off her, and my wee sister as well.'

'Hud oan there, pal, I'm no into sugar daddy scenarios, likesay, I enjoy a bit of luvin with the opposite sex, I think the big yin thair could faw for my kind of patter.'

I walked away, saw him walking behind Karen. He saw me, gyrated his hips behind her, kidding on he was shagging her. He was winding me up and he knew it.

That night after dinner the students got us all to walk along to a graveyard; we didn't want to, but the twats locked the farmhouse door so's we had nowhere to go and had to follow them. They'd been scaring us all shitless with tales about the farmhouse being haunted, blood coming out of the taps, farmers shooting themselves in the barn and all that kind of thing that plays on your mind when you're a kid on your own at night. Pure evil if you ask me. We reached the graveyard on the stroke of midnight,

The Speccy twat was full of bravado.

'I ain't scared of no ghosts,' he was singing. He was at the head of the group, dancing his way up the road. 'C'mon, ya crappers, there's nae such thing as ghosts.'

When we got to the big rusty gates a few of the students shoved them open, scraping away the grass that had grown there.

'Go on then, in you go,' they said.

We stood and looked at them; there was no way I was going in there.

'Come on then, Alex,' said Graeme, 'thought you weren't fraid of no ghosts?'

Speccy's tune changed right there. 'Fuck that,' he said, 'it's dark, might trip over a gravestane, mess my hair up.'

'I reckon you're scared, might wet the bed later,' Graeme said, mocking him, nudging another of the students.

'Fuck off you, I told you no to mention that, it's in the past, I'm a man now. Anyway, there's fuck all to see in thair, only deid people.'

As we looked around to see what was going on, two ghostly shapes at the far end of the graveyard floated towards us. Speccy screamed like a big lassie and sprinted past everybody. The farmhouse was a good half mile down the road, all that could be seen was a big rag tag line of kids screaming and crying, trying to get back to the farmhouse as fast as they could, me amongst them trying to save myself. The ghosts were waving their arms still coming towards us. I dived under a barbed wire fence, ripped my brand new Hibs tracky bottoms; my leg was all cut on the inside but I didn't feel a thing. I scrambled through and eventually got to the door. Speccy had got there before everybody else and had run in, he locked the door behind him – you could hear him piling furniture up behind it. All the kids were banging on the door.

'Let us in Alex, please? The ghosts are comin!'

Muffled: 'Fuck that, no cunt's getting in here.'

Graeme was at the door pretending to be scared. 'Alex, what if the ghosts of the bloody, mutilated farmers are still in the farmhouse beside you?'

There was a scream, we could hear all the furniture getting thrown and dragged from behind the door, it unlocked and we bolted in. It was later that night I pissed on Speccy's bed; we'd barely been there six hours at that point.

Every night of the holiday from there on was crap, I made sure I went to the bog before I went to my kip.

The thing I was dreading most was the trip back home in the orange bus. I was thinking of a way to get out of it, maybe get a lift to the top of the road, get dropped off, say I had to go to the shops for a present for Mum. As it turned out it was dark when we got back to Pilton, I was sure nobody'd see us. I was glad that the bus pulled up right beside our house as the lamppost outside had been dark for months, so there was no chance of anybody seeing us.

As I was slinking out of the bus I saw Andrews' curtains twitch, a few seconds later he pulled them wide open, a big flood of light lit us all up. Next thing I knew, his Alsatian was jumping out of his window and he was shouting 'Achtung! Achtung!' He caused such a racket that a lot of other windows opened, it seemed like the whole street was looking at the Divines. With all of the shouting, the dog barking, and bairns crying it was like a scene from Colditz. I was definitely going to get that disabled limping shite back.

Chapter 2 - Andrews

Awww man, that was so funny, pissed myself laughin aw night, couldnae have planned it better. Aw they Gyppo Divines comin out o that spazzy bus, and aw the neighbours seein it tae. That smart cunt Jimmy thought he'd got off wi it, tryin to sneak oot, look on his face was priceless. I hate him. Think it's the way he always tries to come over as all angelic and that, when I know he's a schemin wee bastard. Glad I'd snaffled that big spotlight from Billy's room, shined it right ontae the trampy bastards. Do anythin to make him look stupid, I would. Cannae wait to tell the boys about this in the mornin...

'Mikey, get the fuck down here and get ready for school. And move that fuckin calliper of yours while you're at it, I nearly tripped over the bastard. Spilt fuckin tea down my peeny. What the fuck is it no on your leg for, anyway?'

'It's no on my leg because I'm no goin to school the day.'

'Fuckin right you are, I'm no havin that po-faced arsehole of a heidmaster of yours comin round here again. If I get the jail for you skivin I'll fuckin panel you before I go.'

Moanin auld tit. Should've kept my mooth shut, I'm defo no gaun to school, got a rondyvoo with the boys lined up this mornin so makes nae difference tae me if she gets jailed or no. Deserves it, meant to be my fuckin granny, right? Christ I could've gone up to the Ferry Boat on a Saturday night for better upbringing. I went upstairs, grabbed the fuckin metal and leather contraption from the spare room, pulled the damn thing ontae my gammy leg to pacify the auld cunt. I hobbled doonstairs, put on a sorty innocent face and went up to the auld boot. 'Can I have my wunch money, Gwanny?' I put oan the small boy petted lip act cos the stupid auld tit always falls for it.

'It's in my purse, I know exactly how much is there, so none of your smart stuff. An dinnae be touchin that fuckin joint that's in the poakit, it's for yer faither, I'm visitin him later on. D'ye want to come and see him?'

'Luv tae, but cannae. Got to go to school, remember? You gaun senile as well as incontinent?' I said, pointin to the wet marks on her smock. I knew I could rip into her cos I'd taken the fiver and the joint earlier, they were safely tucked away in my tail for later. I walked in to the kitchen, grabbed the two slices of warm, buttered toast from her plate, started to eat them. She raised her hand and tried to slap me around the heid but I was too quick for her ravaged auld excuse o a body. As I ran to the door she followed me, tripped over the bag of rubbish that was lying in the hall. I laughed at her lyin there, threw a half-empty tin of beans at her that had skited out of the black bin bag. Hit her smack on the bridge of her nose.

She knelt there in the muck, two hands coverin her beak, breathing heavily … muffled, pained … a bit of blood dripped down her fingers. She looked up at me all Arnie-like.

'Ya fuckin wee cripple, ye,' she said, as she tried to untangle herself from the shit and rubbish that she'd knocked out of the bag. 'I'll tell yer fuckin faither about this, boy, don't you worry about that.' She dabbed the damp peeny to her nose an it came away covered in blood. 'If you're not out of my sight in one second ye'll wish ye'd never been born.'

'Too late for that,' I said. 'Got to that conclusion on my first birthday, lookin aroond at aw you fuckin losers.' I slammed the door an realised I hadn't had enough of slaggin the auld boot. I'd still got too much energy. I opened the letterbox and sang...

'Irish jig, Irish jig, it's no real hair it's fluff on a pig.'

I knew she was so self-conscious about her hair that she'd wouldnae forgive me for a couple o days. But fuck it, if my plans went as I hoped, I wouldn't be back for a couple o days. As I put the letterbox down I felt somethin thuddin against the back of the door. Sounded like the bean can. I laughed at the pathetic attempt. 'Right,' I said, rubbin my hands together. 'The park, the boys, the gear, the burds. Here I come.'

As I headed down the road I turned back, I could hear her shoutin

The Lost Tornado

at me from the stair door, she'd got cat litter on her foreheid and somethin on her hands that she was tryin to wipe off ontae her blood and piss-stained grey smock.

'Dinnae bother comin back here, ya fuckin crippled little cunt, yer no worth the shite that a hope you slip on with yer fucked up legs. I'm getting the lock changed, so fuck you. Come back here and ye'll get my fuckin baseball bat wrapped round your fuckin thick heid.'

A few windows opened, I shouted back to her, in my poshest voice, 'Bye-bye, Grandmama, thanks for the send orf, I'll be back for supper at dusk. Ta-ta old girl,' I gave her the 'get it right up ye' salute. I walked away and saw that weirdo Divine at the bottom of the street. What the fuck was he doin? Looked like he was spewin. He threw somethin ontae the ground, cunt ran away when he saw me comin. I walked down to where he was standin, looked in the gutter, I couldnae believe it, the cunt'd been eatin dug biscuits. Fuck sake, I thought to myself, things must be tougher than I thought in that hoose. Still, it wisnae my problem. I lifted the bit o dry biscuit that he'd thrown away, stuck it in my pocket, hopin that I'd get the chance tae pull it out later in class and embarrass the cunt. More ammo for Mikey boy equals more misery for Divine.

By the time I'd got down to the park the adrenaline had sort o worn off a bit and I was feelin a bit guilty about slaggin that auld cow. Throwin the bean can wisnae pre-meditated so it didn't count in my book. I didn't realise it was half-full. Must have hurt the auld cunt like fuck, though. But maybe the Irish jig thing was gaun a bit too far. She'd had to live with alopecia since she was a wee lassie, couldnae have been easy, especially durin the war and that. I remember Billy and me used to ask her if she ever experienced any hair raids, went right over her head, so did the wig, right enough. We used to piss ourselves. Still, what's done's done, no goin back, as they say.

I'd been hangin around for about twenty minutes an still nobody'd turned up. After another twenty minutes I'd had enough. I headed for Woody's hoose to see where the fuck he was. By then it was almost eight o'clock, we should have been out of our tits. As I was walkin up the green painted wooden path to his hoose, I saw a light goin off in the upstairs bedroom. I walked up the three steps, got to the big black door, always thought it looked like it had been stolen fae Downin' Street or some posh fucker's residence. I hammered on the big round knob as hard as I could, waited for some noise on the other side. Nothin. Looked through the letterbox. Pure silence except for the big grandfather clock in the hall tick-tocking away. I hammered again, stood back onto the path an looked up to the bedroom, I think it was his mum and dad's room. The light goes on, I hear the footsteps of somebody comin down the stair. The door squeaked open an his mum's head appeared, she was standin there in her dressing goon, I was anglin myself to try and see flesh.

Her top lip had got a bit of sweat on it. I noticed that the ends of her blonde hair were darker than the rest, realised she'd been sweatin, heavily.

'Hi Michael,' she said, wantin me to get the fuck out of her sight in the next two seconds. *Looks like I'm no the only yin that's been hammerin on a big knob*, I thought to myself.

'Hi, Mrs Wood, is John there?'

She flicked her damp hair with her hand, swept a couple of loose hairs behind her ear, allowing the dressin goon to open slightly. I got an instant brickie when I realised she'd got nothin on underneath that silk kimono. I spotted her nipples standing to attention waiting for somebody to dial Radio Tokyo on them, my eyes couldnae move from them, I hoped she hadn't noticed.

'He left for school over an hour ago, should be there by now; anything else?' She said, shuttin the door in small percentages, hoping that I wouldn't notice until I was talkin to the black paintwork. I knew for a fact that she'd have liked to slam that big fuckin door in my puss and get back to whoever was bonin her upstairs. But I was in one of they moods, I'd never get a better chance to spy minge.

'No, no, nothin else, I said I'd be round to pick him up like, must've lost track of time. Sorry to disturb you and that,' I said, smilin, inadvertently lookin up in the direction of the bedroom. She knitted

The Lost Tornado

her eyebrows together, pursed her lips, took a deep breath; she probably thought I was too naive to know what was gaun on.

'You should see him if you head to school now. Goodbye, then, say hi to your Nan for me.'

'Will do, Mrs W,' I said. Like fuck I would. I said my cheerios and limped down the path backwards, still lookin at her. The only benefit I'd ever got from my fuckin gammy leg was that I could get a hard on in any situation, limp away, and naebody'd ken. I hung about awkwardly for another minute to see if there was any chance of getting a deek at her tits. She kent what I was after, stretched out to the top step to pick up two pints of milk, grabbin the collar of her kimono, makin sure that I saw fuck all. She stood there, the two pints of milk clutched tightly against her chest.

'Well, IS there anything else?' She shouted, getting really pissed off.

'No, nothin else, Mrs Wood.'

She slammed the door hard. I knew Johnny's house would be oaf limits for a while. I was starting to go all rush of blood to the head way realised that my erection had been there the whole time. This made me even more excited, I could feel my knob getting hot. I ducked behind the big bush on the path hopin to see her naked up in the bedroom window. All I saw was her head pokin around the curtain as she looked in all directions to make sure I'd got the fuck away. I was pissed off with myself cos I could feel that I'd actually chicken souped in my fuckin grollys.

I'd hadnae even seen anything. Fuck sake, man, what chance had I ever got of losin my virginity if I creamed my pants at the sight of a woman's head behind a door? Fuck sake, I was goin to have to address this. I felt dirty and sticky, it was only after nine in the mornin. As I made my way down the path to the gate, I realised that it was only fuckin Monday, I was a day early. 'Stupid bastard,' I said to myself. I said to the boys we'd meet Tuesday, must've been stayin up late watchin they fuckin Divine Gyppos that made me lose track of time. I laughed to myself again thinkin about that barry spotlight, lettin Max jump out the window to go after them.

I suppose I'd better go to the school as I knew two days off in a row would cause big trouble in little China. I reckoned I was probably one or two days from bein expelled. Not that I'd have minded that, of course, but if I got expelled the auld boy would go radio fuckin rental when he got out of the jail. Maggie and Billy got expelled, he was damn sure that at least one of his kids was goin to finish their education. He told me that in no uncertain terms the day he was dragged into the clink. What a fuckin role model he was.

I went up the back way to the school, along the railway bridge, down the big steep embankment. It took me to the back gates, which suited me just fine, nice and quiet, none of these nosey wee fuckin swotty cunts there to grass me up. As I got into the school grounds I could see that I was too early. I was hopin assembly would've started so's I could miss the beginnin, sneak in at the end, couldnae be bothered wi all that religious shite. I hung back a bit, behind the tuck shop, since there was no cunt around I lit up the spliff I stole fae dopey cow. I took a couple of drags on it, made sure I put it out without losin any strands and stuck it back in the bag. I unpeeled a couple of strips of Wrigley's spearmint, the sweet mintiness combined with the smoke tasted sound. I was feelin a bit happier, less concerned about things, I walked slowly along to the main block. As I was passin the registration class I shielded my eyes, looked intae the window. That fanny Divine was sittin in the room on his own, chewin away like he was eatin an elastic band. Probably was, poor cunt, what else can you chew tae get rid o the taste of a fuckin dug biscuit?

CHAPTER 3

I woke up with a jolt, realised I'd kicked Tigger off the end of the bed again. He looked at me like I'd insulted him. I'd been having the usual dream, scoring the winner for Hibs in the European cup final. I could hear the commentator:

'There's only two minutes to go, Paddy Stanton sends a beautiful diagonal ball soaring over the heads of the Real Madrid midfield, they're mesmerised by the artistry and precision of the pass, watching as it rockets over them with laser accuracy, it's instantly pillowed by the magical left foot of Ally MacLeod. Before the ball has time to touch the ground he threads it through the open legs of the right back, nutmegging him in a single continuous movement. The right back pummels the wet grass with his fists, realising what's coming next. MacLeod puts his studs on top of the ball, raises both arms into the air in pre-celebration, the nervous crowd at the green and white end of the stadium are frantically screaming, pass the ball, pass it, pass it. MacLeod is a maestro, though, he has never acknowledged the word pressure. He looks to the crowd, salutes and deftly chips the ball over the advancing goalkeeper's head.

'The keeper launches himself skywards, using the muscle power and agility that twelve years of training have furnished him with. He gets three centimetres of synthetic dimpled rubber fingertip onto the size five leather ball that's twisting, rolling towards its destiny, his intervention adjusts the trajectory by four degrees on the horizontal plane, he knows in his heart that he has not done enough. He knows without doubt that the dream of European glory for his team is, at least for this year, over. The ball bounces once, forcing grass and water upwards into the warm Spanish air, both elements dancing in exquisite abandon as the ball moves on to the next part of its journey.'

At that point in the dream, I always find myself in mid-air. I'm floating horizontally in slow motion, the white sleeves of the Hibs top acting like angel's wings. Hovering, I've got time to take everything in. I'm pulling my left foot back to finish the show, the ball and the path of my foot meet in perfect synchronicity.

The commentator is going mental.

'Divine has only gone and scored another wonder goal'.

The ball slams into the back of the onion bag, there's an explosion of rainwater as it hits the net, the crowd go ballistic.

A noise woke me up, I realised that the noise wasn't coming from the crowd, it was coming from my belly. I hadn't had anything to eat at all last night. I was too busy figuring out ways of making sure I wouldn't be seen by nosey, snidey eyes as I was sneaking off the mongo mobile. So much for that. Failed miserably! I really am going to get that crippled bastard back. Thought I'd escaped from Colditz with that spotlight and then his big Alsatian, Max, launching itself at us. I'm still embarrassed thinking about it and know I'm going to get the crap ripped out of me for yonks. I know fine he'll tell the whole school about it.

I lay there in my kip, looking up at the dark blue wood-chip on the ceiling, sort of admiring the way the yellow damp and red fungus were starting to create quite a nice pattern. I remembered seeing something like it in a programme about the Highlands of Mars. A couple of spiders were walking towards the big red plastic bag that had been sellotaped around the light bulb to stop the leaking toilet from upstairs getting into the electrics. I could hear them talking to each other.

'Come in, Ziggy, do you read me?'

'Loud and clear, Albert. I'm now heading for the red zone, conditions could be exceptionally hot.'

'Not a problem to us, Ziggy, we can survive a nuclear holocaust or an asteroid collision. I'm pretty sure that some red PVC with liquified boiled horses hooves will present very little in the way of a threat.'

The big spider seemed to have got its legs stuck in a loose bit of sellotape.

'May Day. May Day.'

'What's the problem, Ziggy?'

The Lost Tornado

'I've been caught in a trap, my main thrusters have been compromised, I think I'll have to jettison legs six and seven. Here goes … AAAARRGGHHHH, you fucker!'

'Come in, Ziggy… Ziggy, are you OK?'

'Jesus H Christ, that hurt like a bastard. I'll wait for this bleeding to stop, I should be fine when the legs grow back. How long does it normally take?'

'Do you want the good news or the bad news, Ziggy?'

'The good news, please, Albert, I'm in a dark place right now.'

'You're out of luck there, old boy, there's only bad news – two bits, in fact.'

'Eh?'

'Our legs. They don't grow back. That's a different type of spider you're thinking about. If I'm not mistaken, it's the Ganges Bird Eating Red Spider, found commonly in the upper region of the …'

'SHUT THE FUCK UP, YOU BORING BASTARD.'

'You what?'

'You heard me. Here I am, twenty-five per cent down on the old limb front, and you're prattling on about some fucking bird eating spider. So much for the 'we can survive a nuclear holocaust' pish. Are you saying that I have to go through the rest of my life with two wooden legs?'

'Sorry, old fruit, but it kind of looks that way.'

'What's the second bit of bad news?'

'They don't do prosthetics for spiders any more.'

'What?'

'Remember Arachna-Thetics – the company that produced them?'

'Yes, of course I do, they're based in Accrington, if I'm not mistaken.'

'Correct.'

'And?'

'They closed down two weeks ago, due to the recession.'

'Oh, well. Fuckit! AAAARRGGHHHH!'

'Ziggy, Ziggy, no? Can you hear me? Ziggy …?'

I was still looking at the ceiling, one of the spiders fell off. The cat, who'd been busy licking his bits and pieces, watched it as it plunged to the floor. He pounced on it. In a split second the poor thing had been delivered to St Peter's big pearly web. Tigger licked his lips, carried on cleaning his arse. I was lying there trying to think of an excuse, a reason that I could give to people at school when they asked me why I was on a spazzy bus. Nothing came. I lay there with my hands behind my head. Thinking. Scheming …

My stomach growled at me again, I got up. Rolled out of the kip onto the bare wooden floor. I stretched out, trying to ease my back. It was a bit tight after hiding behind the seats in the back of the bus on the journey home. I went into the kitchen, I was scraping at the bottom of the big silver pot with the porrage dregs in it, trying to get that wee bit more with the wooden spoon. I peeled all the dried stuff from the edges of the pot, scrunched it into a bundle and chewed it. The auld man called it 'oat jerky'. It was actually not that bad. I remembered my granddad saying that good porrage had to have the consistency and taste of an auld man's phlegm to be worth its salt.

'That way, son,' he said, 'it sticks to yer ribs, disnae let go for a couple of days.'

My stomach was still rumblin away, there was no sign of any grub. The cupboards were all empty. I pulled a chair over to the big corner cupboard, stood on the middle shelf. The Fablon that was peeling away stuck to my sock, I almost lost my balance and fell off. I felt my way to the back of the top cupboard, reached right back to the hole that was there. I knew the auld man sometimes hid stuff in there, but my hand only came out with an empty Ryvita wrapper. I checked it for crumbs but I'd no luck. Things had been hard on everybody, no jobs for Mum and Dad meant that we'd all got to compromise. The youngest were the first to get fed when there was any grub around, then it worked its way down to the bigger ones, unfortunately I was second from the top, so no grub for me again. You got used to it, though, the rumbling became more of an inconvenience than a hardship.

I'd discovered a way to get free sandwiches from my neighbours who lived on the top floor. Wee Jamesy was an only child, he always got what he wanted. I used to watch him shouting something up to his mum, it was a muffled, nasally whine that sounded like 'Mum Ungry Mum'.

A few minutes later a bag would fall from the skies and land in the back green with two sandwiches in it, sometimes a biscuit or crisps as well. I learned to mimic the noise he made, in no time I was getting free food from heaven. I used to hide in the stair right after I'd shouted in case his mum looked out, spotted the impostor. It all ended horribly one day when I made the noise, a bag dropped into the back garden, I went to pick up my haul, I looked into the bag it was full of old used teabags. I looked up, Jamesy's mum was hanging out of the window with Jamesy. I was rumbled.

'Right, Jimmy Divine, just you wait until I tell your mum about this,' she shouted.

It was good while it lasted. Mum laughed, said she was quite impressed with my ingenuity.

I knew I was going to have to face up to everybody at school and decided to head down there early to get it over with. As I left the house I spotted a bourbon biscuit lying on the big coconut welcome mat of the next-door neighbours. As I was about to bend down and pick it up, I spotted another biscuit, lying next to the mop and bucket at their door. *Ya beauty*. I stuck one in my tail for later, skipped out of the dark stair into the grey drizzly morning with a smile on my face. As I walked out I saw Andrews' curtains twitching. The twat must have some kind of alarm system that let him know when I'm coming out of the house. He opened the curtains of his bedroom, stood there with his arms folded, nodding at me. He was pointing his finger right at me, still nodding. I stuck the Vicky's up and mouthed the words 'fuck you'. He laughed. I could see from the look on his coupon that he was planning a day to remember. He'd waited a long time for this, but now he had enough ammunition on me to make me squirm like a slug on its way to Salt Lake City. As I began to walk away he knocked on the window, he was standing there rubbing his hands together and laughing. Started doing all that mongol stuff with his wrists again. I walked to the bottom of the road towards the school with a heavy pressure in my chest, then I realised that I'd still got the bourbon in my hand. I looked at it, took a big bite, hoping that the energy would get me through the next hour or two. I was walking backwards, looking at Andrews' house, wondering what his plan was, when out of the blue, I began to gag. I spat the biscuit out, looked at the remainder of the biscuit in my hand, sniffed it.

I could see that it was a bit soggy but there seemed to be nothing else out of place with it. It was the saltiness that made me gag, I was wondering why a chocolate bourbon tasted salty. I threw the rest of it into the gutter, took the other one out of my pocket. I sniffed this one, it seemed OK, I took a tiny bite from the edge, avoiding the chocolate filling. Again I spat it right out.

I looked closely at the marks on the bourbon, there was a indented picture of a dachshund with its tongue sticking out, tail wagging. A dog biscuit disguised as a bourbon! I looked again, saw that it said BourBoy, not Bourbon. I felt stupid and violated, rinsed my mouth out with some rainwater that I collected from some leaves in a garden. I could see Andrews limping down the street, so I made a rapid move to school. I wandered down the road, around a couple of corners to the big grey spiked metal gates of St David's, I could see that the padlock had been taken off which meant the Janny was in.

I walked through the quietness of the big empty school, took my shoes off and slid along the corridors in my socks. It was brilliant when they'd been freshly polished. I'd completely forgotten about everything and was in my own wee world until I heard a door slamming in the distance. I listened carefully and heard somebody marching at a fair rate of knots towards me. The echo and the squeakiness of the leather soles on the hard-polished orange lino frightened me a bit. I grabbed my shoes, hid in the doorway of a classroom until I could identify who it was. As the marching got closer I could tell it was the Frank the Janny. I stuck my head out.

'Awright, Jimmy son?' He said to me, rubbing the top of my head, messing my hair up a bit.

'Aye, no bad, Mr Corran,' I said, trying to be as upbeat as I could. I knew if he thought there was something wrong he'd be all over me like a rash, nice but a real nosy prick. Wanted to know everybody's business.

'What are you doin hidin there?'

'I'm no hidin, just slidin,' I said, getting up and making a Hawaii Five-0 surfboard movement. 'I'm in early.'

'No surprise there,' he said. 'D'ye want me to open yer classroom for ye?'

'That would be great, I can get on with my homework; never had time over the weekend.'

'Why no?' He said, raising an eyebrow, looking down over his glasses at me.

I realised I'd said too much already. 'I wisnae feeling too good.'

'You OK now?'

'I will be when a get this homework done.'

'Not a problemo, my man,' he said, as he took out a huge bundle of keys. He fumbled about a bit with them then popped a big silver one into the hole. 'Slam bam, thank you ma'am.'

He pulled the heavy door towards him, turned the handle, then stuck his head around the door to check that everything was alright. 'There you go,' he said, 'if you cannae be good, be consistent.'

I'd no idea what he meant.

He rubbed my hair again, marched along the corridor whistling, always the same tune: 'Tie a Yellow Ribbon round the old oak tree….'

The growl that began out as a minor irritation had now manifested into a yawning chasm in my gut. Felt like it'd got a life of its own, it was clawing at me to feed it. It was starting to hurt and I realised that I hadn't had a decent scran for a couple of days. My granddad always said that yer school-days were the best days of yer life. I sat at my desk with my head in my hands, propped up on my elbows, hoping that he was talking rubbish.

I looked at the brown cupboard in the corner, behind Mrs

McCluskey's desk. I knew that she kept all the sweeties there in a blue Roses tin. I also happened to know where she kept the key for the cupboard. I looked over to the old wooden table, sitting, thinking about the consequences of my actions should I go ahead with the plan.

As I was doing this my stomach lurched towards my throat, I knew I'd no option, I had to eat something, dinnertime was another lifetime away. I walked to the main door, looked all ways to make sure there was nobody about. I wandered back over to the table, pulled the key out. The knot holding the key looked pretty straightforward so I untied it. I was walking slowly over to the cupboard, still not sure if I should do it. I went to the door again, double-checked that all was clear, it was. I then took the big metal yardstick from the side of the teacher's desk and balanced it on the door handle. This would give me a couple of seconds of security if somebody came in unexpectedly. My heart was thumping as I turned the key in the cupboard, removed the big tin. I had my sleeves over my hands making sure that I'd leave no prints. I had to reach up and get the tin as she'd put it on the top shelf. As the lid popped open I grabbed a packet of Dolly Mixtures, opened them while still holding the tin, I ate them in two mouthfuls.

Oh man, that really hit the spot. Sugar, jelly, chewy, crunchy, you cannot beat that feeling in yer mouth. As I was gulping down the last bits I put my hand into the tin, grabbed a packet of cherry lips, stuck them in my pocket, put the tin back. I made sure everything was exactly in the right place, then did the same with the key.

As I was walking back I had an idea. I walked over to Andrews' desk, removed the inkwell from the top of it, placed the Dolly Mixtures packet into it. I put the inkwell back, squashed it down, went back to my desk. I took a jotter from my desk, opened it up to a blank page and poured the cherry lips onto it. They were delicious, not as filling as the DMs but they had a nice tang to them, a real chewiness that made your stomach realise that your jaws were trying to deliver some goodness and sustenance to it, hopefully keeping its pangs at bay. I scattered them around the page into a more aesthetically

The Lost Tornado

pleasing pattern than they currently were and drew around them as I was eating them one by one. Tons of nice crescent shapes, like wee moons in a lovely patterned sky on the lined paper.

As I placed the last one into my mouth I sat admiring the lovely pattern and thought I'd like wallpaper like that. I chewed on the last one, took a bit of time to pick the bits out of the cavities in my teeth. I picked the empty packet up, noticed there was still half a cherry lip stuck at the bottom. Again I walked over to Andrew's desk, opened the lid, stuck the packet away in the far corner, behind his comics. When I got back to my desk I realised the pattern I'd made on the paper could be evidence against me and ripped the page out carefully, went back to his desk, placed the page in one of his jotters. I was really enjoying myself, that spoilt brat had always got his own way, got anything he wanted. I hated him.

As I sat there I felt the familiar rumble, obviously two bags of sweeties weren't enough for the belly monster. I looked up at the clock, figured that I still had about five minutes until anybody arrived, normally the lassies came in before 8.45. I had to decide sharpish, knew it was a tough call, the closer I left it, the more chance of being caught. I ran over to the table, pulled the drawer open, fished out the key on the string, ran over to the cupboard, pulled out the tin and shit myself. It'd seemed heavy when I first took it down from the shelf but now it virtually floated. I opened it, noticed there were only two bags of sweets left. A packet of cherry lips and a bag of Squirrel Horn chewing nuts.

'Stuff it,' I said to myself, 'I've gone this far, it's going to make no difference.' I stuck the chewing nuts into my pocket, went through the drill of getting the key back into the drawer. I took the chewing nuts figuring they'd fill me up a bit better than the lips. I knew I only had a couple of minutes to finish them and hurriedly went about getting them into my gob as quickly as I could. I sat there savouring the lovely smooth chocolate and the hard toffee that eventually softens as the chewing action works its magic.

They were definitely doing the trick, I could virtually feel my stomach swell. I still couldn't hear any life in the school I leaned my chair against the desk behind me, stuck my hands behind my head and enjoyed the same sensation that I think cows have when they're chewing the cud. I only had about six nuts left and was contemplating whether I should eat the biggest one now or leave it till last when I heard the main school door getting scraped open. I almost fell backwards off the chair as I rushed to look out the window. I could hear the lassies getting closer, soon they were running along the corridor to the classroom. I chewed faster, and knew they were getting closer and closer. I was chewing as fast as I could, desperate to get rid of the evidence, chew, chew, the screaming and laughing getting closer, closer, until the ruler clanged to the floor.

The lassies screamed, wondering what the hell had happened, which gave me a few more seconds to finish chewing. My jaws were aching, they were almost seizing up, the jaw muscles were getting so tired. I was gulping and chewing harder than ever before in my life trying to find saliva from somewhere to help me get the sticky mass down my throat and into the safety of my belly.

Three of the lassies from the class, having recovered their composure, looked over and ignored me, as usual. I was still chewing, but doing it at the back of my mouth, trying to hide it from them. More folk arrived, I still had a couple of nuts to get through. I put my hand over my mouth to cover up the fact that I was chewing. I breathed a sigh of relief when I'd finished the final mouthful. 'That was a close one,' I said to myself. I stood up, spoke to a couple of my pals, who had come in behind the lassies. As I put my hand into my pocket I discovered there was still a nut there. It was the big one. As I realised this, the teacher walked in. *Shit. I'm a goner.* My fingers were still on the sweetie, I was too scared to move in case she noticed something.

I could feel it melting and knew the chocolate was spreading all over my fingers. I put my hand up to my hair, tried to discreetly scratch, I made a slick move, slipped the nut into my gob, licked the chocolate off my fingers without anybody noticing, realised I'd got

The Lost Tornado

a bit on my cheek. I wiped it with my sleeve then wiped my fingers on the inside of my jumper. As I was doing that, Andrews came into the room. He looked at me, did the mongo thing with his wrist, then took a bourbon biscuit from his pocket, waved it and smiled, raising his eyebrows as if to say I'm gonnae have fun with this, then he stuck it back in his pocket. I realised that he must have seen me at the bottom of the street and picked up the dug biscuit.

He was going to have fun later, no doubt. He sat down at his desk, I looked away from him as I chewed, ventriloquist-like, on the last bit of the sweet. Shit! In my determination to get rid of the last sweetie, I'd completely forgotten that I still had the chewing nut packet to deal with. I crushed it into a ball in my pocket but it was too big to conceal like that. I opened my desk, carefully folded it into a tiny square. I was about to launch it when the teacher banged her metal ruler on her desk.

'OK, everyone, stand up for registration,' she shouted.

I panicked, I knew what was coming, instinctively stuck the square packet up my left nostril; it seemed the obvious thing to do. I stood at my desk, waiting for my name to be called so as I could sit back down. I could feel the plastic bag slip up and down my nostril with every breath. I was sure somebody'd notice it as it felt pretty big. If it shot out my nostril everybody'd see it when it landed, covered in snotters, if I breathed too deeply it could go down my throat and I'd either choke or be sick, if I was sick, they'd see all the sweeties in a juicy puddle on the floor. I panicked, which was making my throat dry. I decided to breathe through my mouth.

'FLETCHER, CAROL.'

'Here, miss.'

'DOW, DAVID.'

'Here, miss.'

'DIVINE, JAMES.'

'Here, miss,' I replied in a nasally whine and sat down, relieved. We got through registration, Andrews was staring at me the whole time. I was about to ask to go to the toilet when the teacher pulled the gold star book from her drawer. I turned white as a sheet. I knew exactly what was coming. I wasn't expecting it so early on a Monday, but there you go. She banged the ruler again.

'OK, guys, quiet down, we're having gold stars early today as the school examiners are coming around later on.'

She went through her gold star book, said, 'I guess it's not really going to be a surprise to anyone, but the winner this week is …'

'Vivien Middleton,' the whole class said in unison. Swotty cow took it every week. The next bit was the bit I was dreading though. Every step Mrs McCluskey took towards the table drawers then the cupboard was in ultra slow motion to me. I was using every nanosecond I had to think of a way out of this. As she lifted the tin out of the cupboard her face fell a bit. She shook the tin, pulled open the lid, turned it upside down, a single packet of cherry lips floated feather-like onto her desk. As it hit the desk the sound echoed in my head, everybody in the class gasped. She threw the lid and tin onto the desk, making a loud crack, ensuring she had everybody's attention. She stood with her hands on her hips, then folded her arms.

'Explain,' she shouted. 'Who's the thief?'

I kid you not. Every single person in the class looked at Andrews.

'What the fuck are aw you lookin at?' He shouted.

'It wisnae me, miss,' he protested.

She put her palm face up towards him, stopped him in his tracks.

'Nobody's saying it was anyone, but we know we have a thief in our midst. I'll step out of the room for a minute, give the culprit a chance to own up, if they do there will only be minor punishment. When I return I want to see somebody standing on that spot there.' She drew a circle on the floor with a bit of white chalk and walked out, slamming the door.

True to her word, the door opened a minute later.

'I see,' she fumed. 'Nobody's going to own up? This will make things a bit more difficult. You leave me no choice but to get Mr Clark.' She stormed out of the room again. There was much muttering and finger pointing, mostly aimed at Andrews.

'Listen, ya bunch of cunts,' he said, standing on his chair, 'it wisnae fuckin me, right? If I get blamed for this I'll make yir lives fuckin hell on earth, so whae dun it? You better fuckin tell me or I swear I'll fuckin take you out one at a fuckin time and batter yer cunts in.'

Nobody moved or said anything. He got down, picked the chair up, headed towards me to sort me out.

'Andrews! Put that chair down this instant. I might have guessed you'd be involved here.' Mr Clark, the headmaster had been standing at the door for a few seconds, watching everything.

Andrews put the chair down, said, 'It wisnae me that stole the sweets.'

'How did you know what was stolen?'

'McCluskey went mental after pullin the sweetie tin fae the cupboard, what else is gonnae be in it, ya dick?' He said the last bit so's only we could hear.

'It's *Mrs* McCluskey, you ignoramus, and what was that last bit?'

'It was the sweet tin, sir.'

Mr Clark's temper seemed to lower a notch. He realised that even though he knew it was probably going to be Andrews, he needed evidence.

'OK. Mrs McCluskey gave you all fair notice: now empty your pockets onto your desks, leave everything that's in them on the desk. When you've done this you will each walk to the front of the class where we will check your pockets in case you've 'forgotten' to remove anything.'

The room was a hive of frantic activity. All I had was a plastic bag up my nostril that I hoped I could keep hidden for the next few minutes. I saw Andrews desperately trying to hide a plastic bag with something in it, looked like a fag. He took some chewing gum out his mouth, stuck it to the bag, then stuck it to the bottom of his desk. He noticed that the inkwell on his desk was sitting up slightly and lifted it. I was shitting myself. His face went pure white, as he lifted out the Dolly Mixtures bag, not quite sure what was going on.

He tried to press it down again, but only made it worse. He took it out, looked around to see that nobody was watching, then threw the packet under my desk. He winked at me, dragged his finger across his throat. He was looking pretty cool now, thought he'd cracked it.

'Sir, sir? Mikey Andrews threw something under Jimmy Divine's desk,' one of the new lassies shouted.

Andrews' head spun on his shoulders, he gave daggers to the lassie. 'Shut the fuck up,' he whispered. 'I'll fuckin kill you, ya hoor.'

'He said he was going to kill me, sir.'

By that time Clark was tearing his way towards Andrews, the calmness gone. It seemed like he'd wanted to do this for ages. He came over to my desk first, picked up the Dolly Mixtures packet.

'What's this?' He held it in the air. He'd finally got his evidence, he desperately wanted to kick this disruptive influence out of the school.

'Theft is not an acceptable trait here. School rule 7.36 states that any pupil found stealing, lying, swearing or playing truant will be subject to punishment at the headmaster's discretion. Did you throw those packets over here?'

'It wisnae me.'

'Yes it was.'

'Naw it wisnae.'

'Are you denying you threw those packets over here?'

'No. I did that, but I didnae steal the sweets.'

'A likely story; come with me.'

'I telt ye, it wisnae me, I'm no comin with ye.'

Clark grabbed Andrews by the hair, he was beelin, you could sense he wanted to batter the shite out of the crippled twat, but had to show restraint in front of the class. A fight started, nothing major, only a bit of grappling, then Andrews stumbled against the desk, the weight of his calliper knocked it pretty hard, the packet with the chewing gum fell onto the floor. Clark was onto it like a shot. He still had a grip of Andrews' hair. He let go, opened the bag. He put his beak to it, almost fell over when he smelled it.

'MY GOD, MY HOLY JESUS CHRIST! CALL THE POLICE, MRS McCLUSKEY, RIGHT NOW. THIS IS A DRUGS BUST.'

He pulled his belt out from the inside shoulder of his big black cloak, whacked Andrews right over the head.

'Ya fucker!' Andrews screamed.

His swearing made Clark even angrier, he began lashing out with the belt, Andrews was trying to stop him. His hands were all red with welts, he was trying to protect his head. Clarky's head was the same colour, bright red. The lassies in the class were starting to cry, but I was loving it. Another two teachers rushed in, the three of them restrained Andrews, then hauled him out of the class kicking and screaming.

'You're gonnae fuckin get it, Divine, I fuckin swear it, I'm gonnae fuckin kill you, ya schemin wee bastard.'

Teachers' hands were frantically clawing all over his mouth to try and stop the torrent of foul language; it got quieter as he was dragged further and further away down the corridor. I was shaking from the relief and the fear. I'd got away with it for now, but I knew fine I would be looking over my shoulder for the next wee while.

'Well, that was … interesting …' said Mrs McCluskey, looking for an appropriate word to describe what we'd all witnessed. 'Let's try to resume a bit of normality now. Put all of your belongings back into your pockets and get your science books out.'

'Miss,' I said, 'Michael's stuff is still on his desk.'

She walked up the aisle, bent down to lift the chewing gum. I'd noticed a fiver on his desk and jumped at the opportunity, stuck it in my tail and was delirious with possibilities.

She stood up, picked up the half-eaten dog biscuit. 'Some people have very strange eating habits,' she said as she lifted it into the air. The whole class erupted with laughter.

Andrews was expelled, told never to come back to St David's again. The euphoria of the close shave, having a fiver to spend, and the removal of that twat from the class was great, but I knew there would be a big price to pay.

For three days that bloody Squirrel Horn packet was stuck up my nose. Every time I tried to get it out, it'd squirm its way out of my grip, slide back up my nostril. I would sit for ages trying to grip it with my fingers but every time I just about got the bloody thing, it would slither away back up. I'd tried blowing it out by putting a finger over one nostril and blowing hard down the other, but that was too painful, I think the plastic was bonding with the snotters, forming a formidable partnership. On day four I decided that I'd had enough. This thing was coming out today, no matter what. So far I'd tried to blow it out using about level five of my blowing out strength and that hurt. I knew I'd have to go to level ten to remove it and wasn't looking forward to that in the slightest.

Preparation: one old towel, a roll of bog paper, three pillows, a big glass of water and a *Beano*.

I sat on the edge of the bed, took a few deep breaths. I got the towel lined up in front of me to catch the slug. Took a couple of tester breaths, felt it slide up and down my nostril. One, two, three, BlowingDoonMaNostrilAsHardAsICan … 'OooyaBastard!' I screamed as the thing flew down that channel. I heard a doomph as it landed somewhere and thanked the good lord for the release. *Apollo has landed.* I sat there trying to deal with the pain, felt like I'd had a twelve-inch burning poker thrust up my beak, rattled around for good measure. I looked around for the slug, saw it'd landed on the cat's back. It was sitting there looking at me. Next thing we both knew, a big dollop of congealed blood plopped out of my nose, straight on to the same spot on the cat's back. It shit itself and jumped off the bed.

I grabbed it and bent over to wipe it with the old towel, as I bent over, blood dripped from my nose onto the cat. It was freaking by this time. I tried to grab him, but he was out of the door and down the stair in double quick time. There were a few screams of 'the cat's bleeding', and 'call the vet'. My nose was still streaming with blood, so I lay down on my kip, put my head back. I picked up the loo roll, made a twisty rope shape, inserted it into my throbbing nostril. I winced as it went up, but I knew it had to be this way. I lay there for ages waiting for the blood to coagulate and let me get on with my life.

I must've lain on the bed for hours. I felt refreshed. I slowly and surely tipped my head in tiny movements from horizontal to vertical. Slowly, quietly, no blood. I switched the breathing from my mouth to my nose, found I could only breathe through one nostril.

WHOOSH!

Blood gushed down again, it seemed to be even worse this time. I knew this was serious and went downstairs. Mum was sitting having a cuppa and watching *Crossroads* on the telly.

'What's up with you?' She said, as she saw me at the living room door with the towel wrapped round my head. I removed a bit of it to show her the blood.

'Have you been pickin yer nose again?'

'No, honest Mum, it just started bleeding.'

'How long's it been bleeding?'

'An hour.'

'Have you tried putting yer head back?'

'Yip, it makes no difference.'

'Right, get yer coat, were off to the hospital.'

'Eh?' I said, not realising how serious it was. We walked up the road to the bus stop, me with the bloody towel wrapped round my head.

When we got to the hospital, an old nurse took us to a big room with a white ceramic sink, a big three legged stool sitting right in front of a mirror that ran the length of the wall.

'Right, Jimmy, I want you to sit on that stool with your mouth open as wide as you can at all times. Pinch both nostrils with your fingers as hard as you can, whatever you do, DON'T swallow, OK?'

I nodded. I sat there feeling like a right prat as she left the room. All I could see from where I was sitting was the clock in the mirror. My jaws were aching, my neck was getting stiff, but I did what she told me. By the time the clock had gone back two hours I heard the door opening, looked at the nurse in the mirror.

'I'm so sorry young man,' she said, putting her hands to cover her mouth. 'I forgot all about you; thankfully your mum reminded me. Let's see if it's stopped. You can take your fingers away now, but don't swallow. Not yet.' She handed me a glass of something, told me to swallow as hard as I could.

I had my first dry scream there and then. Felt like a slice of burnt toast with glass jam on it. I tried to breathe and couldn't, she handed me the same again, motioned for me to swallow, this time it was smooth, and cooling. It was only then that I noticed the nosebleed was gone, but my jaw was stuck wide open, I looked like a spaz. I tried to shut it by pushing my bottom jaw up with the palm of my hand but it didn't move.

'Don't worry about your jaw, son, it'll ease off in a few hours' time. Off you go.'

I felt a right prick on the way home. People were looking at me on the bus, I was just glad this hadn't happened before I got onto the mongo mobile. When I got back down the road Mum nipped into the shops for more milk. 'Do you want to chum me?' She asked.

I tried to say, 'No, I'll get back to the hoose and hide till the embarrassment goes away,' but came out with something like, 'Doon onae hoose.' She knew what I meant.

As I was heading down to the house I spotted Andrews at the very bottom of the street. I hadn't seen him since he was hoyed out of the classroom and to be honest I didn't want to see him. I knew I was going to get it. He spotted me at the same time. I made a desperate run for the house. It was difficult, I couldn't breathe properly as my jaw was stuck, there were slavers all over my coupon as I was trying to get to the stair door before him. I had a bit of luck; he didn't have his callipers on, he was always a bit slower, without them he walked like a robot, had to hold on to fences in order to stay upright. I got to my house about ten seconds before him, slammed the stair door in his face. There was no banging, no shouting, nothing. I got on my tiptoes, looked out of the glass panel at the top of the door. He was standing there looking at me. Breathing deeply. The silence frightened me, I realised I might have pushed him too far this time. As I walked into the house I put my hands in my pockets, there was a bit of paper there. I pulled it out, it was the fiver! I'd completely forgotten about it, what a bonus. I hid it in my wee secret tin for later.

Chapter 4 - Andrews

I'm gonnae fuckin kill him. Andrews said to Paul Jackson. They both sat on the pavement in the front street in the late evening, drinking from the same tin of Cally Special, Andrews was trying to put as little pressure on his bum cheeks as possible.

'Seriously, I am going to fucking kill that bastard. If he thinks he can humiliate and embarrass me in front of the whole class and get away with it, he's very much mistaken. I don't mind bein expelled, ah'll have to deal with the auld man on that one when he gets out of jail, but I've got time to think and plan for that. I was lucky that fudd Clarky shit himself, didn't bother with the pigs, I could've been in real trouble. I could see the auld loser turn white when I said I'd get Billy to sort him oot.

'Are you THREATENING me, Mr Andrews?' He said.

'I says, I'm no sayin anything other than if you get the pigs involved and I get done for possession, Billy'll have somethin to say about it, that's all. And he knows where you stay.

'That good for nothing thug doesn't hold any fear for me, boy', he said, but I could see he was shitein it after what Billy did to his assistant two years ago.

'Where did he take you after he hauled you out of the class?' Jackson said.

'I was still in Clarky's office, had been gettin interrogated for the past hour, was about to protest my innocence for the umpteenth time, when the door barged open and in walks McCluskey.

'Yes, Jean, how can I help you?' Clarky said to her 'Aw fuckin soppy like'.

'She says, 'I was clearing out his desk, as per your request, sir, when I found these.' She held up my jotters and a crumpled bit of plastic. 'This was hidden in the far corner,' she said as she unravelled and flattened it oot.

'A fuckin Squirrel Horn Cherry Lips plastic bag. She then opened up one of the jotters, took a sheet of paper out of it with scribbles of crescent moons on it, held it up to him'.

'Well?' Said Clarky. 'No ambiguity there. It seems that you prefer moons to gold stars. Not that you ever had a chance to get one of those, of course.' He smirked, winked at that boot McCluskey.

'It wisnae me, I said one more time.

'Thanks Jean, that'll be all for now,' he said. McCluskey left the room. I thought my head was gonnae explode. I know that cunt Divine was behind this, it wisnae an elastic band eh was chewin, it was they fuckin sweeties, he'd dumped the packet in my desk. I could feel my fists tightenin into wee baws. I am going to kill that cunt.'

Paul Jackson stared at him, jaw wide open as he took another slug from the can.

'What happened next?'

'Well,' Andrews said, 'Clarky took his big black cloak off, hung it up on the umbrella stand. He said, 'Bend over the desk, remove your jacket, boy.' I said to him, no way, what the fuck are you gonnae do to me, ya bender?

He said, 'Do as I say and we can sort this out in a civilised, amicable manner; refuse and I'll get the police involved. The evidence is there for anyone to see. Theft and drugs are punishable at my discretion.' I said, how many times am I gonnae have to say it? I'll even say it in English for you, ya Muppet. IT WASN'T ME. He went back to the umbrella stand beside the door, took an auld cane out that had split into a lot of strands at the end from all the beatings the bastard had given out over the years.

I could tell this was gonnae hurt like fuck. He bent it a few times, testin the flexibility, makin me sweat, then he thwacked it three times over his desk. I could've objected or panelled the cunt, but decided to take the medicine. If the pigs got involved I knew I'd be toast. He belted the fuck out of me though, I could tell the sick cunt was enjoyin it. It hurt like fuckery, but there was no chance I was gonnae greet or give the bastard any clue of the pain. Jeez, that psycho cunt always looks like he's one step away from the fuckin nuthoose.'

'How many did he gie ye?' Jackson interjected.

'Fuck knows, lost count after seven; my erse is still blistered to buggery. No aw bad, though.'

'What do you mean?' Jackson said.

'The dopey cunt left me in the room to recover while he went to the secretary sortin out papers to expel me. It took me a few minutes to stand up straight, when I did, I noticed that he'd left his tweed jacket on the peg behind the door.' He smiled at Jackson, put his hand into his pocket. 'He might have leathered my erse, but I ersed his leather. Look.' He opened a fat, worn, brown leather wallet to reveal six crisp ten pound notes, two fivers and some coins. 'Have a look at these,' he said, handing the wallet over after removing the money. Jackson pulled out three small photos of Clark with various family members. There was one, carefully folded, with a heart lovingly drawn onto the well-fingered outer surface. Jackson unfolded it to reveal the headmaster and his wife in younger, happier days, smiling at each other on a sunny summer's evening, swapping ice cream cones through each other's arms as if they were toasting with champagne glasses. Andrews had crudely scribbled a dripping cock over the cone the woman was licking, in blue biro. He'd also added a noose around the woman's neck.

'Stupid cow committed hari-kari years ago. Nae wonder, bein married to that auld fuck. Poor cow had probably never had a good ride in her puff.'

They both sat on the pavement laughing. Jackson handed the wallet and pictures back to Andrews, who ripped them several times, let them flutter into the drain, then he ripped the wallet in two and listened as it dropped with a satisfying plop into the water below.

'So, Mikey,' Jackson said, 'how are we gonnae sort this little fucker Divine oot? I've waited a long time to find a good excuse to panel him, but he's such a sneaky bastard that I could never pin anything ontae him. Dinnae get me wrong, I could easily batter the fuck out of him, but my dad would kill me if a didn't have a good reason. After his years in the Navy he always talks about rules of engagement and ethics.

"You've got to have a sound reason for paggerin cunts like,' he telt me.'

'That's exactly what I'm sayin,' Andrews said. 'He's a snidey, connivin, little prick. If you think about it, how did I end up with aw this shite when I'd done fuck all wrong'? He thought about the consequences of his actions, realising the gravity of the situation. 'Fuck! Billy's gonnae kill me when he finds out that the spliff he got for my auld man is in the hands of Clarky. My auld man's gonnae go radge, tae. I'll huv no hesitation in knockin the crap out of Divine withoot a reason, but the problem wi me is this fucked up thing,' he said pointing to his gammy leg. 'I cannae catch the fucker. We'll have to think of a plan. Mibbe lay a trail of dug biscuits for him,' he said, sniggering.

'Eh? Dug biscuits?' Said Jackson.

'Did I no say? I caught him eatin dug biscuits, munchin oan the fuckers like it was his last meal.'

'I heard it was you that was eatin dug biscuits.'

'What? Where the fuck did you hear that?'

'Pauline heard it at school, some of the lassies from your class were tellin her that you left a half-eaten dug biscuit on yer desk.'

'BASTARD! That was the fuckin biscuit that Divine had thrown away, I picked it up to take to school, must've left it when I had tae empty my pockets. I was gonnae use it to slag him in front of the class, but I never got the chance. Fuck me, I really need to act fast on this fucker. Let's get our heids together, come up wi some kind o trap. We can probably dae somethin that fuck's him up, his auld man's in the nick for a few weeks so that should gie us a bit o leeway. I'll get Lawrie on the case, he's a bit of a mental schemin bastard as well, as they say, it takes one to know one.'

'When did his auld man get put in the nick?' Jackson said.

'Ah fuckin telt ye. Last week, he was caught stealin electricity fae the lamppost ootside his hoose, Billy grassed him an the pigs lifted him a few days ago.'

'Fuck, let's get the wee bastard soon then'. He said, smiling like the Cheshire moggy.

CHAPTER 5

Darkness was shocked into light as John Lawrie speedily dismantled the crude hatch that he'd made from the floorboards in his hallway. He removed the small planks of wood one at a time, carefully stacking them up behind him. As the torch beam angled and scampered across the dusty shapes that lay beneath, he lowered another one in to join them. This shape was different, though; it moved – at least for the time being. It tried to struggle against what it sensed would be its final view of the world, but could utter no sound nor make any movement, as it was bound and gagged with a painful assortment of heavy duty tape, super glue and electrical flex.

It made a final attempt for clemency. Using its last remaining weapon, it beamed its big, brown, pleading puppy eyes into his. The effort was wasted. The guy was immune to emotion. As the small terrier turned its head, it felt the hard reality of metal on bone as a rusty claw hammer came smashing forcefully into its skull. A reservoir of blood flooded immediately into its nasal cavities and lungs. Its claws involuntarily flexed, every sinew and muscle was flooded with trapped energy. The metallic tang of death fizzed across its taste buds, the massively dilated pupils faded from gloss to matt in a matter of seconds. The once-loved life force had been batted away like a baseball into some new dimension.

Lawrie threw the hammer on top of the little dog, rebuilt the hatch, and was carefully rolling a dirty Persian imitation rug over to conceal the entrance when the doorbell rang. He waited, breathing heavily. The excitement of a kill, any kill, always got him high. It rang again. It was an annoying ring, like a bluebottle stuck in a kazoo. He'd meant to change the doorbell when he first moved in, but had never got round to it. He controlled his breathing by taking a couple of deep breaths, like the doctor had told him, although he was meant to do this before he had the urge, not after.

He shouted 'Who is it?' The doorbell rang again. 'Who is it?' He shouted even louder this time.

The letter box squealed open, a muffled shout that sounded like 'Mikey and Paul' wafted its way to the hall where he stood, testing with his left foot that the floorboards were weight bearing again, then, confidently, with both feet.

'Mikey Andrews?' He shouted in reply, satisfied that the floor was good to go.

'Yeah, and Paul Jackson.'

'Who?'

'Paul Jackson, from the top of the road.'

'Who?'

'Paul Jackson – the thick fucker.'

'The muscle heid?'

'Aye.'

'Ah! Awright, I know who you mean. What d'ye want?'

'Can we talk?'

'No. No the now, I'm busy. I'll meet you both in the park at the auld truck in an hour.'

'OK,' came the reply. The letterbox sprang shut like a mousetrap, almost taking part of Andrews' finger with it.

'Who the fuck are you callin thick?' Jackson said, annoyed.

'I was only kiddin.'

'You'd better be, or I'll ...'

Andrews grabbed him by the throat. 'Watch your fuckin mouth, boy – you're forgettin that Billy's out in a few weeks.'

Jackson shrugged him off and walked away.

Lawrie finished rolling the rug over the floorboards, made it look neatish, and walked through the hall, into the dark kitchen. He tugged the ragged cord that hung inside the door, a dim glow issued from the fifty watt light bulb. He flexed his hands as he walked to the sink; this kind of kill always made his hands ache, he reckoned it was the tension that he put into each blow. He squirted some washing up liquid onto his hands, moved them around in the basin of cold greasy water, full of unwashed dishes and cups. He made sure he removed the blood from beneath his fingernails by scrubbing them with the well-used Brillo pad that lay rusting on the bunker. He shook the excess water off, dried his hands on his jeans. He picked up a dishtowel, used it to remove the steaming kettle from the gas cooker, poured water into a mug holding instant coffee granules, added three spoons of sugar, went over to the fridge. He opened the door and lifted out a carton of full fat milk. It had been ripped open hastily, making the spout unusable; he always had trouble following the instructions on cartons, much preferred the glass bottles.

Milk dribbled all over the table top, soaking a half packet of dog biscuits that lay there. Bait, he called it. He threw the half-full carton of milk into a corner beside a pile of festering garbage. There was a jingling sound as the carton hit a fluorescent green dog collar that lay obscured in the trash. It dislodged and slid into view, Lawrie walked over, lifted the milk covered silver disc.

He held it in his palm and read aloud what was there. 'Baby,' he said. 'Baby.' He pondered, as a thought flickered into life somewhere in the deep, dark recess between his ears. *Bye, bye Baby.*

He laughed aloud, ripped the silver tag from the collar, put it into his pocket, tucked the fluorescent strip deep into the bucket. Flies and other insects crawled and buzzed around it, but he never noticed them.

'Where in fuck's name is he?' Andrews said, looking at his watch again. 'Said he'd be here half an hour ago. It's fuckin freezin, I've got to be elsewhere soon.'

'Why are we getting Lawrie involved in this anyway?' Said Jackson, as he pulled the anorak from around his waist, put it on.

'Because he's a fuckin heidcase and it was your idea, remember? That prick Divine'll no huv a clue what's hit him.'

'But Lawrie?' Said Jackson, zipping the anorak all the way up so that the hood formed a tunnel in front of his face. 'Is that no a bit too heavy? Have you heard that he's meant to have cats and dugs buried under his floorboards?'

'Ach, whae believes that rubbish?' Andrews replied. 'He's a nutter, but I cannae see him bein that mental. Mibbe he'll huv a bigger fish to put under soon, though, eh?' He laughed.

Jackson stared at him, eyes wide open. 'D'ye think he would kill him?'

'Dinnae be stupid, he'll get a good kickin and mibbe a warnin, that'll keep him out of oor way for a long time.'

Jackson nudged him, nodded his head to the fence, where Lawrie was making his way towards them. They both jumped down from the burned out truck that acted as a gang hut. Andrews had difficulty getting down past the burnt rubber tyres, his calliper catching in the shreds.

'Fuckin stupid thing,' he said, pulling hard to get himself free. Lawrie looked through the fence, spotted them, took his hands from his duffel coat pockets, slipped sideways through the hole in the fence. He almost stumbled into the puddle as his foot caught the bottom of the grey metal. He managed to catch his balance, stood upright in the old knicker factory yard, assimilated into a gangland meeting place over a period of years by the Young Pilton Crew. Ideal place to meet a prick and a fanny he thought, laughed to himself.

'Awright John?' Jackson said, unwittingly bowing his head, acknowledging his inferiority to Lawrie.

'Awright John?' Andrews said. He tried and failed to keep eye contact, so looked away, pointed to where Lawrie had stumbled.

'Fuckin puddle, eh? I got my troosers soaked with it.'

Lawrie looked back, glanced at the puddle. Took a deep breath. 'What are you meant to be?' He said looking at Jackson, 'a fuckin Clanger?'

Andrews laughed.

Jackson unzipped the anorak, pulled the hood back until it became a collar.

'Aw, for fuck's sake put it back up, I didn't realise you were so fuckin plug.'

Jackson went to pull the zip back up.

'Fuckin stop, ya mongol, I'm only fuckin jokin.'

Jackson was confused, left it halfway up, put his hands deep into his pockets.

'So what's the score, boys? Hope ye've no dragged us down here to talk about fuckin puddles.' He pulled out a packet of Embassy Regal, took an expensive looking gold lighter from inside the packet and lit up, taking a deep draw, blowing the smoke over Jackson, who wanted – but didn't dare – to wave it away.

'Well?'

'Jimmy Divine,' said Andrews. 'The wee fucker that lives over the street fae me.'

'What about um?' Said Lawrie.

'He's a schemin bastard that's got me into a lot of trouble.'

'Aye,' said Jackson, chipping in. 'Wee bastard got Mikey expelled.'

'And?' Said Lawrie. 'What's that to do wi me?'

'We were hopin you could help us sort him oot,' said Andrews.

'He's a wee fuckin laddie,' scoffed Lawrie, sneering at them. 'Why do you's no sort him oot? Yer no scared, are ye?'

'I cannae catch the Hibby cu–' Andrews stopped mid-word, remembering that Lawrie had HIBS tattooed on both sets of knuckles. 'Wee Hibby kid.' The words sprinted from his mouth fast enough, he hoped, to cover what could have been a grave error. 'I've tried to corner him but he gets away aw the time, I feel like the fuckin Roadrunner.'

'He means the coyote,' Jackson chipped in.

'Fuck you, ya smart cunt,' Andrews said.

'So? Lawrie said, feeling that they were wasting his time. 'Go to fuckin Acme an get a fuckin cannon or an anvil, sort it oot. It's got fuck all to do with me, I think he's no a bad wee cunt, done me a couple of favours since his auld man was nicked.'

'Does that mean yer no gonnae help us?' Andrews said in disappointment.

'It means exactly that. And more to the point, if I ever see you touchin him, ah'll fuckin kill the pair of ye.' He grabbed Andrews by the collar, threw him against the truck. 'Got it?' He held a fist up, headed to Jackson, who cowered away from him.

'OK, OK, we've got it,' Andrews said.

As he headed in the opposite direction from which he'd come, Lawrie flicked the remainder of the lit cigarette into the hood of Jackson's anorak, laughed as Jackson danced around trying frantically to get it out. The smoke became dense, eventually Jackson ripped the anorak off, ran over to the puddle, threw it in, stamped all over it. He shook it a couple of times to make sure the fire was out and put the soggy thing back on. Lawrie was creasing himself laughing as he walked backwards away from them.

When Lawrie was well out of sight, Andrews said, 'That cunt's getting it.'

'Aye, right?' Jackson said, dripping wet. 'He's a fuckin nutter, what chance huv we got of getting him when we're strugglin to sort out a sap like Divine?'

Andrews was furious. 'Whae do you think yer talkin tae, eh?' He grabbed Jackson's wet hood, pulled it over the front of his head, dragged him back over to the puddle and hauled him into it. He kicked him a couple of times, as he did so, he stumbled. His calliper caught on a rip in Jackson's jumper, he kicked and thrashed at Jackson's ribs until he freed the calliper, leaving a hole in the cardigan and wool all over his metal support. Jackson was winded and lay in the puddle, curled up as the rain came down on him.

'Be at my hoose the morn at nine,' Andrews said, unwrapping the strands of coloured wool from his leg, throwing them back towards Jackson, kicking some water over the prostrate figure. Jackson coughed a couple of times, got up on all fours in the middle of the dirty water, made his way slowly to the hole in the fence and headed home. As he walked up the street he passed all three houses. Lawrie's was dark, Andrews' curtains were drawn, Jimmy Divine stood at his living room window staring into the distance, biting his nails. He hid behind the curtain as Jackson passed level with the window. Jackson spotted him, but didn't have the energy to turn and look at him.

The Lost Tornado

CHAPTER 6

I spent most days thinking about how the auld man was doing. Mum said he was away on a long distance lorry trip but I knew where he was, that cripple across the road had been slagging me about it. I had got him back though when I took that fiver from his desk. I gave it to Mum, told her I'd found it in a puddle. She was so happy, we ate like Kings that night. I smiled at the memory as I blew on my hands trying to get a bit of circulation going. I was frozen to my core, couldn't seem to get any heat at all. It was no good, I was still freezing. I looked down the street, over the top of the school, a big grey cloud was heading my way; looked like it might snow again. I covered my hands with the sleeves of my jumper, picked the spade up. The garden was a joke. I'd been trying to dig it on and off with a fork since I was seven, I was about to turn ten soon! As usual I couldn't get the soil to break up. I was hammering the fork into the ground as hard as I could, but there was no give. It was all cracked, it looked like a drought scene that you'd see on telly, even the black and white picture looked more colourful than this. I could get the fork into some of the cracks, but I hadn't the strength in my arms to turn the big clumps of soil over.

The only difference I'd made in all the time I'd been there was that I'd managed to tire my arms out. The nearest thing to vegetation that this dump of a garden saw was when apple cores or banana skins were chucked into it. Trying to make it look better was a waste of time. I picked up a soggy teddy bear from the bottom of the garden, think it was Susan's one, it was stinking, some dog must've pissed on it. The only reason I was doing the garden in the first place was that Mum had been a bit down lately, I thought I could maybe grow some flowers for her, cheer her up a bit. It couldn't be nice looking at the desolation when you were stuck in the house all day, hungry, bored and waiting to deliver twins.

The auld man had been whipped into jail, Billy or Mikey Andrews had grassed him up.

'Dad,' I said to him a couple of weeks ago. 'How's it that our lights and cooker only go on and off at the same time as the lamp posts?'

'It's the way the power works in the street, son,' he said.

'But Gary and Snottery Beak's houses can get electricity anytime and they're only up the stair.'

'They're higher up. That's how electricity works.'

'But–'

'That's enough of the questions; go an get the ball, we'll have a kick-about.'

I could never resist those words and went straight to my room, got my Mouldmaster 5 from the top of the wardrobe.

I'd since found out that the auld man had wired our electricity box up to the lamppost, he hid the wire down the side of the fence, it was only discovered when Andrews pissed against the fence one night. The piss dribbled down his calliper, which was touching the wire, gave the stupid wee fanny a shock. Apparently sprayed piss all over his face when his cock jerked wi the shock. He went over to his house crying to Billy about getting an electric shock. Billy went radge, banged on our door late one night.

'What the fuck's happenin here?' He says to my auld man. 'My wee brother's just had an electric shock from your fence, he's fuckin roarin and greetin.'

'Naw that cannae be right son?' The auld man said.

'It fuckin well is. Mikey's a lot of things but he's no a liar.' He stuck his head out of the stair door, shouted at the top of his voice

'Mikey, get over here right now.'

'Keep the noise down pal, there's bairns sleepin here. The auld man said'. A few minutes later Mikey came hobblin over, red eyes, hair all stickin up. I was hiding in the room behind the main door, I could hear everything that was going on.

'Mikey, show Mr Divine where you got the shock fae.' The three of them went away from the stair door, headed out into the garden. I made my way to the front room, opened the window slightly so's I could see and hear them without being seen. They were all standing at the bottom of the garden, right next to the lamp post, Mikey was pointing at the wet bit on the fence.

'That's where it was,' he said. 'I was only standin there and got a shock.'

'Naw,' the auld man said, 'that cannae be right.' He walked over to the fence, rubbed his palm against it.

'See? No shock. You must have been imaginin it.' He put his hand to his nose and sniffed. 'Were you pishin against my fence?'

Mikey said nothin, went red.

'Answer the man,' Billy said.

'Aye, I was.'

'What did you do that for, ya dirty bastard, when your hoose is right there?' Dad said, pointin to the blue door ten feet way.

'Ah felt like it, right?'

'Hey, boy, don't come it with me,' the auld man said, getting a bit heated.

'Oi, calm down, pal,' said Billy. 'Dinnae get too excited, it was only a pish.'

'Only a pish? I want an apology. A man's hoose is his castle, I didn't ask him to fill the fuckin moat, did I?'

'Calm yourself. If anything, it's us that should be gettin the apology. You could've killed him.'

As Billy was sayin this Mikey was pulling away at the grass that was surrounding the lamppost. He pulled a wire up from the bottom of it, as he pulled, he could see that it ran all the way up to the house.

'Looks like you've been a naughty boy. Looks to me like you're pilferin from the electricity board, my man. That could cost ye,' Billy said.

'What d'ye mean, cost me? It's only a wire, I think it's an aerial.'

'Well, let's say that if I keep my mouth shut, you give me a fiver a week for my silence and I won't have to investigate the nature of the wire. How does that sound?'

'Go, fuck yersel, pal. The reason I'm doin it is because I've got eight bairns with another two on the way, no fuckin job, no food, and bills up to fuckin here.' He put his hand above the top of his head.

'Sorry, pal, but your sob stories are no skin off my nose. Money or get grassed, it's up to you.'

The auld man stormed into the house, raked about for a few minutes, returning to the scene armed with a pair of pliers and a screwdriver. The two Andrews brothers were still standing there watching, smiling as the auld boy carefully unhooked the wire from the lamppost. The lights in the house went off, we were all in sudden, unexpected darkness.

'SATISFIED NOW?' The auld man said, right in Billy's face. He stood there nose to nose for a few seconds, breathing hard, staring him out, probably wondering if he should batter him.

'That's better. We don't want any of that kind of behaviour in our neighbourhood, do we, Michael?'

'No, William. It brings down the tone, moves us closer to the working class, it would never do.'

They both pissed themselves laughing, walked back across the road.

'You better not let this happen again or I'll grass you up, no hesitation,' Billy shouted, before shutting the stair door.

Mum was sitting in the darkness in the living room, rocking back and forwards in a chair, her big belly making her look uncomfortable. I could see she was crying.

'Can I get you a cup of tea, Mum?' I said, felt shit as I realised that I couldn't boil the kettle.

'Naw. No thanks, son,' she said, 'I've just had one.'

I knew she was only saying that to make me feel better. She wiped her eyes with the sleeve of her cardigan, went over to the sideboard where we kept the candles. The youngest bairns were howling with the coldness of the back room, the two-bar heater that was keeping them warm had gone off, it was always baltic through there.

Recently it had been great, we'd all been able to have the heater on for a long time, we passed it around the rooms so we all got a share. We got it most of the time in our room as there were six of us, only four in Mum and Dad's room, not including the twins in her belly. Mum lit six white candles from the coal fire, then put two on the mantelpiece, one on the table where John was reading his comic, Karen and Susan were doing thair homework. She handed the other three to the auld man. I could see they weren't talking to each other, again. He took the candles, went through to the bedroom with them. The bairns went quiet as the flame seemed to mesmerise them. He put two of them on the sideboard, made shapes with the other one, drawing patterns and stuff, it was like a magical light show that gave you a nice warm feeling.

Mum went to the cupboard next to the coal bunker an pulled all the coats out. She went round the two rooms putting the coats over the tops of the beds. I went to the kitchen to see if there was anything to eat, but all that was there was a half-cooked pan of chips and some burgers that were defrosting on the bunker. Mum came in behind me, tipped everything into the bucket.

'What are you doing that for?' I protested.

'The meat'll go off, the fridge'll start to defrost and the chips had jist went on.' As soon as she put them in the bin she bent over the sink; I could see her shoulders shaking. I put my arms around her, I couldn't reach all the way round. We stood there in the dark.

CHAPTER 7

It was high summer. I had about two weeks before we left Pilton and moved to Claremont Court in the centre of Edinburgh. The only place I could ever get peace to read my Beano was in the loo, I used to sit with a slice of dry white bread and laugh my way through it. The sun had been beating down for the whole of the school holidays, we had all got used to the routine; waken up, telly on, *Herge's Adventures of Tintin* while eating breakfast, and out to play footy all day. I swear that Hibs strip that I wore could've found its own way home. I almost cried every time I saw the rip on the collar. Mum tried to sew it up for me, but it was a scar that wouldn't heal.

Paul Jackson and Mikey Andrews cornered me the previous week. I was walking back from the shops after getting some bread and marge, I was actually quite happy at the time as I'd discovered these big bars of cooking chocolate in the supermarket. I picked up the bread and a bar of chocolate, pretended to tie my shoelace but was really breaking the chocolate into small chunks and eating it. I put the chocolate on a shelf, kept coming back to it. I didn't see it as stealing as I wasn't taking it out of the shop. At least not in the usual way. After I'd finished it I'd gone past the satisfied bit, moved onto the feeling a bit sick stage. I paid for the groceries and headed home.

I was walking down past the bookies, groceries in the plastic bag, singing about the grand auld team, when something clattered into my head. I thought it was a store detective at first but when I got the bang in the leg with a stick a second or two later, I knew it wasn't. I fell onto the ground, trying not to squash the messages. I looked up, the two of them were over the top of me, looking pissed off.

'So?' Said Andrews. 'Think yer a smart cunt, do ye?'

'What are you talkin about?' I said, as Jackson stuck the boot into my stomach. I spewed up a bit of brown sickness. Wiped my mouth.

'What? What have I done?' I had no idea what it was about.

The Lost Tornado

'Ye know fine, ya connivin little prick,' Andrews said.

'I don't!' Surely he still couldn't be after me for the school incident, when he got himself expelled? That had been months before.

He brought the stick down on top of my head; I had enough time to put my arm up to protect myself.

'You are about to get the kickin o yer life,' he said.

'Aye,' repeated Jackson, as he grabbed my hair, 'kickin o yer life.'

They got an arm each, frogmarched me around the corner to where all the buckets from the supermarket were kept. They threw me on top of a pile of cardboard boxes, both laid into me. My dad had always told me that if you ever got caught in a situation where you couldn't run or fight, the best bet was to think you were a hedgehog and curl up into a tight wee ball; that way you wouldn't really get any serious damage. I remembered after the first couple of kicks, I curled up for the duration. I could feel them thumping kicks and sticks into me but it was true, I didn't really feel anything.

'So, ya bastard, thought you could move away from Pilton withoot payin yer debt, did ye?' Andrews said. 'Think yer a smart cunt movin into the city? Fuckin scum, it'll be nice to clean the street up a bit when you fuckin Gyppos are gone. They'll have tae get Rentokil in to delouse the place.'

I could hear them talking but it was a sort of echoey, muffled noise, as if they were in a tunnel. I felt like I had a shell around me. They got me in the face a couple of times but I could feel the punches and kicks getting weaker. After god knows how long it stopped. I could hear shuffling but didn't feel safe enough to get out of my ball position. Next thing I knew the bastards were tipping a bucket over me. I could smell the old fish and fruit, felt the sliminess dripping down my neck, then a load of tins being poured over me. The two of them were laughing pretty hard. I lay there and took it. I was thinking of a way to get them back.

Even after everything had gone quiet I lay there. I knew we were moving into Claremont Court in a few weeks, to be honest I couldn't wait.

Claremont Court was part of the City of Edinburgh Corporation Housing Committee's post-war housing drive. It is an important example of Continental Modernism in Scottish post-war housing.

The development provided 63 homes through an inward-looking design of two L-plan blocks containing 30 flats and 28 maisonettes and two terraces of cottages, arranged around landscaped courtyards to create a community. It combined practicality and modernity through the provision of basement stores, drying areas to the roof space and in-built storage to properties.

Not everyone was happy with this heap of 'Continental Modernism'. It was a monstrosity. It looked like it had been based on a design by the architect's child using toilet rolls and cornflake boxes. Despite the protests from the affluent neighbouring communities of East Claremont Street and Bellevue it got the go ahead. It was opened in 1962 on the site of Edinburgh's first Zoo and according to the protesters, that's exactly what it would bring back. The only difference being that the animals would not be locked in their cages at night!

Claremont Court looked amazing. Big wide buildings with grass bits to play footy on. As John, Karen and I walked into the place with the auld man, there were a few guys about our age playing three-a-side on the grass.

I was about to ask for a game but the auld man stopped me.

'Leave it the now, Jimmy,' he said, 'there's plenty time for that when we move in.'

We walked up the stairs, came to an orange door with number 54 on it. The auld man went off to check electrical fittings and cooker points, stuff like that. The three of us bolted straight up the stair. Wow! Four bedrooms, all massive. Karen went into the first room at the top of the stairs.

'Jimmy, John, come here, quickly!'

We both ran through to see Karen standing on a balcony looking over Edinburgh Castle.

The Lost Tornado

'Wow!' We said at the same time. It was truly incredible.

'Dad? Dad?' John said, running downstairs. 'Come an see the room!'

'It's awright pal,' he said, 'calm doon, I've seen it, I was here last week getting the keys.' He lifted John up at the living room window, said, 'Look at that view, then.'

It was an even better view of the castle.

'This is the best hoose ever, Dad,' John said. 'When can we move in?'

'Two weeks' time. Have you two chosen yer room yet?'

'Can we have a room each?' John said.

'Naw, It disnae work that way, pal. Karen'll have a room to herself cos she's the oldest, needs somewhere to study.'

I looked round at her, she looked so smug.

'You and Jimmy'll have a room, Susan, Lynne and Debbie will share, Billy and Robert'll share and dependin on what the twins are they'll share with the youngest yins cos they're the wee-est.'

The acrid smell of rotting fish snapped me back. I felt the rubbish all over me, had a look around to make sure that the pair of wankers had gone. The coast was clear, I got up, wiped all the shit and slime from my Hibs top. As I was wiping the crap away I caught sight of a bit of thread. I pulled it, the collar began to come away. That was horrible, it hurt me more than all that kickin. I was mortified, my beautiful Hibs top, ruined. I looked around for the groceries, saw them lying crushed under some cardboard. I picked them up, ran home crying my eyes out. I got busy making a plan to make them regret what they'd done. I had an idea to sort Jackson out, but would have to think of one final plan of attack for Andrews before we left for good.

As I was walking down to the house, wiping my eyes with the sleeve of my ripped Hibs shirt, John Lawrie jumped out from a bush. He had something tucked under his jacket.

'Awright, Jamesy boy?' He said. I tried to cover up the tears and snotters but he cottoned on to it. 'What the fuck happened, pal?' He said it in such a concerned manner that I knew he meant it. I tried to turn my head away from him, but he stepped right in front of me.

'Whae done that to yer strip, pal? This is fuckin not on. After that lesson we dealt oot tae these foreign Johnny's. These fuckers should have more respect for the jersey'.

Hibs had just beaten Sporting lisbon 6-1 at home in the Cup Winners' Cup. I didn't go to the game as the auld man was still locked up. I wondered if he'd heard the score, knew how gutted he'd be that he had missed a brilliant performance against one of Europe's top football teams.

Lawrie took the flapping collar in his hand, it brought back the pain. I began to blubber like a wee lassie, managed to tell him through my tears who did it.

'Fuckin Andrews and Jackson? Bastards,' he said. 'I told that pathetic fuckin cripple and his mong fuckin sidekick to stay away from you. Why did they jump ye?'

'No idea,' I said in all honesty, putting on a pathetic high-pitched voice to get maximum sympathy, starting to blubber again.

'Relax, pal,' Lawrie said. 'They'll no hurt you again, I promise. When I get a hold o they bastards … they think they can tamper with the great Hibernian heritage, but they are not only insulting me, they're insulting Paddy Stanton, Alan Gordon and Lawrie Reilly. Anyone that insults them better have an armoury to back them up.'

'Thanks, John,' I said, by this time I was feelin a bit better knowin that they two were about to get a doing. I was also concocting a plan of my own. Lawrie rubbed the top of my head a few times, walked off across the street to his house. There was something moving under his jacket again. I thought I saw a rabbit's ear pop out, but wasn't sure. Before he got to his door he turned round. I definitely seen a rabbit's head pop out, which he quickly stuck back under his black jacket.

'Jimmy pal?' He shouted over. 'When are you guys flittin?'

'Next week,' I shouted back.

He thought for a while, no doubt devising somethin to do with

The Lost Tornado

those two, then said, 'Alright. They two fuckin halfwits'll have nae idea what's fuckin hit them. Don't you worry about them lad.'

'Thanks, John,' I said. 'You got a new pet there?'

'Naw, pal, lookin after it for somebody.' He went into his house, the door banged shut. A few seconds later he came to the window, waved at me, drew the curtains, even though it was still the afternoon.

After a day or two I had finalised my plan for both Andrews and Jackson.

I'd seen both of them at different times since they jumped me, both of them had black eyes and cut noses. They looked at me with real hatred, I knew and they knew that they couldn't touch me. I smiled at them. My plan to get Jackson back was through his fat sister Pauline. I was sitting on the pavement making shapes in the soft tarmac when I had a eureka moment. I went to the sweet shop, bought a packet of the new liquorice Toffos. I carefully unwrapped the sweets, took out the top one, very precisely removed the wrapper and ate the lovely liquorice toffee. I then got a chunk of tarmac, shaped it to look like a Toffo and waited a minute to let it cool down and solidify before I wrapped it back up, put the whole pack back into a believable state.

As I was setting this up I looked up to see Jackson and his fat sister walking down the street towards me.

'Divine,' he shouted. 'Divine, I'm gonnae fuckin panel you, ya little cunt.'

Pauline was walking behind him, stuffing food into her face, as usual. 'Aye, Divine,' she said through a gobfull of cold chicken, 'we're gonnae fuckin huv ye.'

'Fuckin Lawrie's away till the mornin so he cannae protect you now, ya wee fucker.' Jackson said.

'Aye, ya wee fucker,' Pauline echoed, spitting bits of chicken everywhere.

I was tempted to do the usual thing and run from Jackson, but decided that this would be worth it. He marched up to me, slapped my face.

'Take that, ya cunt.' He slapped again, the other side this time. 'Get yer fuckin mental pal tae batter me, would ye?'

'I've no idea what yer talkin about, Paul,' I said innocently.

'Liar!'

'Aye, fuckin liar!' Pauline said. 'I'll take them,' she added, as she grabbed the sweets from my hand.

'No, dinnae, Pauline,' I said, tryin to sound convincing. 'Geez them back, it's the last of my pocket money.'

I was delighted. As soon as she'd taken the bait I could safely run, but first I had to pretend that I wanted the sweets back.

'Aw, come on, Pauline,' I pleaded. 'They were for the bairns, I was going to give them a treat.'

'Tough,' she said, as she unwrapped them. She stuffed the first sweet into her gob as Paul lunged at me.

'Come here, ya we fuck. I'm goin tae gie you a going away present.'

I did a small dash, knew I was too fast for him. Stopped a bit down the road.

'Forget it, Paul,' I said. 'It's not only your brain that's slow.'

He made a run for me but I was gone. As he was about to come again Pauline started choking and spluttering, holding her throat.

'Paul?' She gasped, pointin to her throat, 'I'm chokin.' I could hear her strugglin to get her breath.

I leapt with joy. 'Take that, ya fat cow,' I said quietly. I didn't want to shout as I didn't want anybody to know what I'd done. I went back towards our house, picked up the packet of Toffos that Pauline had dropped, opened the packet, popped one into my mouth.

About a half hour later an ambulance came screaming into the street, stopped at the Jackson's house. I felt brilliant but terrified at the same time. I was delighted that the plan had worked a treat, but didn't want her to die. The next day as we were preparing to go for good, I spotted Jackson striding down the road, in a rush.

'Divine?' He was shouting, 'your ass is mine.'

He was getting closer, I thought he'd back off when he saw my dad and mum coming in and out of the house to the removal van, but he walked right up to me.

Poomph! He punched me right in the stomach. 'That's for hurtin Pauline, ya cunt.' Poomph! Another. Straight into my guts. 'An that's because I fuckin hate ye.' He was about to go for a third when the auld man came oot.

'Hoy! Jackson, what are you up tae?'

'He tried to poison Pauline,' he said, pointing at me.

'What? Dinnae talk crap, son.'

I was lyin on the ground holding my stomach but not crying. 'Dad,' I said, 'he hates me coz I'm better at footy than him.'

'Ya fuckin liar,' he shouted, moved towards me. Next thing I knew John Lawrie appeared from nowhere.

'Awright, Mr D?' He said.

'Aye, fine, John,' my dad replied.

'Alright, Paul?' He said to Jackson. 'Can I have a couple of words with ye in a minute or two?'

There was a sudden smell of shit, Jackson put his hand to the back of his trousers, brought his hand up to his nose, sniffed, and ran up the street.

'I'll mibbe catch you later, pal,' Lawrie shouted after him.

Jackson looked back, his eyes were about two feet in front of him. Priceless, I lay on the ground pissing myself.

'Sorry to be a pain, John,' the auld man said. 'In a bit of a rush.'

They shook hands.

'Best of luck in yer new place, Mr D,' he said. He leaned over, patted my head a couple of times. 'You look after yerself, wee yin,' he said. 'I'll come an see you playin at Easter Road one day.'

'Thanks, John,' I said, standing up slowly.

'Right, you,' the auld man said, 'let's get this show on the road.'

An hour or two later we were all loaded up. A couple of my uncles who'd been helping out squeezed into the van. There were another two cars with the other eight kids and Mum, all ready to move to paradise.

As we got to the top of the street Jackson, his wee brother Stu and fat Pauline, who was sitting in a wheelchair with an oxygen mask on, looked at us.

'Good riddance, scum,' they shouted.

Dad stopped the van, rolled the window down.

'You boys better watch yer mooths,' he said. 'I'm gonnae be back a couple of times to check the hoose. I'll be asking John Lawrie to keep an eye on you.'

Jackson went white. They turned, walked back into their house. Fat Pauline struggled to wheel herself to the gate.

As we headed up towards Ferry Road and onwards to our new life, I spotted Lawrie taking Andrews' Alsatian, Max, out for a walk. He waved at us as we passed.

'Very considerate neighbour, that boy,' my mum said.

CHAPTER 8

The twins were born a week before we moved into the Court. Might have guessed it would be one of each; it evened the score up for the 5-a-side team that we seemed to be forming. It was a strange feeling having all of these people in such a small space, it really was just as well we were moving to a bigger house. We now had a bigger family than The Broons! The hierarchy was similar though; Dad, Mum, Karen, me, John, Susan, Billy, Robert, Lynne, Debbie and the twins, Gordon & Catherine. Thing was, there was only about a year between us all.

The first few days after we moved in were a complete blur. My whole life had been spent in Pilton in a two bedroomed house with bairns all over the place, but here I found myself with a room to share only with John. It was a dream.

As we walked around the neighbourhood and back to the house there were a few guys playin footy. I'll be honest, I was amazed at their skill. These guys were playing like professionals. I thought I was pretty good, but after watching these guys I had to re-assess myself. As we walked back up the slope, passing the guys on the way, one of them, a big guy with perfect hair stopped us.

'What are yous doin here?'

'We live here,' I said, 'just moved in to number 54.'

'Are all yer cousins and stuff helpin ye?' He said.

'No. What makes you say that?'

'Only that there's about a hundred bairns gone into that hoose.'

'That's all our family,' John said.

'All your family? Christ!' The guy said, 'I take it yer mum and dad dinnae have a telly?'

We both looked at him, confused.

'Aye, we've got a telly,' I said. 'What do you mean?'

The other boys pissed themselves laughing. He walked up to John and me. 'Paddo's the name,' he said. 'Remember it.'

With that, he did three keepie-uppies, foot, thigh, knee, belted the ball into the goals. Turned his back, hands in the air, saluted the imaginary crowd. I was seriously impressed. If I could learn from these guys, the Hibs position was in the bag. John and I ran all the way to the top of the stairs, all around the adjoining landings, around the whole perimeter of Claremont Court. Some of it was covered, some was open with patches of grass, there were tons of nooks and crannies that looked so exciting to us. We were delirious with possibilities.

We went back up to the hoose, handed out some of our sweets to the kids. The next day was a Sunday. I remember it well, I walked over to the bakery to get two dozen rolls and a dozen eggs, as well as six pints of milk and my dad's paper. It was so peaceful. The church bells were ringing not far away, with the lovely warmth in the air I really felt like we'd arrived in heaven.

On the way back a few of the guys who'd been playing footy were walking down the hill towards me; they all had football strips on and boots hanging around their necks. One of the smallest ones stopped me.

'Any good at fitty?' He said.

'Aye, pretty good,' I replied. 'Left back or winger.'

He threw a ball at me, I tried to chest it down. In doing so I dropped the bag with the milk in it. The bottles smashed, as I put the other bag with the rolls in it down, the milk spilled downhill, soaked the rolls as well as dad's paper.

'Shit, sorry pal,' the guy said. 'I didn't mean to do that.'

'Christ!' I said, 'Mum'll go mental.'

He tried to help clear it up, but it was a big mush.

'It doesn't matter,' I said. 'I've still got plenty of change to get more.'

'What's yer name, pal?' He said.

'Jimmy. Jimmy Divine.'

'I'm Jimbo. How about comin for a kickabout the mornin?'

'Aye, that would be brilliant, where?'

'At the bottom of the ramp, ten sharp.'

The Lost Tornado

'Aye? OK.'

'OK, JD. Be there or be square.'

I watched the group of them walk away and felt elated. I went back to the shops with the bags and smashed glass, bubbling my eyes out.

'What is it, son?' The woman behind the counter said.

'I chased a cat from the middle of the road. There was a car coming, and when I dived to get it out of the way I dropped all the stuff. My Mum'll kill me,' I said, really turning on the water works.

'Dinnae you worry, son,' she said. 'What colour was the cat?'

'Black and white,' I lied.

'That'll be my wee Suzy,' she said, 'she's always doing that. Thanks, son, yer a lifesaver.'

She took the soggy mess from me, put it in a silver bucket. 'Now, what was it you had son?' After she'd put a new full shopping into the bags she handed me a handful of pick and mix, rubbed my hair.

'Yer a hero son, you dinnae get many like you to the pound.'

I had no idea what she was talking about. I went back up the road, things felt great.

After breakfast, Dad was reading the paper, having a cuppa.

'See the Hibbies won again yesterday, son.'

'Aye?' I said.

'Beat Rangers 2–1 at Easter Road, Cropley and Duncan last ten minutes.'

'Is Easter Road near here, Dad?

'Aye, sure is. Ten minute walk. I think we could be goin there next week with yer uncle Rab.'

'Really? Wow, that would be brilliant.'

'If you play yer cards right, anyway.'

'I will, promise.'

I grabbed my Hibs top and a ball, sprinted downstairs to train for tomorrow. That whole night I hardly slept, thinking about how I would impress those guys.

I got down to the meeting place about seven in the morning, way earlier than I was meant to. There was nobody there. I went back up to my room, read a comic, decided to get a bit training in before the meeting and went down about half nine. I waited for ages and ages, there was still no sign of anybody.

I went back up the house to get the time, it was almost eleven. I was so sad that I'd missed them. After lunch I wandered back down. There were about a dozen guys playing footy on the grass in the middle of the Court.

I ran excitedly over to them, asked for a game.

'Fuck off,' one of the guys said. His words stopped me like a bang in the face.

'Paddo said I could play.'

'Well Paddo's no fuckin here. I'm in charge, so fuck off.'

The guy who'd thrown the ball to me yesterday had scored a goal.

'Great goal, Jimbo,' the nasty guy shouted. Jimbo turned around and saw me, he sort of waved.

'Can I get a game, Jimbo?' I shouted.

The other guy said, 'I thought I told you to fuck off'.

Jimbo came over. 'Awright, JD?' He said.

'Aye, good, but he said I can't play,' I said, pointing to the nasty guy.

'Come on, Mikey. Paddo likes the wee cunt.'

'Well, I dinnae,' said Mikey.

'Aw, come on, Mikey,' I said. 'Give us a game, please?'

'Don't you fuckin Mikey me, boy,' he said. 'It's 'Mr Corrie tae you.'

'Sorry,' I said. 'Goin to give us a game, Mr Corrie? I really, really want to play.'

'Have ye got any fags?' He said.

'Naw, I dinnae smoke.'

'Well, fuck off then,' he said, an booted me right up the backside. I walked away, my world in tatters. I'd have to find out where Paddo stayed in order to get my career back on track.

A few days later, after realising that I was not fitting in quite as smoothly as I'd hoped, I was walking back from the school. The same guys were all playin footy again, including Paddo.

'How's it gaun, JD?' He shouted, whilst jumping up to head the ball.

'Alright,' I said, 'but I cannae get a game with yer pals.'

'How no?' He said, stopping suddenly, grabbing the ball. He put it under his arm, walked over to me. 'Right, who said this guy couldnae play wi us?' He said, lookin around.

'It was Mikey Corrie,' Jimbo said.

'Fuckin Corrie?'

'Aye,' Jimbo replied, 'booted the wee cunt up the erse, too.'

'Big fucker. That cunt couldnae play fitbaw if his life depended upon it. I'll soon sort this out pal,' he said. 'Where were you on Sunday? We were waiting for you?'

'I was here,' I protested. 'Ten o'clock. Sharp.'

'Ten? I said eleven?' He winked at Jimbo.

'You said ten,' I said. 'I waited for hours, but nobody came.'

'Well, tell you what,' he said, 'we're goin down to Warriston later on to play the Rodney Street gang; fancy it?'

'Aye, that would be great,' I said.

'Right see you here at six, sharp.'

'Six?' I said. 'Sharp?'

'Yip, six sharp,' Paddo said. He winked at Jimbo again.

I turned up at six, again there was nobody there. I was gutted, felt so low. I knew now that they were taking the piss out of me. I felt so deflated. Went up to my room, took off the Hibs top, kicked my ball into the corner, slumped onto my bed to read a comic. I spent the next few days playing with John, he was crap at footy but better than nothing. On the way back from playing in the school grounds the gang were playing footy at the usual place, bottom of the ramp. There were some new guys who I'd never seen before. What was different about them though was that they were taking the piss out of Paddo. They were slagging him and were also destroying him at football.

Here was me thinking he was top dog when he was actually like me, much bigger though, about a foot! John and I walked up the ramp, past all the guys playing. I spotted Jimbo looking up, he gave me a sort of nod, it seemed to me that he was alright. I looked at

Paddo, he was looking sheepish.

'What the fuck are you lookin at?' He shouted, trying to deflect the attention to me.

'I've no idea,' I shouted back, 'a shitty footballer?'

The other guys laughed. Paddo made a run for me, but I was way too quick.

'I'll get you, ya fuckin white Paki,' he said.

The other guys looked at him. 'White Paki?' One of them said.

'Aye,' said Paddo. 'There's about a hunner of them. Fuckin trampy bastards, no only that, they're Hibby trampy bastards.' Paddo looked at me and smiled. He'd succeeded; the attention was now on John and me.

Everybody started laughing and singing. 'White Paki bastards, yer only white Paki bastards, white Paki bastards.'

The two of us walked towards the stairs, heading for the house, dejected. This paradise was fading fast.

As we passed the communal bin I spotted a discarded mince pie supper with brown sauce splattered all over it. It was still in the wrapper, looked like the grease had congealed overnight. The chips were almost gone but there was only a single solitary bite out of the pie. I looked back at the guys, they'd forgotten about us and were getting on with their game. I picked the supper up, slid the old bits of chip onto the ground and got a nice firm hold of the pie, still in the greaseproof wrapper. I opened the door of the bin cupboard, hid behind it, trying to get as near to the guys as I could without being seen. I waited a few minutes, then my chance came. It was Paddo's turn in goals, he was only a few feet away.

'Oi, Paddo,' I shouted. I launched the pie. It flew over the fence, as Paddo turned around it caught him smack in the side of the head. I could see the pastry and mince in slow motion, hitting his perfect hair, then his face, and finally his ear. It was magic. I laughed so loud, mainly I think because I'd never done anything so dangerous in my life. John was looking at me like I'd killed somebody, in truth maybe I'd signed my own death warrant. At that moment I couldn't have

The Lost Tornado

cared, it was amazing.

All the guys stopped playing, began to piss themselves laughing. I was king for the moment.

'Oi, Paddo,' I shouted. 'Now you can say you're a pioneer.' I've no idea where that came from but it was brilliant. Every single person except Paddo and John were killing themselves laughing.

Some of the other gang were saying, 'Pioneer? That's class.'

It seemed like the laughter went on forever, but eventually I focussed on Paddo. He was standing there not saying a word. He was wiping the old meat, pastry and grease from his face with the sleeve of his Celtic top, staring at me. Eyes getting narrower. He tipped his head to one side as if removing water after a swim; some grease dropped onto the ground, he put his finger in his ear to clear the rest. By this time the laughter had died down, but there was still some residual chuckling from the new gang.

One of them jumped up onto the fence, I took a few steps back thinking he was coming for me.

'Wee man,' he said, 'that was fuckin superb. What's your name?'

'Jimmy.'

'Well, Jimmy, your life's gonnae be a fuckin misery from now on.'

'Too right it fuckin is!' Paddo shouted. 'I am gonnae kill you three times over, ya stupid little fucker. When I'm finished with you there won't be enough o ye left to bury in a crisp bag. Your life is mine.'

'Scary stuff, Pioneer,' I said. 'You'll never catch me. I'm way too quick.'

'Don't you worry, boy,' he said, pointing. 'It might not be today. Might not be the morra. But I'll fuckin have ye.'

By this time the realisation of what I'd done had sunk in. I was dead, but I still felt I had to go with the bravado thing.

'What's that, Paddo?' I said, cupping my ear. 'I can't hear you. Must have something in my ear.'

I could see his head getting redder and redder.

'Eh? What's that?' I shouted. I walked right up to the fence, knowing that there was a barrier between us, which would allow me to get away.

He hurled himself at the fence, jumping up, grabbing hold of the wood at the top; he was about to launch himself over it but the grease on his sleeve made him lose his grip, he fell down, cracking his head on the ground.

Again everybody pissed themselves laughing. He got up straight away, bombed after me, up the ramp. I was too quick for him, though, and got up the stairs to the landing easily. John was way ahead, waiting at the door.

'Come on, Jimmy,' he shouted, 'he'll kill ye!'

I looked over the balcony at the scene below. Ten guys looking up at me, the leader of the other gang was shaking his head at me. Paddo was still picking bits from his hair and ear, staring directly at me.

I leaned over the balcony, waved at the boys.

'See you later!' I shouted. Some of them gave me a thumbs up.

I knew as I headed through the front door that I'd made my life a lot tougher. I closed the door, letting the lock slip into place slowly, the click it gave was like a gun being cocked, Paddo's gun. I stood with the palms of my hands on the frosted glass of the door and breathed out the word 'shit'. As I walked away towards the living room I heard the letterbox squeak open, I turned to look, Paddo's eyes were staring at me, he looked at me for a good while then put the letter box flap down.

The Lost Tornado

Chapter 9

The first official day at St Mary's was a real eye opener. The school was a good mile and a half from the house and for a posse of five kids all walking at different speeds it was quite a task getting there in time for the school bell. The school was built in the days when pupils were treated like prisoners, there could be no other explanation for the state of this place. The playground was virtually underground, the only sky we could see was through a horizon completely covered with chicken wire. As soon as the Janny locked the school gates we said cheerio to any lingering thoughts of sunlight. I hated it.

The only blessing for me was that they had an under-twelve's football team, and from what I'd heard, they were pretty decent. I was determined to get in there, make my mark. The downside, though, was that because of the Paddo trauma I was undergoing, I hadn't kicked a ball in a long time. Sure, I'd played in the hall and the stairway, but that was it; I was fast losing my skills.

I was still petrified of Paddo's revenge. Every single time I stepped out of the door, I was always on the lookout for him, it was so serious that I'd created a precise drill: Look left, look right, look up, look down, look sideways, finally look behind me at every single corner I went around. I was sure he was out there planning my painful and lingering death, who could blame him?

When I did go out, I only went with Mum or Dad.

I used them like pilot fish use sharks, not the cleaning bit, the protection bit. I would walk along with them knowing fine well that Paddo would never attack me while a stronger force was protecting me. As soon as he was out of sight, I'd peel off from them, get on with whatever I had to do. He always acknowledged my mum and dad every time he saw them. 'Hi Cath, John,' he would say, 'nice day,' when he knew they weren't looking he'd threaten me by pulling his finger across his throat, pointing at me, mouthing the words 'you are so fuckin dead'.

This went on and on, I was becoming more reclusive and less skilful every day. One beautiful bright sunny Saturday I decided to end it, I was so sick of the restrictions that were being put on me by my self-imposed incarceration. It had been weeks, the only time I almost relaxed was when I went over to St. Mark's Park. It was a massive open space with three football pitches. If Paddo showed up I'd spot him a mile away and easily get away. Mum and Dad had noticed a difference in my behaviour, thought I was suffering from depression.

That morning after *Swap Shop* I looked at myself in the mirror. Told myself if I wanted to play for Hibs my chances were running out quickly, I had to get myself spotted playing, there was no chance of that happening as things stood. Mum and Dad were even threatening to take me to see a doctor, a special one! That put the shits up me.

'Come on now, Jimmy,' said Mum, 'it's not normal for a boy of your age to be in the hoose all the time, maybe there's somethin wrong with ye.'

'I'm alright, Mum, I really want to play for Hibs, but I don't know how.'

'Have ye ever thought that ye might not be good enough?'

I laughed at her.

'OK,' she said, 'but if yer not any happier in a week I'll have nae option but tae take ye tae the hospital. OK?'

'OK,' I said. Knowing that if I didn't get this sorted I could end up in the loony bin, that terrified me more than a beating from Paddo.

I'd been chased by him probably twenty times since the incident, although he'd never caught me he had got pretty close, had grabbed my jacket, but I was slippy enough to get out of it. Enough was enough.

So here it was, moment of truth, as Noel Edmonds was saying cheerio till next week I walked outside, spotted Paddo sitting on one of the stone bollards at the garages. I very slowly walked down the four sets of steps, onto the pavement, along the big wooden fence, getting slower and slower as I approached him. After a long drawn out walk where I'd made wee bits of eye contact with him I got right up to him. He was on his own, staring right at me. He didn't move. I thought he would make a beeline for me, but he sat there smoking, looking at me.

'Awright, Rab?' I said.

He said nothing.

'I didn't mean to hit you in the ear with that pie, I threw it anywhere, it was a really lucky … sorry, *unlucky* shot.'

Still nothing. I got to within a foot of him not knowing if I'd bottle it and run when the time came. I tensed my whole body, waiting for his weeks of vitriol and hatred to concentrate his fists, teeth and nails on my petite body. Seconds passed. I opened one eye, caught him running towards me, he jumped onto me, pinning me to the ground. Finally he had his quarry. He drew up his fist, surprised me by putting his arm around my neck. He tightened his grip, hit me a couple of blows on the head, then he stopped.

'I cannae hurt you,' he said.

'Eh?' I said, surprised, almost disappointed at his reaction.

'You're a real cheeky wee fucker,' he said, 'but I quite like your cheek. If you can run with a ball as quick as you run from me, yer in my team. But if you ever try anything like that again, I'll be dancing on your fucking heid with my pit boots, get it?' He punched me in the guts.

'OK, Rab, I get it,' I said, recovering enough to get my breath. He let me go, then grabbed me again. Rubbed his knuckles hard into my head, then slapped me a few times, getting rid of the last of his anger, no doubt. It seems we had, unbeknown to me, developed some kind of bond over the period. I figured it was a bit like Tom and Jerry. I was so relieved. It felt like I was given the chance of a new life. I felt so free. I got up from the tarmac, tucked my shirt back into my trousers.

'Rab?' I said, 'stay there a minute.'

I was really happy, ecstatic in fact. I went over to the tuck shop, brought him back a thirty pence mixture.

'What's this for?' He said, opening the paper bag, popping a Chelsea

Whopper into his gob.

'We're buddies,' I said, 'buddies do stuff like that.'

He raised his eyebrows, ripped another packet open, emptied some space dust into his mouth.

'Don't forget,' he said in a crackly voice, 'do anything like that again and yer Mum'll be picking yer teeth out of my fuckin boots. Got it?'

'Got it,' I said, 'nae problem, Rab. I'm a learner.'

I walked away lighter than ever, picked a couple of Black Jacks from my pocket, sailed up the stairs three at a time, got my Hibs strip on, ball under the arm and off out to heaven.

After the ecstasy of that Saturday morning, being free to go where I wanted and to do what I wanted to do again, I couldn't wait for Monday.

Monday was school football trial day. I never slept a wink the night before. How would I measure up to these guys? My preferred position was left back or wing, but to be honest anything would do.

I never had a pair of football boots, the nearest I had were some black trainers that Uncle Richard had dropped off, along with a big black bin liner full of clothes. I think they were Adidas Sambas, they were a bit too big but a bit of newspaper in the toe area soon fixed that problem. After the lunch bell went, we all walked down to Warriston. Those pitches were magic it was like being at Wembley or Hampden. As soon as we got into the park we kicked the ball all over the place. A whistle blew, loudly.

'OK, boys,' Mr Stevenson, the headmaster shouted. 'I want you to all line up at the eighteen yard line.'

OK, I thought, *he's going to pick the trial team.*

He lined six of us up along the eighteen yard line.

'OK, we'll begin alphabetically,' he shouted.

I turned to Paul Coletti. 'What is he doing? I thought it was a trial for the team?'

'This is Stevenson's idea of how to pick a team,' Paul said. 'We all have to kick the ball as hard as we can, the further it goes, the further back in the team you are. If you kick it too hard you'll end up in

The Lost Tornado

goals.'

'Really?'

'Yip. It's always been this way ever since I was in primary one.'

'What position do you play?'

'Right back. I accidentally toe poked the ball at my first trial, the ball flew over the bar, into the tennis court.'

There were sixteen of us at the trial, fourteen got picked, me included. Stevenson put me at left back for the team, I really had quite a good game. I felt my career was shaping up very nicely, I smiled when I saw the team sheet on Saturday morning. My name was third from the top.

We were all getting changed into our Arsenal strips when Stevenson came through to the cold, wooden changing rooms. We were all sitting freezing on the benches while he gave us a team talk about facing some great opponents – I think it was Sciennes or something – he told us they were unbeaten this season, had only conceded three goals in fourteen matches. I shit myself.

'Mr Stevenson,' I said, 'where are we in the league?'

'We don't talk about that,' he said, and carried on talking.

Massimo, our goalie, turned to me, put his hand to the side of his mouth. 'Bottom of the league. No points.'

I put my head in my hands. I thought they were only mucking about at the trial, surely they couldn't be as bad as that?

We got humped 10–1. I was slipping all over the place as I was wearing my trainers; it was quite muddy, they were smooth on the bottom, every time I kicked the ball my shoe flew off. I soon realised there was no way this team would be looked at by any professional outfit. I had to make another plan.

School, despite the lack of sunlight, turned out to be a good laugh, though. All of the kids had holes in their shoes, Mum n Dad just could not get enough money together to sort us all. When we walked to school in Winter the wet pavements would soak in through the holes and eventually our socks would become so saturated and heavy that they'd be dragged through the hole, it was really irritating having to stop every twenty feet and drag the wet socks back up your shins. Worse would follow when we got to school. After sitting down for ten minutes, the water would form a puddle from the hole in the shoe and inevitably someone would shout out 'Jimmy's peed himself again miss'.

There were a lot of foreigners there, mostly Italians. Every Friday afternoon after school we'd have a match on Calton Hill, Scotland vs Italy. Scotland won easily every time. Those Italians were mummy's boys, diving about, crying every time they got nudged. They had something I never had, though: money.

One of my best friends, Big Massimo, was a lovely guy. I used to sit next him in school. He reminded me of a young Oliver Hardy. And never so appropriately had a name been given: 'Massimo' means 'maximum' in Italian, he was huge. His family were well off, he always seemed to have expendable income. One day I stumbled upon a way to tap into this rich vein. We were working on a science project that involved determining the direction of magnetic north or something like that. We had a small magnetic testing kit and some magnetic dust that you could move with a magnetic pencil.

Massimo became fascinated by magnets after that. I had nicked a magnet from the experiment, Massimo wanted to buy it from me. He paid me ten pence for it, which was brilliant. I occasionally got ten pence to last me the whole week and here I was getting the same for a small thing like a magnet.

When I was making a mug of tea for myself after school that day, I had put the milk back into the fridge when I noticed a nick in the corner of the plastic seal as I shut the door. I realised there was a magnet sticking out of it, that was what kept the fridge door shut. I checked the whole door, found that there was magnet all the way around it.

I measured it, discovered that there was approximately fourteen feet of magnet in my very own kitchen! The next morning before I left the house for school I cut the plastic seal a bit more, pulled out a huge strip of magnet, snapped about six inches off, slid the rest of

The Lost Tornado

it neatly back into its plastic sheath. The door shut perfectly; no one would notice.

On the way to school I snapped the six-inch magnet into six lengths of approximately one inch. When I got into the playground I showed Massimo one of the magnets.

'How much?' He said.

'Ten pence,' I replied.

'Is it really a magnet? It feels plastic.'

'Try it,' I said, he did. He put his hand into his pocket, pulled out a handful of silver; I was mesmerised. He gave me a ten pence piece, put the magnet into his shirt pocket. Later on during milk break I took another two magnets from my pocket, began to play with them. I was captivated by the way the two opposite sides of the magnet repelled each other. I nudged Massimo, showed him the two magnets jumping away from each other. His eyes lit up, if he was hooked before he was now obsessed! Once again he pulled out a pile of silver coins, handed me two ten pence's. I couldn't believe my luck; in one morning I had tripled my pocket money. My head was swimming, what would I do with this wealth? I put my hand into my pocket, pulled out the remaining three inches of magnet.

'How much for the lot?' He said.

'I'll give you the three of them for twenty pence.'

He handed the money to me, began making a magnetic jumping sandwich.

'Petroccelli!' Shouted the teacher, startling him. 'What have you got there?'

'Nothing, Miss Noble' he said.

'Of course you've got something. Bring it out here immediately.'

Massimo handed her two of the magnets.

She looked at them, said, 'See me after class. I want to know where you got these.'

'I got them from my house,' he lied.

'You can collect them at the end of the week,' she said. 'Now go and sit down, pay attention to me in future.'

It was approaching lunchtime, there I was sitting in my classroom with fifty pence in my pocket. I was delirious; I could not concentrate on my work. In my head I was already in the tuck shop picking the best sweeties that money could buy. I couldn't wait to get home; I'd discovered a magnetic gold mine.

The next morning I got up before anyone was awake, sneaked down to the kitchen, removed another six inches from the other side of the fridge door, then went to school.

I was nervous. I'd tapped into a massive vein of wealth, didn't know how to handle it. If anybody at home found out that I had great sweets and plenty of them, there would be suspicion that I'd stolen money from Mum's purse or something. I didn't want that, not after the last time, when I'd convinced John to steal fifty pence from her purse. John had gone ahead without realising that it was the last of her money; he'd also handed me a five pence piece that had been there as well.

None of the kids would admit to taking the money so the auld man had grabbed everyone before we left for school, lined us up in the kitchen.

'Alright, empty your pockets everyone,' he said. All eight of us turned our pockets out. Billy got a slap across the head when two cigarettes appeared. Poor John was at the end of the queue and did not realise that I had put the coins back into his blazer pocket. I had also, when I realised we were going to be searched, put the five pence into the cavity in the roof of my mouth, sucked the air out, causing a solid vacuum. The five pence piece was solid. The auld man searched everyone, when he got to John and found the money in his pocket he took off his belt, smacked him three times right across the arse. John was howling. I felt guilty as hell, but also relieved that it wasn't me. To his credit John never said a word.

By this time the five pence was starting to hurt the roof of my mouth. I waited until the auld man disappeared, had to get the money out by using a teaspoon to wedge it down. I decided that I would sell the magnets to Massimo for a lower price as I couldn't

The Lost Tornado

trust myself to keep this wealth hidden. I felt that my lust for sweets would betray me.

We agreed the price of seven pence for a one-inch magnet. That day I picked up another fifty pence! By the end of the week I had a stash of cash of over two pounds hidden in my cupboard! It was of no consequence to me whatsoever that the fridge door did not shut any more. Mum and dad couldn't understand it. I told them I had seen Gordon, my youngest brother, playing with the door. The next week I took the first six inches of magnet from the bottom half of the fridge, the freezer compartment, and took it in to sell to Massimo. I knew it was the end of a good thing when he only offered me thirty pence for the full six inches. I was horrified, but decided to go with it. Friday morning I was counting the money I had gathered, deciding how much I'd take to school and what I'd buy. It was a beautiful sunny morning, I bought the kids an ice lolly each, Fabs all round.

When I got into the classroom Massimo was sitting there, looking glum. The whole pile of magnets was sitting in front of him. I knew for certain that there was at least seven feet of magnet broken into one inch strips sitting there. He was not making eye contact with me, I knew something was up.

'Alright, Massimo?'

He still did not look up.

'My mum said I've to give you these back and get all of my money. She said if you didn't give me it back she would go to your house to speak to your mum and dad.' He pushed the eighty-four small black strips back onto my desk, they clung to each as if they were terrified. I quickly figured out that I'd got around twelve pounds in total from him over the weeks and dreaded the thought of having to get that kind of money together. It was impossible. *Shit*, I thought, *I don't have the money*. I'd spent most of it at the weekend on massive sweet mixes, and had bought the latest Hibs Bukta top. I'd also paid my debt to my sister Lynne for ironing my shirts for me. After the spend on the ice lollies that morning I tried to calculate how much I had left, figured out that it would be no more than forty pence! I was in deep shit.

'I'm sorry, Massimo,' I said, 'but I don't have your money.'

'My Mum'll kill me if I don't bring the money back by tonight,' he said, almost crying.

What could I do? The magnets could not be put back into the fridge as the sealed units which originally held them were split wide open, never to be closed again, there was now a brick at the bottom of the fridge keeping the freezer door shut.

I asked around the class to see if anyone would be interested in buying some magnets at an amazingly low price. I was laughed at. Massimo was determined that he was going to get his money back, my mind was once again swimming, although this time it was in deep shit rather than exuberance. I decided that the best ploy was to fake illness and hope to get time off school, thereby avoiding the issue while I figured out a plan. I left the magnets sitting on Massimo's desk. As far as I was concerned they were his problem.

As I left school, I completely ignored him. He tried several times to push the magnets onto my desk, but I shoved them back using my elbow. For some reason I thought if I didn't touch them with my hands they were still his. I left school nursing an anxiety that I hadn't experienced since the Paddo incident. Crap weekend. No energy to play footy. Hibs got beaten by Brechin in the cup, John had kicked my ball into a barbed wire fence and burst it. I was so down.

Sunday morning was miserable. I could not afford to go to school tomorrow. I knew that my mum and dad were too long in the tooth to fall for the usual stuff, decided that I would have to really get ill in order to achieve my goal. As a small boy, I'd discovered somehow that by licking certain ornaments in my Nana's house I could get sick. The taste of them was very strange, kind of salty and sweet at the same time, but it also tasted cold. That evening I paid my Nana a surprise visit, cut her grass for her while I was there. Before I left, I put my master plan into action. I pretended to go to the toilet but sneaked into one of the rooms where she kept her ornaments; strange blue fish and several fairies on the mantelpiece. I picked up the biggest blue

The Lost Tornado

fish; it looked like a goldfish with big rubber lips and bulging eyes. I licked the bottom; it tasted really weird. I licked and licked until I was thirsty. I then went on to the small fairy and licked the wings, which were made of a different material to the rest of it. The fairy wings also made me feel sick, I was glad, as I would not have to work too hard to get off school. After I had licked the ornaments enough I went to the toilet, had a big drink from the cold tap. I looked in the mirror, I was delighted, my face had turned deathly white and my tongue was blue. I went into the living room where Nana was sitting watching *Crossroads* and smoking. She looked at me.

'Are you feeling OK, Jimmy?' She said.

'I was feeling OK before I cut your grass, Nana,' I said, 'but now I'm feeling quite sick.' I stuck my tongue out. She dropped her cigarette onto her pinny in alarm.

She took me back round to my house, told my mum that she thought I'd worked too hard in the garden and had made myself ill. She gave me ten pence for cutting the grass and another ten pence for being a brave boy. Inside I was doing a somersault of jubilation. It worked a treat, I was off school the whole week, by the time I returned Massimo had gone back to Italy to visit his family for his two month summer holiday. Talk about luck! Mum got the insurance company out to see about the problem with the fridge and freezer. We'd lost a lot of food with the mysterious leaking. I made sure I was nowhere to be seen when the engineer came. For my own insurance purposes, I put the bag of magnets into the bottom of John's cupboard, left them there to get him the blame or to use them in the future. Either outcome would suit me.

CHAPTER 10

I was sitting in front of our new four-bar electric fire, settling myself down on the blue canvas rug with a big bag of pick 'n' mix that I'd bought from the tuck shop. This was one of my favourite places in the whole world, although having said that the only other places I'd been to were Pilton and Kinross, so there was no real competition. I loved the simplicity and comfort of sitting in front of a nice warm fire, eating some great sweeties, watching my favourite TV programmes – in colour, mind you, nothing but the best.

Halfway through eating that rubbish I was beginning to feel bloated and sick. I'd long since made my peace with Paddo and could now wander anywhere I wanted without the fear and loathing that once consumed me. Life was great. As always, I'd got my Hibs top on, a massive cup of tea sat on the fireplace at my left hand, lots of milk and three sugars.

Earlier that day after a bit of luck, I was financially flush. I'd found some money that I got John to steal from mum's purse; he'd hidden it, I'd then taken it from his hiding place, put it in my own one. I'd completely forgotten about it until I put on the jacket that was my hiding place. The good thing about the situation was that John couldn't complain to anybody. The tuck shop had a vast array of sweets. I stood there, heart beating fast. I had one pound, seventy pence to spend. I stared at the jars of sweets lined up on the shelves like condemned men standing to attention. Eventually after much eye squinting and calculating I decided on a quarter pound of pear drops, a quarter pound of cola cubes, another quarter of sherbet lemons and a quarter of soor plooms. That was the boiled sweets taken care of, now for the chocolate and chewies. I got a dozen Chelsea Whoppers, six foam bananas, a handful of shrimps, some toffee Rolos and some mint creams, four Drumsticks, twelve Black Jacks, twelve Fruit Salads, ten fizzy cola bottles and finally a big bar of chocolate-covered nougat. I got Maggie to put them into a plastic carrier bag.

'I hope you're going to share them with your brothers and sisters,' said Mags as I left the shop.

'Of course.' I laughed. 'As if anyone could eat this lot on their own.'

I looked left, then right, then left again, ran over the road, made my way over to the house. The weight of the sweeties held me back from a full scale sprint. I was hoping that Debbie had guarded the prized position in front of the fire for me as she'd said she would. *Scooby Doo* was about to start. I worried about that as I ran home. Some of the sweets were almost slipping out of the carrier bag. When I got into the house I heard raised voices. John was fighting with Debbie, trying to move her from the front of the TV and fire.

'No. I'm not moving,' she screamed, 'I'm keeping this seat for Jimmy.' She was holding on with all of her might to the chair legs, John was desperately trying to pull her away by her ankles. He was ten years older than her but she was a determined wee character. As I walked in, she kicked out at John, caught him right in the heehaws. He bent over, his face turning pure white. He walked out of the room slowly without saying a word.

'Well done, Debs,' I said. She got up, I settled myself down in the prime seat. 'Get me a cup of tea, will you, doll?'

She went through to the kitchen, made me a big cup of hot, sweet, milky tea. I placed all of the sweets around me in a big semi-circular array, felt like a king. I took a few from here and there, handed them to Debbie. She was delighted. The other kids looked on jealously.

For some reason John had been annoying the shit out of me all day, I don't know why, it was really unusual as I was normally annoying him. He appeared at the door, face flushed.

'That's my seat,' he said, 'I was there first.'

'Well, I'm here now,' I replied, 'and there's nothin you can do about it.' I refused to get drawn into his arguments and concentrated on concocting confectionery cocktails. I was sitting there watching *Scooby Doo* followed by *Grange Hill*, jaws going twenty to the dozen, no doubt crunching my way to buying some future dentist a holiday home. After two long hours of jaw action, it was beginnin to take its toll. I'd finished all of my sweets except for the soor plooms. I kept them to last as they were really hard on the teeth. They also had a high content of citric acid, tended to make me pee, I had no intention of letting my spot go. I didn't offer anyone any of my sweets, I sat there, scoffed the lot.

To be honest, by then I was thinking about using the bag for its alternative purpose, I felt so sick and bloated. The electric four-bar fire was on three bars and was burning a very authentic fireside tartan onto my left thigh. It hurt like hell, but I knew that if I got up I'd lose my place to John, who was sitting waiting on the edge of the couch like a vulture.

I put my hand at the side of my thigh to shield the pain from the fire but my hand got burned more quickly. I was busy trying to reach up to the couch for a cushion to use as a shield when John sneaked up on me. I tried to hit him with the cushion, ended up knocking half a cup of tea onto the fire. It hissed like hell, smoke bellowed from it. I got up quickly, turned it off at the plug.

As I was doing that, John grabbed my bag of soor plooms, ran to the living room door with them. He held up the bag, removed two of the little green balls, popped them into his mouth. 'Thanks for the sweets, greedy guts,' he shouted.

'Oi, put them back,' I shouted. He stuck his two fingers up at me, threwe the bag onto the couch, walked out of the room. I got up, chased after him.

He looked round, laughed at me, headed for the front door, before he ran out of the house, he ran back into the living room, grabbed the bag from the couch, took another two sweets. I'm not sure if it was the sherbet lemons or the cola bottles that tipped me over the edge, but I was absolutely fizzing. He knew that if he asked he would never have got one. I found myself running after him with one thing in mind, getting my damned sweets back. It was as if I was possessed.

I looked over the balcony, there was John with his pals. He took the sweets from his mouth, held them aloft, like four small green

The Lost Tornado

saliva-covered trophies. I ran downstairs after him; he jogged his way to the steps at the bottom of the road. I was catching him, but he put on a burst of speed, headed towards the school. He jumped over the closed school gates, I followed. I looked around, couldn't see him. I spotted him at the gates at the other end, he was jumping over them, heading back towards the court. By this stage we were both knackered, having run almost a mile. My belly was aching with all that gunk I'd eaten, I wasn't sure if I needed to fart or shit, but I was determined not to let him get the better of me.

I pushed myself, managed to sneak past him, dodging behind a car, unseen. I waited on top of the small bridge that linked the top of the court with the bottom. I spotted him coming towards the bridge, he had no idea that I was standing above him. He was laughing to himself, looking around, thinking he'd got away with it.

I leapt onto him from the side of the fence, flattened him, knocking his breath out of his body. His face was now as serious as mine. I pinned him down on the grass, pushed his head down, rubbed it into the mud. He was way too tired to fight back so I put my dirty fingers into his mouth. He was shocked, but not as much as I was. I forced his teeth apart with a discarded ice lolly stick I'd found lying nearby.

I pulled out the shrunken, dripping sweets, held them in my hand. I looked at them, I was now seeing them as trophies. I surprised myself as I put them into my mouth, crunched them into a pulp! It was extremely liberating. John lay there gasping for breath, surprised. He was experiencing a violation of his mouth for the first and, I guess, last time in his life. I looked up, John's pals were watching us. They were chanting; 'spot the weirdo' at me. I didn't care a jot. I lay on my back, Hibs top soaked in sweat and mud, crunching, getting my breath back, looking up at the sun.

John gave me a weak kick as he walked towards his friends. They all looked down at me from the high fence, some shaking heads, arms around John's shoulders. They headed off somewhere.

I punched my fists in the air, shouted, 'Yyyyyyeeeesssss!'

One morning, a fancy envelope was delivered to the door, I remember it as it had to be signed for, this had never happened before. We gathered around the kitchen table as mum opened the lovely white embossed envelope with a kitchen knife. One of our aunties was getting married, she had invited the whole family to the wedding, the whole twelve of us! Very unusual, normally it was only Mum, Dad and Karen that were invited to any weddings, the rest of us being pretty uncouth by comparison to the 'golden child'.

Mum had taken delivery of a new catalogue. 'Right you two,' she said to John and I. 'You can pick a shirt and suit each from here'. There was a section of the catalogue that had been marked with some ripped up newspaper.

After flicking through the book countless times, I decided on a pink shirt with multi-coloured dots and a three-piece pinstriped suit while John chose a shirt with hockey players and a pale blue jacket and trouser suit. Mine looked so cool on the young model. He looked a similar build to me. I could picture myself in it, no problem. *The girls would flock to me, the guys would be so jealous.* I nodded to myself a few times, put a big fold in each page to mark it.

Mum took the book, filled out all the forms, that left me waiting in anticipation of my new beautiful life dressed like a model.

After almost a week of waiting the parcels arrived at nine o'clock on a Sunday morning, in time for us to wear them as we went hiking into the Pentland Hills. Mum had no idea that we had our shirts on, our anoraks covered them nicely. When Mum gave us the catalogue we were told to pick a shirt and a suit. I went for this brown pinstriped suit, again, it looked so cool on the guy. The shirt was a magnet, but both items combined would keep me snogging for weeks. Although tempted, I decided not to wear the suit up the hills as Vincent, the guy who was taking us, said it might get a bit muddy in the swampy bits that we were going to be walking through.

Eventually my pinstriped suit arrived, I took it out of the plastic bag, mesmerised by it. It was a beauty, dark brown, very thin cream pin stripes, Crimplene perhaps? I wasn't sure about the material, but it was magic, a three-piece suit, nice jacket, lovely waistcoat and a pair of the most fashionable flares. There was also a surprise for me in a box next to the bag; Mum had bought me a pair of brown platform shoes. *Matching footwear? What will people think of next*, I thought to myself. I really could not wait to put them all on. I had never had any clothing before that had got me truly excited.

Mum was at work. Now was my big chance to try it all on. I carefully opened the bag up. I had to make sure that after I'd tried it on Mum would have no way of noticing that I'd even disturbed it. I opened the tissue paper, making sure not to rip the sellotape, took out all of the pins and clips that were holding it in place, making sure that I knew where they all had to go when I put it back. I pulled a cleanish pair of pants from under the bed, put them on, put the trousers on, buttoned up all eleven buttons, looked in the mirror. They were perfect. I checked myself out, moving my hips a bit, the flares swung nicely to and fro. I put on a T-shirt, then the waistcoat. It had two nice little pockets that I could just about get three fingers into. The look I wanted was almost there. I made a note; have to get a watch on a chain to make me look the business. I put the jacket on, then the platforms. Walked into my dad's room, borrowed his big sunglasses. My image was complete. I made one final adjustment as I looked in the mirror; my hair needed a quick brush.

After strutting around the bedroom looking in all of the mirrors, I looked out of the window, noticed a whole gang of kids sitting around. I had a great idea. I'd go downstairs for a minute to show them that I really had taste.

'Who's this guy?' They'd say. 'Did someone walk out of a Hollywood set?'

I managed to get my balance with the platform shoes quite easily, at least it was OK when I was on the level, but when I headed downstairs it got very tricky. Holding onto the rail, I eventually got down. I stumbled down the outside steps, hiding the wobbling from the group of kids who were sitting at the garages, walked nonchalantly into their midst as if I did this every day. As expected I got a few wolf whistles from the girls.

'Who is this guy?' Sharon shouted.

'Cool suit,' April said. 'Great platforms.'

I felt superb. This ex-ugly duckling had shed its grey wispy down and turned into a beautiful swan.

I was now bonding with the look, and believed that this was where I was meant to be. Claremont Court was no longer big enough for me. I wanted to get out into the main street, show off the new image, perhaps wander up to Princes Street to meet some amazing foreign girls who would in all probability drag me into the bushes and take their helping of JD love.

Jeez, who'd have guessed that some fake leather shoes and Crimplene could feel so good? My ego erupted. Who cared if Mum was back soon? This was the new me. How dare she think she could limit me and my potential? My heart was thumping harder inside the waistcoat, I was driven. After a couple of minutes walking around strutting my stuff I decided Princes Street was a step too far. I could feel the shoes forming a blister on my heel. The football socks I'd put on were riding down into the front of the platforms, bundling up. I had to reach over a few times to pull them up to my calves, almost falling over.

I went from the Court to the main street, moved swiftly over to the tuck shop, then into the school playground.

Some of the guys were playing against the softies from Broughton Road; Toby, Weeps, Bellie, Woody and McCowan were all there. They turned around, stared at me when I came through the gates. An obvious jealousy pervaded the atmosphere. I stood stock still with my hands squeezed into the waistcoat pockets, looking sooooo cool. I was sure they had no idea who it was. After a few minutes staring, they turned round, carried on with their game of football on the tarmac.

I walked so slowly towards the guys. Clint Eastwood never made a better entrance in his life. Alex kicked the ball, it came straight towards me, I stopped it with my big shoes, two of the Broughton Road guys ran towards me, I did a shimmy, nutmegged one of them, which was very impressive in platforms. I decided to use the monster weight of the platforms – they were like two mallets tied to my feet – to hammer the ball into the top corner.

As I prepared to balance myself for the shot, I shifted the weight from one leg to the other, finding the middle ground. I leaned back, pulling my left peg into the strike position. As I let go, my left shoe got caught up in the flared bottom of my right trouser leg. The momentum of the kick spun me around, I felt the material on the right leg ripping, my hands were so tight in my waistcoat pockets that I couldn't get them out. I could feel momentum, gravity and a spinning sensation forcing me to the ground. I tried to get my hands free again, but to no avail.

I was twisting in slow motion. As I went down, I tried to manoeuvre myself onto my back as I knew I couldn't use my hands to cushion the fall. I was spinning precariously on one platformed foot. I couldn't even put my elbows out for protection. I sensed the rough tarmac getting closer and closer to my face.

Crunch! I hit the tarmac, teeth first. Not a straight down plummet, I had to do it in style. The spinning motion caused my head to act as a brake against the rough ground. I could immediately feel the burn against the pristine skin on my face. I heard laughter in the distance. I jerked my left hand from the waistcoat pocket, heard another rip; the pocket flapped about like an autumn leaf. I put the fingers of my left hand towards my mouth, found that I was covered in blood. My right hand was still firmly embedded in the other waistcoat pocket. I pulled it out, getting blood all over the pocket. My face and mouth were burning. I involuntarily reached up to my mouth, found a space which was not there a minute ago. A gap in my teeth, but on closer examination it was only half a tooth that was gone. Still hurt like a whole tooth, though.

My nose was scraped and bleeding as well.

The Broughton Road losers were laughing their tits off at me, Woody was getting them going by mimicking a spinning idiot, eyes crossed, tongue lolling. *I'll get that wee shite later*, I thought. I made a mental note. As I stood up I heard a sickening crunch, my left platform shoe had crushed Dad's sunglasses to a pulp.

Fuck! How bad could this get? I thought.

As I picked the glass and metal remnants up, figuring out how I could fix them, my mates Higgy and Alex came to my aid, asked if I was OK. I dragged myself to my full height slowly, painfully. With them supporting me on either side I shuffled out of the playground, around the back of the school so that none of the girls would see me in that state.

As I was hobbling, whining my way out I spotted Mum talking with one of her school cleaner chums. They were deep in conversation, I got an icy chill as I realised what I'd done. I hoped she hadn't noticed me. I sent Higgy and Alex away while I waited in the coal-shed out of sight until she'd gone. *Shit*, I thought, *how am I going to get back into the house without getting spotted?*

During the hour and a half I spent in the coal shed I had the chance to examine the damage. It was bad. Very bad. The trousers had a big hole in the right knee, that being the first point to impact the ground, closely followed by the right elbow. Once again there was collateral damage; in fact, it had an even bigger rip. The seam of the right leg was ripped up to the shin, caused by my shoe getting caught. I remembered that as I lay on the ground frustrated, embarrassed, I stupidly tried to kick my way free, adding an extra foot and a half to the rip.

The right waistcoat pocket was covered in blood, the left one was literally hanging by a thread.

The left shoe had a big scrape on the front where I kicked the tarmac instead of the ball, battered it against the ground. To top it all, my mouth and nose had swelled up to double their usual size. I thought

The Lost Tornado

about the consequences, I couldn't make it sound good, no matter what scenarios or excuses I came up with. Although I was cold, sore and hungry I waited until it was dark to make my way home. I knew that if I timed it well enough, I could sneak in via the boys' balcony while the rest of the family were busy at the teatime trough.

An hour and a half later, I attempted to climb vertically up the three flights of fences to their balcony. I couldn't get a grip in the fence with the big stupid shoes. I raised my arms but they hurt too much, I was obviously in no fit state to climb anywhere. I went to the door, lifted the letterbox. Silence. A good sign. It meant everyone was eating. I seized my chance, got out my key, tried to pop it into the keyhole. I pushed and pushed but it wouldn't go in. I held it up to the light. *Shit! It's bent, must have fallen on it.* I looked through the letterbox again; still silence. After a moment or two Gordon wandered into the hall with his plate.

'Gordon,' I whispered.

No reaction.

'Pssst, Gordon!'

He came over to the door, opened it, looked at me with wide eyes, put his hand to his mouth, pointed at me, then pointed to the rips. I could see he was about to shout something. 'Shhhh,' I whispered. I grabbed him, covering his mouth with my hand. His plate and spoon crashed to the floor, dripping tomato soup all over me and the stairs. I heard somebody get up from the couch, I ran upstairs with him under my arm, him trying to bite me.

As I locked the room door I wiped my tomato soup covered hands onto the trousers. *Fuck it*, I thought, *it's a lost cause now.* I dropped him onto the floor, got my sweetie jar, handed it over to him. He was silent as he got stuck into my sweets. I took the suit off, Laid it down, shook my head. I put my head into my hands as I sat on the edge of the bed.

'You silly, stupid bastard,' I muttered to myself. 'What do I do now? What *can* I do?'

Gordon was chewing a Mojo.

I said to him, 'Stay here, don't let anyone in, OK?'

He nodded, I went into the toilet, washed the blood and snot from my face, then made a decision. *Let's pretend that didn't happen.*

Great idea. I thought back to earlier in the day, as I recalled, I was the only one who saw the suit being delivered. Could I pretend it didn't arrive? Hope was beginning to grow. I calmed down a bit, dried myself, went back into the room. Gordon was still chomping on my precious sweets. I took the jar from him, gave him two Refreshers.

'I'll give you two of these every day for a week if you keep quiet. OK?'

He nodded twice. Seeing him tiring out his small jaws on my sweets really annoyed me, but it was a price worth paying. I fetched the suit box and bags from my cupboard, folded the suit into the shape that it arrived in. Well, I tried to; folding was never a strength. It sort of resembled what had arrived, I made sure all of the pins and clips went somewhere believable. I made doubly sure that all of the rips were well hidden. It still looked new from certain angles, especially in a dimly lit room. I bundled it back into the plastic bag, which now seemed way too small, forced it into the box, putting masking tape around the edges to keep it from exploding out. I cleared a bit of space under my bed, pushed the box way into the corner, past the cups, plates and dirty clothes, making sure that nobody would find it.

I convinced myself that nearer the wedding I'd get some brown pinstripe thread, repair the damage myself. I'd take classes on embroidery and thread-work, there were still weeks to go, yeah, plenty of time for all that. I was high on my own bullshit, actually believing it!

I ventured downstairs, Mum came over to me.

'You've missed your tea,' she said. Then she stepped closer. 'What's happened to your face? Have you been fighting?'

'Of course not!' I said. 'I tripped.'

She pulled my chin towards her, examined my mouth closely, poking the half tooth that sat there.

'Ouch!' I shouted.

The Lost Tornado

She went through to the kitchen to get some TCP. I think she was surprised that I didn't flinch much, but I was way past that particular pain threshold, getting practice for the different pain that would, no doubt be coming my way in a few weeks when she discovered the truth.

My injuries really didn't hurt that much, even though I'd smashed a tooth, cracked my nose, elbow and knees.

Time passed, I wasn't sure how long, maybe weeks. I waited until the house was empty, dragged the suit from under the bed, cleaned off the debris, unwrapped it for a second time. I was horrified at what I saw. In my mind, the passage of time had healed a lot of the rips and cuts. The reality of what I was looking at right then made me practically shit myself. I knew that Mum had paid a lot of money for it and that she'd be paying it off for the next year or so. I got the purn of brown thread that I'd borrowed from my Nana – not that she knew I'd got it, of course, I threaded the needle. The courses on embroidery and stuff that I swore I'd take never happened, to be honest I'd forgotten all about those ideas and kicked a ball about most of the time until a few minutes earlier, when Susan had mentioned that Theresa's wedding was at the weekend. Her words had sent a lightning bolt down my spine, through my half tooth, propelled me upstairs at breakneck speed.

With a new perspective and a clearer head I realised the first thing to do was to try to get rid of the blood before I began repairing it with the needle and thread. The only thing I'd ever sewn in my life before was two washers onto an old sock to make a glove puppet. I didn't really want to sew, but I had no choice. I took the suit into the bathroom, ran the hot water. There was no soap or shampoo, but there was a bottle of conditioner. I thought it was similar to shampoo. I put some onto the blood-soaked material and left it, ears pricked, alive to any movement around the house. After a couple of minutes steeping, the blood-soaked cream stripes turned pink.

I panicked and ran the whole suit under the hot tap. The brown dye now started to run into the cream stripes, they began to turn light brown and pink. I dropped the suit into the water in a complete and utter shitstorm, turned the taps off, locked the bathroom door. I had to think of something fast. I went through my whole repertoire of blaming the kids for the things I did, but this time there were none suitable for this extreme and desperate situation. I heard a key in the door followed by loud chattering; a group of siblings had come home. I dumped it, dripping, into a bin liner, threw it out of the bathroom window. It landed near the cages.

The cages were a part of Claremont Court where very few people ventured. Originally designed to be kind of garden sheds for flat dwellers - 'Basement Storage' they called it. They were situated directly under the main building. They were prison-like, one per household with a big padlock on each cage that contained mostly household items, worth keeping, but too big or did not go with the house decor. They stunk of old piss and shit, the reason for this was that drunks would often piss and shit there when they could not hold their toilet parts in check after a night on the tiles. The most unnerving thing was the feeling underfoot, hundreds of packets of yeast had been stolen from Redbrae's bakery over the years and for some reason it was dumped in the pitch-black cages, it grew there like some kind of sticky silent monster waiting to gobble up your footwear, it also smelled like puke.

It was a well-known fact that people on the run tended to hide in the cages as it was a labyrinth that nobody wanted to go into, including the pigs.

I ran downstairs, ignoring everybody. I opened the cages door, looked for a far corner, threw the bag, splashing and sloshing, into the piss-stinking underground. I couldn't deal with it then.

I'd leave it there, pick it up when I had a plan.

The pressure of the wedding was building and building. Mum said at least once a day, 'Wonder when your suit'll arrive, son?'

And I replied, 'No idea, Mum.'

Pressure, pressure. Day after day after day. Only a day or two to go before the wedding.

I was sitting on the toilet pan, eating a slice of dry white bread, as that was how I did my best thinking.

Bang! A brainwave took shape; I'd get Ronnie or Andy Duke to nick me a suit before Mum ever found out about the disaster that was festering in the cages. That definitely seemed like THE Eureka moment in my life. I ran downstairs to their house, punched my fist in the air as I saw Andy sitting watching telly.

'How do you fancy doing me a favour, pal?' I asked. Andy and I got on well, he'd always help if he could. He was the youngest in their family, relatively inexperienced at the nicking lark. 'I've had a bit of bad luck with a new suit; Tigger peed on it and Mum would get rid of him if she found out,' I said. Andy loved Tigger, which is why I'd told a small white lie.

"Yeah, no problem, I'll go up town in the mornin'."

'Thanks Andy, yer a real pal.'

The following day he headed up to Marks and Spencer to see if he could nick me a suit. Well, didn't he blow the whole gaff by getting caught! He tried to nick us a suit each and was spotted waddling towards the exit wearing two suits under his duffel coat! To his credit he didn't grass me up, he took the blame firmly on the chin.

I felt so guilty, I was obviously in his debt. That night, after he'd been released by the rozzers, he went out 'snowdropping', managed to nick a pinstriped suit from the washing line of a well-off family along the road. The next morning he turned up at my door, handed it to me. I could see immediately that it was at least three times too big for me, but I took it anyway, sneaked him a half box of Sugar Puffs for his efforts.

'That's from Tigger,' I told him, 'he says thanks.'

I took the suit upstairs to my room, put it into the cupboard. The next morning I was sitting there wondering what to do when Mum shouted on me. I went down to the living room to see what she was after.

'I've been in touch with the catalogue, they say the suit was sent ages ago,' she said.

'Ah, that's right,' I said, 'it arrived yesterday, I forgot about it. I took it up to the room.'

'Great! You'll have to try it on. There's not long to go until the wedding, if it doesn't fit you, I'll have to send it back.'

Her words set off *Psycho* shower scene noises in my head. *Shiiit.* It felt like somebody had pulled the handbrake on in my mind. My brain froze, I couldn't think.

'Try not to make it too obvious that there's something wrong,' I said to myself.

She can tell by your face that there's something up, my mind whispered to me. *Do something to throw her off the trail.*

'The kittens are stuck to the hall wall,' I blurted out.

That should do it, my mind said, *at least it'll give you another minute to be pain free before the beating begins*

One of our cats had four kittens about three or four weeks previously. Mum told us that as soon as they were old enough she'd be getting rid of them, but we all knew she was too soft, would let us keep them. There were enough to go around, one for each room. That morning I was first downstairs, had laughed out loud at the sight that greeted me. During the night two of the kittens had climbed up the wood-chip wallpaper with their brand new claws and had no idea how to retract them, leaving them dangling like mountaineers. I laughed to myself as I thought about it again, but quickly snapped out of it as my dilemma demanded attention.

'Eh? What are you talking about?' Mum said. 'What do you mean?'

I rushed out of the living room, desperately looked for one of the kittens. I found the ginger and white one, the weakest of the litter, hurriedly held it up to the wood-chip, tried to get it to grip on.

'Come on, you little weakling,' I whispered, 'get a grip.'

It meowed helplessly. I heard Mum coming into the hall, I squeezed its paws gently to push its tiny claws out. They were too small. I tried again, but this time it pissed all over me, wriggled out of my grip, fell to the floor, ran away as Mum came into view.

The Lost Tornado

'What are you talking about?' She said, looking puzzled as the kitten rushed past her.

'I've taken the small one down,' I said.

She looked at me, as if I was mental. 'Sometimes I wonder about you, son,' she said. 'I really do.' She stared at me then said, 'What's that all over your tank top?' She walked over, stopped as soon as the smell of pish kicked in. 'Go and get changed, I'll put that tank top into the wash. How did that happen? Were you tormenting those kittens again?'

'No, I told you what happened,' I said.

She shook her head, dragged the tank top over my head, catching my ears. I bolted upstairs three steps at a time, changed into my Hibs strip, handed the dirty clothes to Mum on my way down, grabbed my football, ran out of the door.

'What about your suit?' She shouted.

I pretended not to hear her, running quickly along the landing while shouting some football commentary about myself to make sure she knew that I hadn't heard her.

'And it's Divine, with a penalty for Scotland in the last minute of the World Cup ...'

I got downstairs, congratulated myself on the ingenuity of my escape.

'Remember, lad,' said my mind, 'T' grim reaper will eventually catch up with 'ee.' (For some reason the voice in my head speaks in a Yorkshire accent.) 'Ye think ye've escaped, but he even caught Houdini in the end.'

I ignored it, ran off to play football.

Pressure, pressure, dribble, swerve, goal!

Pressure. Pressure ... I knew it was inevitable; I would at some point have to show Mum how the suit looked on me. I'd delayed it for days, using wit and guile. I knew time was running out. By then I'd brought it back up from the cages, dried it out in the airing cupboard, the material felt as crispy as a giant poppadom.

After Mum shouting on me for the fourth time I went downstairs with the suit in the dust covered box. It was still folded so that the size of the suit was not possible to determine. I slowly opened the box, showing her the suit under the plastic.

'What do you think of the material?' I said to her.

'It looks quite nice.' She said, ripping the plastic bag, feeling the material between her fingers. 'Hmmm! Actually, it seems a bit rougher than I'd thought it would. Take it out, try it on.'

I took out the jacket that Andy had given me, put it on.

'What in hell's name's happened here?' She said, holding the jacket up to the light. 'That suit's far too big for you; it doesn't even look new. Put it back into the box, I'll send it back to the catalogue tomorrow. We only have a day until the wedding. I hate to say it, son, but if we can't get a replacement you might have to miss the wedding.'

I handed over the box with Andy's suit in it, feigning disappointment. 'If I can't go, will you bring me some cake and stuff back?' I said.

'Of course we will, son,' she said.

I turned my back, walked out of the room, congratulating myself on my ingenuity. The pressure was gone, wiped away. It felt marvellous, but I knew that one day the catalogue people would come calling.

As I headed upstairs singing happily to myself Dad was walking down.

'Have you seen my sunglasses? John said he saw you with them earlier.'

CHAPTER 12

I was outside at the garages kicking the ball against the doors, they acted as make-piece goalposts, there was a satisfying bang every time I hit the sweet spot. I turned around when I heard Weldo's squeaky window opening.

'How's it goin?' I said.

'Ach, no bad', he shouted back to me. 'The auld boy's still takin my Mum's passin a bit hard, though. They'd been married thirty-four years. Would've been thirty-five next week.'

'Ach I know, sad but what can we do, eh?' I said.

'Aye, I ken,' He said. 'Not a lot.' 'How D'ye fancy chummin me up tae Albert Street for a haircut?'

'My god. Are you running a temperature or somethin?' I said, walking over to the window, ball under my arm.

'Nah. It's getting on my tits now. I'm getting a sore neck from flicking it over my shoulder.'

'Aye, OK, ah'll chum ye,' I said.

'Cool' he said, ah'll get my jacket.'

We did the usual stuff, kicked the ball all over the place, across roads, getting in the way of people, but we were in the zone, didn't care about upsetting people. We got to Albert Street about one o'clock, the barber had two customers sitting on the red leather bench and one auld baldy boy already in the chair. Frank Sinatra's singin in the background and the auld boy thinks he can sing like him.

'Go yerself, Scottish Frank,' the barber says to him.

Weldo and I looked at each other, raised our eyebrows.

'OK, boys,' the barber said to us, 'be with you in a couple of minutes.'

He was chat, chatting to the auld boy. Robbin him, charging him for basically combing his baldy heid. Eventually the auld boy got up fae the chair, pleased as punch.

'Cheers, Fergie,' he said. 'See you next week?'

'Will do, Aldo, my son.'

The next guy sat down, got a short back and sides. The barber was chat, chatting away again. I noticed that while the Fergie was chattin he kept lookin at his watch.

The last boy on the bench went up to the chair, sat down. Another baldy auld coot.

'Just a trim, pal,' he said.

I thought, *what a waste of money, the auld boy's as bald as my plastic ball.* Eventually, after a lot of fluffing about, making the auld boy think he still had hair, Fergie winked at us, showed the auld boy a photo, pretending to the auld boy that it was a mirror reflecting his new haircut. The auld boy must have been half blind.

'Aye, that's magic, Fergie,' he said, 'you've still got it.' He got up from the chair, gave Fergie a tip.

'Anything for the weekend, sir?'

'Nah, I'm fine, Fergie. Still got the yin from last month,' he said, taking a rubber Johnny out of his wallet, waved it about a bit then buggered off.

Fergie fumbled away at his till, washed his hands, walked over to us.

'Right, boys, the bad news is that I've only got time for one haircut.'

'Perfect,' I said to him. 'Only one of us wants a haircut.'

Weldo wandered up to the chair, sat down. Fergie got a clean smock, wrapped it around him. He stood for a few minutes, cleaning his equipment.

'So, what can I do for you today, young man?'

'Skinhead, please.' Weldo said.

'Are you sure?'

'Yeah, I'm sure.'

'OK, you're the boss.'

He got his clippers, removed the guards, he turned the power on it sounded bloody scary. He began to shave Weldo's head. First cut was right across the top and middle of his head, ear to ear. He then took off everything in front of it.

I was still looking at Fergie looking at his watch. This big American

Jeep thingy screeched to a halt outside his door. There were two big burly guys in the Jeep, they were looking out of the rolled down windows. The horn blared BEEEEEEEP! Then blared again.

Fergie stopped cutting Weldo's hair, went outside.

He looked round at me. 'What's gaun on there?'

'No idea' I said. 'I saw Fergie looking at his watch a couple of times, must've been waiting on his mates.'

Fergie came back into the shop.

'Right, boys,' he said, 'we'll have to leave it there.'

Weldo looked at Fergie, laughed. 'Aye, right?'

'Nah, seriously boys, I've got to go. No charge.'

'Eh?' He said, 'What about my hair?'

'Come back Monday, I'll sort it out for ye.'

'Nae chance,' He shouted. 'We're goin out tonight. I cannae go like this!'

'You'll have tae. Oot with ye.'

Weldo sat in the chair, not moving a muscle. Looked at his hair. It was terrible. Looked like a red Indian about to go on the warpath. He was baldy from the front of his head to the top, the back was still long black hair, shoulder length. 'I'm stayin here,' he said.

'Oh, are ye now?' Fergie said. 'We'll see about that.'

He went outside, came back with one of the big meat-heads. The big guy stood at the door, slowly rolled his sleeves up. 'Right, pal,' he said, 'ye've had yer freebie, oot ye fuckin get.'

'Fuck off,' Weldo said. 'Look at the fuckin state o my hair, I look like a fuckin mong!'

'True,' the guy said, 'but do I look like a give a fuck?'

'Fergie,' I said, from the sidelines, 'why don't you do a quick skinhead for him?'

'Whae are you callin Fergie, ya familiar wee cunt?' He said. 'Fuckin oot, the pair of ye.'

The two meat-heads grabbed us both by the scruff of the neck, hoyed us out. Weldo was fighting and kicking, but I was glad to get out of there.

As soon as we were on the street, Fergie went back inside, got a few things, then locked up. He got into the back seat of the Jeep, the three of them were laughing, pointing Weldo as they drove slowly off. As they were passin us, the window wound down, Fergie shouted, 'I'm on holiday Monday, ya mong! Come and see us next Wednesday.'

They were all laughing in the Jeep. The horn blasted, they disappeared around the corner.

Weldo stamped about, he was furious. He walked over the road, picked up a crash barrier that'd been left from the previous week's derby match, hurled it into the window of the shop. I looked over and stared at him.

'Fuckin hell, Weldo, what are you doin?' I said. He'd lost the plot, He couldn't stop himself though, kicked the window until the whole shop front caved in. I heard this roaring noise, saw the Jeep come back, screaming around the corner, almost up on two wheels.

'Looks like Fergie's forgotten somethin, Weldo,' I shouted. 'Look – they're back.'

Weldo turned around, picked the crash barrier up again, threw it into the glass in the door. It made a massive bang, the glass came tumbling down, shards everywhere. The Jeep was screeching into the street now. It slowed down at the shop, they saw what'd happened, didn't stop, came right after us. We legged it down Albert Street, me and the mong. There were a couple of auld boys sitting on a bench on the other side of the road observing, sayin nothing, being entertained.

As we were running along between all the cars the Jeep was trying to keep up with us, but we were pretty quick. Albert Street was a real mess, narrow street, cars parked in every available space. We used this to our advantage, knew the guys would have to get on Shanks's pony to catch us. A minute or two later they also realised that. The three of them got out of the Jeep, ran towards us.

'See you back at the Court?' Weldo said.

'Will do,' I replied, we split up.

The meat-heads had decided to go after Weldo, as it was only Fergie that headed towards me. He was an old guy, maybe fifty or something like that, I knew he'd got no chance of catching me. It was Weldo I was worried about. These other two boys looked serious hard nuts. I wouldn't mess with them on any level. Tattoos, shaved heads, pure muscle, testosterone, probably mince for brains.

A minute or two into the chase I could see Fergie leaning over a car bonnet, out of breath. I gave him the wanker sign as I strolled past within a couple of yards of him. He looked about for his mates, but they were nowhere to be seen.

'I'll get you, boy,' he said to me, taking deep breaths, desperately trying to get air into those ancient, creaking lungs.

'Nah, don't think that'll happen,' I said to him. 'Not in this lifetime.'

'Don't you worry, boy,' he said, 'I remember faces.' He stared at me, looked like he was taking a mental note of my coupon. Truth was, I was crapping it; what if he did remember my face and him and the meat-heads came after me?

He couldn't do anything about it right now though.

'Piss off, ya decrepit auld fanny,' I said to him. 'It's yer own fault for being a smart arse. I hope your shop's getting raided.'

I could see that this was not something he'd thought about until now. He got up from the car bonnet, running towards his shop as I laughed out loud.

I was really concerned about Weldo. It'd been a good five minutes, there was no sign of any of them. I'd noticed the way the tough boys ran, knew that I could outrun them if I had to. I decided to go looking for Weldo. I walked all the way up Albert Street, couldn't see them. I walked down Dickson Street and along Iona.

'Jimmy D? Jimmy D?'

I could hear somebody shouting, sounded like Weldo.

I looked around for a while, followed my ears, looked up to a roof in Iona Street, saw him standing next to a chimney stack. 'Where are they?' He shouted.

I shrugged my shoulders. 'Haven't seen them,' I shouted back.

Right where Weldo was standing a top floor window opened up, a boy stuck his head out. He tried to crane his neck to see who was on his roof.

'Oi,' he shouted. 'What are you doin on my roof? Get the fuck off. Ye've ruined the picture on my telly.'

I could see that Weldo was holding onto the aerial. 'Cool it, pal,' he said to the guy.

'Dinnae you tell me to cool it.

'Fuck off,' Weldo said.

'You get down right now, ya little nyaff, or I'll come up and boot yer baws.'

I couldn't believe what I was seeing.

Weldo was yanking the aerial from the chimney stack, dangling it down by the cable to where the boy was, he lowered it to the boy's eye level at the window.

The boy went mental when he saw the metal strip dangling.

'Ya fuckin little cunt,' he shouted. The window slammed, the boy was obviously heading to the stair to get onto the roof.

I shouted up to Weldo, 'What did you do that for? You're in enough trouble as it is.'

He shrugged.

The noise and commotion had got the attention of Fergie's pals, I could see them on a roof along from Weldo. One big bulldog head appeared over the top of the roof, followed by the other one.

'Weldo,' I shouted, 'behind you!'

He looked over, saw the boys. He headed for the side of the building, began to shin his way down the drainpipe. As the two boys got to the roof, the glass window on the roof opened, Mr Ruined TV picture stuck his head out.

'Right, ya bastards,' he shouted, 'I'm havin ye. Destroy my fuckin aerial would ye'

I could see his face dropping as he saw how big those guys were.

'Sorry guys I didnae mean tae shout at ye'.

'What are ye on about?' One of the boys said, 'It's that fuckin mong wi the red Indian haircut we're after'.

The roof-boys were speaking to each other, it looked like we'd now got another enemy. They piled down through the roof window, I was hoping Weldo would get down in time. As he hit the gardens at the bottom, the stair door flew open, we were on our way again, me with my ball tucked under my arm, Weldo with his mong haircut.

They chased us all the way back to the Court. When we got there we knew for sure that we were safe: it was a rabbit warren, we were the rabbits. As the three boys were standing there looking bewildered by the complexity of the place, the big Jeep roared into the Court. The driver's door opened, Fergie jumped down, looked at the boys.

'Forget it, lads,' he said, 'it's pointless, you'll never catch them here. This place has got more escape routes than Colditz. We'll have to wait, get the bastards some other time.'

The four of them looked up at us, shielding their eyes from the glare of the sun. Weldo and I looked down from the roof, he shouted, 'Oi, stooges? Ye've got no chance of catching us. Get back tae yer fuckin caves or we'll fuckin have ye.'

The guy with no TV signal lost the plot at this point. His head went bright red, he began to run about, but ended up at the same spot. We were killing ourselves laughing.

Fergie and the other two bulldogs looked up at us, taking note of our faces. Fergie shouted up to us, me in particular.

'The next time we meet, you little cunt. I'll kick your arse so hard that when you cough it'll smell like shite.' He pointed to me, held his finger there for a while. The threat built as he did so, but was nicely diluted when Weldo dropped a water balloon on him, soaking him, knocking his trilby and glasses onto the road.

CHAPTER 13

ohn and I had shared a double bed ever since we moved into the court, before that we shared a single bed. We had an ancient record player at the side of the bed and used to go to sleep listening to music mainly to drown out the sound of mum and dad arguing and fighting downstairs. We always left the arm up so that whatever record we put on would play and play until morning, letting us drift into oblivion without hearing shouting and screaming.

At some point Mum was able to get an account on the never-never, and surprised us after school one day when we came home to find two single beds in our room. It was really exciting, so much so that John decided to do a flying Kung Fu kick, landed on his bed, cried, swore and shit himself when three spars of the bed cracked in half. We locked the door, inspected the damage. No way could these be repaired. John left the room, came back ten minutes later with a pile of bricks to support the mattress.

'We'll have to keep this quiet,' he said, worriedly.

I tapped the side of my nose. 'Silence is golden, brother, silence is golden.'

Days later, I found myself hiding under that very bed. I'd taken a black crayon from one of the kids rooms, rubbed it all over my face, dug out my big red chunky jumper from the bottom of the cupboard where it was lodged underneath a whole pile of winter stuff, put the jumper on back to front, squeezed under the bed. The stench of the mouldy jumper wool was overwhelming, it made me gag, but it was definitely going to be worth the pain.

John and I had decided a few days ago to conduct an experiment with one of our thickest 'friends', Mikey Meek. His usual attire was a pair of dark brown jeans with big turn-ups and a crease that could cut bullshit, a dark blue checked cowboy shirt, and a pair of brown sandals with white socks. He was chunky, 'puppy fat' his mum called it, but by my reckoning he'd had his puppy fat for about a hundred and twenty dog years.

I used to pop over to his house now and again. I was there one day when his wee brother Mark stripped off, jumped into the bath; nothing unusual in that, but his mum was already there! The door was open slightly, she waved to me.

'Hello, Jimmy,' she shouted, in her posh Edinburgh accent, 'how are you?'

That was the first time ever that I'd seen a naked lady. Fair enough, I couldn't see anything per se, the soap was so foamy that everything was covered up. I could only see her long elegant neck and that she had her hair tied up with a red ribbon.

'Hi Mrs M, I'm good thanks,' I said, hanging about making small talk, hoping the bubbles would disperse a bit and I would at least get a deek of her tits. Mark was about ten at the time. He jumped straight into the bath, making a huge splash, then jumped on top his mum. I still saw nothing except his scrawny little arse. He leaned over, flicked the bathroom door with his soapy big toe, it slowly creaked to a close. I felt like opening it again to continue the chat but knew that she'd know what I was up to. I never forgave the little shit for that.

I was under the bed prepped and waiting. We were expecting Mikey to arrive at five past six, after he'd had his tea. He always had the same tea, sausage, beans and egg, if any of the separate items touched each other he couldn't eat it. *Spoilt weirdo*, I thought, many times.

It really pissed me off because every time he came over he always had a bit of egg on his shirt, same spot every time, some bean sauce at the left side of his annoying gob. I don't know why it annoyed me, but when I saw it I always wanted to give him a slap, then wipe his face on that stupid checked shirt.

I was getting impatient under the bed, it was hot, the spars of the frame were digging into my back a bit. Thankfully the bricks were doing a good job. Eventually, after a bit of back cramp eased off, I heard the front door going downstairs. I knew it was Mikey as he had no motor control and the touch of an elephant wearing boxing gloves.

BANG! BANG! BANG! BANG! BANG! BANG!

'Shut up, ya fuckin mongo,' my dad shouted from his room. John ran downstairs, answered the door. I heard a slow, thumping footfall coming upstairs, knew he was on his way. The door yawned open, the clumping continued. This guy's lack of energy and motivation made me so tired, no wonder I was ready to turn the inside of his knickers brown. His lethargy made me want to punch and kick him, to get some kind of reaction or sign of life. I watched secretly from under the bed. He blundered into the room, John went downstairs to make him a cup of tea. Before he left, John spun this yarn to him about some Borstal guy who'd escaped and was believed to be in the area.

'Yeah, he's really dangerous,' said John. 'Killed three people already with his bare hands.'

Mikey stood stock-still, eyes wide open, breathing hard. 'Is he scary?' He said.

'Of course he's scary, he'd probably kill us without hesitation.'

'I better go and tell my mum,' said Mikey, panicking, waving his T-Rex arms.

'Sit down,' said John, 'calm down. The chances are that he'll be with the guys from the Fort. You know, the troublemakers, Jimmy Henderson n that? What d'ye want, tea or coffee?'

He knew fine well that the answer would be tea.

'Tea, please,' he said, and flopped onto the bed. His vast bulk scored a direct hit, the spars offered little support, I felt his weight bang down on me, almost collapsing a lung. I was suffocating, gasping for breath. I had no choice but to haul myself out from under the kip. I crawled out, lay on the floor gasping, staring at him. I was trying desperately to get my breath back. After a minute or two I was in control again. During this whole time he had not said a single word. He flinched on the bed as if there was an invisible person hitting him.

Why the hell did I muck about with this moron? I guess it really was honestly the fact that I might get to see his mum naked, eventually.

'What the fuck are you lookin at?' I said, in a real hard nut Weegie

The Lost Tornado

accent.

'Nuffin,' he replied, still batting away the invisible attacker. He got his whole body onto the bed, squirmed his way into the corner beside the dodgy headboard.

'Well?' I shouted.

'I'm waiting on my wee cup of tea and a wee biscuit.'

The saddest thing is, Mikey and I had been mucking about together for years. He had been in my primary class, held back for a year or three, he still had no idea who the tough guy on the floor was.

I restrained a belly laugh. Eureka, the experiment had worked. I was ready to milk this, get some of my real feelings for him out there. 'You better no be lookin at me, ya fat fucker,' I said. 'Are you lookin at me?'

'I'm not,' he said in a terrified whine.

'Who the fuck are you fightin then, ya dick?'

'I'm scared,' he whimpered. Just then John kicked open the bedroom door, Mikey shit himself, screamed. A bit of snot came down his nose, shot back up again.

John walked in with three cups of tea and a packet of biscuits clamped in his teeth. He spat the packet of biscuits onto the bed. Mikey jumped up, screamed again. He hid behind John, almost knocking the cups out of his hands.

'Mikey, this is Chavvy,' he said, putting the three cups down onto the coffee table. I went to shake hands with him, felt his pathetic weakness, it was like shaking a four-day-old lettuce leaf that'd been left in a hot room. I pulled my hand away, looked at it in disgust.

'Have you got a cloth there, Johnny Boy?' I said, still using the rough Weegie accent. 'Ah have tae wipe the sweat off my hand from Mr Puniverse here.'

John and I sneaked an incredulous look at each other.

How could this guy, who we'd spent every single day that summer going up to the Chambers Street Museum with, be fooled by some black crayon and a jumper turned back to front? I jumped up, grabbed him by the collar.

'Did you hit my wee brother, fat boy?'

'No, I never,' he said. 'I never touched him.'

'Geez yer tea, fatso,' I said. He reached down to the table, lifted his cup, with shaking hands, gave it to me. I gulped it down in two mouthfuls, spilling a lot of it down the front of the jumper for effect, wiped my mouth on my sleeve, not taking my eyes off him, gave him a hard man stare.

'Do you think you're a wido?' I grunted.

'What's a wido?' He said. I could see he wasn't far off pissing his pants by this time.

'A smart arse. Somebody who thinks they can take the piss out of me.'

'Nut, I'm no a wido, I never said anything,' he said, still whimpering. 'John, tell him I never called him a wido or hit his wee brother.'

'No, you did not, Mikey,' said John. 'It wisnae him, Chavvy, must have been somebody that looked like him,'

'Alright, ya fat waste o space, I'll gie ye the benefit o the doubt, but any mair smart arse comments, I'll knock yer teeth that far doon yer throat that you'll be able to chew yer shite on its way tae the pan. Understand?'

'Thanks, Chavvy,' he said

I sniggered, had to hold back a full laugh, disguised it as a big roar. 'AARGGHH.' Then I said, 'Are you gonnae grass me to the cops?' I made it sound threatening.

'No. I dinnae even know who you are,' he says, his voice getting higher, more anxious. At this point he was blubbing like a big bairn, I felt guilty.

'Stay where ye are,' I said. 'Do not move a single muscle, if you have any that is.'

I went into the bathroom, washed my face. I still kept the red jumper on.

A minute or two later I went back into the room, he was sitting with his head down, chin on his chest. I stood right in front of him, didn't move. He raised his head very slowly, took in the red jumper

The Lost Tornado

as he did. He eventually looked up, saw that it was me, he was really happy. He grinned from ear to ear, pointed at me once or twice. I could almost see his tail wagging.

'Jimmy,' he said, 'it's you. John? It's Jimmy.' Then he asked, 'How did you get that guy's jumper?'

I looked at John, we both pissed ourselves laughing. How thick was this boy? His relief was palpable.

I went downstairs to make three fresh cups of tea, brought some black bun with them. My sister Susan worked in Crawford's bakery, got about twenty kilos of black bun, way past its sell by date, for pennies. It used to last us for the whole year, it was what we dipped into when the digestives were gone. That biscuit tin sure saw a lot of action in a year.

After tea and black bun the three of us wandered off to the park for a kick-about. I had to keep practising hard if I wanted to fulfil my dream and play for the Hibees. To be perfectly honest, if I had to choose two people to play football with, John and Mikey would be chosen marginally ahead of Old Mags from the tuck shop and my granny, she'd died three years previously! Still, I had been a real shit to the guy and John was my favourite brother at that time.

As we reached the park, John, Mikey and I had walked across the big wooden swing bridge and kicked the ball about. Playing football with these two was pretty boring, but Mikey was enjoying himself, running and fetching the ball. I felt I owed it to him after being such a bastard. Eventually he was too tired to run anymore so we stopped playing football and sat on the swings eating the strips of red liquorice that I'd nicked from the tuck shop.

Mikey was pushing us on the roundabout. From the corner of my eye, in the far corner of the park I spotted a gang of guys coming towards us; there were about six of them.

'Let's get out of here,' John said. 'That's the nutters from the Fort.'

We jumped off the roundabout and moved quickly back to the safety of the bridge; not too quickly, though, as it would have looked like we were scared. They were singing some songs, looked like they had cans as well. They ran towards us, so we started jogging. Mikey couldn't run at the best of times and the fact that he'd pushed us around the roundabout for half an hour put him at a distinct disadvantage. John and I picked up the pace, ran as fast as we could, easily outrunning the gang. Mikey wasn't so lucky. They caught him pretty easily, laid into him with their hobnail Doc Martens, kick after kick, punch after punch, they kept it going until eventually he crumbled and fell to the ground.

The biggest guy took a leap, jumped right on top of him, pushed Mikey's face into the grass, making him eat the mud.

After they'd beat him up and had their fill of violence, they wandered off, back into the direction they'd come from, back towards the Fort.

They were laughing and singing cheerio, cheerio, cheerio, waving as they went. One of them threw a can, hit Mikey smack on the head. John and I waited, hiding under the bridge, until they were out of sight. When they were gone we sheepishly went over to see if Mikey was OK. He was lying in a heap, curled up in the foetal position. I lifted up his head. There was mud all over his face, he now looked like I had when I'd crawled out from under the bed. Amazingly there were no tears.

John and I were so delighted, we laughed at this. If it had been us we'd have been blubbering like Girl Guides. When we were sure Mikey was OK, we shouted at the gang.

'Ha ha, ya bunch of fannies, he's no greetin.' We shouted this a few times, began to wander home, patting Mikey on the back, congratulating him on his courage. We headed back over the bridge. As we approached it something caught my eye, I looked around. The gang were all running back to us, shouting and swearing.

The leader was the fastest and loudest.

'He's no fuckin greetin, eh?' He shouted. 'He soon fuckin will be.'

Once again we ran, with exactly the same result. John and I got away, but they caught Mikey, made sure this time that there were tears and blood – lots of both.

After a good ten minute beating the leader looked menacingly at

The Lost Tornado

John and I before holding Mikey's hair, head-butting him, bang on the nose. He then spun in the air, unleashed some kind of Bruce Lee kick, Mikey's bottom lip burst like an over-ripe tomato. As he was being held there, Mikey looked at John and I with pleading in his eyes, then the rest of the gang rained blow after blow down upon him.

As the savage beating went on and on, clouds rolled by, blood flowed. We waited; it was all we could do. Eventually we made our way over to Mikey as the vultures had picked every scrap of dignity they could take from him. They'd ripped his shirt and given him a wedgie, had virtually tucked his underpants under his arms.

I ran over to the far corner of the park, made sure that the gang had gone for good. They had, thankfully. We picked Mikey up, he was semi-conscious. There was blood everywhere. His nose looked like a burst balloon, his eyes were black and blue. The shirt he wore had been ripped to pieces, one of his sandals had been thrown into the river. I went down to the edge of the water, but it had disappeared. We took an arm each, slowly, carefully, walked him back to his house. He was crying the whole time.

'I didn't greet first time did I?' He said, trying to hold on to some kind of positive.

'No, you were so brave,' John said.

'Aye, brave,' he said. We struggled to get him up the stone steps to his house. As we went up and up, getting more and more tired with carrying the fat pig, an old woman poked her head from her door, quickly closed it again, a whiff off mothballs and Mint Imperials wafted out of her house. We knocked on the door of the top floor flat, the one with the brass engraved sign that said 'McCluskey'. Waited anxiously.

There was a woman singing behind the door, the singing stopped abruptly as the door opened. His mum, wrapped only in a towel, put her hands to her mouth suppressing a cry.

'What happened to my beautiful boy? What have you done to him?' She cried out.

'Sorry, Mrs M, it was the gang from the Fort,' I said. 'We tried to protect him, but there were too many of them.'

'He only went out for a cup of tea and a biscuit!' She said. 'You poor, poor boy, let's go and get you cleaned up.'

'They left me, Mum,' he said, pointing to me and then to John.

'What do you mean, they left you?'

'The gang battered me, then when I didn't cry they asked them to batter me again.'

'That's rubbish!' Said John.

'Yeah,' I agreed, 'rubbish.'

'Why are you saying that, Mikey?' John said.

'Because it's true,' he said. 'And their pal was going to kill me in their room. He escaped from prison, threatened me with a knife.'

'That was a joke, Mikey,' John said.

'A joke!' Shouted his mum. 'You think this is a joke? I thought you were his friends.' She went to the bathroom, ran the hot water, pouring in heaps of blue Radox.

'Can we stay for a cuppa?' I said. 'We'll explain it all.' I was hoping that I'd see her in the bath again.

She looked at me with fury in her eyes. 'I'll say one last thing to you two. Go.'

'But we …'

'Go!'

Mikey wandered into the bathroom. I could see in the reflection of the bathroom mirror that he'd removed his clothes and was about to step into the bath.

'Please, Mrs M,' I pleaded. 'We did all we could.'

I was still hoping to see her knockers. She stood there still as a statue, pointing to the door.

That was the end of the friendship as far as I was concerned. I would never see his mum naked. Mikey was absolutely no use to me any more.

The Lost Tornado

Chapter 14

New to secondary school, summer, girls, hormones, new fashions, boys with growth on their faces, exciting music; Bowie, Bolan, Brotherhood of Man! The invention of fluorescent green and black striped socks and Sta Prest trousers, but none of this bounty for me. No pubes yet, but hoping desperately. I was so underdeveloped for my age that I looked like I should still be in primary 6, looked like I'd wandered into the wrong school gates. People looked at me when I turned up for a class. 'Hey wee guy, should you not be at primary?'

'Heard it a hundred times mate' I squeaked with my puny wee voice.

The nearest I got to stumbling into anything fashionable was when my Uncle Richard brought his usual black bin liner full of second hand clothes to the house. Rifling through the bag, I spotted this tank top. I couldn't believe my eyes, tank tops were in fashion at the time. I looked around to make sure John wasn't around, stuck it up my jumper. Next day I could not wait to get to school, *fashion icon coming through*, I thought. I went to school thinking I'd found my ticket to fit seamlessly with the in-crowd, but as soon as I got into the playground I was hounded by guys trying to get a look at my top, pissing themselves when they saw it. It was brown, very woollen with two white horizontal lines across the middle, in the centre was a massive yellow star which stood out against a cream background. They all began to call me 'Jew boy' and 'Star of Zagreb'.

'Dinnae wear that in December or you'll have three men on camels following ye,' someone shouted; they all pissed themselves at that. The thing was, I couldn't take it off as I had big holes in the shirt I wore underneath it. I wandered away to the far playing fields alone, kept my blazer buttoned up all day.

I'd tried to fit in before. A few of the 'in-crowd' were talking about cycling into the countryside to go fishing. I knew one of them;

Franny, who was on the periphery of the group.

'Why don't you come with us Jimmy?' He said, 'It's always a great laugh.'

'Nah, I don't know where Flotterstone is', I said, 'and I'd have to borrow John's bike. Plus, I'm not even sure these guys know me'.

'Of course they do, meet us on Sunday at Hillend Ski Slope, nine sharp'.

I asked John if I could borrow his bike but he said no. I took it anyway, left the house at six in the morning before he was awake, just managing to catch them all before they left the meeting point. It had taken me over three hours to cycle less than ten miles. Franny waited as the rest of them sped off as I approached.

'Look at your front wheel?' He said.

'I had a look, the wheel was buckled beyond belief. 'Jeez, that must have been hard work, what time did you leave?' Franny said.

'Six' I said, 'no wonder it felt hard riding up those hills'.

'And what's that?' He said pointing to the fishing net and bamboo cane I had strapped to the bike.

'It's a fishing net of course? I thought we were going fishing?'

He laughed out loud, some of the guys who'd cycled off turned around.

'You'd better dump that pal' he said.

'But it's my wee sister's'.

'Trust me, if you bring that along you'll regret it. Stick it under a bush and get it on the way home, preferably when none of the guys are around. This is what you need'.

He pulled a three-part fishing rod from his backpack.

'Ah!' I said. I hid the net under a tree making sure I'd noted where it was.

'Come on, better catch them up' He said.

I struggled along as the hills increased my speed decreased. I hoped the wheel was bent like that at the start as John would go ballistic if it was my fault. God knows how much a new wheel would cost. Franny let me use his rod for a while and told the guys my rod had fallen from my bike. I could hear a few of them talking quietly about the state of the me and the bike, knew they didn't want me there. I was never a great socialiser at school, most of the time I was with my best mate Stevie Ross. We spent a great deal of the time away from the main body of the school and used to wander towards Duddingston Loch and the peaceful haven it provided. Two minutes from the school gates and a million miles away from lessons and hassle. I was only interested in playing for Hibs or being a Commercial Artist, but no teacher was interested in me, while swots like Alan Inglis, Harry Dickinson and Renzy were getting photography classes set up especially for them.

My voice was so weak and puny that I never spoke, there were many times when I had an opinion or a funny comment but was too embarrassed to speak up. Eventually my non-participation was viewed as disinterest and I was dumped into the rubbish chute to the remedial Maths class with the school's thickos, who weren't deemed worthy enough to merit a classroom and met in the dinner hall. I quickly figured out that if you put two of these guys together they wouldn't make a half-wit. As I was swirling down the plughole of my life a couple of guys in my class were going in the opposite direction; Mike Scott and Chick McLaughlin had started up a band 'Another Pretty Face', they were getting headlines in New Musical Express - even got single of the week! And Paul Coletti one of my St. Mary's Classmates was going to Vienna or somewhere to play the viola with Yehudi Menuhin.

I was making music of a kind I guess, one of the thick'os grabbed my plastic comb from my back pocket, twisted my hair into the teeth of it, and proceeded to stoat my head off the dinner table a few dozen times, he was getting a nice rhythm going. Each time my head thumped onto the formica I didn't feel pain, I felt a strange calmness, a moment on which to reflect on my life so far. The rest of the thickos sat around chewing gum and smoking, barely noticing 'Big Rab' smackin' Jimmy's heid off a dinner table. I looked hopefully, helplessly towards the teacher, as that was the direction he'd pointed my head in.

Mr. Rawlinson glanced up briefly from his Daily Record, jiggled his glasses a bit, nothing to worry about there, back to his crossword; 'Six letters? Sounds like distant drums...'

Maybe the thumping helped dislodge the crustiness that clogged my brain. I got smart after that, managed to get a D+ in the subject, which got me away from those morons, into a class where inertia and sleep ruled, rather than violent musical experimentation.

My English class wasn't much better. Stevie and I spent most of our time making comics about one of the weird guys in school. There were all kinds of drawings and stories about what his mum got up to with the milkman, postie and whoever turned up at her door while Brian was at school. We got really good at drawing knobs, tits and fannies. The comics began to get a good following, more often than not our school chums would be reading the comics, pissing themselves, rather than reading *Shadow of a Gunman or A Clockwork Orange* as they should be. One day Mrs Buchan caught us drawing, ordered Stevie out into the front of the classroom. She made him read one of the stories out to everyone, when he'd said the words 'fuck me' or 'tits' for the second or third time she stormed off for the headmaster.

We stopped the comics after that. We did get her back, though. She had nipped off to the loo, I noticed that she'd left her handbag under her desk. I had a peek inside, realised she had a packet of Dr White's fanny pads in there. I took them out, hid them around the room, one under her registration book, one on the back of her chair, one on the blackboard and so on. When she came back in there was utter silence with an edge of subdued belly laughs. She lifted the regi book up, the fanny pad slid onto the floor. She was mortified. She kicked it under the table; everyone burst out laughing.

She scooped it up with the jotter, noticed there were others around, used paper towels to gather them up. She then left the room. I never saw her again after that.

School lay in the centre of the city, which was a big volcanic area that had a park with hundreds of acres of grassland, great places to hide from teachers, gangs and general school thugs. Stevie and I used to marvel at the beauty, sitting on a summer's day watching the clouds float by, listening to the birds and wildlife with the distant muted excited hum of Edinburgh during the festival fluttering away in the background. How many kids had the opportunity to spend time in the company of an extinct volcano?

A sandwich, can of juice and a sweetie. Who could ask for more? Occasionally the school gangs passed nearby, we hid, fearing that if they caught us hiding they'd think we were bum boys and give us a kicking. We used to play a lot of football using a tennis ball instead of the real thing, a great way to develop ball skills. Even though I loved football and wanted to play professionally I never had the confidence to play it at PE as I was so small.

I was good, skilful, took the piss out of people when dribbling, but more often than not got a smack in the face for nutmegging them. I only played footy after school and at weekends. Of all the school sports there was only one I liked – tennis. The school tennis courts were over towards the loch and were protected by a big ten foot metal fence, to stop the wayward tennis balls from going out, the Gyppos from the nearby 'camp' getting in.

Stevie and I were playing tennis one morning during a PE lesson when I spotted a young scruffy boy of about ten trying to throw something alive into the rubbish strewn stream that oozed along the back of the courts. He looked like he was from the gypsy camp, despite our shouts and threats he paid no attention to us. Stevie hit a tennis ball way over the fence; this gave us an excuse to retrieve it, despite the fact that we were not allowed outside the school boundaries under any circumstances. We ran over to the guy, checking that there were no teachers watching us. As we sneaked up on the wee bugger we saw that it was a tiny black and white puppy that he was throwing in.

'What are you doin?' Stevie asked.

'Oi'm drownin my poap,' he said in a strong Irish accent.

'You're doing what?' Said Stevie.

'Oi don't want it no more,' he said. 'It only ever shoites and eats.'

'You cruel little bastard!' Stevie said, pulled the puppy from the stream. The little shit grabbed the puppy back from him, tried to run away. We ran after and grabbed him, took the puppy, let it go. It ran into the undergrowth, hid under a bush, shivering and cowering. We then dragged the little shit down to the stream, put him face down into the water for a few seconds, to let him see how it felt.

He began to scream muddy bubbles. We got some mud, rubbed it all over his face. He screamed again. We let him go with a couple of boots up the arse, he ran towards the camp, rubbing his eyes.

'Oi'll get me brudders to beat the shoite out of yous,' he said, through tears.

'That taught the little bastard a lesson,' Stevie said.

'Yip,' I said. 'He won't do that again in a hurry.'

We tried to get the pup, but it ran away to where the boy had gone.

'Poor wee felly,' Stevie said. 'It's gonnae have a shit life.'

We walked back to the tennis courts a few feet taller, feeling like Clint Eastwood and Charles Bronson, although we probably didn't look like them as I can't recall these guys wearing purple shorts, purple vests and matching socks, swinging tennis racquets. We were almost back when I heard someone shouting. I looked around, saw that there were a few big scruffy guys coming from the gypsy camp. They looked like they meant business. They were pointing towards the school, a couple of them had sticks.

'Shit, Stevie,' I said, 'run!'

'Eh?'

I nodded for him to look around. We dropped the racquets and legged it. There were six burly guys heading our way at full speed. As they got closer one of them picked up both racquets, gave them to a smaller guy, he bolted back to the camp with them. *Shit*, I thought, *how are we going to explain that?* At least the delay gave us time to run away from the tennis courts, over across the playing fields into the relative safety of the school.

It had gone dinnertime so there were hundreds of pupils around. Stevie and I hid in the River Dee lunch room, still wearing our purple shorts and vests. We hadn't time to get our clothes from the tennis lockers. As we hid, there was a commotion, it was gathering momentum through the school. Somebody in the dinner hall shouted that there were gypsies in the school grounds looking for two tennis guys. There was a rush towards the doors, everybody wanted in on the action. Stevie and I huddled under a table, which we covered with the big heavy brown blackout curtains which were lying waiting to be put up. We made a gap in the curtains that allowed us to see into the main school-yard. The janitor and head teacher came out to confront the men. They stopped, facing each other on the school boundary. The gypsies were talking to them, animated, throwing their hands up, shaking fists, pointing. I honestly thought I'd shit in my shorts. Stevie held his nose.

'Was that a …?'

'No. Wet fart,' I said, relieved. After a lot of 'calm down' movements from the headmaster, the waving arms stopped. It looked like they'd agreed on something. The leader shook the headmaster's hand. He pointed to the four corners of the school; it looked like they were going to launch a search for the thugs who had tried to …

'Drown an innocent wee boy.'

That's what people were saying as they flocked back into the dinner room to finish their meals. We were shitting ourselves, waited ages until after everyone had finished. After a cramped eternity we peeked around from behind the curtains. Everyone had left the dining room and were out following the mob. We ventured into the now deserted main school area and could see the small boy with the mob. A few of the girls were holding his hands.

'Poor wee soul,' they said. 'We'll find the bad boys.'

It looked like he was there in order to identify the thugs. Not only were the gypsies after us, we now had the entire school looking for potential murderers! How could we escape? Our school clothes were still sitting in the pavilion while we were standing quivering in our purple PE kits.

Someone must have been watching over us. In another part of the school the school jester, Squiddly Diddly, was about to give us an escape route. Squiddly Diddly had been offering his usual challenge to the bullies; if they could catch him they were allowed to beat him up. This time they made sure he would not wriggle free. They had some rope with them, when they caught him four of them tied him up. They each got a hold of an arm or a leg, pulled his legs wide apart, began to bang his balls against a tree, again and again … They kept this going until he was unconscious, apparently he went into some kind of coma.

Unbeknown to us, this had happened about five minutes before the gypsies arrived. The ambulance and police were in attendance. By the time the headmaster, janitor and gypsies had even completed a first sweep of the school, the attention was immediately deflected to the bullies who had committed this horrific crime. During the double commotion, Stevie and I snaked and laddered our way around the periphery of the interlocking schoolrooms using some large box files and curtains to hide behind. After a few lucky escapes and a pint of sweat, we headed back over to the pavilion, got dressed, back into our school uniforms. As we prepared to leave the changing rooms we spotted the gypsies coming back across the field swearing that they would find out who had done this.

We ducked back in, waited until the coast was clear. We had to make sure that the little shit never spotted us. The two of us were shaking through hunger and fear. We looked at each other as the gang passed by. We were hiding under the pile of tennis nets that were lying there. We knew how lucky we were, breathed a big sigh when they were gone. Before we headed home we went to the registration book in the tennis pavilion, ripped out the page with our names on it. Nobody would ever find out we were here.

On the way home, we were quiet. We got off the bus at Elm Row, we wanted to look at the equipment and gadgetry in the camping shop as we were planning on going camping in summer. After we had been there for a while, talking about our trip and what equipment we'd take, we left, went into the Post Office next door for a sweet. As we walked into the shop, there was no one about. I looked around, *could be an opportunity*, I thought. Raised my left eyebrow high. Stevie copied. Bottom lip came up over the top one, we raised both eyebrows, nodded to each other. I let go of the door, as it slowly creaked shut, a woman popped her head up from the hatch in the floor.

'Can I help you boys?' She said, smiling.

'Jeesus!' Stevie shouted, putting his hand to his heart.

'We only want a sweet,' I said.

'OK, boys, I'll be with you in two flicks of a kitten's tail.'

'No hurry,' said Stevie. 'Take your time.'

'Good boys,' she said, smiling, popped her head back down the hatch to finish her task. We both decided to take the opportunity to fill our schoolbags with free sweets. We were about to start when the woman popped her head up again. We each had three or four chocolate bars in our hands, quickly put them back on the shelf. It must have been obvious as we both instinctively put our hands behind our backs.

'Would you boys come here a moment?' She said, and popped down again.

'Fuck,' said Stevie. 'Now we're for it, she must have seen us.'

We walked slowly over to the hatch. Looked down.

'I wonder if you could help me to shift some boxes down here?' She said, her voice muffled.

'No problem,' we said together, relieved.

We climbed down the wooden ladder to the damp basement.

'You see, boys, the shop is about to get pretty busy, I have to serve up there,' she said, pointing to the top of the ladder. 'If you could move all of these boxes from here,' she pointed to perhaps twenty cases of Cadbury's chocolate products, 'to that shelf over there,' she pointed to the shelf, 'I would be very grateful.'

'No problem,' I said. 'You OK with that, Steve?'

'Fine with me sir,' he said.

'Good boys,' she said again. She went upstairs, left us to it.

Almost immediately we heard the shop doorbell ringing again and again. It was near teatime so people were no doubt coming in for the Evening News, chocolate and fags. I lifted the boxes while Stevie snooped around checking out a whole lot of other packages that were lying around.

'Stevie,' I said, 'this could be a trap. She could be some kind of evil old witch looking for fresh ingredients.'

'You're right,' he said. 'Think about it … this is the perfect trap if you need young meat.'

I looked around in the darkest corners to make sure there were no skeletons lying around wearing school ties and blazers. Stevie was doing the same thing in the other corner.

'Christ, Jimmy,' he said, 'look at this.'

I went over to where he was standing, gazed lovingly at a pile of open boxes of chocolate. Stevie opened the zip on his Celtic schoolbag, put handfuls of the chocolate bars into it. I went back to the other side of the room, continued to move the other boxes. After he'd loaded his bag up, Stevie came over for my schoolbag, filled that up as well. We must have been there for twenty minutes, moving the boxes, filling our bags.

When we'd finished we climbed back up the ladder, sweating.

'Is that it, boys?' Said the woman.

'Yep. That's it done and dusted,' said Stevie.

'Thanks very much, boys, I really appreciate your help,' she said, handed us each a can of ice cold Coca Cola.

'No problem. Only too happy to help, ma'am,' Stevie said.

'Please, help yourself to chocolate or sweets, it's the least I can give you for your help.'

'No, we wouldn't dream of it,' said Stevie.

I nodded in agreement, said, 'I think we're ready for our tea now, chocolate would only ruin it.'

'What school do you go to?' She said. 'I'll have to write to your

The Lost Tornado

headmaster and compliment him on bringing such well-behaved pupils into our society. All you hear about these days is the bad side of youngsters, but look what we have here,' she said holding her two palms heavenwards, 'angels. Now, now, don't blush boys. You are. Truly angelic. What are your names?'

We gave her our names: Ross and Divine.

'Divine? How appropriate,' she said. 'What did I tell you?'

We were both well aware that it was easy to sacrifice her offer of free bars of chocolate for the wads that we had in our bags.

'Thank you again, boys,' she said. 'You'll be hearing from me. Bye-bye.'

We swaggered out of the shop, ecstatic. She was delighted. We were delighted. It was a win-win.

We ran down the road, laughing all the way, heavily laden bags banging against our legs. *Has anyone in the history of the world ever had a better win than this?* We thought. All the chocolate we could eat. Praise from the headmaster, who would no doubt call us into his room and give us massive compliments. When we were almost home we stopped in a shop doorway to investigate our haul, examine what we'd plundered.

I had sixteen Mars Bars, fourteen Twixes, fourteen Bounty Bars and twenty-one Crunchies. Stevie had forty-two Marathons and seventeen Mars Bars. We were delirious.

We put all of the chocolate bars into a big pile and looked at it, sat on the pavement in the early evening sunshine, then divided our loot equally, put it all back in our bags except for one bar each, which we were going to celebrate with. I picked a Mars Bar, Stevie a Twix. I ripped open the wrapper, stuck the first half of the Mars Bar straight into my mouth, began to chew. I was ravenous after missing lunch.

As I chewed, my brain registered some kind of alert message. A few seconds of hard chewing had passed before my eyes and brain between them realised that the colour green was poking out from the remaining half of the wrapper. Green in a chocolate bar without a minty taste was not really a good thing. A furry chocolaty type of realisation hit my taste buds. I involuntarily boaked, with green furry chocolate sickness spilling all over my bag.

I spat the remaining bits of Mars Bar from my mouth, ripped the rest of the wrapper from the other half, which was being crushed in my hand. I was faced with a furry green thing. I tried to be sick again, but couldn't. I opened the can of Coke, gulped it, down burping up more sickness.

'Fuckin hell,' said Stevie, staring at me.

He unwrapped his Twix, it was exactly the same. It was obviously a furry, green, two-fingered gesture from some higher being, telling us that we had erred on the wrong side of karmic balance by being too greedy. We emptied our bags onto the pavement, ripped open the wrappers.

Every single bar had the same flaw. We looked at each other.

'For fuck's sake!' Stevie said. 'All that work for fuckin nothing.'

'And to make matters worse, we handed back our other stuff,' I said, still burping up bits of fungus.

We sat there, stunned, silent, feeling cheated. Then we looked at each other, began laughing, we looked at all of the useless chocolate bars around us and laughed harder, we piled up the chocolate and jumped all over it, laughing and jumping, crushing it into a big messy sticky lump, getting it all over our shoes, we rolled on the pavement, exhausted with the laughter.

'All that stuff must have been ready for the bucket,' I said.

'And us mugs put it straight into our bags. She must have known we would do that, conniving old witch. Next time I'm in there I'm going to steal twice as much.'

We sat there picking the stickiness from our shoes, throwing it against a garden wall.

'Still,' I said, 'we did get a Coke out of it, and she's going to phone the headmaster, we should get some Brownie points.'

I looked at Stevie, realised I'd cracked a joke.

'Brownie points,' I said, 'get it?'

We rolled around laughing for a long time.

CHAPTER 15

I was standing in an old rooftop attic in my pyjama bottoms and a T-shirt. Six a.m. Shaking and shivering in the freezing morning air. The rumour had gone around that the cops were going to do a house-to-house search in order to find stolen goods.

A few days before, Ronnie Duke, Paul McDonald and another couple of guys had peeled away the lead from one of the skylight windows on the roof of Clapperton's toy factory, lifted the glass out, gained easy entry. They suspected, and confirmed, that the alarm system was a dummy box. Once the window pane was removed they dreeped down onto the top shelves with ease, strolled into the factory. They were face-to-face with a complete toy store, anything and everything you could possibly want was there in multiples of hundreds or thousands. What a scenario. Anything you ever wanted as a kid, right in front of you, free of charge.

Initially as they walked around there was a real hesitancy as there was still a danger that the alarm would go off. Was it a silent alarm that only went off at Gayfield Square Police Station? Ronnie and Paul left the building, got the dim-witted McCowan to walk around picking his favourite toys.

They knew that he was incredibly clumsy, if anyone was going to set the alarm off it would be him. After twenty minutes or so, McCowan's head appeared from the skylight window. He threw three Adidas Samba football boots onto the roof, along with an Action Man doll.

'Why have you got three football boots?' Ronnie said.

'In case I lose one of them, stupid,' said McCowan, clambering up onto the roof.

'You've got two left shoes and one right one,' Ronnie said curiously. 'What if you lose a right one?'

'Oh! I never thought about that.'

It was now obvious that the coast was clear, they could go for it.

Word soon got around, after a few nights every kid for miles around was lining up on the roof, climbing into the factory after it closed, helping themselves to a never-ending dream Christmas list. The older kids tried to keep it hush-hush, but extravagance and complacency set in, the value of toys began to plummet. If somebody felt like getting a new leather football, they would simply wait till closing time, climb through the window and help themselves to a big bag of them, perhaps a dozen at a time.

By the end of that week there were toys all over the place. Everywhere you looked you would see a brand new toy lying there unopened, a whole collection of brand new footballs with penknives sticking into them. Things really got out of hand, eventually no one appreciated new toys. The parents of the Court kids began to ask questions as they could not figure out what was happening. The people from Clapperton's became suspicious when their stocktaking showed up glaring discrepancies. Every one of us had kept strictly to the rule: always put the glass back on, fold the lead back into place as soon as you leave the building, so that the staff would not notice.

Eventually one of the younger kids slipped up when they were asked what they wanted for their birthday.

'Don't bother, Mum. I can go and get anything I want from Clapperton's.'

This was the single sentence that ended the shark feeding frenzy. This was also the reason I was in the attic at Clapperton's at six in the morning.

John and I had gone into the toy factory every night for six nights, helped ourselves to all kinds of toys, for some reason, a whole lot of penknives. We had planned that we would go into the store every night, get some future Christmas presents for all of our siblings as Mum and Dad could not afford decent stuff. Christmas was always tough with so many kids to buy for, our plan was that we would leave the toys in the living room a couple of days before Christmas and not say a word to Mum or Dad.

When all of the other kids in the Court began to abuse the privilege we knew our plan could not possibly work. It would be obvious where the stuff had come from. For days, rumours were flying around that the cops would search all of the houses in the Court on the Friday after lunchtime.

Friday morning, John and I got up at five-thirty, loaded all of our loot into a couple of stolen duffel bags. I was to take them all back to Clapperton's, make sure that I wiped our fingerprints from everything. John was keeping shottie from the bedroom window. After half an hour of sneaking around in the Clapperton's attic area, contemplating whether to put the stuff back or hide it, I heard an owl hoot from our bedroom. This was John's signal that there was trouble. I stopped what I was doing, looked out of the attic up to our bedroom. John was very animated, pointing at something. I couldn't figure out what he was trying to tell me. A few seconds later the kitchen light went on, I could see Dad getting ready for work. *Shit*, I thought, I had completely forgotten that he'd started a new job delivering papers to the newsagents. I was snookered. I looked up at John, he shrugged his shoulders.

I had no choice, I had to sit and wait it out. I had stuck on a T-shirt and a pair of jammie bottoms as I was sure I was only going to be a few minutes. An hour later I must have been close to hypothermia.

Eventually, after a few rounds of toast and several cups of tea, Dad left, as his noisy, clapped out car smoked and struggled its way from the Court, its echo stirred a few light bulbs into action. People emerged from drowsy sleep into their kitchens. The downside was that most of the kitchens in the Court faced the attic in which I was hiding. How could I even attempt to get out of there when I was sure that at least one person would look up and spot me? And I could imagine what the story would be when the police came around to interview them.

'Yes, officer, I definitely saw the eldest Divine boy in Clapperton's attic in the early hours of this morning. Looked pretty suspicious, had a couple of bags, if I'm not mistaken.'

I would have no alibi and would be held responsible for all the wanton destruction that had gone on, which would lead to a hefty fine, a massive bill to pay and no doubt Borstal, where I would get an unwanted sex education. No thanks. By comparison, hypothermia was not a bad option.

I had spotted an alternative getaway, but it involved a ten foot drop onto a ledge, then another seven or eight foot drop from there to a concrete path. I was never very good with heights and would only use it as a last resort. I tried to wait it out, but it became ridiculous. Each time a noise was made in a kitchen, a kettle going on or a toaster popping, it would create a chain reaction; it was almost like watching a very slow firecracker – lights go on, toaster pops, kettle cracks, another light goes on and another tap fills another kettle, and so on. It was also getting lighter by the minute. I had almost forgotten, but I still had to get back up to the house to get ready for school.

I had no choice, I had to go the long way round and take the drop. I was petrified. I hung from the guttering on the roof, concentrated hard to make my arms stretch like Stretch Armstrong in order to lower myself down rather than drop and perhaps miss the ledge and commit myself to an horrific injury. To my disappointment my arms didn't stretch at all, I had to dreep down, but thankfully I landed on the ledge.

I then had to manoeuvre myself to a squatting position, jump the remaining eight feet. I was sweating so hard that my T-shirt was saturated, then I noticed it had some ice crystals forming on it. I ran back to the house in a strange drunken-like state.

John had prepared my school clothes and made me some breakfast. Our problems were not over, though. I told him that I had not managed to get the stuff back into the factory, and worse, I had not managed to wipe away our fingerprints.

'Why don't we skive school?' He said.

'I've got a maths exam today,' I said. 'I sit my prelims next week so I can't miss it.'

'What time is your exam?'

'One o'clock, why?'

'Well, we could skive after your exam, get back to the attic, wipe away all of the fingerprints.'

We had only skipped school about three times each in all our years and always felt guilty, but this time it was essential.

'OK,' I said. 'Where should we meet?'

'The science block at two?'

'OK,' I said. 'See you there.'

I couldn't concentrate on the exam and would have got exactly the same result if I hadn't turned up. I kept looking at my watch as I knew my future depended on it.

'Are we finished already, Mr Divine?' The adjudicator shouted to me after ten minutes. He said the same thing three times within an hour. I ignored him. I knew where my priorities lay.

After the exam John and I met at the science block at two on the dot. Four beeps went off with barely a second in between. We'd synchronised our four stolen 'A-Team' watches that morning, both wearing one on each wrist. I borrowed John's diary, which he always kept in his inside blazer pocket, and drew a few lines on the grid paper, we both agreed on the quietest, most secretive route out of the school. We would sneak under the windows of the science block, hide behind the reeds and rushes of the pond until it was clear, then make our way on hands and knees, past the music and PE blocks. We knew the music block might be tricky as Philly Moffat, the head prefect, was always looking out of the window for escapees.

We'd then head over behind the woods to the playing fields and beyond to the gypsy caravan site, although I was always nervous about that place in case that guy that tried to drown the dog spotted me.

We had negotiated most of the route, but as we were heading across the playing fields we were gripped by a cold, debilitating terror.

'Where do you two think you're going?' Boomed a big familiar voice. We both looked round at the same time, saw that the headmaster was striding purposefully towards us.

'Well?' He shouted. Where are you going?'

"Maths," I said, while at the very same time John said, 'PE.'

'Well? Which is it to be,' he said, 'maths or PE?'

'PE,' I said, because that was the direction we were heading in, but unfortunately John said, 'Maths,' right at the same time.

'Let me see your timetables,' he demanded. 'Now!'

'I haven't got my timetable with me,' I said.

'Why not? You know you the rules, you must have your timetable with you at all times.'

'I forgot it, sir.'

'What about you?' He said to John.

John handed him his little cream diary, he opened it up onto the inside back page, showing his timetable. I was shitting myself as I knew the map was right next to the timetable, if he spotted that we would be rumbled. The headmaster studied it for a few moments, then pointed at John.

'You should be at double woodwork. Why aren't you there? What's all this tosh about maths and PE?'

'I don't feel well,' John said, feigning a sore stomach.

The headmaster had seen this act a million times, he ordered us to hold our hands out straight. We knew what was coming.

'Boys, boys, boys,' he said, shaking his baldy head while simultaneously reaching into the inside of his devil's cape. 'You'll be so sorry you ever crossed me. You,' he said, pointing to me with his forefinger as he pulled the strap from his shoulder. 'Hands out.'

I put my hands out, right hand on top of left. As he raised the strap I swapped them over. I felt that because I was left-handed my left hand could take the pain. This really irritated him.

'Make your mind up, boy!'

I swapped a few times, decided that my left hand was the one that could take it.

The old twat belted me three times, caught me on the wrist with the second blow. It hurt like hell. I balled my fist to try to lose the pain.

'Get back to your classes this minute, report to my office first thing tomorrow morning,' he said.

The Lost Tornado

'It's Saturday tomorrow, sir,' I said, with my hands in my pockets. The headmaster looked at us both and held his hand out, pointing towards the school.

'Go!' He said. 'I'll see both of you in my office nine o'clock Monday sharp.'

John and I walked towards the school, as soon as the headmaster was out of sight we slipped away past the music department, waving to Philly as she gestured frantically to the head of music.

Inadvertently the real bonus for us was that the headmaster didn't take a note of our names, he had no idea who we were. As we saw it, we would be idiots to turn up at his office, so we decided not to, just kept out of his way for a long time.

We arrived back home after four, there was no sign of any police activity. All of the burst footballs and all kinds of dolls and hero action figures, which had been strewn all over the place, were now gone. A clean up had taken place. We changed into our jeans and Hibs shirts, went quietly back up to the attic, collected all of the stuff in the duffel bags which had been sitting there all day, brought it back to the house. The main culprit, Paul McDonald, was eventually caught and sentenced to some time in a young offenders' institute. Clapperton's bought a state of the art security system and had the lead windows replaced by plastic double-glazed fixed units.

As I walked back to the house I spotted McCowan staring at his feet, looking bewildered. A solitary Adidas Samba shoe was dangling from a telephone wire – a left one. McCowan had thrown the wrong spare away and was now wearing two right shoes. I laughed to myself, headed up to the room.

CHAPTER 16

I was sitting on the top deck of the number six, bus. I'd come out of the Victoria baths and was on my way home, I opened my Hibs school bag and examined the contents. I moved the wet towel and trunks out of the way, reached in, pulled out the jar of slime that I'd nicked from Clapperton's. I'd seen some kids playing with it in the Court. It was a chemical goo that was very sticky and was meant to look and feel like snotters. This was the first time that I'd had the chance to inspect it. I remove the plastic lid, smelled it: no scent. I dipped my finger in, it was cold and slimy, felt fabulous, it really did look and feel like snotters. I discovered it made a farting sound if you squeezed it right down into the bottom of the plastic tub. I sat there for a good ten minutes squeezing it in different ways, getting lots of great farting sounds. The people on the top deck looked around, half-wondering why the bus was not full of eggy smells.

Once again, that wee devil inside me popped up, gave me a great idea. There were only four people sitting on the top deck of the bus; me, an old guy, and two other kids about the same age as me, both with nuclear ginger hair. I decided that I would test my goo.

I sneaked up behind the old guy very quietly, began to sniff as if I had a cold. He turned around, looked at me, obviously wondering why I'd moved from the seat I was in to the one right behind him. He was sniffing as if inspecting the air for farty smells. I was pretending to look out of the window. I increased my sniffing and spluttering intensity until he looked around at me again with a real knitted brow. I wiped my sleeve across my nose, he snorted at me. I let out a couple of pretend sneezes to see what his reaction would be. He looked around for a third time.

'Can you go and sit back at the back of the bus?' He said angrily. I ignored him, continued to pretend to sniff and splutter.

'Go on,' he said, 'get back to where you were, I don't want to catch your germs.' He got his hankie out, blew his nose, muttering under his breath. He kept the hankie at his nose as if it was going to protect him. There was silence for a while.

'I like sitting here,' I said, 'it's a free country. Anyway, the radiator is here, it's too cold at the back.'

He looked at me, gave me an old man's stare, growled a bit.

I stayed where I was, leaned over the front of his seat so as my head was pretty close to his. I carried on sniffing and spluttering. He pulled his collar up around his ears. A couple of stops before I was due to get off I decided that now was the time.

I began to exaggerate the loudness of my sneezes, then I leaned back for a second, pulled out a big handful of the slime. I poured it into my cupped hand and produced an extra big sneeze. At exactly the same time I threw this stuff all over the back of the old guy's head! It hit him smack bang on the bald patch. He ducked involuntary and immediately put his hand to the top of his head where he felt the stickiness hit.

'You disgusting little bastard,' he shouted, and rang the bell on the bus non-stop to get the driver's attention. He made an attempt to grab me, but I got past him. He was too busy wiping the goo onto the metal of the seat in front of him and onto the seat that he was sitting on. The two kids at the front of the bus looked round and began killing themselves laughing, pointing at him. This made him even angrier.

He pulled chunks of slime from his baldy head. He put his bunnet, which he'd been carrying on his lap, to his mouth, a small dribble of sickness spilled into it. He turned the bunnet inside out, emptied the dribble onto the floor, ran past me and off the bus. I watched him bent over, throwing up. I felt incredibly satisfied The bus moved on, I watched him leaning, steadying himself against the bus stop as he looked at me with a grey face. By the time he had gained his composure. I waved to him from the back window. He responded with a half-hearted fist in the air, then bent over again. I laughed for a good five minutes, this had gone much better than I had planned.

CHAPTER 17

My auld man had bought that crappy unreliant, Reliant Robin from one of my uncles, It was an embarrassing heap of fibre glass and small parts of metal and glass. I got slagged by my mates for the next three months.

'Jeez, Jimmy does yer dad think he's Del boy?'

One day in summer he decided that he was going to take us all up to Arthur's Seat. I was mortified. John and I refused point blank, but he said if we didn't go along with everybody else he'd stop our pocket money. No choice. The only person that didn't have to go was Karen. She was studying. So there we were. All eleven of us, traipsing down the stairs, having to pile into a Reliant Robin. A crowd gathered, watching in disbelief as we all somehow got in. I'd like to say the car started first time, or even second. Four times the auld man tried to start the bloody thing, eventually it remembered it was meant to be a car, somehow the engine spluttered, chugged into life and we struggled forwards. Smoke was billowing out the back of it. No wonder; it was probably the equivalent of one donkey power, no way would horsepower have associated itself with this pile of crap. There was a cheer from the gang as we made our way out of the Court. The younger kids thought it was great.

After a long half hour we reached Queen's Park. A few sheep looked up from their munching on the football pitches as we noisily chugged past them. Dad aimed the car for the upper reaches of the extinct volcano. We cruised past St Margaret's Loch, not really an achievement, as it's only around two feet above sea level. The problems arose when he tried to get the car to climb a real hill. After stopping for a few minutes for a fag and to rest his accelerator foot, we continued uphill, this time aiming for the dizzy heights of Dunsapie Loch, elevation three hundred feet!

Halfway up, the car was showing signs of cardiac arrest. It was coughing and spluttering like a hundred fags a day pensioner who'd tried to sprint for a bus.

It slowed to about two miles an hour. There was a massive queue of cars behind us full of people hoping to get to the top

'Come on pal' one guy shouted. 'Do ye think you'll get tae the top before Christmas. They could see nothing for the smoke. We were going so slowly that some people got out of their cars, walked past us to see what the hell was going on.

The auld man had got the message by this time, pulled in to the grass verge to let everyone pass. When it was clear again, John and I got out, shoved the car back onto the road, got back in, there was a mighty ping. God knows what it was, but the car started to roll backwards. The auld man put the handbrake on, it stopped it from rolling back too fast; it was still heading back down the way, but in a controlled fashion. John and I leapt out, pushed the car all the way to the top loch. When we got there we were so embarrassed as there were some hot chicks sunbathing and hanging about. We grabbed a couple of sandwiches and a drink, headed off up to the rocks to get as far away from that crowd of gypsies as possible.

Man, we'd never live this down. What made it worse was that our school was opposite Arthur's Seat, there was a gang of boys from the school there. A few fingers pointed in our direction. We walked home that night, no surprise, we got back first.

CHAPTER 18

Billy had been missing for five days, nobody had seen or heard from him since Tuesday night. Mum was worried. Christmas had passed, she was planning to spend New Year with her brother Gordon in Innerleithen. The last anybody had heard of Billy was when he and Robert had been fighting in Mr Abdullah's corner shop, along East Claremont Street. Billy had been doing a job for him, painting the interior and exterior of his shop. He'd taken Robert along to help him, thinking that he could wrap the job up a bit quicker.

'You paint the windows with this white gloss paint, Robert, and I'll paint the doors with the red,' Billy said. He'd always been a very good painter, even at fourteen, he really took his time and was pernickety about clean lines, no streaks. The job was meant to start a week before Christmas and end on Christmas Eve. This never happened as Mr Abdullah had not moved anything in the shop, Billy had to paint and move stuff as he went along, which made things really difficult in a busy grocery shop. They'd agreed that Billy would get an extension to January third in order to give him a fair chance. He'd become immersed in painting his second red door when Mr Abdullah came running out of the shop into the main street.

'Vot your brudder do veet my fucken vindys?'

'What?' Said Billy.

'Vot your brudder do veet my fucken vindys?' He grabbed Billy by the arm, pulled him from the front of the shop, around the corner to where Robert was working. There were around a dozen people at the bus stop opposite, pointing at the windows, laughing. As Billy turned the corner, trying to get out of Mr Abdullah's grip he looked around, to his horror, he saw three full window frames, where the glass in them was covered in white gloss paint. He put his hand to his mouth. 'You get that off my vindy now or you pay me for noo gless,' said the irate shopkeeper.

'Fuck,' said Billy, shoving Robert out of the way. 'What did you do a stupid thing like that for?'

'You said that you were going to paint the doors and I was to paint the windows,' said a totally oblivious Robert.

'I said paint the window *frames*.'

'You said paint the windows,' said Robert, defiantly.

'How thick are you?'

'Don't call me thick,' Robert said, he threw a paintbrush at Billy. It actually missed Billy as he ducked just in time, caught Mr Abdullah right on the chin.

'Ya wee bastars, get the paint off my fucken vindies or I get polis. I'm no payin you for fucken shyte joab.'

'But I've almost finished the inside of the shop,' Billy protested. 'I want paid for doing that.'

'No munny. You fuck up my vindies.'

Billy walked up to Robert, planted one right on his nose. It escalated from there, they managed to fight their way back into the shop and do a bit more damage by knocking over a couple of shelves and display cabinets.

'You're going to pay me for the money I've lost here,' said Billy.

'No way. You told me to paint the windaes.'

Billy stormed off. Robert came home later, told me the story.

Billy had not surfaced since.

Five days later Robert ran into the living room shouting that Bobby Thomson had seen Billy with Pugwash and Ronnie Duke.

'Get Bobby up here right now,' Mum said. A few minutes later Bobby was explaining to Mum where he got this information.

Pugwash was a criminal. He lost his leg in an accident when he was a boy, had gone off the rails, into a life of crime. Ronnie Duke was one of my best mates, but I refused to follow him onto the dark side. Billy on the other hand was easily led. He was fourteen so he still had things to learn. He was always the kind of guy that would be on the verge of doing something bad or dangerous, then crap out of it. Outsiders thought he was a tough wee character but nothing could have been further from the truth.

Billy shared a room with Robert and Gordon; they had the messiest room I had ever seen. Their bed was an island in a sea of clothes, toys, cups, plates and god knew what else. It was so messy that one time Billy let an escaped borstal boy into the room via his balcony, he hid in the room for three days. It was only after Gordon had heard a lot of strange noises under the bed, noticed a few things going missing that it clicked. He grassed the guy to Mum, they were all grounded for a week.

The three of them shared an old double bed, the bed that John and I had parted with six months earlier as the mattress was getting threadbare, the main springs were beginning to poke out, sharply. Gordon slept in the bed with Billy and Robert but, as he was the youngest, he was made to sleep in the middle of the bed as the springs were ripping through the material, those two had no intention of getting their legs and bums scraped. The unfortunate thing was that Gordon peed the bed a lot, after a week or two the springs got so rusty that every time he moved, he scratched himself. Every morning he'd get the scrapes wiped with TCP to avoid infection.

Bobby spilled the beans to Mum, letting out that Billy had been hiding in the cages at night, going to Princes Street shoplifting at M&S during the daytime.

Mum gave John and I specific instructions: when Billy came back to the cages that night we were to wait for him, bring him back to the house. If we didn't do this she said she'd go down with a torch and drag him out by the hair if necessary. We didn't want Mum to go anywhere near the cages.

At the same time, we didn't want to go either.

'But it's Hogmanay, Mum,' I said, 'can't we wait till the second or third?'

'No. I don't want him spending any more time with those two,' she said. 'If you get him early you can still enjoy your Hogmanay and I can head to Uncle Gordon's.'

'OK, Mum,' we both said; it seemed fair enough.

We headed downwards towards the abyss. After a lot of face-pulling, squelching and standing on things our feet did not recognise, we hid in the middle of the cages, cage number 45. There was a black piano cover in it and, most importantly, no padlock. Before we shuffled under the cover I checked my luminous watch hands. Eight o'clock. That gave us around two and a half hours to get Billy, get washed, changed and ready for Hogmanay action.

We had a flask of tea and some black bun.

Ninety minutes into the shift we heard voices. It was without doubt Pugwash, Ronnie and Billy returning.

'You are a natural, Billy, my son,' said Pugwash. 'You really fooled that woman into thinking you'd lost your mummy, how did you make it look like real tears?

'Just did,' Billy said.

'Yeah, that made it really easy for us to nip out with the coats,' Ronnie said.

As they walked in, we couldn't believe our luck. Ronnie got a key out of his pocket, fumbled with the padlock on the cage almost directly opposite us. He dropped the key.

'Fuckit,' he shouted. His voice echoed all along the long corridors of the cages.

'SHHHH!' Hissed Pugwash. 'You'll have everybody down here. Shut the fuck up.'

'But I've lost the key,' Ronnie said. A beam of light appeared. 'Ya beauty!' He shouted.

Billy held up a small key ring torch, pointed to where Ronnie was fumbling. John and I were hiding in the shadows, shitting ourselves in case he shone it onto us.

'Right,' I whispered to John. 'Wait till Mum finds out, helping these two crooks to steal from M&S, he's for it.'

It was getting late by this time, we were conscious that Hogmanay was only a few hours away.

'I'm heading up the road', Ronnie said and headed out of the door.

Pugwash and Billy disappeared into the cage, they were talking quietly. A long time had elapsed, the voices were getting quieter until we heard no sound from them.

We decided to go in and get Billy before it got too late. We made our way stealthily into their cage, the smell was overwhelming, in fact it was not a smell, it was a taste as well, it clung to the back of the throat like a lump of sludge. By this time, our eyes had adjusted to the low light, there in the far corner we could see three shapes under a quilt, they were silent. The shapes under the sheet rose and fell at different times. They were sleeping. Soundly.

Manoeuvring ourselves like SAS men, we made a move to get Billy. We knew it was him by the tiny shoes sticking from the bottom of the quilt, size threes. We grabbed him, attempted to run out, John holding his legs, me with his top half, my hand over his mouth. As we got to the cage door we clumsily banged it shut instead of open. Shit! There was a movement from under the quilt. I dipped into Billy's pocket, took the key ring out, shone it onto the cage door to see, then we dragged him out. In the dim glow from the minimal light, I spotted somebody sitting up in the bed. I pointed the key ring at the bed, Pugwash was sitting there rubbing his eyes, shielding them from the light.

'Hold it right there, Nazi scum,' he shouted, sleepily. 'Where do you think you're going with the wee felly?'

'We're taking him home,' John said, dragging a squirming younger brother along, squelching noises on the ground. Pugwash was now standing up and shout-whispering. 'He doesn't want to go home, this is his home.'

'Our mum says he's got to be in the house by midnight or she'll call the cops,' I said, hoping that the mention of the law would strike fear into him.

'Fuck the pigs man,' he said. 'Forget your 'Mummy''.

He said the word 'Mummy' slowly, making me feel really small.

'He doesn't need a Mummy. I'll be his daddy. Don't you two wankers give this kid the fuckin third degree or I'll kick your arses into next week.'

Despite being petrified of him, John and I, with Billy under our arms, ran out of the cages, up the stairs. Pugwash was high on something but still managed to put his leg on in double quick time and chase after us. I slammed the main cage door shut, it took him a few seconds to hammer it open again, which gave us time to escape and get Billy back into the house. It was now about quarter to ten, Mum got a taxi to Innerleithen for Hogmanay, leaving us with instructions not to let Billy out of the house. We gave her a hug, wished her Happy New Year.

The auld man had been out most of the day, after a half day at work he had gone out to the pub with a couple of his mates. As we had the house to ourselves with no adults, John and I invited a few of our friends around for a New Year party: Higgy, Alex, Stevie, his brother, Jimmy and a couple of other guys. It was a great laugh, we watched Ricky Fulton, waited for the bells and were currently waiting for some female company to arrive. Not many of us knew girls that weren't related so we waited, and waited.

In vain, as it turned out.

And unbeknown to us Billy, the bugger, had untied himself from the rope and masking tape, somehow got out of the house and run away again. But it was of no immediate concern as we had a few days until Mum got back.

One o'clock became two o'clock, two o'clock became three and so on, no sign of girls yet. Higgy was falling asleep on the couch, tongue lolling about like a Rottweiler having a Kennomeat dream. I shook him, told him to go upstairs, crash out. There was no chance of any lassies turning up now. He reluctantly agreed, but getting him upstairs in a comatose condition was no easy task.

Most of the kids were at our auntie's house, which left plenty of beds to choose from. Typically, Higgy chose the wrong bed.

Three thirty, the auld man returned from the pub, pissed. He always believed he could play the guitar and speak Spanish when he was pissed.

'Adios amigos,' he shouted, falling through the living room door. 'How's about a sing song?'

John and I were so used to this; he'd strum the guitar, realise that he couldn't play it and end up smashing it on the staircase bannister. Things went as expected, except for a small deviation in the guitar's death scene. He had finished playing, nobody was taking any notice, as usual. Some of our mates thought this was great fun, but we discouraged them from communicating with dad.

He staggered out of the room with the guitar under his arm. We heard him go upstairs, heard the sound of a guitar hitting something repeatedly. Normally it was the bannister and the guitar would be destroyed in five or six hits. This time it kept going. After ten, eleven thumps there was a muffled cry. The sound of the strings poinging and twanging actually made a better sound than him playing. I ran upstairs, found him thumping the guitar onto a quivering body hidden beneath the bedclothes on Billy's bed.

'Where – the fuck – have you – been – for – the last – five – fuckin – days?' The old man was finally getting rhythm, he was thumping what he thought was Billy, with his guitar. Each word was a different thump, each thump brought a different a cry from Higgy.

When I got into the room the auld man looked at me, turned around, went downstairs into his room, locked the door. I peered under the blankets, there was Higgy, sobbing.

'Why didn't you tell him that you weren't Billy?' I said.

'I couldn't,' he said. 'Every time I tried to get out from under the blanket the guitar would come down on ma heid.'

'Well, see if you can sleep now,' I said, trying to be sympathetic but pissing myself inside.

'I think he bust one of my new teeth,' Higgy said.

I ran downstairs killing myself laughing, burst into the room, had the guys on the floor in kinks.

The Lost Tornado

CHAPTER 19

The auld man seemed a bit hacked off these days. He was out a lot more than usual and came back drunk a lot more than usual. It was obvious that he and Mum were no longer on speaking terms, or any other terms for that matter. The fact that they'd got separate rooms for the first time in their married life proved it. It was a very difficult time for him as there were still eight of us bouncing around the house, they all sided with Mum. Karen, the eldest of the sisters, had gone to live with Stuart, her new boyfriend, in Qatar, the auld man was pretty pissed off that his eldest daughter had gone, and the Qatar thing stuck in his throat.

John had moved to Gorgie. Five of us helped him to move into his two bedroomed flat, around the corner from Tynecastle stadium. I really envied him. There I was, a year older than him, still years away from being independent, although the good side of that was that I was still only paying a fiver a week dig money.

The auld boy always locked his room door when he was going out. Nobody knew what he was hiding in there and to be honest, they didn't want to know. He'd been locking the door now for a year or two. Gordon was the only one that was interested in finding out his secrets.

For quite some time now he'd been trying to get into the room, but the auld man locked up every single time. He put the key, which was on a chain around his neck, down his black polo-neck jumper, then double-checked the door.

One day, when Mum and Dad were standing arguing, I decided to try to get my Hibs career back on track. Nothing had happened on the Hibs front. No scouts had come along to watch me. John Hagart, the Hearts boss, and brother of our BB Captain, Haggy, had been sacked and that route was now firmly closed. I was still playing great stuff with the BB team, still learning new skills and to top it all I was running three to four times a week to increase my fitness. I was beginning to realise that if Hibs didn't discover me soon my chance would have gone. I decided on some drastic action: I would write a letter of introduction to Eddie Turnbull, manager of the legendary Turnbull's Tornadoes Hibs team. I sat down on the couch, pulled a chair over, put the pad onto it, began to compose the letter.

I sat writing and re-writing until I got it right. Lots of crumpled pages ended up on the floor, but eventually I cracked it.

Mr Eddie Turnbull, Manager
Hibernian Football Club Easter Road Stadium
12 Albion Place
Edinburgh
Midlothian EH7 5QG

Dear Mr Turnbull,
My name is Jimmy Divine, I've wanted to play for Hibs ever since I was a wee laddie. I am a really good player. I'm nearly seventeen and currently playing with the 46th BBs. I've spoken with the manager and he said he would have no problem if you wanted to sign me.

I am not looking for any pay or anything, maybe some boots or something would do. I prefer to play on the left wing, Arthur Duncan is not as good as he used to be, I think I am better than him. Alternatively, if Erich Schaedler gets injured I can fill in at left back, or anywhere else if you have space. I can come to Easter Road for a trial anytime you need me.

P.S. What bus do I get from Claremont Court to Easter Road?

P.P.S. You don't need to get me a strip either as I have a Hibs strip (and it already has the Bukta logo on it).

P.P.P.S. If you don't have a place for me right now do you have any spare tickets for the cup game? The game against Leeds United in the UEFA Cup would be preferable to the League Cup game against Stranraer.

Thanks, look forward to meeting you.

Jim Divine, left winger (or left back, or whatever you need).

I ripped it from the pad, folded it in half.

As I was looking around for an envelope Gordon ran through, all excited.

'It's open! It's open!'

'What's open?' I said.

'The auld man's room, he's gone away and left the key in the door. Ya beauty,' he shouted.

'Opportunity knocks!'

Although he was sure the auld man was away he knocked to make doubly sure. He turned the key, popped his head in then out again, then confidently he strode in.

'What secrets do we have in here then, Daddy dearest?' He said aloud. As he walked in Catherine, his twin sister, followed him.

There was silence for a minute or two, they were busy rummaging through all his stuff when quite unexpectedly the auld man came back in. He speeded up when he saw that his room door was open. He went straight for it. At that point Gordon popped his head around the door again to check. The auld man was almost upon him. Gordon saw him in time, slammed the door shut. Right in his face.

'Let me in ya bastard,' he shouted.

'If I'm a bastard you're not my dad so I'm claiming this room,' said Gordon.

The auld man pushed hard against the door ripping the wood-effect Fablon that was covering it. There was a lot of rustling going on behind the door, a bit of paper made its way underneath.

Gordon shouted, 'Stick that on my door, ya auld dick.'

The auld man lifted it up. It was a scribbled note that said;

EVICTION NOTICE FOR DANDRUFF MAN – THIS ROOM IS NOW GORDON'S

The auld man crumpled the paper, threw it onto the floor. 'I'll give ye ten seconds to get out or I'll come in there and kick your arse all over the wall. Are you listening?' He shouted.

There was silence.

'I said, are you listening to me, ya bastard?'

Still silence.

The next thing I saw was the auld man's nudie mags being pushed under the bottom of the door. By that time there were six of us sitting in the living room watching TV.

Images of all kind of lady bits were coming through the door, tits, fannies, the lot. It was fairly serious stuff, but we were all creasing ourselves while the auld man tried to hide the images that were coming out. He was in such an awkward position. He lost the rag. As he shouted a final warning his false teeth fell out. He picked them up, wrapped them in his dirty hankie, put them into his pocket. He began to push the magazines back under the door, the pages began to crumple and rip. Naked women, naked women and naked men, naked men and naked men, naked women and naked women, he couldn't stop them, they flooded through too fast His finger was in the proverbial dyke.

He gave up trying, began to kick the door as hard as he could, but he only had his faded blue slippers on and hurt his toes, he took a few steps back, ran forward, shoulder charging it. He bounced right off, no impact whatsoever. He picked up all of the dirty mags in a bundle, stormed out of the house, avoiding eye contact with everyone.

He returned a few minutes later after putting on his steel toe capped boots, which he kept in the car. He bent down outside the door, tied the laces very slowly and deliberately, then attacked the shit out of the door, aiming mainly for the lock area.

After half a dozen kicks the door caved in, the lock fell to the floor. He ran through the gap and to his surprise there was nobody in the room. He ran out again quickly, looking bemused. 'Where is the wee bastard?' He said to the room in general. No one said a word.

He ran out of the house looking for Gordon, he had no idea that Catherine had been in there as well. His bedroom had a balcony that linked to the living room balcony, Gordon and Catherine climbed over his balcony onto the living room one. When they knew the coast was clear, I let them in.

The Lost Tornado

'That wasn't the cleverest thing to do,' I said to them.

'He deserved it,' said Gordon.

I grinned. 'It was a great laugh, though.'

'You know he'll kill you when he comes back,' I said.

'He'll have to catch me first,' Gordon replied, out of breath with the exertion and fear.

The excitement died down a bit, the auld boy returned a lot later, nothing more was said of the incident.

The following week the auld man was constantly looking for Gordon, but could never catch him. Gordon was scared shitless, but at the same time was really enjoying the thrill of the chase, even though it meant sleeping in different friends' houses, watching his back every single moment of the day. His friends treated him as if he was some kind of rebel.

One afternoon Gordon had been playing rounders in the square with some of the kids and had come up to the house to dig out a tennis ball. He'd been in and out of the house many times, especially when he thought the auld man was away. He sneaked up to his room to get the ball, as he came stealthily downstairs he spotted the auld man in his usual betting slip writing position; facing the fireplace, writing a slip on the mantelpiece. The back of the auld man's head bobbed up and down as he chose his horses. Slowly, silently, Gordon raised his arm, the tennis ball primed, took aim and WHAM!

The tennis ball blootered the back of the auld boy's napper like a cannonball, the front of his head smacked hard against the wood-chip wallpaper in front of him, a big red mark appeared on the wallpaper directly in front of his forehead.

'What the fuck?' He screamed as he spat the chewed, red plastic pen from his mouth. He looked round to find Gordon sticking the vicky's up at him with both hands.

'Fuck you asshole, fuck you asshole, fu–'

'Come here, ya wee bastarding prick,' the auld man bellowed as he ran towards him.

'Like that makes sense!' Gordon laughed, then he put on a mock posh accent, said, 'Later, Pater,' and ran from the room.

The auld man raced after him, in a single movement scooped up the leather-effect wooden stool that he ate his dinner from. As he ran from the house he manoeuvred the stool until he had a firm grip of one of the legs. He hurled it at Gordon, missing him by inches.

As the stool smashed into smithereens against the hall stairs, it knocked down a big bundle of coats and jackets that were piled on the bannister. His forehead now looked like the inside of a pomegranate. It was oozing blood, he wiped it with his cardigan sleeve, to his credit he almost caught the bugger, grabbing a hold of Gordon's tracksuit hood, luckily for Gordon, he was able to unzip it speedily before the auld man could get a grip of anything more substantial. The auld boy was left standing at the front gate in front of around twenty of Gordon's pals with the tracky top in his hand, a ripped cardigan, and a face dripping blood.

'Don't you worry,' he shouted. 'I'll be waiting for you, time is on my side.'

Gordon, playing the big man in front of his pals, shouted, 'Why don't you piss off, ya auld loser, come near me again and I'll hit you even harder next time.'

The auld man wiped his still dripping head with the cardigan, ripped it to shreds, threw it to the ground, turned, then went back up the stairs. As he walked away a tennis ball missed his head by inches. He barely noticed.

I waited an eternity for a reply from Eddie Turnbull. Nothing ever came through. I wondered to myself if his reply got lost in the post or if he was still considering the offer. I decided to give it until my eighteenth birthday, if I'd still hadn't heard by then, I would come up with a better plan.

The Lost Tornado

Chapter 20

School had come to an end, I'd walked out halfway through the last exam. I realised that whatever I did there would make no difference to my life. I'd turned the paper over an hour before and literally only understood one of the twelve questions. Instead of completing the paper, I spent the time trying to remember what options the careers officer had given me.

Bricklayer, shop worker or cleaner; that was it.

'James,' she had said to me. 'I think it's best if you try to find a position of little skill. Your attention span is hardly even a span, it's more like a small portion of a span, then you go back to dreaming.'

I had no idea what she was going on about.

'I've arranged for you to go and see the council about a position they have for an apprentice bricklayer. Failing that, Campbell's butchers need a boy for the front shop.'

I ignored those interviews; I wanted better. Surely somebody would come knocking at my door? *Eddie? Where are you?*

As I sat there in the exam, I doodled on the back of the paper, drawing random shapes, then trying to make them look like something. A rabbit, a cock, a football. This exam thing was shit, a complete waste of time. I imploded. I put my pen down next to the paper, walked out of the room.

'Where are you going, boy?' The old beardy adjudicator shouted. 'You can't possibly be finished, come back here.'

I didn't even turn around, not to say 'up yours, pal', or even to wave cheerio to the school pals I'd leave behind for good. I walked, and walked and walked.

I had no idea what I was doing or what I wanted to do, I was trapped in a child's body. At PE I used to shit myself at the size of my fellow pupils, they were men, almost all of them. They stood there, head and shoulders above me, with their hairy chests and man-sized toilet parts, I was still struggling to coax a couple of pubes out. They shed more hair in a slide tackle than I'd grown in my whole life. I once contemplated collecting their cast-offs from the changing room floor, gluing them onto myself!

I used to read the problem pages about adolescents struggling to cope with impending adulthood. I yearned for it.

One time I actually rubbed salt into my groin after reading a story about a sea captain who rubbed salt onto his chin to make his hair thirsty, then when the hair came out for a drink he'd tie it in a knot and keep it as a beard.

The salt nipped, went red, itched for a few days, but I was still bald as Kojak's head.

I was completely lost, nobody to guide me, no idea what the hell I could do. After a few months on the dole I had no hope, no prospects, and no ideas. Eventually after having to go to the dole week after week and be humiliated and embarrassed by the morons on both sides of the counter I'd had enough. I needed a job, any job.

Davie Duke, my mate from downstairs, approached me one day. 'Hey, Jimbo,' he said, 'how are you doin for cash these days?'

'Crap. Why?'

'I may have a bit of good news for you. Meet me up town the morn's morning, say ten thirty outside the George Hotel. How does that sound?'

'Is there money to be made?, Legally?'

'Yeah; meet me there, got to go now.'

That night I was pretty excited. I'd been in a few scrapes with Davie, mainly to do with us thieving or breaking into places for bits of cash. Not much, mind you, but I had broken into two places, Timberland joinery shop and Clapperton's toy factory, both using the same ploy: take off the lead from the attic window, dreep into the building and nick stuff. This time it seemed legal.

I was there well before ten. Davie turned up, pretty well-dressed. I followed him into the Hotel, scratched my head a bit.

'What's going on?' I said.

'Go through there', he said pointing to the ballroom.

I walked through, admiring the elaborate decor of the hotel and into this stunning ballroom, with it's tables laid out perfectly. The stage was being set-up for a four piece band, I walked over to a guy dressed in a penguin suit at the back of the room with a stack of forms laid out in front of him.

'Seet down'. He said pointing to a chair opposite. I guessed he was Italian

'So tell me, Master Deevine,' said the Italian head waiter, 'how much do you know about seelver serveece?'

After fifteen minutes bluffing my way through the interview for a job as a commis waiter I thought I'd finally been caught out. I knew more about the inner workings of a snail's inner eardrum than I did about silver service.

'We never use silver in our house, it takes too much work to clean, especially with ten kids, I said.

I couldn't quite believe it when he offered me a position. Davie winked at me from behind a curtain at the side of the stage

I was now somebody! The George was the best hotel in the city.

He told me the job was shift work, usually about a ten-hour day. The waiters had their own rest room, which had a jukebox, pool table and Coke machine. My main motivations in life were watching *Noel Edmonds' Multi Coloured Swap Shop* and cramming as many sweets into my mouth as possible, I was thinking about how many visits to the tuck shop I could make when the head waiter jolted me out of it.

'Sign here,' he said, as he concluded my offer of employment. 'Twenty-five pounds per week basic, and teeps depending on how you perform,' he added, handing me a copy of the contract.

I couldn't take my eyes off the agreed payment line. Twenty-five nicker a week. Wow. I was walking on air.

'Can you start thees evening, Mr. Deevine?' He said.

'Yes, sir,' I said. I offered my hand but he turned away. I was dying to get home to tell Mum I'd finally got a real job.

I got home, washed my face, put one of John's white shirts on, looked out his black shiny shoes, lay on the bed thinking about what

I was going to do with all that money. I took a deep breath, smiled and realised I was happy. For the first time in years, I was happy!

After a few weeks at the hotel, the smile and happiness had gone. It had all turned shitty. Early starts, late finishes and shit money. The only bright points had been when the Bay City Rollers stayed in the hotel, It was mental, I felt like I was part of the CIA as I could wander in and out at my leisure with my special access badge, straight past security and all of those screaming girls. Another big star also stayed a couple of nights. I had no idea who he was at the time. I'd finished my shift and headed to the rest room to chill a bit. A guy who'd wandered through from the upper part of the building with a glass of wine in his hand asked if I fancied a game. Reg seemed a nice enough guy, I thought he was a guest trying to get away from everyone. We had a couple of games, he drank his wine while I had a Coke from the machine. We were on our third game when the hotel manager came down with a security guy, Reg shook my hand and that was the last I saw of him. Turned out he was Elton John!

Because of my lack of stature and general naivety, there were people who took advantage of me. The head waiters took a dislike to me, but the worst was Martin, the big fat slob of a chef, he hated my guts. I never did anything to offend him, he seemed to hate me, had done from day one. Every time I went up to collect a meal from him he hit me over the knuckles with a bread knife.

'Dinnae put yer fuckin grubby hands on my shiny surface, you little cunt,' he said.

It had been going on for weeks, every time I had to go up to his kitchen to pick a meal up, off he went with the abuse. I took so much, then one day I decided I'd had my fill of the big fat shite. I complained to my headwaiter about his behaviour.

'Don't you worree, Meester Deevine,' he said, 'I weel look after you.'

I watched him as he walked to the kitchen; he went straight to Martin, the two of them stood laughing together.

The next morning as I was getting my bow tie and maroon jacket on for my shift I was cornered by one of Martin's good friends.

His name was Iain, a Glaswegian. He was about six foot two inches in his stockings. Martin had convinced this guy that I was a 'sneaky little cunt' with a 'hidden agenda'. I honestly didn't know what an agenda was let alone know how to hide one.

This guy Iain was also a waiter, so I thought he'd be on my side, part of the brotherhood, but no. There were many times when he kicked and punched me for absolutely no reason.

On that occasion we were in the changing room putting on our waistcoats and dicky bows when he walked over to me, grabbed my hair, twisted it round in his fist a couple of times. He pulled me over to a table with my hands behind my back then frogmarched me across the room, forced my face right up against the Coke machine. My nose was pressed flat against the ice-cold glass, I could hardly breathe, my breath was making long condensation marks on the glass every time I breathed out.

I tried to say something but he pushed harder.

'Listen to me, you pathetic little cunt, when Martin tells you to do something you'll do what you're told, say nothing and like it. Do what he says, do what I say and do it without question, OK?'

I nodded. He whacked my head against the machine. I got up, walked back towards my locker, he used some kind of judo move to trip me up, laughed, slammed the door behind him on the way out.

I'd felt small and shitty enough before, but this lowered my confidence another few notches. *How low can I go*, I wondered. I lay there, almost sobbing, angry as hell and powerless. Eventually I got up, brushed myself down, made it upstairs a good half hour later than I should have. My headwaiter was furious.

'Where have you been, Deevine?' He whispered so that none of the lunchtime clientele could hear him.

'I lost my bow tie, sir,' I said.

'Your pay weel be docked accordingly, get over to station three. Now!' He fumed.

As I walked over to station three that big bastard Iain was standing looking at me with an evil grin on his coupon.

'Hello, Mr Divine,' he said, enjoying his power trip. 'A little late, aren't we? Delayed by anything important?'

As he laughed, I avoided eye contact, got my order pad out, began taking orders.

The area I grew up in was quite a rough one from an outsider's point of view. There were gangs of teenagers trying to prove things to each other, the usual stuff. The leader of one of the gangs, Davie Duke, also stayed at Claremont Court. Davie was not much bigger than me but he had this tough guy attitude. It really worked for him. Davie had been at the George Hotel a lot longer than me, but as we were on different shift patterns we rarely saw each other.

As I finished that particular shift, I wandered back down to our communal room to get changed ready to go home, losing confidence with every step. I was aware that Iain was finishing up, I rushed to make sure I got away before he came down.

I felt a tap on my back, cowered instantly, expecting a thump.

'What was all that about?'

I turned around, it was Davie.

'Sorry, Davie,' I said, 'I thought you were that big bastard Iain.'

'Jeez, what the hell's he been up tae?' He said.

I told him everything. He shook his head, knitted his brows. I could see his fists balling and unclenching as I told him the story.

'Well, you might cheer up soon,' he said.

'Why?'

'Stu Lothian is starting in the next few days, he'll be on the same shift pattern as you.'

'Really?' I said. I could feel the smile return to my face for the first time in ages. My spirits lifted immediately, I knew I was going to be OK.

Stuart was a really nice guy, he seemed to take a shine to me in a brotherly kind of way. He was tougher than anyone I knew, including Davie, plus he'd got the build to look after himself.

'Ya beauty,' I said.

'I thought you might like that' Davie said. 'Fancy a game of pool?'

'Yeah, why not,' I said. Things were looking up.

On Stu's first day, all three of us were working together. We showed him our staff room.

'Wow,' he said. 'How cool is this? Pool, Coke and a jukey.'

For the first time I was aware that I was not as weak as I thought I was. These two guys were giving me confidence.

We were sitting around drinking Coke and playing pool.

'So, Jimmy lad,' Stu said, 'tell me about this big wanker, Iain, or whatever his name is. Davie says he's been gein you some real hassle.'

Iain had actually punched me in the ribs earlier that day. I lifted my T-shirt up, showed them the big bruise. 'He did this about half twelve this afternoon,' I said to them.

Davy put his cue down, the two of them were very attentive, they sat down beside me.

'Go on,' says Stu, 'tell me about it. You've never mentioned any of this before.'

'I told Davie a while ago but I didn't want to tell you because you'd think I was a sap,' I said.

After I gave them the whole story of Iain and Martin's hate for me both of them looked at each other, Stu said, 'Don't worry, wee man, your troubles are over. It might not happen today or even tomorrow, but it will happen.'

I was ecstatic, I so wanted that pair of bastards to get their comeuppance.

A week or so later we were about fifteen minutes from going on duty when Stu tapped me on the shoulder. 'Follow me, wee felly,' he said.

We walked silently into the underbelly of the hotel, the parts where nobody ever went. We walked for a good five minutes, through a couple of small doors, into a boiler room. I almost shit myself when I looked in. Davy was standing over this big guy, Iain, he had him bound and gagged, tied to a chair. He looked absolutely terrified, his eyes were on stalks. He was sweating profusely.

'What do you want us to do with him?' Said Stu.

I was caught in a dilemma. I really appreciated them looking after me, this big bastard deserved all he had coming. I wanted to see him harmed, but something inside me had already forgiven him. I couldn't let these guys see that I was as soft as a melted marshmallow. I hated him with a passion, but my anger would only work in the heat of the moment, not in cold blood.

'Do you want us to chib him?' Davy said.

'Or cut his balls off?' Said Stu, laughing.

Iain's face went pure white at that suggestion, his eyebrows arched like a cat's back.

'Why don't you two leave me with him for a while?' I said.

'Are you sure?' Stu said.

'Yeah, definitely.'

As they were leaving the room I walked up to him. Looked the big twat in the eyes for the first time.

They both looked at each other and walked out. As the door closed I picked up the broken pool cue that'd been used to jam the door shut.

'Listen, you big ugly bastard,' I said to him, brandishing the cue. He ducked to one side as if I was going to hit him.

I walked up to him, whispered in his ear, 'If you pretend that I'm hitting you these guys will be happy with that.' I knew for a fact that Davy and Stu were on the other side of the door waiting and listening for me knocking seven different colours of shite out of this boy.

He nodded.

'If they think I've let you off too lightly, they'll do the rest.'

He nodded again, vigorously.

'I'm going to have to mark you,' I said. 'You'll have to scream and shout as if I'm giving you a kicking. I don't know if you know, but these guys are my mates, Davie's the leader of Young Leith Team'

His eyes popped like Marty Feldman's, his ears seemed to fold back a bit at this news. He now understood the gravity of his position.

'Do you understand who YLT are and what they could do to you?'

He almost nodded his head off.

'I'm going to take the tape from your gob and start hitting you. Even if it's not sore, scream and whimper as if it is, OK?'

More nodding.

I removed the gaffer tape from his mouth, kicked and punched him a few times. I realised how pathetic it was, so did he. He looked at me like he wished the two behind the door didn't exist, knew I was way too puny to cause any real damage.

I knew he wanted to kill me, I could see it in his eyes, but he knew that he couldn't afford to convey that feeling and tried to disguise it. We were now playing a game. He shouted a bit, made more noises, forced a cry or two and that was that.

'Roll the chair onto its side,' I said. 'It'll look more convincing to them.'

I could hear the door handle rattle a bit. They both burst in as I was laying into his gut with a few additional kicks. He retched and I walked away. For effect I ran back over, gave him another boot in the balls.

'And if you ever look at me the wrong way again, I'll boot your balls so hard that the next time you get on your motorbike you'll need a fuckin Mickey Mouse crash helmet.' I walked away, stopped, turned dramatically, pointed to him and added, 'And you can tell your mate, that fat fucker of a cook, the same thing.'

Davie, and Stu high-fived me as I walked to the door.

'You'd better get up to your station, man,' Stu said, rubbing my hair.

'What are you going to do with him?' I asked.

'Don't you worry, we'll look after him, teach him how to be nice to people,' Stu said. 'If he as much as forgets to say good morning to you, let me know, OK?'

'Cool,' I replied and looked back at a quivering wreck. I was chuffed.

Iain's head was hidden in his chest, he was sweating, had a wet patch on his crotch, looked like he'd pissed himself. I laughed out loud, pointed to him, feeling a hundred feet tall.

I found out later that they kept him locked up in that room all night, the biggest bonus was that he got a written warning from the headwaiter for skiving.

After that night he was always very helpful to me. Most accommodating.

One thing I really hated about the job was the fact that customers did not have to leave the hotel until they'd finished their meals. This was perfectly acceptable in normal circumstances; however, every first Tuesday of the month this arrogant obnoxious toffee-nosed twat, probably a lawyer or something, came into the hotel with his chums, they stayed and stayed until coffee was coming out of their ears.

The downside for me was that he always sat at the same table, at MY station, the rule was that the waiter could not leave his station until the last guest had gone. They sometimes went on until three in the morning; I only got paid for an eight-hour shift. I hated the guy, he never left a tip either.

He always sat, stared at his sweet for a seriously unhealthy length of time, sometimes for twenty minutes, not saying a word to anybody, staring at his sweet. He always had the same thing, 'Death by Chocolate', then he sat sipping brandy, staring at it. It really pissed me off. I was waiting to get home after a day's work and that old twat was trying to stare out a fucking pudding, putting my life on hold in the process.

At this point in the night, my mind drifted, I often went over my favourite scenario of what I'd like to do to him:

'What's that? You want a sweet sir? Death by chocolate? Really? How unusual,' I'd say, spooning on a dollop of sarcasm, smiling as I cleaned up his main course dishes. 'Our sweet chef says he's made something extra special for you tonight sir, something you'll never forget.'

'Oooh?' He'd say, dribbling main course coloured saliva down his napkin. 'Give it to me, give it to me.'

I'd take the plates away, around the back of the stage, head to the kitchen. I'd then sneak down to my locker, remove a Hibs football sock from my sports bag, take out the four Yorkie bars that I'd bought from the tuck shop earlier in the day. I'd open the wrappers, slowly break the bars into big chunks, eating a couple as I worked. I'd place them one by one into the sock. I'd weigh the bulging sock in my hand, shifting the big chocolate chunks, getting the balance right, then put an elastic band around the top of the sock to stop the chocolate from escaping. Then I'd sling it over my shoulder, head back upstairs to my eager customer.

I'd keep a single, pristine rectangle of chocolate aside, the one with a 'Y' engraved into it. I'd wander upstairs nodding, acknowledging the people I met on the stairwell. Calmly walk back to my station, watch the old twat's face as I placed a porcelain plate in front of him and lay the single slab of chocolate in the centre. Saliva would still be dripping onto his chin, onto the tablecloth. I'd put the cutlery, very precisely, either side of it. A silver dessert spoon and knife, making sure to polish them with my white cotton cloth before laying them down. I'd then carefully observe as his face slowly twisted into an angry, evil contortion.

'WHAT'S THIS, BOY?' He'd shout, in his posh Edinburgh accent.

'You misunderstand, sir,' I'd say, calmly, collectedly. 'Take a closer look,'

'Y?' He'd say, looking at the typography on the slab.

'Explain, boy, or you'll be looking for a new job tomorrow.'

'Sorry, sir, look again,'

As he bent his decrepit old dandruff-infested head towards the table, I'd pounce.

I'd smash that green sock into the back of his head over and over again. Watch as his false teeth flew into the plate and disintegrated on impact. The blood would pour out of the gaping wounds on the front and back of his head. It would take a dozen blows to kill the old bastard, but I'd go for fourteen to make sure.

Then there'd be absolute and utter silence.

His friends sit around open jawed, hands up at their mouths covering their whimpering, quivering lips.

I'd drop the now red and green sock to the floor. Look at them one by one.

'Anyone else fancy death by chocolate, then?' I'd say, removing my white gloves, throwing them onto the corpse.

——- I LOVE YORKIES ——-

The job was becoming a complete bore, I hated it and everyone I worked with. Stu and Davie had long gone, so had Iain.

The final straw for me came on a nice summer's evening. I'd agreed with the headwaiter that if I worked three afternoons I'd get the Wednesday evening off to see Hibs in the cup. I did my three afternoons and on the Wednesday afternoon I worked as agreed, finished cleaning up my station and had polished all of the silver condiment holders. The headwaiter sat and had a big three-course lunch watching me working. I put the cleaning stuff back into the trolley and wheeled it to the back of my station. I was on my way out, removing my bow tie as I left the empty restaurant.

'Where do you think you are goeeng?' He shouted to me.

'I'm off home, going to the Hibs game, I've got to get back to get changed.'

'No, no, no, no,' he said, waving his pathetic nicotine stained finger at me. He walked right over to me, came so close that I could smell the smoke on his breath. 'You are workeeng tonight.'

'No, I'm not,' I replied. 'We agreed that if I worked those afternoons I could go to the game.'

'No, no, no.'

'Don't start that again,' I said, knocking his finger away from my face.

'How dare you heet me, boy?' He said, getting angry.

'I never hit you,' I said, pushing my way past him. As he grabbed my arm I swung round, shoved him in the middle of his chest. He fell into a table that I'd set for the evening meals. The whole thing collapsed with him falling into the centre of it. The dishes and cutlery went everywhere. I put my hands to cover my mouth to stop myself from laughing.

He lay there, tried to get up; with his fat belly and full garb on he looked like a penguin, the white table cloth was like an ice island that he struggled to get onto. I could just about hear David Attenborough doing a voice-over.

After feeding, these penguins find great difficulty getting back onto the ice covered mainland, their bellies so full that they slither and slide....'

'Help, help,' he shouted.

I couldn't move, pissed myself laughing. I know I shouldn't have as it could cost me my job, but I kept on going.

'You bastard, Deevine,' he shouted in his Italian accent. 'Getta me up'.

I couldn't, I was helpless with laughter. He rolled onto his fat belly, amidst the smashed crockery and glass, eventually made it up.

'You are toast,' he said.

'Eh?' I said? 'Toast?'

'You arra fayerd, sacked, kaput, understand?'

'Big deal,' I said, accepting that my job was over. I didn't care, I wanted out, this was the perfect way of doing it. I walked over to the big silver tray where about twenty silver condiment sets sat. I lifted the tray up, tipped everything onto the floor, then threw my maroon jacket and bow tie at him.

'You know what, Luigi?' I said. 'You can stick yer shitty job up yer arse. 'I'm off to see the only silverware I'm interested in.'

'You'll be back, Deevine, I know youra typa,' he shouted as I walked away. 'You arra rubbeesh waiter, nobody will geev you a job, you'll see.'

I walked out of the George Hotel that afternoon, never looked back.

Later in the year Hibs won the cup, they had their cup final party in the George Hotel.

Shit, I thought. That could have been my last chance to speak to Eddie Turnbull, I could have got speaking to him, arranged a trial, impressed him with my skill and work ethic, not many waiters became footballers.

I still harboured the last dregs of ambition to play for Hibs, but realised that time was running out.

Chapter 21

I spent almost a year on the dole after the George Hotel job, found it impossible to get anything I wanted. Nobody wanted me; after all, what had I to offer? I spent most of my days playing footy, drawing, watching TV, and training, with the outside hope that I'd still get signed. I had no way into Hibs, I used to hang about Easter Road waiting for the players to come out, do a bit of keepie-uppie to impress them, thinking maybe they'd tell Eddie about this wonder-kid in the car park. Long shot, I know, but it was the only shot I had.

One day I got a phone call from Tam Graham an ex-member of the BBs.

'Hi Jimmy,' he said. 'I've got you a trial.'

'Who with?' I said excitedly.

'Newtongrange Star.'

'Are they any good?'

'Yeah, top of their league.'

'OK, when and where?'

'I'll pick you up tomorrow night at six o'clock outside the Court, OK?'

'Perfect,' I said, 'see you then.'

I was pretty excited as this was the first trial I'd ever really had. They seemed a good, hard team by all accounts. We went along, the first thing that hit me was that they had their own stadium. It was cold and icy, I was a bit worried about crashing onto the icy pitch, ripping my legs open. I got to come on as a sub and couldn't get to grips with the pitch. I'd only brought small rubber studs, I slipped about all over the place. The other guys were hammering and smashing into each other as if it was a battle. I preferred silky one-touch stuff like Hibs played and was not really interested in or equipped for warfare.

The next day Alex appeared at my door.

'Tam called, said they didn't think you were that good,' he said.

'Thanks, Alex, I didn't really want to play with them anyway, a bunch of nutters crashing into each other; no silky skills, a bit like the Jambos, actually'.

He headed downstairs.

I leaned over the balcony. 'Fancy a kick-about after tea?'

He gave me a thumbs up.

My year on the dole was almost up, the pressure they were putting on me to get a job was ramping up. They offered me all kinds of shit jobs with terrible pay. I refused to go along to the interviews. They were pointless.

Another Monday morning came around, I had to sign on at ten-thirty. I hated it, demoralised me every time. I'm sure I actually lost height as I traipsed the twenty minute walk to the Leith dole office, shoulders slumped against the wind. As I waited in the queue I spotted one of the guys behind the desk point me out to one of his colleagues. A girl opened the door, shouted my name.

'James Dean Divine?'

I looked around, embarrassed as always when my full name was called out in public. I caught her eye, walked over to the door.

'Hi James,' she said. She stood back to let me in.

'Jimmy,' I said, as I followed her to her desk. 'My name's Jimmy.'

'OK. Hello, Jimmy,' she said, sitting down. 'Do you want the good news or the bad?'

'The good,' I said, slumping into the chair, knowing fine well that there would not be any good news, only two different levels of bad.

'We have a job for you.' She smiled, thinking I'd be happy; all it did was fill me with dread.

'I said on my form I only wanted to be a designer or play for Hibs.'

She looked at the wad of files in her hand, my files, flicked through them.

'Yes I can see that,' she said, laughing. 'That's the bad news. The government are starting a new programme, everyone aged between sixteen and twenty who has been unemployed for over twelve months must register and begin work within a four week period; if not, your dole money stops.'

'Oh,' I said, shitting myself. 'What kind of jobs are on this programme?' Dreading the next words that came out of her attractive mouth; the red lipstick looked hot.

'Well, there's a whole range of jobs specifically designed to get you fast-tracked onto a career path.' She flicked to the back of the papers. 'I see that you wanted to become a bricklayer when you were at school.'

'No, I didn't,' I said, aggressively, way too quickly. 'That was my school careers officer, I never said anything of the kind.'

'Well, there are slots available on the programme starting a week on Monday. I've pencilled you in for the path building programme; how does that sound?'

I looked away from her, feeling really angry. They were forcing me to do something I didn't want to do. I knew deep down that if I took this job my life would go away onto the wrong path, it would be impossible for me to get back onto my true path, even though my true path was not something I was really clear about. One thing I did know for sure; this was somebody else's path I'd be building, not mine.

'Do I have to?' I pleaded.

'No,' she said. 'But if you don't, you'll not get any money, you'll also be unable to sign on for six months, minimum.'

Shit, I thought. I was now getting older, money was a necessity. I knew that if I had no income my life would change for the worse, and if I took this job my life would change for the worse. I sat there with my head in my hands, looking at her like she was the enemy.

'Well?' She said.

'Can I try it out, see if I like it?'

'Of course you can, if you don't like it we've got another eleven sites around Edinburgh that you can go to.'

'Path building?'

'Yes,' she said, filling in a big twenty-odd page document. 'You'll start at Duddingston Park on Monday the twenty-fourth at eight a.m. OK?'

'Duddingston Park?' I said, alarmed. 'Isn't that near Arthur's Seat?'

'Yes. It's right next to Holyrood High, do you know it?'

'Yes, of course I do, I said, 'I only left last August!' I was mortified. Imagine meeting any of the guys who'd stayed on to sixth year to sit their higher exams? They'd see me as the thicko who left with no qualifications and was now digging a path on Arthur's Seat! What a fucking sad loser. I had no choice though.

On the Monday I headed up to London Road to catch the seven forty number five bus. I had a heavy heart and an overwhelming sense of dread. My head was slumped towards the ground, my hands were firmly in my pockets. I had a red plastic Tupperware box tucked under my arm containing a couple of cheese sandwiches that I'd hastily made up for lunch. I was really grateful for the early start as it meant there was nobody on the bus going to school, it was forty-five minutes too early for them, which suited me perfectly.

I had no idea what to expect when I got there. I was to ask for Davie, the charge-hand, who'd give me instructions. I thought I'd be first to arrive, but was surprised when I got to the bothy and found five guys sitting around. They all ignored me. I looked for eye contact and caught one of the guys.

'Is this job creation?' I said.

He nodded. They were all facing in different directions to avoid having to speak. I sat on an old railway sleeper, a pile of them had been laid in front of the bothy. During the long wait for something to happen, some of the guys smoked a few cigarettes, this allowed them to speak to each other, finding a common denominator.

I had my ears tuned for any snippets. I had no confidence, didn't want to make an arse of myself. After a long silent wait a maroon Jaguar came into view. It was heading for us.

'What the fuck's this?' One of the guys said. The car drove over the grass all the way up to the bothy, slammed the brakes on a few feet from where we sat. A guy in a deerstalker hat and a donkey jacket jumped out.

'OK, lads?' He shouted. 'Ready for action?'

'Fuck you!' The same guy shouted. He was a blonde guy, looked full of confidence, like nothing could touch him.

'What the fuck are you meant to be?' He said. A couple of the other guys laughed.

'I'll tell you as soon as I find out,' the Jaguar guy said, laughing. 'I presume you are Mr Charles Milligan?'

'I am indeed,' he replied.

The Jaguar guy walked up to him with his hand extended, they shook. 'I'm Davie Mac,' he said in a posh English accent, 'your boss.'

He walked around everybody, introduced himself. *Seems a decent bloke*, I thought, *not a bad start*.

There were seven of us in total. I was beginning to get a bit taller by now and was about the same height as three of them.

Davie opened the bothy, asked us all to go inside. The first thing he did was to attach the gas canister to the cooker, put the kettle on. He pulled a big bag of teabags, a jar of coffee and a bag of sugar from his bag.

'Anybody got any milk?' He said.

'There's a shop down the road,' I said.

'Perfect,' he said. He reached into his pocket, pulled out a pound note, handed it to me. 'Nip down, get two pints, there's a good lad.'

As I walked down the hill towards the shop, I became aware of growing numbers of school kids heading to school, but heading to the shop first. *Shit*, I thought. *What if somebody sees me?* I ran down to the shops, by this time I was looking out for faces I knew, thinking of reasons why I might be there.

I almost got away without being seen. I'd bought the milk and was on my way out when I spotted a guy from my class last year heading towards me. I tried to ignore him.

'Jimmy,' he shouted, 'I didn't think you were staying on?'

I thought I'd bluff it.

'Hi Mike,' I said. 'Yeah, I got a holding job at the George Hotel for a while, the late, late results came through and I was able to take the highers'.'

'Wow, well done. Thirsty?' He said, pointing at the two bottles of milk.

'Nah, this is for home economics,' I lied.

'See you around,' he said.

'Yeah, sure.' I legged it out of the shop, swore I'd never go back there during school hours.

Turned out our job was to create a walkway through a wood on the hill. It was easy work, manual labour with plenty of time to skive. They were a weird bunch of guys, though. I used to hate it at tea break, we'd sit in the bothy eating our rolls, having a cuppa, but most of the guys were smokers, I'd be forced to inhale all that shit. I tried sitting outside but the weather was so bad I was forced back in.

I complained, but was called a poof and a fanny.

As the time went by, I found out more about the guys. We had an ex-prisoner, an orphan, a guy with learning difficulties who fitted in perfectly, and a guy on parole for rape. Again, like the George Hotel, there was one guy who hated me from day one. Luckily the others all liked me, I was able to ignore that guy most of the time. The one exception was when I annoyed him so much that he attacked me with an axe. Thankfully Chas was there to stop him bringing it down on my head. I almost got him back one time, but ended up being glad it didn't work out.

He was sleeping on the hill in the long grass on a warm summer's day, skiving as usual. I noticed that the big pile of logs that we were going to use as steps were lined up on top of the hill in line with where he was dozing.

I quietly crept around the front of the logs, thought about dislodging the wooden pins that were holding them in place. I put my hand on one of them to see how hard it would be to move them, the damn thing broke off as I pulled. I tried desperately to keep them in check, but they were heavier than I thought.

Fuck! I could feel the weight of them building, it was only a matter of time before I had to get out of the way or get crushed myself. I thought about the embarrassment of that scenario and dived out of the way. They hurtled away from me downhill, quickly gained momentum and were out of control. The whole pile was heading directly towards Kevin, got to within twenty feet of him when the rumbling woke him up.

'What the fuck? AAAARRGGHHHH!' I heard him scream, thankfully he managed to scramble to the side and avoid them. I was so relieved they missed. They continued down the hill, smashed into the bothy, almost knocking it off its feet.

Kevin was going mental. 'Who the fuck did that?' He was shouting. 'I'll fucking kill whoever did that.'

By this time, I'd run around the other side of the hill and had made my way back to the bothy.

There was nobody about when I got there, so I went inside. It had been totally whacked by the impact, the tables and cooker were all over the place. I had an idea. I lay on the floor, waited. There was a lot of shouting and running outside. The door flew open, Davie the gaffer ran in first.

'Jesus, lads, Jimmy's in here,' he shouted. 'Give me a hand.'

Another few lads came running in, they removed all of the debris, put it outside.

'Are you OK?' Davie said.

I acted as if I'd just woken up. 'Yeah,' I said, faking a dazed expression. 'What happened?'

'You are a very lucky lad, that's what happened,' Alistair, the learning difficulty guy, said. 'You could have been squashed like a bug on a bit of road kill.'

'How? What happened?' I said again, rubbing my eyes and head.

Kevin came storming in. 'Some cunt tried to fuckin kill me!'

'What are you talking about?' Said Chas. 'Some cunt tried to kill Jimmy.'

Kevin looked confused. I could see that he thought it was me, but logic told him that I couldn't be in two places at the one time.

'Calm down, lads,' Davie said. 'It must have been an accident.' He scratched his head. 'I don't want anyone saying a word about this,

OK? If they find out that those pins were not stable, they'll shut us down, we'll all be fucked, so we say nothing, agreed?'

'Agreed,' everyone said.

He nodded. 'Good. Alistair, go and check the holding pins for the logs.'

Alistair was the only one apart from me who didn't smoke. He was a massive Hibee, we spent a lot of time talking about them. He was the simplest guy I'd ever met, but he knew all of the Hibs teams stretching way back in time. I could never figure out how he could be so thick, but so clever, too. He was the perfect guy for me to wind up. A godsend. When we were nearing completion of the pathway, I had a quiet word with him.

'Alistair,' I said, 'has anyone said anything to you about the Lord Mayor's opening of the path yet?'

'No,' he said.

'I'm not supposed to tell you this, but Davie has nominated you to hand the scissors to the Lord Mayor as you're the best worker here.'

'Really?' He said, beaming a massive smile that took up about fifty per cent of his face. 'Me? Me's gonnae meet the Lord Mayor?'

'Yip, you sure are, tomorrow afternoon. Do you have a white silk suit and a matching top hat?'

'No. Why?'

'Because that's what you wear when you meet him,' I said. 'Can you ask your mum and dad to get you one? You can probably hire one.'

'OK, I'll ask Mummy tonight.'

He never turned up for work the next day.

Two days later Alistair came to work with perfectly packed sandwiches, all individually wrapped, his biscuits were neatly laid out, they and his container of soup all fitted like a glove into this plastic Hibs lunch box. One day for a laugh, when he was up the hill, I slipped one of the guys' used fag packets into his empty lunch box, imagined the scene when he got home. Hilarious. I couldn't wait for him to come in the next day, would his mum and dad ground him or give him the belt?

The next morning he came in without a word.

'What have you got for your piece today, Ali?' I said, trying not to laugh.

'The usual.'

Just then Rab came into the bothy with a full kettle, he'd filled it up at the river as our water supply had sprung a leak and all the clean water drained away.

'Anyone for a cuppa?' Everybody put their hands up. Rab stuck it on the cooker, got a fag out from his jacket pocket, popped it into his gob, lit it on the cooker. I could not believe what I was seeing.

Alistair went into his lunch box, pulled a twenty packet of Embassy Regal out. I sat there, probably with a very strange *not sure what I'm witnessing here* look on my face.

At first I thought it was the packet I'd put in yesterday, but he was unwrapping the cellophane so it couldn't be.

He took out a fag, stuck it in his mouth, then bent his head to the cooker for a light; his hair got singed but he managed to light the fag.

'What are you doing?' I said, really confused.

'My mum and dad saw a fag packet in my lunch box yesterday, said it was about time that I started smoking.'

'Good lad, Ali,' Rab said.

'No, not good. Not good at all,' I said, completely taken aback.

I walked outside. I'd been breathing in all this shitty smoke for months but refused point blank to breathe in any from this thick shithead. I sat outside shaking my head.

The Arthur's Seat job lasted around six months, as the job creation project mandate said, it was time to move on.

On our final day, Davie sat us all around the table in the bothy, took out a whole pile of papers. He informed us where our next part in the project would be.

I'd assumed that we'd stay together as a team, but no. We were all going to different places. The really good news for me was that I was going to build a path along the Water of Leith, at St Mark's Park, two minutes from my house.

Ya beauty, I thought, envisaging long lie-ins, money saved on bus travel, taking a ball with me, getting as much practice as I needed. The job was going to be easy, I was beginning to like the outdoor life.

I turned up at the park on the Monday, the gaffer seemed to be a sensible looking guy. He introduced himself to everyone, made us all feel like we were worth something, a unique feeling for me; I liked it. Again, there was the usual hotchpotch of people. One guy had recently left the army, after a few hours I'd grown tired of his stories of sexual prowess, how many women he'd shagged in all various positions and places.

There was a ginger guy called Paul, who was nodding his head to all of them, knowingly.

'What the fuck are you nodding yer heid at, ya ginger cunt? Ye've probably never even had yer hole.'

'Course a have, plenty times.'

'Aye, right? Prove it.'

'How can I prove it, ya daft cunt?'

Before the last word faded away, army guy was right over to him, holding him against the wall, forearm jammed into his throat. 'Who are you calling a daft cunt, ya ginger prick?'

'Easy lads, easy.' Graham, the gaffer, came into the room as it was all kicking off. 'The last thing we want is any friction, especially on the first day. Shake hands.'

Nobody moved.

'Shake hands or I'll have to let one of you go.'

Army guy extended his hand, they shook. I could see ginger wincing as army guy squeezed a bit too hard.

After a week or two everything settled down. They weren't a bad bunch, the work was much easier than the last job, I was able to spend tons of time with a ball at my feet.

I used to go for the filled rolls in the morning as it got me away from the tedium of work. I could walk along the pathways next to the river, watch the wildlife. Most of my mates thought I was a bit soft in the napper, looking at birds, trees and nature in general.

One breakfast time I had a brilliant plan. I knew what the guys had for breakfast every day. Why not buy a dozen or so rolls, some bacon, cheese, sausage and tomato, nip home, make them up myself, keep the substantial profit? A big light bulb was going off in my head, my mind was giving me a huge thumbs up. What could possibly go wrong?

I waited for a particularly big order before I knocked the plan into action. Everyone bar none was having at least two rolls each. I quickly did the sums in my head. I would make about half a day's wages from this. Easy.

I took the order. Went to the shops. Bought the raw materials and headed home. There was nobody in so I put the cooker on, began cooking up. It was a lot more complex than I thought, keeping all of these different things hot and aiming for them all to be ready at the same time. I lost control; the bacon was burnt, the butter was so hard that I couldn't spread it, there were chunks of it sitting on the ripped rolls. The knives we had were blunt, when I tried to slice the tomatoes thinly they burst. I was rapidly running out of raw material and had spent so much of their money on it that I could not give up and go to the real roll shop. I thought about how mad army guy would be when he saw the state of his rolls. I began to shit myself because I knew he'd probably thump me. Panic set in and the whole thing went to pot.

Even something as simple as wrapping the rolls nicely in brown paper bags became difficult as I'd completely forgotten to grab any. Shit, what was I going to do? I looked at the fourteen different rolls all sitting on the worktop in the kitchen, some hot, some cold. It looked like something that had been pulled from a bin. I opened up the cheese and tomato rolls, sighed heavily as a big chunk of cheese, half a tomato and a lump of butter looked up at me. This was a disaster. I had no choice. I had to go with it. I got around the packaging issue by putting the rolls on one of my mum's metal trays, covering them with tinfoil. I nipped upstairs to the loo, peed, washed my hands, and realised I should've really washed them before I started, but it was too late now. I looked at my watch, speeded up when I realised how long I'd taken. I ran downstairs just in time to see Tigger dragging a sausage roll into the living room. I dived in after him, fought him under the couch until I got most of it back. Fuck! That was army guy's roll. I washed it under some hot water, to disinfect it and keep it warm. The roll was buggered so I swapped it with mine.

I was shaking like a leaf as I walked back over to the park, the tray hidden up my jumper to preserve any lingering heat.

I reached the path that we were working on in the park, the boss spotted me. He whistled.

'All right, lads, grub's up.'

Everyone threw their tools down, headed towards me, most were rubbing their hands in anticipation. I went into the hut, put the metal tray on the cooker to try to heat the stuff up.

Army guy was first in. 'Go to the palace, did you?'

'No,' I said, thinking he was complimenting the look of the tray.

'You could've done; you were fucking long enough.'

'There was a new guy in the shop, wanted to impress me,' I lied.

One by one they came in, took their rolls. I waited tensely for the comments. Initially there were none. *I may have got away with this*, I thought, but right at that moment army guy shouted out.

'This roll's fuckin freezin, and the sausage is fucking raw in the middle.' He pulled it out, showed it to the rest of the guys, spat the remnants from his gob. He looked carefully at it, close up. 'Is that fucking teeth marks there?'

'Don't be a knob,' I said, although after thinking a bit, it was probably Tigger's fang marks, 'that's from the strange fork the boy in the shop had.'

'Mines tastes shite,' said somebody else.

They were beginning to look at what they were eating. One of the guys opened his cheese and tomato roll.

'Look at the fuckin state of this,' he said, taking out the half tomato and lump of cheese. 'Did the boy have boxing gloves on and use a spanner to make these?'

'There's a fucking big ginger hair in mine,' Wee Gus shouted.

Shit, I'd forgotten to wipe Tigger's fur from the tray after he'd been up at it.

Everyone looked at Ginge accusingly; he chewed away, oblivious to the accusations.

'Where the fuck did you get these?' Army guy shouted at me.

'I thought I'd try the new place in East Claremont Street,' I said, acting as if there was nothing different about the grub.

'Right? That's it,' army guy said, 'I'm taking this shit back to them, getting my fuckin dosh back. I'm no paying good money for this shite.'

FUCK!!! I thought to myself. *What am I going to do?*

'You can't,' I blurted out in a panic, 'they're shut.'

'Eh? What dae ye mean? You're just back.'

'The guy had to go to a funeral,' I conjured from somewhere, and continued without a pause, 'he was about to close the shop when I pleaded for him to make our rolls.'

'I suppose if the guy was upset and in a hurry it might explain things,' said Graham, the gaffer.

I jumped onto the crest of his wave. 'Yeah, he was gutted, think it was his wife who kicked it,' I said.

'Poor guy,' Graham said.

'Takes the time to make our breakfast and we're sitting here slagging him.'

I could see a few of the guys were feeling guilty, they sat silently and ate the rolls.

'I'll give it a couple of weeks, then go back again,' I said. 'Maybe get a discount or something.'

'Like fuck you will,' army guy said, 'ye'll get back to the usual place, pronto.'

'Fair enough,' I said, 'Monday morning normal service will be resumed.'

I wiped the sweat from my brow. Looked at my hands as they shook, promised myself never to do anything like that again.

We'd had tons of time to play footy in St Mark's Park during the building of the paths, there was probably three times too much manpower for such an insignificant job, but it did what the politicians wanted – kept another few lost souls off the dole for a while.

I was dribbling away on my own one day during a lunch break there were a couple of teams playing a rescheduled league game. I went over to watch, as I stood on the sidelines a guy, turned out to be one of the coaches, began talking to me.

'Saw you dribbling away there, pal, looked pretty good. Are you playin for anybody?'

'The BBs,' I said.

'BBs?'

'Aye, 46th,' I replied.

'How d'ye fancy a trial with us?'

I'd never played for another team other than primary school and the BBs; this could be a good opportunity. I was hitting late teens, my chances of playing for Hibs was dwindling fast.

'Aye, sure,' I said, not quite knowing what I'd be getting into. 'When and where?'

'Tuesday night, six o'clock at Warrender Park, you know it?'

'Of course.'

'My name's Jock,' he said, offering me his hand. We shook. 'See you Tuesday.'

I went around the other side of the pitch to look at his team, my competition for a place. *I could do well here,* I thought.

I went to the trial, easily got a game with the team. I played left-winger. It was hell of a rough league. I played about four games with them then gave up. I'd already been kicked and booted in the air more times in the first three games than I had in my whole career to date.

On the fourth game I was getting to know my team mates, building a bit of an understanding. The right back I was up against was a fat guy with bow legs, ideal for nutmegging. I did this three times in the first half. As we were about to kick off the second half he wandered up to me.

'You try doin that again, ya little shit, I'll break yer fucking legs.'

This was the first time I'd been threatened on a pitch, I thought about it for a few minutes.

The opportunity to nutmeg him arose again, I went for it. Not only did I nutmeg him, I ran on, scored from there. He was raging.

The next time I got close to him I could see he was intent on flooring me, but I was three steps ahead of his Neanderthal brain. I dribbled the ball close to his feet, got so close to him that he couldn't tackle me. He threw a hay-maker of a punch, which I saw coming all the way. I went down like a sack of spuds, but in reality he'd hardly touched me. I lay on the ground clutching my face. There was a barney, the ref came storming over, blowing his whistle.

'Right, you, number two, early shower.'

The guy really thought he'd hurt me, but I was lying there laughing to myself. He came over to me on his way off the pitch.

'Serves you right, ya bastardin show oaf cunt. Come near me again and ye'll get more than a sore face.'

I stood up, shook my head a couple of times to show my team mates that even a punch in the face wouldn't keep me down. A couple of guys came over, showed a bit of concern.

'Alright there, Jimmy? That looked a sore one.'

'Nah, it was nothin,' I said.

That was my last game of football.

After those four games I'd decided that I wasn't prepared to put my well-earned health and fitness on the line for some numbskull to cripple me. I'd always been one of, if not the, fittest guy on all of the teams I'd been in.

I decided I'd keep on running, see what happened, if Hibs came calling I'd be as fit as a butcher's dog.

CHAPTER 22

The St Mark's job came to an end after about six weeks. I still had some time to go if this project was to last a year. That meant I was going to have to go to yet another Job Creation team. Graham got us together in the bothy on the last Friday, he rolled out a big sheet of paper on the table, keeping the edges down with a couple of mugs, a bag of sugar and a hammer. It showed the locations of all the projects that were on the go in the Edinburgh area.

Everybody gathered around wondering where they'd be sent to next. There were about twenty projects in all. There was a big red circle drawn around the project in Niddrie, at the Jack Kane Centre.

'I'll tell you one thing,' army guy said, 'there's no fuckin way ye'd get me to the fuckin Jack Kane Centre, no danger, too many radges and arse bandits there.'

'Me neither,' Ginger said.

'You'd mibbe enjoy it, ya poof,' army guy said. 'Probably lose yer virginity through the back door, unless yer a giver.' He looked around to see if anybody was laughing with him.

'So how can I be a virgin and a poof?' Ginger said. 'Ye cannae have it both ways.'

'I bet that's what you say to yer boyfriend,' army guy replied. Everybody laughed except Ginger and the gaffer.

'Right lads, come on, calm down, you two are never going to be best of friends so can we maybe get through our last day without a fight.'

Ginge was sulking.

'Put the kettle on, Rab, would you?' The gaffer said, knowing fine well that the noise of the kettle boiling would ease the tension. 'Right, back to business.' He took a sheet of A4 paper from a plastic folder. 'Here are the results.'

He called the names out and where we'd be going. I was hoping

I'd get anywhere but the Jack Kane Centre. It was a community and sports centre in the heart of Niddrie. There were green fields all around, but the centre looked like a big concrete wart on the Green Giant's arse. I'd passed through it a lot, even played football there.

It was rough, no doubting that, one of the areas in Edinburgh where violence was never far away. Growing up in Pilton I'd experienced the dangerous, violent underside from a kid's perspective, that was bad enough.

I was pulled back to the moment when I heard my name.

'What? Are you sure?' I said, failing to believe that I was the only one of the group to be allocated to Niddrie.

The boss showed me the sheet of paper, true enough it had my name and the words Jack Kane next to it.

'Look,' I said taking the sheet from him, 'it might not be me.'

'What do you mean?'

'They've spelt my name wrong. They've put 'Devine' rather than 'Divine'.'

'Sorry, pal, that's a typo.'

'Can I appeal?' I said desperately.

He shook his head. 'Sorry. It's within five miles of your house so your only option is to stick it out or pack it in, you know if you pack it in you'll get no dole money for a long time.'

I was shell-shocked. I had no option. 'How long is the project to last there?' I asked, hoping it would be a week.

'Three months, max.'

'Shit,' I said. It was coming up to winter, the last place I wanted to be was sheltering in the fort when the Indians attacked. 'When does it start?'

'Monday.'

I sat on the bothy table, head in hands, wondering if I had the strength for this. I decided I had no choice, had to accept it; I'd been here too long, put too much into this to walk away.

I said cheerio to Rab, he was the only one I got on with, he had a brain and could do things the others couldn't, like think and talk in a cohesive manner.

'Tough luck, buddy,' he said, meaning it.

'Well, nothing I can do, I guess,' I said, resigning myself.

Rab was a wee guy, but tough. He took no shit from anybody.

I found this out one day when army guy tried to shove him around. Army guy was over six feet, looked pretty toned, turned out his toughness was all bullshit, he probably hadn't even been in the army, nobody had ever seen proof, he'd slipped up a few times when asked what regiment he was in. He told different people different things.

Para's, SAS, 401 Squadron, HMS Belfast.

It was one of the most surreal sights I'd witnessed. Rab, a tiny guy, lying on the ground with big army guy in an arm lock, screaming for mercy.

'Don't you ever try to fuck me around, d'ye hear me?' Rab said as he tightened his grip.

'Aye, aye,' army guy said, 'let me go. I'll never dae that again, promise.' Tears were beginning to form.

My respect for Rab shot up about a thousand per cent in a split second. I liked hanging about with tough guys that never showed it until they had to. I wondered if I had that toughness deep down, wondered if I could be a hero when I needed to be.

'If I could swap you, I would,' Rab said. 'Niddrie's no that bad.'

'Maybe for you.'

'Ye'll be alright, keep yer head down, get on with the work. It'll be over in a flash.'

I raised my eyebrows.

'Ye want the good news, though?' He said.

'Good news? At Niddrie? Are you joking?'

The next thing he said floored me.

'Hibs train there every Tuesday.'

'Seriously?' I said, getting excited. 'The first team?'

'Yep. Turnbull takes them into the five-a-side pitches for two hours every Tuesday during the winter.'

Was Karma trying to tell me something? I wondered. I now couldn't wait to start. My heart beat faster.

Monday morning, I'd hardly slept, thinking about the opportunities for me getting into the Hibs squad at long last. As I walked up to the bus stop at Elm Row I'd popped into the Post Office, the one Stevie and I had nicked the chocolate from not so many years ago. Golden Wonder had been pushing some new flavour of crisps that I wanted to try. Sausage and baked bean! I scoffed them as I walked. After a couple of bites I decided that would be my last packet – they were shit – but I'd paid for them, they were edible so I scoffed the rest of them quickly, trying to avoid my taste buds. It was freezing that morning. I'd run out of the house in my excitement not bothering to wrap up for the cold, I had my American football jacket, designed for warmer climes. I'd no gloves or scarf. To be honest I had thought about it but thought that if I turned up wearing gloves and a scarf my new, presumably tough, workmates might think I was a poof, I would have sealed my fate before I'd even begun.

It was a different bus to Niddrie, one I'd never been on before. It went all ways and every-ways. I could see the Jack Kane Centre up ahead, the Hibs euphoria wore off as reality kicked in. At that moment I felt a surge in my stomach. The sausage and bean crisps wanted back out.

There was a real bubble-up in there, I could feel it. I needed to get off now. I reckoned I was about two or three stops from my destination. I tried to hold on as long as I could, every stop less was a bigger walk to the bothy in cold, inhospitable territory, but eventually I had no choice; I rang the bell about twenty times.

'Haud yer horses,' the driver said, 'I heard ye the first time. Fuckin impatient twat!'

As soon as the doors opened I sprinted off the bus, spotted a small stone bridge, ran over to it, wiped some snow from the top of it to give me grip, jumped up onto it, pulled my head and shoulders over the parapet, puked every remnant of sausage and bean crisp into the burn below.

I felt much better. A couple of ducks that had been sitting on the grass verge at the side of the burn immediately jumped onto the frozen water and scoffed the puke.

I could imagine a customer after eating from the local chinky that night.

'How come my crispy duck tastes like baked beans, maw?'

'I don't know, son, but if it farts we're takin it back.'

My hands were so cold, though. I pulled my Redskins American football jacket around my neck, zipped it up to the gills. I loved that jacket, wore it everywhere. I'd seen it in Top Shop months before and had to have it.

I headed over towards the centre, holding on to my fragile guts. I'd no idea where our bothy would be, but figured that it would not be too hard to find. The whole landscape was deserted, not a soul to be seen. I spotted the bothy, wandered up to it. It was locked, the padlocks were firmly in place. First time I'd seen three padlocks on the door of a bothy. Wondered if we were mining for gold!

I waited a few minutes, getting colder and colder, the heat wouldn't return to my hands no matter where I stuck them, up my jumper, down the front of my pants. I shook them vigorously to no avail. Decided to wander around, see if there was another bothy. I wandered all around the perimeter of my new environment; ironically the snow had added a cleanliness to the place, hid the dark bits with a white overcoat. In truth it didn't look as bad as I'd imagined. After a fifteen minute walk, I was getting close to hypothermia. I wandered back to the bothy, there was still no sign of life. I couldn't feel my face, I felt tears dripping down my cheeks, didn't even realise I was crying.

I decided to head home, forget this shit, I walked towards the bus stop, it was the only thing to do.

As I got halfway down the path, a maroon Jaguar was making its way up. *That looks like Davie's Jag*, I thought. As it got closer, I got a glimpse inside, spotted the deerstalker hat, waved him down. The window rolled down, smoke billowed out.

'Hi, Jimbo, my son, how's it goin?' Davie said to me, knowing I'd be surprised to see him. 'Jump in.'

The Lost Tornado

I needed no second invitation.

As I sat in the heated passenger seat, my bum warmed up in a second. Davie extended his hand to shake mine.

'Christ, man, you're freezing,' he said. He took a half-smoked fag from his gob, put it in the overflowing ashtray, took off his scarf, wrapped my hands in it. I heard a cough behind me, looked to the back seat.

'How's it gaun, Jimmy, my son?' I recognised the voice immediately. It was Alistair, fag in hand.

For fuck's sake, I thought to myself. I'd completely forgotten about the newest member of the smokers' club. My lungs had been given a real treat at St Mark's; there were only a few that smoked including Ginge, even then it was only Consulate, the fag of the effeminate. I could see army guy's on-going argument to an extent. I'd taken the clean air for granted.

Alistair reached over, went to shake hands, I offered him my scarf-bound hands. He laid his pathetic hand with the fag in it onto the scarf.

'Watch you don't burn Davie's scarf,' I said, pulling my hands away. I didn't want to touch him, breathing his smoke in was punishment enough. I cursed myself inwardly, vowed to keep that lesson in mind. As always, I had to get some kind of positive from the situation, it came quickly. If I thought I was vulnerable in a place like this, Alistair would be like a baby turtle amongst the Galapagos Skuas. That thought calmed me down a bit, I relaxed, kept the window down with my head sticking out. My hands began to warm up nicely, my arse had never been toastier.

It took three days for me to get the proper feeling back into my hands, I must have been damn close to hypothermia. On the first Tuesday the Sports Centre was still locked. No Hibs team had appeared. I wondered if Rab had been winding me up, making my task slightly easier to bear, cruel to be kind in a way. The cold winds and snow kept the place as silent as the grave. We saw only the occasional dog walker. The older ones would knock at the bothy door, try to blag a cup of tea, get a bit of info on what we were up to.

'Building a path? Around here? Ha! What's the point of that? Bloody waste of money if you ask me.'

'Make it easier to walk your dog, pal,' Davie said.

Time and time again, we heard the same words. Obviously the community hadn't been involved in the consultation.

On the Friday the weather had eased up a bit, there was still a lot of snow around but the temperature was a bit more bearable. I made sure I had scarf, gloves and good warm boots every day.

I got to the bothy first, as usual, but unusually the door was wide open; somebody had got there first. I walked in.

'Hope the kettle's on,' I said removing my gloves. There was no light on, it was freezing. The padlocks were still in place, but the door was open, I looked more closely, only then realising that the door opened left to right when it should have opened right to left. Somebody had broken in by removing the hinges on the other side of the door.

The padlocks now acted as the hinges. It was too dark to see anything, so I sat there until Davie and the gang arrived. The cops were called, but didn't come out.

'Pointless,' they said.

We were all sent home until the place was up to scratch again. 'We can't work without tools,' Davie said. I looked at Alistair's dippit coupon, thought, *can't work with them, either.*

It took ten days to get fixed up again, it was fab. Ten days holiday, paid as if we were working. I felt great. Christmas was coming, I had money for the first time in ages, I could get Mum and the wee yins something for Christmas. I was also going to be going out with my mates for a few drinks for the first time in years at Christmas time.

I'd had my first pint the summer past, an experience I'll never forget. Tam Townsley was one of the very few non-football guys in the Court. This immediately placed him in the vicinity of gay; anyone that didn't like football was seen as suspicious. Tam, in my opinion, may have been, but he took up the sport of drinking to balance things out. He was always trying to recruit new people into his new gang, by the first summer he'd a good half-dozen folk in the gang. They spent a lot of their time in the pub, or at the bookies. I had always seen what the sauce did every time my auld man imbibed. It was not a path I wanted to stray onto. My fitness was always paramount to me, not for a particular event or reason, it felt great to wake up every morning and feel like I was breathing fresh air for the first time, at least as soon as I got out of my room. It had a whole wall of fungal spores, a throwback to when the houses were built without damp proofing.

That summer I was flying past everyone on the training runs we did at footy practice, I could give most of them a good half-mile start and still catch them easily.

We had a great kick-about at Warriston. One of the boys had dropped a six-pack of Cally special and a Playboy off to the parkie to let us play on the best pitch. Tam was on the sidelines encouraging anybody who'd listen to come to the Northern Bar afterwards.

'There's a stripper there tonight, guys,' he shouted. He was on his normal crusade, like a town crier.

'Roll up, roll up. Tits, fannies, the lot. All for the price of a pint.' This got attention, a LOT of attention.

'What time?'

'Seven. Sharp.'

Glances at watches.

'Right, lads, next goal's the winner.'

Everyone except me had been going to the pub on an at least semi-regular basis. Harry, who was my training partner and a really good sprinter, asked me if I fancied it.

'Come on,' he said, 'one pint'll no do you any harm.'

'Nae money,' I lied.

'I'll buy your first pint.'

'OK,' I said, not quite believing I'd committed to it. I was over eighteen, but was still a bit under developed, slowly growing up though.

After the game we headed to the pub. I was pretty nervous. I'd seen the inside of a few bars but never sat in them for any length of time. As the boys filed in I smelled the foost and the smoke, almost backed out. Harry grabbed me.

'Come on. You get used to it quickly, pretty soon you'll not even smell it.'

I let him pull me in. We commandeered a corner next to the pool table, quite a distance from the TV. The footy was on, think it was Brazil in a friendly. I got up to move closer to the telly.

'Stay here,' Tam said.

'But the football?' I said. Nobody else moved.

I looked at them in disbelief, a colour telly, Brazil, football. Not one of them paid any attention to me. Harry came back from the bar with two pints. He put mine down in front of me.

'There you go pal, bottoms up.'

'I'll be saying that to the stripper in a wee while,' Tam piped up.

'Hah? No chance,' Gary said.

I'd completely forgotten about the stripper. *Crikey*, I thought. Was I really prepared to see real tits and a fanny in the flesh?

What if I got excited? Christ, how embarrassing would that be, hobbling off to the toilets? The TV was switched off, the barman was handing empty crisp boxes over the bar to the boys. *What the hell are they doing with those?* I thought, watching as they ripped them open to make them into big flat cardboard strips, laid them on top of the pool table.

'It's so as the stripper disnae mark the felt,' Tam said to me.

They put three layers on. As the Salt 'n' Shake box was laid down, the music started and the lights dimmed. I don't know what I was anticipating, but it was certainly nicer looking than the thing that appeared. She was at least twice as old as I'd hoped and dressed in a cowgirl outfit; *at least she got it half right,* I thought to myself. *Ach well, at least it can only get better from here.*

I'd taken the first sip of my pint when the room lit up. 'Shut the fuckin door,' someone shouted. A young woman pushed through the heavy, stained-glass doors, flooding the place with unwanted evening sunshine.

'Help! Help!' She shouted, looking around the pub to catch somebody's attention, anyone's by the look of it. I couldn't believe it; not one person showed any interest. Even my mates were too busy watching the 'action' on the pool table. The woman was frantic. I got up, walked over to her.

'What's wrong?' I said.

She looked me up and down, as if measuring me for a task, but as nobody else was paying the slightest bit of interest she grabbed my arm, pulled me out of the pub. 'It's my husband,' she said, tears rolling down her cheeks. 'He's kidnapping my daughter.'

'Eh?' I said, not realising that you could actually kidnap your own kids. 'Why, how, whe …' I had no idea what I was saying or what I could do.

She grabbed my arm again, as it seemed to be the quickest way to communicate with me. We only walked about fifty yards from the pub, stopped at one of the big main doors of the posh houses on the Crescent.

'In there,' she said, pointing, trying to push me towards the door. I dug my heels in and approached the door very cautiously.

'Stay away, whoever you are,' came a posh Edinburgh accent from behind the frosted inner glass door. 'The police have been called.'

'That's him. My husband,' she said.

'And he's called the police?' I said, confused.

He opened the door and was standing there brandishing a knife.

'Where is she?' The woman screamed at him.

'You stay away, you bitch,' he said. He then pointed the knife at me. 'You don't want to get involved, sonny.'

Tell me something I don't know, I thought.

I heard myself utter the last words you should never say to anyone brandishing a big kitchen knife and in a state of utter radgeness.

'Calm down, pal.' I put my hands out in front of me, palms down, as if I was playing an invisible piano.

'Calm down? Calm down?' His head went even redder. 'Fuck off, you little toe-rag,' he shouted. 'Fucking child. Telling me what to do.'

He walked towards me as I walked backwards, matching his pace but knowing for a fact that I'd be able to sprint away from him if he got too close.

Just then I heard the sirens. Blue lights were all over the place in minutes, my relief was palpable. An old cop was first on the scene, he jumped out of the Panda and was at the door in two strides.

'Get lost,' he said to me, 'rubberneckers are the last thing we need here.'

'I … I … I …' I tried to explain, but in the end I walked away.

Jeez! How hurt was I? The woman completely ignored me as well, she was too busy cuddling her kid, who'd walked out of the house completely oblivious to the fuss around her. The Fuzz stormed in. I stood back, watched as a dozen cops bundled into the house and wrestled the man into a meat wagon. I strolled back to the pub, shaking my head, angry. I pushed the heavy door open, disturbing everyone as the light flooded in again.

'Shut the fuckin door!' Someone shouted from the pool table area. *Christ, are these losers vampires as well as wasters*, I thought. I sat down.

'What was happening along there?' Harry said, whispering, not taking his eyes from the half-naked stripper.

'Some guy was kidnapping his daughter,' I said. 'Cops are all over it now.'

'Get a good view?' He said, sipping his beer.

'Nah,' I said. 'They were all over the place, couldnae see a thing.'

I went to pick up my pint from the table; it looked flat. I felt the weight of the pint in my hand, thought, *do I really want to put that weight of liquid into my guts*? I'd gone off the idea. I looked up to the pool table, the stripper was slowly removing her star-spangled pants. I got a good look at her baps, they were almost as flat as my beer; given the choice I'd rather stick an onion in my mouth than either the beer or the boob.

The Lost Tornado

Tam lifted my pint up, shouted up to her, 'Gonnae stick a head on that, doll?'

She took my pint, removed the fag from her lipstick-covered gob, took a long slug and squeezed one of her saggy tits into the half-empty glass, dislodging most of the remaining lager with her ancient flesh. She then shook it about. A cheer went up. 'There you go, pal,' she said, in a rough Weegie voice, that sounded like a dried coconut husk being rubbed against a metal cheese grater. She handed the beer back to Tam.

'Cheers, doll,' he said. He handed me the remains of the pint.

I shuddered. 'Nah, you can keep it,' I said.

The boys were still so engrossed in the act that when I slunk out of the side door nobody noticed. I felt puny again. I'd found a bit of hero inside me, but unfortunately it was only me that recognised it. I didn't want to tell anyone about it as I'd be letting out that I'd been to the pub, I knew Mum would be disappointed in me. I wandered home, looking forward to a nice cuppa and a chocolate biscuit.

I'd been at the Jack Kane Centre for three Tuesdays now, I'd decided to count my time there not in weeks or months but Tuesdays.

After the Hibs had failed to turn up again, I asked the manager of the centre if they really did come to train here.

'They sure do, sonny,' he said proudly, putting both of his thumbs under his blazer collar.

'So where are they? I've waited weeks to see them.'

'Too cauld,' he said. 'These are finely tuned athletes we're talkin about and because the weather is so inclement, they could pull muscles and stuff. Sure, they've got technology on their side with those tight Lycra shorts that stop their muscles from flapping about. They're no help in these conditions, though, no son, no good whatsoever. They're gonnae wait till the weather picks up.'

'When will that be?' I said, desperately hoping that I was still going to be working there.

'Probably a week or two after Christmas.'

'Good,' I said. 'Thanks.'

That would give me time for a final attempt at pulling on the joystick of this plummeting Turnbull's Tornado, try to get it flying again. Roll on New Year. New life?

Chapter 23

Christmas had come and gone, it was still bollocks freezing but not as bad as it had been before the turn of the year. I'd been hatching a plan to see if I could get myself noticed by Eddie Turnbull. I arrived at the bothy a bit later than everybody else; the bus service was still on holiday mode, I'd missed the number thirty-three by a minute, had to wait another half hour. I was freezing and grumpy.

When it arrived I went straight upstairs where it was always that wee bit warmer, sat in the front seat, hood up, hands as far down into my pockets as they could go. Figured the deeper, the warmer. I got to the Jack Kane Centre eventually, made my way up the winding path, slipping now and again on the ice, shut the door of the bothy behind me, said 'Merry Christmas' to Davie and the two lads sitting there, no shaking hands or anything, though. After a few cups of tea I warmed up a bit, inside and out.

'Where are Alistair and Chas?' I asked.

'They went out about ten minutes ago, said they were going to start pathway three today,' said boss man Davie.

'Fancy another cuppa?' Bob said.

'Sure, that would be dandy, Bob.' I took my jacket and hat off, sidled up to the gas heater, making sure I got a good heat before I joined them in the bitter cold. 'What are you three up to then?'

'Bob and Mikey are going to make sure that the hole in path one is filled in and flat, aren't you?' Said Davie, looking at them.

'Of course we are, boss,' Bob said, standing up, flexing his puny biceps. 'Dream team in action, nae worries.'

'You, boss?' I said. 'What are you up to?'

'I've got urgent paperwork to see to.'

'Aye, bettin slips. Yer off to the fuckin bookies, ya chancer,' Bob said, slapping Davie on the back.

'No, honestly.'

'Aye, right? And we're building the yelly brick road,' Bob said, laughing.

I finished my tea, wrapped up, headed out. I walked over to the wheelbarrow which always stood outside the bothy door, picked up my tool of choice, the mattock. It was a great tool, looked like a pick but it had a big broad head instead of a sharp point. What I loved about it was that with very little work it looked like you'd been working your bollocks off. I slung it over my shoulder, wandered down to the mucky brown river where I spotted the other two lying on the frosty grass.

'Alright, boys?' I said.

'Happy New Year, Jimster,' Alistair said, wandering over to shake hands.

'Happy New Year to you too,' I said. I walked the other way, didn't want to shake hands with him. Tony lay there, put his hand up in the air in acknowledgment, trying to sleep.

'Watch it, boys,' Alistair shouted, 'boss alert.' He put his hand on top of his head, turned his fingers to face the sky, opened and closed his fist.

'What the fuck are you doin, ya mong?' Tony said.

'Silent siren.'

Tony threw a rolled up fag packet at him, Alistair stood there as it banged off his specs and bounced onto the grass. He nudged the specs back onto his nose.

Davie came bounding over, rubbing his hands, a big rolled up sheet of paper tucked under his arm.

'Team three, path three,' he announced. 'We have something very special here.' He rolled out the plan on top off an upturned wheelbarrow, revealed a drawing of a river and a path that ran parallel to it. 'This is the river,' he said, running his finger along a squiggly line.

'Really?' I said, sarky as you like.

'And this is the path that we shall create,' he said, moving his whole hand over the area. 'We are about to make history here, boys. No one has dug, here since Roman times.'

He took a metal pin and wheel contraption with a long wrapping of bright white string, stuck it into the ground, walked along the side of the river, with the string slowly unwinding itself. About a hundred yards upriver he stuck the adjoining pin into the ground, came back to us and said, 'Let us begin.'

'What if we find coins or centuries?' Alistair said.

'Centurions,' Tony said.

'Eh?'

'You mean Centurions,' he repeated.

'What if …?'

'Don't even go there,' said Davie. 'If we find stuff, work will have to be delayed, we'll be out of a job, so if you find anything, keep it or chuck it. Clear?'

'Clear,' Tony and I said in unison. Alistair scratched his head.

'Right, lads, I'm off to do that paperwork,' Davie said. 'The Times waits for no man.' He disappeared over the horizon.

Alistair won the toss of the coin to see who would begin the work, took his spade and gave an almighty grunt as he broke ground. Tony and I sat back, watched him most of the day, giving him the odd bit of encouragement when it looked like the penny might be dropping. It never did.

It took days to work our way along the string line. Eventually the whole squad joined our team. Bob had a good eye and was really slick at digging straight lines with the spade, my role was to hack the tuffets to pieces with my mattock, stick the smaller bits into a skip. Tony put all of the divots into the wheelbarrow, Alistair wheeled them away. A perfect team. When I thought of the word 'team' it unexpectedly hurt.

'Team' to me equalled Hibs.

It was Tuesday number five now, not including holidays, I'd still seen no sign of the Hibbie boys. I was losing hope, I had to remind myself constantly that I was 'the undiscovered kid'. I was putting a bit less into my footy now, limiting my training to four hours a day because of the dark nights and the long bus journey home, with the objective disappearing fast, my motivation was wavering. Less ball work and more running.

Tuesday number seven arrived. I got in pretty early, opened the bothy, put the kettle on. I opened the metal shutters that had been put up after the break in, as I was lifting them I could see that the Centre was open. *That's unusual*, I thought, *first time it's been open before ten*. I spotted the manager of the centre picking up litter, he had a helper cleaning the reception windows. 'Could this be the day?' I muttered to myself, moving my head around to see as much as I could. It was too exciting, I couldn't wait. I put a single padlock back on the door, headed over to the centre.

'Hi, Sam,' I shouted, catching the manager's attention as he disappeared into his office.

'Hi, lad,' he said, smiling.

'Is this the day then?' I said, holding my breath.

'Could be.' He walked over to a big ledger, opened it, showed me the page. It was a booking form. He ran his finger down the margin, but my eye got there way before his finger.

Hibernian first team + coaches:

10.00 a.m. – 1.00 p.m.

Pitches 3–6 £17.50 Exclusive use.

Pies/sausage rolls/coffee/tea/OJ at Break 11.30 a.m.

Showers 1.10 pm.

'Yes!' I shouted, pumping my fist.

'Thought you'd like that. But remember, don't go near them. Mr. Turnbull has a temper on him, if he thinks you're disrupting anything he'll come down on you like a ton of bricks.'

'No worries there, Sam,' I said. 'I'll keep out of sight, work away like a good boy.'

'You make sure you do. If you're lucky I might get an autograph or two for you.'

'Would you?'

'Maybe; don't build your hopes up, though, these are focussed athletes we're talking about.'

'Thanks, Sam,' I shouted, as I floated back over to the bothy.

Davie was sitting smoking in his car, reading The Times. He got out as I approached.

'What are you so happy about?' He said, rolling the paper up, sticking it under his arm.

'Nothing,' I said. 'Just thinking about my new career.'

'Eh?'

'Nothing,' I said, 'only joking.'

'Get the bloody door open, it's fucking freezing,' he said.

I was buzzing. I'd been pretending to work for hours. My eyes were peeled, looking for any signals, a big diesel engine noise or the sight of a luxury coach. I was busy wheeling my barrow to and fro along the new path. I'd almost worn a groove into the damn thing the amount of times I'd gone up and down it. Hours passed, I was knackered. My hands were aching from holding the metal handles of the barrow. I threw it down, really annoyed by the lack of Hibby sightings, I headed back to the bothy for my soup and sandwiches.

The main reason I was annoyed at their no show was that I'd arranged with Davie to work on my own, feeling this would give me a better chance to carry out my plan. He'd be pissed off at me as well because I hadn't done a single stroke of work all day. I decided to go to see Sam, see what had happened.

'Did Bob not tell you?' He said.

'Tell me what?' I said.

'They're not coming until next week. Bob had put the wrong date in.'

'Ahh,' I said, relieved rather than disappointed. 'Thanks, Sam.'

As I approached the bothy I knew Davie would want a path one progress report. *What do I do?* I thought. I feigned injury. Held my forearm as I pushed the door open with my shoulder.

Davie stopped talking when he saw me hobbling in. 'Well?' He said, 'what happened?'

'Fell against the sharp bit of the mattock,' I said, pretending to wince.

'Is it broken?' He said, concerned, coming over to me, about to take hold of my arm.

I pulled away. 'It's OK,' I said. 'Badly bruised.'

'I knew this would happen if you worked on your own, that's why we have teams of at least two. I knew I should've said 'no'. That's it, fuckit. Listen everyone,' he said, standing on the wooden bench at the table. 'From now on any job that involves big tools …'

Laughter.

'I'm serious. Big tools equals two men, got it?'

'Got it, boss,' we said.

Shit, I thought, *that's blown my plan for next week; I'll have to think of getting away from my partner when the time comes.* I knew who I wanted to team up with so I'd have think of a plan to ensure that Alistair and I were teamed up.

Tuesday number eight. My plan had worked a treat, Alistair and I were team three, perfect. I'd spent a lot of my spare time dumping earth close to the training pitches during the week, I knew we were due to upgrade the path there pretty soon, I suggested to Davie that as Alistair was such a good barrow man, we could remove the debris in time for the phased operation. As everybody hated moving earth from place to place we were a shoe-in. The other guys looked at me, they knew I hated doing this as much as they did. There were a few raised eyebrows.

'What you up to, Divine?' I could hear the thoughts, stayed schtum. Alistair was oblivious. He sniffed a few times, pushed his glasses back onto the bridge of his nose, rubbed his hands together.

'Right, Jimbob, lead the way.' The guy was a gullible sap but, more to the point, right now he was MY gullible sap and my passport to fame and fortune.

We started work close to the five-a-side pitches after nine. I was wired. Every sound or movement brought a jerk from me, looking in every direction for the vision that I'd longed to see for so long.

'You OK, Mr D?' Alistair said.

'Fine. Why d'you ask?'

'Nothin, really. You look a bit edgy, that's all.'

As 10.00 a.m. Approached I had to get this gibbering buffoon out of the way. I knew he'd fuck things right up, especially if he knew the Hibs were within a mile of this place. I was a Hibs fan, he was a Hibs Fanatic, he had everything the club shop could offer, all the versions of the strips, the calendar, the mug, even the bed sheets! I had to dump him somewhere. There was no way I could send him to the bothy or Davie would realise I was a one-man-big-tool danger. If I sent him to the shops he'd have to go past the bothy, and those big windows would give the game away, as Davie would be in there as usual, 'planning.' Sure, he was. All he ever did was smoke, write betting slips and pick up a decent pay packet.

I knew what shops were in front of us, along the main Niddrie road, but had no real idea what was behind us. I knew that the road, at the side of where we were working, went into the countryside, and eventually led to Dalkeith.

I thought, *can I do that to him? How long would it take?*

I decided to go for it. Half an hour before they arrived, I called him over.

'Alistair, you know how you love the cabbage and ribs?'

'Uhuh?' He said.

'How would you like to meet some of them?'

'What? The Hibbies? Turnbull's ACTUAL Tornadoes?' He screamed. 'The Hibbies? Here? Really?' He was rotating his head in all directions.

'No, not here.'

'Where then?'

'Near here. Dalkeith.'

'Where's that?'

'You'll never believe it, but it's through that gate there,' I said, pointing to a gap in the wall. 'You go through that, walk towards the signs for Dalkeith.'

'But Davie–'

'Shh. It's all right. It'll be our wee secret,' I said tapping the side of my nose. 'I'll work away, when you get back you can finish the rest off. How does that sound?'

'Magic. You're a real pal, Jimbo.'

'Can I ask one favour from you, Ali pal?' I said. 'Can you get me Paddy Stanton and Ally McLeod's autographs when you see them?'

'Done,' he said, 'a friend indeed.'

He went to shake my hand; I took it after noticing he had gloves on, then handed him his jacket, scarf and woollen bobble hat, helped him do his laces up nice and tight, walked over to the wall with him, making sure he went in the right direction.

I spotted a road sign way in the distance; it read 'Dalkeith 4.5 miles', which confirmed my thinking. That would give me hours of free time to set things up. I helped him through the hole in the wall, pushed him towards the countryside. As he walked towards the sign he looked up at it, but before he could take in the information I shouted to him, 'Alistair? Take your glasses off, you might get recognised, somebody might grass you to Davie.'

I watched as he popped the glasses into his coat pocket.

'Good luck, pal.'

He turned around in the distance, gave me a double thumbs up.

'What a loser,' I said out loud. I dumped the tools into a bush and got on with my plan.

I was busy stretching and warming up, getting ready for my trial, when I heard a loud whisper. It was the last voice I wanted to hear.

'Jimbo? Pssst? Jimbo?'

I knew who it was, I turned my head over my shoulder as I was lying on the path stretching my hamstrings.

'What are you doing back so soon?' I whispered back.

'I got up to the top of the road and didn't know what way to go.'

I looked at my watch, he could still fuck things up. 'Right, what did the sign say?'

'I dinnae ken. I couldnae read it.'

'Why not?'

'I didn't have my glasses on.'

Jeez, how thick was this turd of a bloke?

'Right, Ali pal,' I said, taking him by the shoulders. 'You go up to the sign, in fact when you get to any sign, put your glasses on to read the information then hide them in your pocket again, OK?'

'AHHHH?' He said, astounded. 'That's a brilliant idea.' He ran for the wall without any prompting.

I looked at my watch twice, three times, in a few seconds. 'Come on, Jimbo,' I said to myself, 'this is it.' I walked over to the wheelbarrow, removed the black bin liner that I'd hidden underneath our tools. Took out the camouflage jacket and trousers that I'd borrowed from John. He didn't know of course, I hoped he didn't need them for his Territorial Army meeting that night. I was about to smear the green and black paint on my face, but had a thought. I ran over to the hole in the wall to make sure that numpty wasn't on his way back again. The coast was clear. I ran back to the path, applied the greasy paint, put my other clothes into the bin liner and hid it back in the wheelbarrow.

I put all of the tools that were lying around into it, wheeled it into the bushes. My last action was to take the small pair of binoculars and pop them into my trouser pocket.

My plan was two-pronged; first I'd find out all about the training, see what I needed to do should the trial opportunity arise. I also had to find out what to wear as I wanted to blend in. I put some branches and twigs over the barrow and tools, making sure that any casual observer would see nothing. Not that I expected anybody to come along this far at this time of day. My heart pounded faster as I heard the unmistakable sound of a big engine. I looked along to where the sound was coming from, saw the bus wend its way up the long, winding road to the front door of the centre.

My heart jumped with pride as couple of guys in Hibs trackies got off the bus. I didn't recognise them, but then Eddie Turnbull got off, wearing his purple Bukta tracky. *Wow, how cool does he look*? I thought. I kept on looking, noticed I was shaking; fear and excitement? I wasn't sure, maybe anticipation as well, but I'd have to get this bit of the plan right first.

Ally MacLeod, Des Bremner, Tony Higgins, Alex Cropley, and Pat Stanton all stepped from the bus. I counted every one of them, it was almost the full team, only Arthur Duncan was missing. They all headed into the community centre; I figured I'd have about five minutes if they began to walk to the pitches now. I had no idea how I looked, I didn't think a mirror would be needed as the camouflage paint was well mixed up, should easily hide my face and hands. The one thing I realised I'd forgotten, as I was getting changed, was to put on dark socks. I looked at my feet, the white socks did stand out pretty brightly compared with all of the camouflage gear.

I scraped up some mud, rubbed it over the socks, instant invisibility. I could hear a lot of raised voices as I ran over to my hiding place. I backed myself into the base of a tree right on the halfway line, about a foot from the fence. I covered myself with leaves and any other foliage that lay around. The voices got louder and louder, the footballs were getting booted from a long distance, some of them flew over the fence and onto the pitches. I could hear them bouncing all around, I desperately wanted to get in there and have a kick about. Alex Edwards was the first onto the pitches, at first he had a bit of trouble getting the snib of the gate open.

'Ooyah fucker,' I heard him say as he pulled his hand back quickly. He must have jammed his finger in it, I knew it was quite a stiff lock. As soon as he was through he ran straight for a ball, booted it into the goals, sucking on his bleeding finger. I heard myself whispering 'Goaaallll! Edwards scores another beauty, it's now Hibs four, Celtic nil. The Scottish Cup is surely now destined for Easter Road.'

As more and more of the players came into the fenced-off area I got comfortable, I thought I'd be shitting it but was surprised at how calm I was.

They all had small man-bags with them, dropped them into a bigger leather case that someone had brought in. Must have been their valuables; I didn't blame them, there was no way I'd leave

The Lost Tornado

anything of value in this place without keeping eyes on it. *Man what an amazing view*, I thought, *wait until I tell everyone about this.* I sat back as they got into a big circle, Eddie in the centre of it. He bellowed out numbers and they all did various things. After an hour of this I could feel myself nodding off. I must've dozed off as I felt my head slump forward. I over-compensated to get it upright, smacking the back of my head on the tree, before I knew it I'd shouted 'Aargh!' And involuntarily put my hand up to rub it.

'What was that?'

I froze in absolute terror, hand in mid-air. I sat stock still for a few seconds, then I raised my head very slightly, slowly. *FUCKIN HELL!* I thought. I could feel my eyebrows go into orbit, my arm began to shake.

Eddie Turnbull and Pat Stanton were standing with their backs to the pitches, both had their hands on the fence, pushing it, to get closer to whatever was moving out there. They were both looking right at the tree I was sitting at. *Dear God, Jesus and Mary, mother of Joseph*, I thought, not really knowing if that was an actual phrase that you used in such emergencies, *I promise to be really good if you don't let them notice me. Please, please.*

'Didn't hear a thing boss,' Pat said.

'I thought I heard something, probably a squirrel or something, they look for their nuts around this time of year I think,' said Eddie.

'They're not the only ones, Boss,' Pat replied. They laughed, Eddie screwed his eyes up a bit, took half a step nearer to the fence pushing the flexible green wire nearer to me, by now his face was about three feet from mine. He was so close that I almost gagged with the heady mixture of Old Spice and the lashings of Brylcreem that locked his famous quiff into place. I figured he was a vision-based hunter, similar to T Rex, if I resisted movement I'd stay hidden. It seemed to be working. I looked at his knuckles as they forced their way into my eye line, I couldn't believe what I was seeing. The two sets of knuckles were gripping hard on the wire, the tension in them made each letter stand out proud.

Looked like it had only been done yesterday, but it was a good five or six years since that victory. The fence sprung back as he stood away. I held my breath. They both had their backs to me now, but were still as close. I dared not move, although my arm was going numb. I could hear them talking, I moved my eyes and eyebrows about as if somehow this would help increase the volume of their voices. I was tempted to turn my nearest ear towards them, but resisted.

'So boss, do you think Mr Hart will go for Bestie?'

'I'm no sure about that Pat,' Eddie said. 'He wants two grand a week. That's silly money in anybody's language.'

'I know boss, I get it.

Eddie continued. 'I spoke to Mr Hart yesterday, he's convinced that if we can sign Georgie Best, the crowds will surge, says the money's not an issue.'

'He's not wrong,' said Pat.

'The trouble is,' said Eddie, 'he's trouble. 'A nice guy, would give away his last penny, but that's the problem. There's no control. I've got to think of the effect he'd have on the whole team, I'm not sure, and one thing's guaranteed; if he did sign, there's no way we could keep coming here, it's way too exposed. We'd have these bloody photographers flocking all over us, like flies around shite.'

They continued talking. Pat unconsciously mimicked Eddie's steps, they walked in perfect synchronicity away from me, hands clasped behind their backs. The volume dropped, so did my arm.

'Phew!' I let out a massive sigh. Jeez, that was way too close for comfort. I sat for a few minutes gathering myself. Rubbed the blood back into my dead arm. The good news was my plan had worked. I'd found out what kind of training they did, what stuff they wore and, more importantly, there were a couple of trialists there. This meant that if I timed it right I could appear as a trialist, the first team players would have no idea that I wasn't meant to be there, and if I shone like a star, I'd get noticed! Who'd care if I didn't go by the official scouting channels? Surely it would be about the Hibbies unearthing an undiscovered talented nugget? A gold one, I hoped rather than a plain nugget. But I was worried. If Georgie Best signed soon my opportunity would be gone. I had no choice but to plan my move for the next week.

I got onto all fours, crawled like a sloth along the ground, kept checking all around that nobody had spied me. It took time, but I made it back to the wheelbarrow.

It was far enough away for me to get dressed into my originals without being seen. I put the camouflage stuff into the bin liner, wheeled the barrow back to the bothy for lunchtime. When I got in Bob and Davie were the only ones sitting there, kettle bubbling away, some tomato soup on the boil. The place was fugged with their fag smoke. Nobody looked around, too engrossed in their activities.

'Where is everybody?' I said.

'Chippy,' Bob said, mouth full of banana roll. I'd had enough of breathing all that shitty smoke in, as I stepped out of the door I spotted Sam was on his way over.

'Jim, lad,' he said, 'just the man I'm after. How would you like to meet a couple of the players?'

Shit, I did not want this to happen, not now. If I was introduced to them as a numpty working on a Job Creation Project, then turned up in a tracksuit waiting to play with them the next week, I'd be spotted a mile away. It was against every fibre in my being, I'd always wanted to meet some of the players, but I had no choice. I consoled myself by imagining that after next week I would be meeting them on a regular basis.

'Sorry, Sam,' I said, 'I can't. I have to go to the hospital.' I had to think on my feet, I pulled my trouser leg up a bit, showed him my muddy ankle and sock. 'I tripped over a pick, think I might have broken it.'

'Sorry to hear that, lad,' he said.

'Can I do it next week?'

'I'll see what I can do. Let me know how you get on at hospital.'

I hobbled away as he looked on sympathetically.

The week was spent remembering what I'd seen the players doing at training, trying to get some of the awkward moves right. After watching them running I knew I was fit enough, no problem on that score. I ran a lot, did a lot of press-ups and sit-ups. I was down to the final two ideas of how to get myself in with them.

Plan A, the easiest, relied on a bit of luck, but I eventually decided against that. If the luck did not happen at the right time then that would be it.

I decided on plan B.

During that whole working week, I was at the centre a good hour before anybody else. I'd been putting bits and pieces of equipment into the football pitch area, within the fenced pitches where Hibs trained. I'd noticed last week that they only used certain parts of the pitches. By Monday I'd designed a very small 'pitch under repair' sign and construction set-up. It had a tarpaulin, two parking cones and a plastic red and white barrier that I'd nicked from a construction site up the road.

My set up was pretty close to the gate; I had to think about an escape route should things go wrong. The pitches were a good five-minute walk from the centre and the staff were lazy; it could go for weeks without anybody checking up on it. I couldn't sleep on the Monday night, going through everything, checking and checking again.

I got up at six, went downstairs, made some porrage and sat chewing it. Gulping it down was tough as my throat felt pretty tight. I'd packed a bag the night before with the stuff I'd need. I was too early for the bus, decided to start walking along London Road, as the sooner I got there, the sooner I could begin the plan.

I got there well before eight, opened the bothy, had a cuppa, got on with the job in hand.

Ten on the dot the bus pulled into the centre, made its way up the long winding path to the front door. My sphincter was tying itself in knots. I'd managed to team up with and get rid of Alistair again. I knew he wouldn't fall for the same trick twice, so I sent him towards a garage; you could see it over the hill where we worked. I'd found an old punctured wheelbarrow wheel a few days earlier, stored it in my armoury.

'Can you see the giant in the distance, made out of tyres?' I said to him.

'Where?'

'There?' I said, pointing him to the horizon where a big rubber man that was some kind of landmark stood, arms folded like some kind of rubber sentinel.

It was only about half a mile away, but given the stupidity of the man, the task I'd asked him to complete it would give me a good ninety minutes. More than enough time.

Ninety minutes, I thought, *imagine, in the time it takes to play a game I could have changed my life for ever.* I smiled, sent him packing with the tyre tucked under his arm.

He turned back after a few paces. 'New inner tune and valve?'

'Inner *tube*,' I said, emphasising the word 'tube'.

The speccy twat had no idea that I'd given him a solid rubber tyre. I'd deliberately kept it attached to the wheel as it added a good seventy per cent extra weight. I was hoping this would slow him down.

After I sent him packing I looked at my watch. Ten minutes max to get into action.

I wheeled the barrow into the woods, stuck it behind a big oak tree. I undressed, carefully removed the purple Bukta tracksuit from the bin liner, making sure then I didn't get any mud or dirt onto it. That could jeopardise things. I wanted to look pristine when I joined the boys. I put my Hibs top on. I was so proud every time I did that, it made me feel massive, my chest swelled, confidence grew, I could take on anybody.

We were the first team in the UK to have a sponsorship logo on the front of our shirts, I thought the Bukta logo added an element of elegance that no other team had.

I could hear the boys in the distance; they were making their way up to the pitches. I sat down, using the bin liner as a blanket as I didn't want to get my shorts dirty, put on my Adidas Sambas, slipped the purple tracky bottoms on. Put the tracky top on, zipped it up. I pulled on the tracky waistband. *Hold on a minute,* I thought, *there's something wrong here.* I looked down, it looked like my cat had died. Strike that, it looked like my Sabre tooth tiger had died!

The fucking things were so small that I wasn't sure if they were long shorts or short longs. I'd obviously picked up my own tracky top, but my wee sister Lynne's tracky bottoms. I looked like a mental patient. A few footballs banged against the fence and another couple bounced into the pitches. If last week was anything to go by, Alex Edwards would be up in a minute. I tucked the bin liner into the bottom of the wheelbarrow, ran towards the pitches, the tightness of the tracky bottoms nipping my heehaws.

I opened the snib, closed it, ran over, tucked myself under the tarpaulin at the construction site I'd assembled in the corner during the week. I manipulated the tarpaulin to make doubly sure that I'd never be seen, then sat down with my back against the plastic barriers, tried to control my breathing. Fuck! My arse was soaking. Rain had gathered in the small hole I'd made in the pitch, I was sitting right in the middle of a puddle three inches deep. I was about to shift when I heard the gate opening then a shout of pain.

'Ahh, fuck it!'

That idiot, Edwards, must have trapped his finger in the snib again. I would've laughed, but couldn't. I heard his footsteps getting closer to where I was. *Why is he coming here,* I thought? *They were away at the other side of the park last week.* I saw a hand reach under the tarpaulin, it let in a bit of light, he put his black bag under it. A second or two later there was another bit of light, another bag. This went on for ages. Eventually there were a pile of leather bags and all kinds of stuff, wallets, rings and watches right next to me. I felt myself getting shoved forward. Again and again. *What the fuck is going on?* I thought.

'Right, lads, stop kicking the balls into the tarpaulin.' It was Eddie's voice. 'Warm up time.' He shouted.

This was my cue. I could hear the footsteps on the asphalt, the plan was to let them do a single lap, then when they came back around to where I was I'd sneak out and blend with the running circle. I waited until they were at the farthest away point, positioned myself under the tarp, timing it, waiting for the seamless blend. For some reason I began to whisper-sing the Hibee's song, I think it was to get myself mentally ready;

United we stand here, divided we fall,
we play for each other, when we're on the ball.
Our fans are the greatest, they cheer us each game.
We're Turnbull's Tornadoes, Hibernian's the name.
Hibs, Hibs, Hibs for the cup.

As I sung the chorus I got myself into a sprinter's starting position, waited for the moment … this was it. My heart was thudding harder than ever before, they were getting closer and closer and 'GO!!!' I said to myself.

I let fly from under the tarpaulin and got into the circle easily, there was a big gap between Alex Cropley and Ally MacLeod who looked like he couldn't be bothered. I jogged along at the same pace, got my head down hoping nobody had noticed me.

I heard somebody shouting something from way over the other side, couldn't make out a word. After a hundred yards or so of this I raised my head. I'd tucked my tracky bottom trousers into my long green socks whilst under the tarp, which wasn't great, but looked acceptable. It was then that I realised there were only two people wearing purple trackies. Me and Eddie Turnbull!

He was busy looking at his clipboard, as I jogged past him the colour change in his peripheral vision must have caught his attention. A few seconds later there was a shout.

'That's him,' someone said. I continued jogging, noticing that there was a building momentum of noise. I looked up again, there were fingers pointing towards me. I was a good hundred yards from Eddie by this time, I slowed as I saw him storming towards me. He was pointing and shouting something. I slowed to a jog-walk. Listened intently, was he inviting me into the squad?

I heard clearly what he was saying.

'Stop him. Thief!'

I looked around, the players were all slowing up, not quite sure what was going on.

'Stop that thief!' Eddie repeated, throwing his clipboard to the ground.

'Pat saw him coming out from under the tarpaulin, he's stolen our stuff,' he said.

'Eh?' I said.

I was oblivious, wondering what the hell was going on. I was jogging on the spot backwards now, as the players were realising what was happening. I made sure I was getting to the gate first.

'Fucking hell,' I shouted out loud, angry at them 'Nothing was nicked'. I ran to the gate, got there well before anybody else as my alert glands were up at full tilt. I stuck a twig into the snib. As this was the only exit point, it would give me those few extra seconds to get away. As I put the twig into place my hands shook like Al Jolson on speed.

I watched and fumbled it into place as Turnbull's Tornadoes ran screaming towards me. I'd seen this scenario many times in my dreams … after I'd scored the winning goal in the cup final. I thanked God Arthur Duncan was still injured, I reckoned he'd have caught me easily, but as it was I had about thirty seconds to disappear. I bolted into the woods, ran towards the wheelbarrow.

I realised with a heavy heart that I was now the Lost Tornado.

There was no way I'd ever get the chance to play with them after this.

'It's their loss,' I said out loud, confirming my thoughts; Eddie's misunderstanding had seen to that. To be honest, I didn't care now, after all those years of yearning, I wanted to get as far away from them as possible. As I ran, I peeled the tracky off. I got to the wheelbarrow, grabbed the bin liner, pulled out the camouflage stuff that I had from last week. I thanked myself for my forward thinking, I was going to take the outfit home last week but thought better of it. They'd no idea what direction I'd gone in, which gave me time to get blackened up.

Voices rose and fell, before I knew it I was surrounded by angry footballer's voices. I was in a ditch full of branches and dirt that we'd been clearing earlier. The wheelbarrow was sitting right next to me. Again, I prayed that I wouldn't be spotted.

I stilled my breathing to a fraction, although my heart was going twenty to the dozen. There were voices all around now, I recognised some of them. I heard rustling.

'Look, boss, he's nicked one of our tracksuits.'

Sounded like that wee shite Alex Edwards.

'Any sign of the wallets and stuff, though? That's the important thing.'

'No, nothing, boss, a spade and some tools.'

I was lying there reddening; I could feel the injustice bursting me, I wanted to get up and tell them to fuckin look under the tarp! There were a lot of people now going through the undergrowth, kicking bushes.

'Let's get back to training for the time being,' I heard Eddie saying. 'Pat? You and I should go back to the centre, alert the police.'

'Sure, boss,' he said, then there was silence.

I crawled out slowly, again making sure they hadn't set a trap for me, waiting until I moved, then all pouncing on me.

I was in deeper shit than I'd been in for a long time. It was obvious to me that the wallets and stuff were still there, all they had to do was check what was missing and I'd be OK, fuckin thickos. I felt blood dripping from the back of my hand, looked down, I was scratched to buggery. Hands and face ripped to shreds by the gorse and rosebushes we'd cleared from the path and dumped here last week. As I was hurriedly contemplating my next move I heard rustling in the bushes ahead of me. I was about to jump back in when that big ugly mush of Alistair's appeared, covered in dirt.

'I couldnae find it,' he said, barely registering that I was wearing camouflage.

'Nae worries,' I said. I was in a tailspin. Confused. I threw him a bottle of water from the barrow. 'Better wash your face.'

As he was doing that I dipped into the bin liner, got changed back into my jeans and jumper. I was gutted, the tracksuit and my trainers had gone. They'd taken them. *Shit, what will I tell Lynne*?

As I was puzzling my next move sirens could be heard coming into the centre.

'Police,' Alistair said. 'Wonder what's happened?'

'No idea,' I said. I decided the safest thing would be to go back to the bothy. I needed to somehow get Alistair to be my alibi. I tried to figure out what I'd got on him that could make him keep his trap shut.

I rummaged through the memory banks, came up with a beauty. When we first started on the Arthur's Seat job, way back in the summer, it was roasting, I was constantly drinking bottles of water. I'd run out one afternoon, jogged down to the bothy to fill my bottle up. When I got there I looked in the window to see Alistair with his tackle out, rubbing it all over the page three girl in The Sun. He never spotted me, he thought we were all at the top of Arthur's Seat. I deliberately kicked the door open, watched as he tried desperately to get his tadger back into his pants. He was panicking, knocked his tomato soup all over the poor lassie.

'Aye aye?' I said. 'What do we have here then?' I was loving it.

'I was just … just …'

'Tadger baiting?' I said.

'Eh?' He said.

'Wanking. It's the posh word for it.'

'No, I wasn't, I was fixing my belt.'

'I'll believe you,' I said. I filled my bottle, went back up the hill laughing. Alistair stood there with a beamer, his jumper tucked into his breeks.

I was jolted back to the present by the doppler effect of the siren that had passed us on the other side of the wall, must have been two or three cop cars there by now. *Shit! Must get moving here.*

'Alistair?' I said.

'Uhuh?'

'Do you remember that time I caught you tightening your belt when we were working at Arthur's Seat?'

He went pure red, it began at his neck, within a second, had reached his glasses, looked like his specs would pop off with the blood pressure from his embarrassment.

'Sort of,' he said, looking away from me.

'Well, you know how I sent you to get the tyre fixed?'

'Uhuh,' he replied.

'Did I go with you?'

'No.'

'Wrong answer,' I said. 'Did I go with you?'

He looked confused. 'I went myself.' He put his arm out, closed one eye, pointed to the rubber man. 'Up there.'

'If anybody asks, I want you to tell them that we both went, OK? If you don't I might have to write a note to your mum and dad telling them about that loose belt.' *Christ*, I thought to myself, *the fag thing had backfired on me so drastically that if I tell them about this they'll probably be ordering him a subscription of Playboy.* 'Deal?' I said, extending my hand.

'Deal,' he said. We shook. I made sure I squeezed his hand so tight that it hurt, I wanted it to be imprinted in his wandering brain cell.

'Ouch!' He said pulling his hand away.

'Sorry pal.'

We gathered all of the stuff that was lying around, while his back was turned I threw the camouflage outfit into the ditch. I'd pick it up after all of this had blown over. We headed back to the bothy.

Just before we walked through the door I said, 'Alistair, did we go to get the tyre fixed together this morning?'

'Yes,' he said nodding his head too many times, looked like one of those wee nodding bulldogs in the back of a car.

'Correct answer,' I said, 'but don't nod so much when I ask you next time.' I felt my conscience prick slightly, remembering how I'd been bullied at the George Hotel. Was I guilty of doing the same to Alistair?

'Nah. He deserves what he's getting, I'm actually helping to develop him.' I reasoned.

The boss was in the middle of telling the rest of the squad that the police and security guards were out looking for a thief as the Hibs boys had tons of stuff nicked. He turned around as we walked in.

'Have you heard?' Bob shouted. 'The Hibby bastards have had all their valuables nicked.' He laughed loudly. 'Their shell suits and knock off Rolex's have been choried. Wait until the thief tries to pawn the fuckers and gets offered hee haw.' He was decking himself. I ignored the comment.

'How did that happen?' I asked. There was a knock on the bothy door, Sam was standing there.

'Hello, lads,' he said, inviting himself in. 'Can I have a word with you, Dave?'

I shit myself, did they know something? I thought back to all of the things that had happened today, wondered if I'd left anything that'd give me away. Davie left with Sam, they headed over to the centre.

Davie returned a while later, we'd all been sitting about discussing it. I'd had to make like everything was a surprise to me, widen my eyes, lift eyebrows up to the forehead and all that. At one point I almost said, 'But nothing's been nicked!' Caught myself in time.

'Well?' Bob shouted as Davie came through the door. 'What's the score?'

'Looks like somebody's been setting them up for a while, there's all this stuff at the pitches that nobody knows about, been pretty well organised by all accounts.'

'Have they caught him?' I asked.

'No, they know what he looks like though, a lot of the Hibs players saw him. He had the cheek to goad them, then lock them into the pitches. He nicked their valuables, a couple of tracksuits, trainers, some other bits and pieces. The police are going to do some sort of identikit picture.'

That was all I needed, more pressure.

Surely they'd look at everything and realise there was nothing missing? Surely? I thought.

'But lads,' said Davie, 'there is good news.'

What's that then, boss'? Tony said.

'You're all on a half day.'

'As of when?' Bob said.

Davie looked at his watch. 'Five minutes ago.'

There was a mad scramble of guys getting their belongings, bolting for the door. Dust flew. I was taking my time, wondering what the hell was going on. I hung back. Davie thought I was hanging back to cadge a lift, said, 'Need a lift into town?'

'Nah, I'm fine Dave. Why are we getting a half day, though?'

'The police want all of our guys gone as they think we'll get in the way.'

This thrilled me, as it seemed to indicate that we were not the suspects. I was elated.

'On second thoughts, Dave, if you're going into town I will take a lift.'

'No problemo.'

I grabbed my bin liner from the barrow, hid it in my Hibs shoulder bag, jumped into the Jag.

An hour later I was sitting having tea with the family, only the eight of us tonight, watching some documentary while shoving grub into our mouths.

'Is John not having his tea, Mum?' I asked, noticing that things were a bit quieter than usual.

'He's at the TA at seven, so he says he'll get something there.'

A jolt zipped through my body like a firecracker, starting at the base of my neck, working its way down to my sphincter and back up again, all in a split second. I rushed upstairs, realising his TA camouflage suit was sitting in a ditch in Niddrie. He'd go ballistic. He'd got such temper on him at times that the kids around here called him 'psycho'.

I looked at my watch; four thirtyish; that'd give me roughly two hours to get up to the JKC and back again. I didn't think it was enough time as I wasn't sure what time the buses ran at night.

While I was running upstairs I remembered that the cops were conducting their investigations and could still be there. It'd be dark when I got there, so might as well be prepared for it. I dived into my half of the wardrobe, pulled out all of my black stuff; jumper, balaclava, gloves, black trousers and … shit! No black shoes!

I used to wear my Sambas, but the fucking Hibs team nicked them. *Bastards*, I thought, even though I didn't mean it.

I was still feeling guilty as hell about losing my wee sister's tracky bottoms.

I grabbed John's TA army boots; *might as well go the whole hog*, I thought

I got a bus right away, got to the JKC after half five. It was pitch black. I got off one stop further away from my usual one as it was nearer to the hole in the wall where I sent doolally Ali. I figured that I could get in that way unnoticed. Seemed to be working. I walked through no problem, not a sign of anybody. I couldn't see if there were any Panda cars as the centre was hidden from me. I got onto the path, realised I'd forgotten to bring a torch. It was darker than John's mood would be if I didn't get home in time. I couldn't see an inch in front of me. I tried to go all Jedi, closed my eyes, seeing if I could let the Force take me to the right spot. Almost immediately I tripped on something and lost my balance, felt my face and hair being thwacked and ripped by sharp twigs and branches.

'Fuck!' I shouted, annoyed at myself for being such an arse, realising I'd no chance of finding anything in the darkness. I decided to walk hands in front of me, one protecting my face as that last thwack stung like hell. A light bulb went on, not literally, if it had that would have solved the problem. I remembered something army guy told me way back.

'*When you're in darkness, take a moment to still yourself. Close your eyes and wait a few moments. In this period of time your inner eye will take the available light into consideration, sample your last visual input and create a seamless border between both, allowing you to see in virtual night vision*'.

He actually said 'If ye shut yer eyes for a minute it's easier tae see in the dark'. I thought it was worth a try. I shut my eyes, waited, even though I knew that the second hand was zipping around the face of my watch like an Aberdonian in a trolley dash.

I opened one eye, then the other. Couldn't believe my eyes, it worked, I could actually see a bit more, certainly enough to find my way to the area where I'd dumped the suit. I still had to keep one arm out in case I got the smack in the puss again. I thought I was at the right spot, did a couple of checks, thinking about what should be there. We'd almost completed the edging of the path on the right hand side and had finished it completely on the left hand side so theoretically there should be a gap in the edging almost at the right spot. I used my boots as the gauge, dragging them along the edging like a rail line. Eureka, a gap! I'd found the right spot. Then:

BANG!

The world lit up. On instinct I dived into the undergrowth. I was sure the pigs had been hiding, waiting for me to recover the suit, to then pounce. A trap in which I was the prey. I could now see the camouflage suit clearly. I thought it was ironic, given what kind of suit it was. I grabbed it, covered myself up with it, hoping that it would do as good a job as it had last week. I knew I was kidding myself. I lay there waiting on plod marching up in their droves. Nothing happened. There was sound in the distance, shouting and such like, but no sirens or anything like that. I lifted my head; still nobody around. I tried to stand up but there was nothing substantial to grab onto, the thorns and spines of the cuttings were ripping me to shreds again. I wrapped the suit around my hands, crawled out. I peered over the bushes, into the distance, saw there were a lot of guys playing five a side on the pitches ... the floodlights had gone on. 'That's what the big light was,' I said to myself, I laughed, shook my head.

I stopped laughing when I looked at my watch, though. I had about forty minutes to get back home. The only way that was possible was to get a Joe Baxi.

I hailed one down on the main Niddrie drag, asked him to get me to Claremont Court as quickly as possible. He was a grumpy old bastard.

'I'll do thirty miles an hour as fast as I can, pal,' he said, sarky old bugger. I ignored him, I had major worries of my own to deal with without this shite. For a start I had no money to pay for the taxi. Secondly I had to get John's suit back into his half of the cupboard in approximately twenty minutes and counting. I held my watch hand into the air, hoping that gravity would slow it down a tad. As we approached the Court I had to deliver his bucks, or at least make him think I was going to.

'Can you stop at a cash-line, pal?' I said.

'Is there one nearby?'

'Yip, if you go to the Claremont Hotel, they've got one in the foyer, I'll nip in there.'

'OK,' he said. He put the meter off as we turned into the hotel.

'How much?' I said.

'Three-fifty.'

'Cool,' I said. 'We'll make it four quid since you stuck to your guns.'

He drew right up to the front gate of the hotel. This was now my territory. I opened the door, took all of my bits and pieces, headed into the hotel. Looked at him, gave him a 'one minute' signal, walked into the foyer, all the way through to the back of the hotel. Out through the back door, over the 'hundred walls' and into the Court. 'Muppet,' I said to myself.

I had my key ready as I took three stairs at a time, bounding up like a greyhound. Ran straight up to the room, removed the suit from the bin liner, dug out the coat hangers and suit bag from John's side of the wardrobe. I undid the spaghetti laces from his boots and had to leave some of the knots that had formed, they were way too tight to sort at a time like this. I put the suit into the bag, only noticing then how muddy and slightly ripped it was. Zipped it up, hung it neatly in place. I looked at the boots, there was a big long scrape along the side that I'd used to find the edge of the path. I rubbed it with my jumper, spitting on it, which kind of worked.

I wasn't really concerned with details right now. I was relieved that after the day I'd had, things were now calm. I shut the cupboard doors, went downstairs, put the kettle on. I knew John would be back soon, but figured that scenario would take care of itself later.

Chapter 24

I finished the project at the Jack Kane. It lasted a month longer than we thought it would, which left two months before I was back on the dole again. On the final Friday, the boss man came along with the sheets of paper that let us know our next posting. This time it was a breeze, especially after the fear and tension I felt when I knew I was going to Niddrie. Unrolling the A4 sheet, Davie stood on the table which was by now, the custom.

'Jimbo, my son,' he shouted, 'you are off to Inverleith Park.'

'Yes,' I shouted, pumping my fists. I'd been down there a couple of times to drop off things for other jobs. Wee Paddy, who I'd worked with a while ago now, worked there full-time. He was the first intellectual schemie I'd ever met. I was mega impressed with his general knowledge, wanted a bit of that brainpower myself. It was probably the easiest posting in the entire Job Creation Project.

It went by so quickly; nothing happened. Not a single thing of interest. I spent my time learning from Paddy how to fill in a crossword and how to look at things differently.

'When you're looking at a tree, Jimbo,' he'd say, 'don't look at the tree, look at negative space of the tree, the small gaps of air between the leaves, the divisions in the bark.'

It sounded daft but I really did begin to see what he was talking about.

The last day of Job Creation arrived like lightning, I was elated. I'd served my year for Thatcher. What did we achieve? Who knew? Wondered what kind of reward they'd give me when I turned up at the dole on Monday, almost felt like a serviceman returning from some far flung outpost, returning wiser and better equipped for the next phase of my life.

When I arrived at the dole on the Monday, I about fell off the seat that I was about to sit on. The lassie was sitting at the desk with a pile of job cards for me. Could this be this right? I sat down. Pulled the chair closer to her desk, trying to get a look at what kind of jobs the cards offered. She pulled them away, teasing me.

'Uh, uh,' she said. 'Wait.' She dug my file from her drawer, flicked through it. 'Very good, James. I'm impressed.'

'With what?'

'You've spent an entire year on JCP.'

'And?'

'Not many people stick it out, well done. I'm Clare by the way.'

'Nice to meet you Miss by the way, unusual surname?' I said testing her humour.

She didn't respond, just looked through the cards.

Maybe I had achieved something with this path building carry-on. She picked up the cards, held them like we were playing Rummy.

'Pick a card,' she said. I dipped into the pile, pulled one out. She laid the rest of them face down on the table.

'Burton's Biscuits, Product Quality Response Manager.'

'That sounds pretty fancy,' I said. 'What does it involve?'

'Let me see,' she said looking at the job sheet. 'You quality check the biscuits as they go past you on the conveyor belt. If they do not meet the specified standard, you have to re-assimilate the low quality product.'

'Re-assimilate, what does that actually mean?' I said.

She sighed. 'It means you remove the duff biscuits, sweep them up at the end of your shift.'

My face must have said it all. 'Nah,' I said, 'not for me.'

'OK, fair enough. Pick another.'

'I picked another two, it was the same shite. I was about to resign myself to another spell on the dole when she flicked through another pile she had sitting at the side of her desk.

'How about this one?' She said. 'Kenworthy's Grocery Store. Apprentice grocer.'

It was by far the best I'd heard yet. I thought about it. Albert Arkwright and Granville from *Open All Hours* came to mind, I liked the thought. 'I'll take it,' I said, smiling at her. I was already thinking about the nice cosy job and all the perks, cakes, sweets, and juice.

'Hold on,' she said, 'it's not as easy as that.'

'Eh?'

'You have to go for an interview, see if you're suited.'

'Suited?'

'Yes. Do you know where Kenworthy's is?'

'Don't think so.'

'It's off East Claremont Street.'

As soon as she said that I knew exactly where it was. 'Did it used to be Babbette's?'

'I think so. Why do you ask?'

'No reason, want to make sure it's the right place.'

The real reason was more than I dared let on. Babbette's was a shop out-with its time zone, an anachronism. The old French woman who owned it, Babbette, only sold wool and sweets. They were all contained under one massive wooden and glass counter that she had to lift up every time she sold something. I had no idea how she did it. The lid must have weighed a ton.

One day I was heading up to the vet with John's hamster. Lady had developed a big lump on her leg, as John was working, he gave me a couple of quid to get her checked out. As I was passing Babbette's I had an idea. I pushed the door, which set off a few clanging bells. I expected this, knew she'd be through in exactly twenty seconds. Her room was behind the counter, which was so high that she couldn't see anything that was in front of it.

I took advantage. I hid in front of the counter silently. I waited for her to come through. She obviously thought there was nobody in the shop so headed back. This allowed me time to help myself to the sweets. I grabbed a couple of MB bars and some Raspberry Ruffles. As I put the lid back down I had a brainwave. I went over to the door, opened it, the bells clanged, I hid at the front of the counter again. Just before I ducked down, I put Lady on top of the glass counter to toddle about. I heard Babbette walk through again, heard a gasp then a thud. She hit the floor. I looked over the big counter but couldn't see anything. I looked under it, saw a pair of shoes looking skywards attached to a pair of wrinkly old legs. I grabbed Lady, stuffed her back into my pocket and legged it. The shop was sold soon after. I didn't want to know why.

Clare, the Job Centre girl, looked at the phone number on the job card.

'Are you sure about this?' She said, as she picked up the phone. I nodded. She was chit chatting with the person on the other end, answering questions about me, I guess. 'Tomorrow at three? Hold on a second please, Mr Kenworthy.'

She put her hand over the mouthpiece and spoke to me. 'Are you OK to go along for an interview tomorrow?'

I gave her a double thumbs up.

'Yes, that's splendid Mr Kenworthy. He'll be along, three sharp.' It's Divine. James Divine. OK, thanks.' She hung up.

'Well, that's that,' she said, handing me a card which I was to take along with me. I can honestly say I was a bit excited about being an apprentice grocer. In my mind it was the perfect job, it sure beat being on the dole.

I had a kick-about down at the garages with a few pals, they laughed when I told them where I was going.

'Not bothered what you lot think,' I said. 'I'll be earning big bucks, and think about the products. I'll be able to cherry pick.'

Tuesday afternoon, two minutes to three, I was on my way down the stairs into the basement grocery shop. It had certainly changed since it was Babbette's, it looked quite clean, I couldn't get over how big it was now. They'd opened up the back of the shop. It looked really good, I could see myself working here. Cracking sweets, too. There was nobody around so I walked the shop examining the merchandise. I heard a door open behind me, there was this tall, lanky army Sergeant Major looking guy, complete with white moustache. I went to shake his hand.

'Hi, I'm Jimmy Divine,' I said.

'No, no, no,' he replied.

'Pardon?' I said, putting on my best manners.

'No, you're definitely not what we're looking for.' He furrowed his brow, frowned as he backed away from me. 'I hate when that bloody dole office wastes my time.' He muttered.

'What's wrong with me?' I said, feeling unnerved.

'You're not what I'm after. You're too … too … can I be honest, lad?'

'Of course.'

'You don't look bright enough.'

My anger rose in a second. I wanted to punch the old twat in the puss, kick his spuds all over the place, but instead, I stormed towards the door.

'Good day to you, lad,' he said, as he walked over to the door, held it open for me.

I grabbed the handle from him, slammed the fucking thing until the bell fell off.

I thought I'd lost all of that shit, the lowness of spirit, the self-esteem that had scraped its knuckles on the gutter so many times. I walked home utterly dejected. A year in Maggie's New Model Army had only gone and pushed me further down the food chain. I was hopeless. I stayed away from the dole for a long time, giving up on any idea of employment, suffering the consequences of having no money. My lack of funds for all these years came home to roost one Christmas. I was so down that I stayed in bed on Christmas day. I had no money to buy Mum or any of the kids a gift. I wanted to hide beneath those covers until springtime. There were excited knocks on my bedroom door, kids asking me when I was getting up.

'I'm not'. I said.

'There are presents downstairs for you though'.

This made it even worse. I slunk deeper into the covers and cried for a long time. My sister Karen had come back from Qatar for a flying visit and had bought everyone a gift. She stormed into the room and pulled the covers off me. Thankfully I was wearing my jammies.

'Come on then?' She said, 'Get up'.

'I can't' I said pathetically, 'I haven't bought anybody anything.'

'So what?' She said, 'what does that matter? People only buy you things if they want to, if you can't afford it they'll understand'.

I felt a huge lump in my throat, gave her a cuddle and blubbered like a wee lassie.

I was spending a lot of my time drawing and painting, getting bits of cash from shops and friends that wanted a card or a poster designed. I still wanted to be a commercial artist. The money I earned went mostly on materials, big A1 Daler boards, paints, inks, spray cans. I was obsessed with science fiction illustration. Couldn't get enough of artists who could create incredibly realistic Sci-fi worlds. Roger Dean was my hero in that regard. He'd designed tons of album covers. I loved letting my mind delve into worlds that nobody owned or dictated how things should be. It was magical. My mates were getting their escapism from dugs, slugs, and drugs, I was doing art and ornithology. Although I was a sound guy, they could not grasp why I'd want to walk about the paths and rivers looking at birds and animals. It was amazing to me. I felt alive.

I noticed everything around me, within three hundred yards of the Court there were rabbits, kingfishers, water voles, foxes, bats. They noticed nothing, perhaps the occasional flap or scream or a 'whatthefuckwasthat?' As a bat came too close to their kebab on the way home from another night on the piss. I didn't want that; I wanted knowledge and awareness.

I spent most of my time on my own, trying to learn. I guess I was hoping that by doing this stuff some of it would sink in. I knew I wasn't a thicko.

It worked. I kept on drawing and painting, listening to music, reading. I was educating myself without really knowing that was what I was doing.

One day I plucked up the courage to get in touch with a few design agencies and printers. Maybe I'd go looking for an apprenticeship.

That was the faraway dream in my head, which seemed much more unachievable than playing for Hibs had ever been, look what happened there! I phoned and wrote to a few companies, and got so excited when two people got back in touch saying they'd see me. I was ecstatic. I had a week to get my 'portfolio' ready, although first I had to look up the word to see what it meant. I couldn't afford a portfolio as such, but as my paintings were big I put them in a black bin liner to keep them together, stop them getting wet.

The first place I went to see was a print company, Image Printers. When I went through the door I loved the smell. It was fresh ink on freshly cut paper. It did something to me. I guess it was a similar smell to the spray paint I'd been using in my room with the windows shut. I discovered that I'd been a spray can junkie, that's why the ink gave me a buzz.

The guy liked my ideas, but said come back to see me in a year or two. 'Ye've still got a bit o development to do, son.'

He was nice enough, but I'd gone in thinking I'd walk out with a job. It was OK though, not another downer as such. The other guy I was to go and see cancelled on me three times, but eventually he called me to ask if I could see him in half an hour. It was eight at night, but I didn't care. I got all my stuff together, ran along to London Street Studios. It was a graphic design place. I looked at the address, couldn't figure it out, it definitely said number sixty-three.

The number sixty-three I stood in front of was a funeral parlour.

I paced about outside, thinking it had been a wind up, when I spotted this guy with a cracking village people moustache waving at me from a room within the funeral parlour. He didn't look a happy chap. I walked to the steps, he met me at the door.

You Jimmy?' He said, looking pretty pissed off.

'Yeah, that's me.' I wiped the sweat from my brow, trying to compose myself for the interview after running there.

'Can I tell you one thing, pal?'

'Sure.'

'I do not like latecomers'. He looked at his watch. 'You've got fifteen minutes to impress.'

He walked into the big, horrible dark house and I followed. I was raging a bit because It wasn't even twenty past eight, I'd bombed it along the road, I was ten minutes early. There were coffins lying in the hallway, one open, but thankfully no bodies in them. It still creeped me out.

I sat down in front of his desk. He cleared a space and I dipped into the bin liner, removing the paintings one by one, talking him through the images and ideas. He kept looking at his watch. I was not getting good vibes. No feedback, no comment on anything. I was about to go onto the next painting when he put his hand up.

'Can I stop you there?' He said. 'I'm going to give you a bit advice that'll save you a lot of time and heartache.'

I looked at him, knew he was going to say 'no job'. I was relieved, this place felt awful, drained of any spark.

'OK,' I said, waiting.

'Put your things back in the bag, leave it at the front door as you go out. The bin men are coming in the morning, they'd be happy to usher that stuff into the afterlife.' He smiled.

I thought he was joking. I half-smiled back, not really sure what was happening here.

'I'm not joking,' he said, with a serious coupon. 'Your stuff is not good. Leave it at the door.'

Inside I split into bits. I felt the foundations of confidence I'd slowly and deliberately built up explode into a million pieces below me, all the dreams and hopes, plans for the future, and the joy of doing something I loved fell away like a skydiving team into the abyss. I watched them all disappear into the distant void below me. It was, after everything I'd ever been through, the most hurtful thing anyone had ever said or done to me.

I wanted to rip his fucking head off, stick those Daler boards into the hole where that ugly fucking face had been. I wanted to, but didn't. I did not want to show that ignorant, arrogant bastard that he'd wounded me. I picked the paintings up carefully to try to show him that no matter whether he placed any value on them, they were valuable to me. I did not look at him at all, placed everything neatly back into the bag, tied it in a knot at the top, walked out. I tried to act as if I didn't care. When I got out of sight, around the corner to the big empty playground of Bellevue School, I went to pieces.

I sat on the steps, cried my heart out. I opened the bag, pulled out what up until five minutes ago had been the most valuable thing in my life. All this time I thought I'd been developing currency, after all, was that not what currency was? I thought about the investment of time I'd put into these paintings, with each stroke of the brush or swipe of the pencil I was building my future, I really believed that. I laid the paintings out on the steps and looked at them. I wanted to rip them into bits.

'Fucking shite!' I shouted at them.

I kicked the empty bag, threw it down the steps and sat there for ages. I went through the paintings with a hatred that had never been there before. My favourite one was of my all-time Hibs hero, Ally MacLeod. I looked at it with new eyes, saw how shite it was. He looked more like Prince Charles after a night on crystal meth. I ripped it to bits, threw it over the fence and watched as the wind took it away. I examined every bit of 'art'. I laughed at that. ART. What the fuck did I know about ART? This stuff was absolute shite. I went through all of it, destroyed it piece by piece.

I sat on the steps, head in hands, wiping away tears. They were tears of fear that I was crying. I'd set my heart on doing two things in my life that I loved, it looked like I had failed at both. I was terrified that I'd have to get an ordinary job, be an ordinary person, and that scared the shit out of me. I walked away from the debris that lay in the school playground, not once looking back. The bin liner blew towards me almost tripping me up, seemed like it was taking the piss, I picked it up and ripped it to bits on the school fence.

I was on a downer for weeks. The vibrancy I'd been seeing in everything had gone. The world was permeated with a greyness, it was a bland, stark place that offered me no hope. I didn't run for all that time, never went over to the park, never played footy.

I was walking down Leith Walk one afternoon after meeting the dole people, passing Boston's second-hand shop, when something in the window caught my eye. It was something beautiful. There at the back of the window sitting amongst a lot of bric-a-brac was an incredible looking camera. *Wow*. I thought, *how professional does that look?* I knew nothing about photography, but this device had my attention, I could see it offered me the possibility of getting some colour back into my shit life.

They wanted twenty-five quid for it, which was way out of my league.

Every time I signed on I passed the shop to look at it: ZENITH 35MM SLR. Those words were like candy. I wanted that camera. If my painting was not much good, I thought maybe capturing images, rather than creating them was more my thing, maybe that was how I was supposed to express myself.

CHAPTER 25

I saved and saved but never quite got there. I was terrified that by the time I'd saved the dosh, the camera would be gone. I was at the dole, waiting to get it over with as usual, looking forward to visiting the camera. I was not far away, another ten quid and I'd be able to buy it; I hoped it could hold on. My dole officer caught me totally by surprise. She brought a bundle of cards over to her desk. We hadn't played the card game since my experience at the grocery.

I raised my eyebrows.

'I know what you're thinking,' she said, 'but bear with me.'

We went through a few, my eyes lit up.

'Say that again?' I said.

'Assistant photo-processor.'

'Is that developing photos and stuff?' I asked.

'Yep. That's exactly what it says,' she said, checking the details on both sides of the card.

'Where is it?'

'EastPoint Photos, North Bridge.'

'Edinburgh?'

'Yep.'

This was it; sounded too good to be true. The wage was pretty good as well. She arranged the interview for the following week. I wanted the job so badly I got a haircut, borrowed some of John's good clothes and headed up to North Bridge.

It was a nice looking shop with a whole range of cameras in the front window. It had a lot of machinery in it, too, technical looking stuff. I was mega pleased with this. I looked in, there were three women behind the counter. Two of them looked pretty fit, the other was a wee dumpy thing who I didn't really look at. I went in, asked for Linda Fergus, the manager. She seemed nice, fairly attractive, kept flicking her hair over her shoulder, looking at me and smiling. The interview seemed to go really well, I left the place feeling pretty cool. *This could be it*, I thought. I stepped outside onto the bridges, looked around at the other shops in the vicinity; there was a bakery next door, a chemist the other side, restaurants across the road and Princes Street round the corner. The location and premises were top class.

I got a call from Linda the next day.

'Hi, Jimmy,' she said. 'We're really meant to give you and the other candidates a second interview, but me and the girls think you'll fit in perfectly. Can you start Monday?'

'Of course, Yes,' I said, 'definitely, thanks.'

Fit in perfectly? I'm in there, I thought.

I was ecstatic. I borrowed a tenner from John's savings, nipped down to Boston's and bought the camera and as a bonus, the guy in the shop gave me a huge pile of photography magazines for free.

'Look out for the glamour shots, pal, apologies if the pages are stuck together, like,' he said, winking at me. I'd no idea what he meant. I was floating home.

When I got the camera into my room, I unpacked it. He'd given me a metal briefcase to carry it about in, I felt like James Bond. I opened the case, clicking open the two silver locking tabs, flipped the lid up, there sat this beauty of a machine. It was held lovingly in place by a piece of grey foam and a couple of ripped up Yellow Pages.

I lifted it up and was shocked and pleasantly surprised at the weight of it. It was solid, Russian built. No plastic Kodak 128 shit here, this was the real McCoy. I dumped the packaging into the bin, sat the camera on my kip, then went down to the kitchen, made myself a cup of tea, giving me time to appreciate the newness of the thing. I sat on the bed all night, winding the camera and clicking the shutter button; it was the best sound I'd ever heard from any machine.

Man, it soothed me, it also got me excited. I opened the back and had a look at the mechanism; I'd never seen anything like it before. I read up about it in the mags the boy had given me, pausing a few times to admire the glamour shots.

It was an SLR – single lens reflex. How cool and sexy did that sound?

'Hi ladies, Jim Divine at your service.

'What's this?

'It's a single lens reflex camera, ma'am.

'Me? A professional?

'You could say that.

'Portraits? Sure.

Just lift your top a bit more, doll, I'll snap tastefully.'

I could see myself growing in confidence with this beauty, wondered what doors would it open for me, especially now that I was also working as a photo processor. I clicked away. Tigger got about a thousand shots of himself that night taken from all kinds of angles, with hats on, tucked up under my blanket, a pair of pants on his head. I had no film for the camera yet, but I'd be able to get as much as I wanted from the new job. Happiness was all over me like a fat man locked in a sweet shop. My non-camera eye twitched all night, I had been winking it shut while I used the other eye to peer through the viewfinder. I couldn't sleep.

The next morning I woke up, I still had the twitch. It wore off eventually but not before I'd had some funny looks from customers.

I'd been at the job for nearly a fortnight, it seemed more glamorous before I started. The job description gave it an air of sophistication and glamour. I was a bit annoyed, if the truth be told, but it was better than the dole and there were some perks, none more so than Judy. Her real name was Pam, but she looked like Judy Tzuke. Lovely looking lassie and didn't believe in the bra! Hallelujah! I gave her belief system two thumbs up and her chest reciprocated, even more so on cold days.

Subtlety for a teenage guy is difficult, I hoped I didn't make it too obvious as I stared at her thruppenny bits for hours.

There was a downside. She was manky and smelly. When she ate there was always something escaping from her roll, dripping onto her top: egg, grease, brown sauce, mayonnaise. She never wiped it off. I secretly called her *Judy Puke*, an anorexic could survive for a year from the food on her top.

I wasn't sure if she had a boyfriend, wondered if I could change her. First thing I'd change would be her black, manky, egg-stained jumper. Her smell could be overwhelming at times. One morning I got in early, only Linda was in. I'd watched *Apocalypse Now* with a couple of mates the night before. When I walked through the door of the shop I took a big lung-full of air.

'I love the smell of *nae Pam* in the morning,' I said in a big Sergeant-Major American voice, mimicking a line from the film.

Waited on the acknowledgment and laughter. Linda sat there flicking through a mag, sipping her coffee, not looking up. 'What are you on about?'

'Nothing,' I said. Went downstairs to put on my smock.

I was sitting behind the counter waiting on the Gazza the delivery boy to bring in the day's films and photos. Today was a special day for me. Last week, I'd borrowed a couple of 35mm films for the new camera, took a load of great pictures; Landscapes, sunsets, animals, people. I was half thinking about entering them for some of the competitions in the photography magazines. Depending how the photos turned out, of course. Gazza was due between half-nine and half-ten.

The van pulled up outside the door, it was Gaz. A fellow Hibs fan. He put the hazard lights on, walked in with a big box.

'Awright, Jimbo?'

'Could be, Gazza. Depends what you've got in yer box.'

He grabbed his tackle with his free hand and shook it. 'If Judy's around she's free to rummage.'

We laughed, shaking hands as he walked past. I'd let him into my secret about her not wearing a bra last week.

'Is she around?' He said.

'Nah. Day off.'

'Pity. It's fucking freezin out there. I was lookin forward to asking her if she'd get me a couple of baps from the bakery.'

We laughed again, both of us raising our eyebrows, smiling at the thought. He put the box on top of the counter, I went through the delivery, signed the delivery note.

'See you tomorrow, pal,' He said. He went out of the door, walked to the shop window, grabbed the front of his jacket with his thumb and forefinger, pulled out two huge material boobs, twisting the ends as if he was dialling into Radio Tokyo. I gave him a wave, he disappeared in the van.

I skipped all of the urgent notices and emergency stuff that we were meant to check as soon as a delivery came in as I spotted the two packets with DIVINE on them, looked around to make sure neither Linda nor Angela were watching me. I could see them yapping behind the frosted glass in the office, so I was fine. I ripped the elastic bands off the first packet. I knew these were the photos, the other, smaller packet would be the slides. As I flicked through them I was getting slower and slower. There was only half a photo on every print! Why the hell was that? I checked the negatives, they were the same.

'Shit!' I shouted, a bit too loudly, but nobody came out. I grasped for the slides, they had cost me a fortune and taken even longer than the prints. I popped the green and white plastic case open, pulled two or three out. The first two were perfect. Bright vibrant colours, incredible saturation, but out of focus. I'd hoped for an award-winning sunset, but had failed. I flicked through the rest of the slides, while half of them were full slides, the others showed only half the image again. *Must be the camera*, I thought. *I'll go to Boston's later, find out the score.*

I felt so flat. I'd had a vision in my head, all the time and care I'd taken over these. I was sure the awards would flow.

'Basically, pal, it's your shutter that's the problem, looks like it's jammin up.' The boy from Boston's said.

'But I only bought it a couple of weeks ago,' I pleaded.

'Did you get a guarantee?'

'No. Did I need one?'

'No guarantee, no refund or replacement. Rules are rules.'

I was raging, but he was a big guy, looked like he took no shit from anybody.

'Look at the sign as you're leavin pal.'

I picked up the camera, walked out. There was big red sign at the door. NO GUARANTEES – GUARANTEED.

I went home, threw the camera, slides and prints into the cupboard, lay on my kip. I fell asleep. I must have been thinking about solutions in my sleep. When I woke up I thought, *how come some of them were perfect?* There were a few with full pictures. I went to the cupboard, pulled the camera out. I opened the back of it, began clicking away, changing the settings of the shutter speed, looking to see what was happening.

I'd found the problem! I would see light getting through the lens on every setting except two. I tested the theory hundreds of times, it was definitely the problem. 'Yes!' I shouted. Game back on. As long as I avoided those two settings, I'd be fine. I was happy all over again.

As the days and weeks passed the job was getting more and more boring. All I did was stand behind a counter, looking at other people's shitty photos, handing them over or taking in spools.

I had to censor a set of prints that came in one Friday. The whole set of them involved a beardy guy wearing white ankle socks and nothing else, he was inserting various different types of bottles up his girlfriend's jacksy. The most revealing were the Cream Soda and Red Cola ones.

I showed them to Linda to ask what I should do with them. She put both hands up to cover her mouth. 'My god,' she said.

'Should we call the cops?'.

'We can't. It's not illegal. Put them in the drawer, if they come in for them, let me know and we'll make a decision.'

'Cool,' I said, putting them away. I'd have a closer look later, the girl looked pretty tidy. I Wouldn't take a drink from her though, hairy juice? No thanks.

Weeks went by. I'd now been there ten weeks, two days and three hours. It was a drag, even the thought of Judy's raspberry ripples was not enough to keep me interested in the job. I was bored like never before. At least with Job Creation I was outside all the time; here the only stimulus I got was from the bakery next door, even my daily pineapple slice and macaroni pie were becoming dull. So dull in fact that I had to invent games to keep me occupied. My favourite was *Toilet Pan Jedi's*. It's designed for men but women are free to try it.

1. Go to the loo.

2. Take three sheets of toilet paper, fold them over each other so that you have what looks like a single piece of toilet paper, three sheets thick.

3. Place it carefully onto the surface of the water in the toilet pan.

4. Take a moment to steady yourself, then BLAST THE SHIT OUT OF IT with your piss-stream light Sabre. If somebody'd left a bit of shite on the side of the bowl, you get extra points for wiping out the dark side.

I still hadn't made time to re-take all of my photos, but planned on doing it sometime soon; the holidays were coming up, I promised myself to take some time then to learn my camera for real.

It was going-home time on Friday night. I was looking forward to the Hibs game but Linda asked me if I could work Saturday afternoon. I was meant to be off every third Saturday, it was what we'd agreed from day one.

'I'll give you double time,' she said.

I waited.

'And a day in lieu.'

I hadn't been to see the Hibs for almost a month now and was getting withdrawal symptoms. 'I'm not sure Linda,' I said.

'Please? It's my birthday, my dad's taking me out to the North British for afternoon tea. I promise never to ask you again.'

'OK,' I said.

'Thanks. Really appreciate it,' she said, trying to give me a hug.

'What time should I come in?'

'Well, dad's going to pick me up at half-twelve, so can we say twelve?'

'OK.'

She grabbed me, planted a smacker on my forehead. 'I'll phone him now, he'll be chuffed.' She went to her office beaming. It made me feel pretty good, if I'm being honest.

On Saturday morning I tried to sit and watch *Swap Shop* in peace, but the brats were fighting. I wandered up to the shop a bit early; it was a bit more relaxed at weekends, you were allowed to wear more casual clothes. I never really had any decent stuff, usually waited until John was out the door then helped myself to his wardrobe, which was really up to date and fashionable. My wardrobe was 'basic', to put it mildly. A lot of brown things. I didn't believe in spending my hard earned cash on fashion. It was brilliant that we were the same height and build. Only a year between us.

When I got in Linda was ready to go.

'Looking pretty hot, Miss Fergus,' I said. She did too. She was always dressed in her EastPoint Photos garb, and she looked ordinary. But now, with make-up and some dinky rags, she looked do-able. As if I'd know! Jeez, nineteen and the closest I'd been to a naked lady was watching a hag on a pool table. I'd have to do something about the situation.

I was interrupted in my thoughts by a triple-beep of a car horn outside the window. A big black Jeep thingy sat there.

'Here's my dad now,' she said, waving to him to come in. 'I'll introduce you to him, he was happy as Larry when I told him that you'd agreed to stand in. Said he'd like to meet you 'it's unusual to get a well-mannered young fellow these days.' He said.

I felt the warmth of my action tingle nicely up my spine. As her dad climbed down from the step of the truck, the tingle turned into a jolt! A cattle prod jolt. A fingers in the plug socket jolt.

It was fucking Fergie from the barber's shop off Easter Road. If he saw me he'd kick seven different colours of crap out of me, he'd literally said so. I could remember the exact words he'd shouted up to me when we'd last met. Looking me straight in the eye, even though I was thirty feet up on a roof, his threat still carried.

'The next time we meet, you little cunt, I'll kick your arse so hard that when you cough it'll smell like shite.'

I ran down to the toilet, giving no explanation to Linda. Locked myself in. I heard her high heels clicking on the steps as she made her way down. She knocked on the door. 'Are you OK, Jimmy?'

'Yeah, sorry Linda,' I said, trying to make my voice sound strained. 'Diarrhoea. I had a Vesta chicken curry for breakfast, I think the chicken was off.'

'I didn't think there was any actual chicken in those curry's, you going to be alright?'

'Yeah, sure. You go, I'll be up in a minute.'

'OK,' she said, I heard her clumping upstairs.

I sat there hoping that Fergie hadn't clocked me. Even this far below the shop front I could hear the big pulsing roar of the Jeep's engine disappearing into the distance. I stuck my head out of the toilet door, crept up the wooden stairs from the basement, looked around like a penguin chick in an elephant seal colony. The coast was clear. I got behind the counter and realised I was shaking.

'Jesus H Christ!' I said, 'I did not see that one coming.' I stood with both hands on the counter, calming down, deep breaths, in through the nose, out through the mouth … in through the nose, out through the mouth …

'How are you feeling now?' Linda said. It was Monday, I'd calmed myself down; I figured that the threat of this happening had always been there. If he'd come in any other time I would have been done for. I was lucky, but I had to make sure that it would never happen again.

'I'm fine,' I said. 'My wee brother had the curry and the runs as well, must've been that. How was your birthday?'

'Och, it was great. Ended up at the Sheraton instead. My dad says he'll meet you next time.'

'What does he do for a living?' I asked.

'He's got a barber shop down Easter Road, I'm sure he'd do your hair for you, as a favour.'

'I might look into that, Linda, but I'm growing my hair now, thinking of getting into heavy metal.'

'Really?' She said, looking astonished.

'If he's ever picking you up again, let me know,' I said. Thinking I could do with the advanced warning. 'I'd like to shake his hand.'

She looked at me, paused. 'Yeah? Sure?'

Every Wednesday morning there was a grumpy old cow waiting at the shop door before we opened.

'Morning, Mrs Whitworth,' I'd say, as I pulled the metal shutters up. I was always the first one in Wednesdays, so had to open up.

'My photos in yet?'

'Sorry, Mrs Whitworth, you know the rules. I'm not allowed to speak to you until the shop is officially open and that's not for another four minutes.'

This had been going on for weeks. She'd said that I, me personally, had taken her Kodak 128 film from her, sent it off to the lab, therefore I was responsible for getting her prints back or giving her a full refund. It was rubbish, we had records of every transaction between customer and lab going back six years. Sure, some things did go missing, but we knew what was missing from our records and her prints were pure invention. I always took my time on Wednesdays.

After the shutters were up, I'd unlock the front door, then lock it behind me so that she couldn't get in, turn the alarm off, go and make a coffee in Linda's office. The frosted glass was a great veil. I'd sit there unit 9.02, then slowly wander up to the front door, fumbling with the keys, getting another two or three minutes out of it. I enjoyed it. It was a power thing, I loved pissing the old cow off. By this time I'd decided that I was going to look for another job. I was looking for things to do, have fun, this was getting more and more boring as the days went by.

I'd decided last week that Mrs Whitworth would never come back to the shop. Certainly not after this visit.

I let her in, walked round to my side of the counter, asked for her receipt.

'You know fine well I don't have a receipt,' she said, the fixative in her gritted false-teeth almost foaming with hatred for me.

'You did have a reference number, though, didn't you?' I said, pretending to flick through the pile of print packs, hundreds of jobs never yet collected.

'Yes. You know what it is.'

'Can you tell me again, please? We have hundreds of files here.'

'Three four six two,' she said, resigned to getting the same answer as always.

I flicked through the files and stopped, acting surprised. 'Well, well, well,' I said.

She jerked her head towards me. 'Pardon?'

'Looks like we owe you an apology, Mrs Whitworth,' I said, pulling a fat packet of photos from the pile. I wrapped it in a plastic bag with a sticky seal designed to stop the prints from falling out. 'This should keep the prints dry for you until you get home.'

She was animated. She went into her bag, pulled her purse out.

'Stop right there, Mrs Whitworth,' I said. 'It was our mistake, there will be no charge. And as a way of making up for this discrepancy, here are some rolls of film, on us.' I handed her four 128 spools that were duds; we used them for window dressing, but she'd have no clue if they were real or not. She never said thank you or uttered a word. Never even waved as she left the shop.

I'd grown sick and tired of her ugly mug. I'd decided to make it go away. I remembered the juice bottle shots had still not been collected, they'd lain in the drawer for such a long time that I knew nobody would pick them up. Even if they came for them and they were gone, what would they say when I asked them to describe the shots?

'Err … one had a juice bottle sticking up my wife's arse.'

I don't think so.

I'd made up a false pack with the reference number that she kept going on about and simply put the juice bottle pictures into it. I laughed for days at the thought of that old trout collapsing from her chair when she opened the packet up, even better if it was in front of her church cronies. I knew she wouldn't be back, either. Same scenario.

'Describe the pictures you received by accident to me, Mrs Whitworth.'
'Juice bottles arses and fanny's? Is that right? Can I have a look? Oh! These are disgusting, If you hold on I'll have to call the police, this sort of thing has to be reported...'

There was no chance of her returning, I was clear. This was great therapy, but it happened so infrequently, the good times were a coloured blip on my very flat, grey horizon.

CHAPTER 26

Y ou've got a good camera, haven't you?' Angela said to me one day when the two of us were on shift together.

'Yeah, not bad,' I said. 'Single Lens Reflex.'

'SLR?' She whistled. 'Any good with it?'

'Yeah, pretty good,' I lied. I still hadn't got round to testing it after that shutter malfunction.

'Do you do weddings?'

'Yeah, weddings, landscapes, animals, glamour, stuff like that,' I lied. 'I'm thinking of putting some stuff in for competitions,' I said, trying to impress her.

She was the fat one in the shop, decent enough, but I'd rather stay a virgin than do it with her. She was repetitive, fat and boring. I wanted to elevate and distance myself from people like her, people who were content to have a life that revolved around *East-enders* and *Coronation Street*, where having a job in a photo processing shop allowed your family to think you were doing well.

'Aye, our Angie? She's assistant manager now. Works aw they photy machines with computers and stuff, bright lassie, don't ye know.'

Big deal. It was a shite, boring job, with shite boring people. I couldn't stand it much longer. I felt my spirit was being pulled backwards through my arse. Every day I was getting flatter and flatter. Spotted a dead hedgehog on the roadside one morning, said, 'I know how you feel, pal.'

'Why do you ask, Angie?' I said.

'One of my pals is getting married, they cannae really afford a lot for photography and I said to her that I knew somebody who could mibbe do it cheaply.'

'How cheaply?' I said, knowing that if I fucked it up I could afford to at least give them their money back.

'Thirty quid?'

'Thirty quid? That is cheap,' I said. 'How many photos do they want?'

'Not many, mibbe twenty? Wedding, signing the paper, reception, and some family ones. How does that sound?'

'Can I think about it?'

'Aye, sure. Can you think about it before tomorrow?'

'When's the wedding?'

'Saturday.'

'This Saturday?'

'Yip.'

'The day after tomorrow?'

'Yip. Sorry,' she said, patting my arm. 'I should've said, I meant to ask you sooner.'

'OK, I'll tell you what,' I said, 'I'll go home, have a think about it and tell you in the morning.'

'Perfect,' she said. 'Thanks.'

'OK, Angie. I'll do it,' I said next morning as she walked through the front door.

Her face lit up. She ran around the counter, gave me a big hug.

'Brilliant,' she said. 'Pauline'll be chuffed, I'll go and phone her now.'

'How do I get the money from her?' I said. 'Do I get it today?'

'I think they're gonnae send a cheque. Do you have a name for your photography company?'

I hadn't even thought about that. She did have a point, though, in all those magazines I looked at, most of the good photos had a company name on them rather than an individual.

'How about JD Images?'

'That sounds good.'

We said it to each other a couple of times. Nodded.

'OK. JD Images it is,' I said.

I turned up on the Saturday at the registry office in Queen Street. The wedding was at three, so I got there an hour early to scout about, look at the best angles to shoot from. The one massive thing that worried me, though, was I'd forgotten which two settings on the camera didn't work. I was sure I'd remember when the time came, instinct kicking into action and all that. I'd brought a few things along to help me get good results. A brolly to reflect light onto the bride and groom, a baseball cap to keep the sun out of my eyes, and a tripod that I'd borrowed from somebody I didn't want to borrow it from as he was a creep. He had a train set in his attic with all the paraphernalia; stations, people, countryside, farmyard, plastic animals but the most worrying thing was that he'd painted pubes and red nipples onto a tiny model of a naked sunbather in a back garden.

'Realistic don't ye think pal?' He said to me when he first showed me.

'That's my back garden she's sunbathing in, no bad eh, bet you wish you could get burds like that tae sunbathe in your gairden eh?'

I knew there'd be consequences for borrowing the damned thing from him but I needed a tripod. The consequences could wait.

I'd completely forgotten to ask Angie the bride's name! I knew her first name was Pauline and thought it would be easy to find a Pauline getting married in Queen Street at three on this particular Saturday afternoon. Thankfully it was. As I walked about the vicinity of the registry office a car pulled up.

It was an ordinary car, not a limo or wedding car, it was dirty, hadn't been washed properly in quite some time, bumps and dents bits of rust on it. The door opened and an incredibly fat woman struggled out of the door; they must have covered her in butter and squeezed hard to get her in there. She got out, removed the veil from her face. Something deep inside me shuddered and I found myself backing away. I had no idea what it was.

I paused involuntarily while my brain ticked away;

working in the background, blowing dust from, pulling up, and comparing files from my dusty memory banks.

It speeded up rapidly as the next car pulled up. As soon as I saw the next person get out of the car my brain had completed the maths and linked the memories to the present moment. It was Paul Jackson. He'd obviously taken up weightlifting, he was huge. I was getting towards six feet tall, but a broom handle looked well-built compared to me. I estimated he'd doubled in size since we'd last met, maybe ten years ago when he and his sister Pauline had shouted abuse as the Divines had ridden out of Pilton. I was kind of relieved that the liquorice toffo hadn't killed her.

A lot of his income had been spent on Indian ink. He had more tattoos that I'd seen on any one person. He looked menacing. His dad, who was now fat, wrinkled and on walking sticks, got out from the other side of the car. I hurriedly went into my bag, pulled the baseball cap out. I stuck it on my head and was about to make my way past them, get out of the building. The memories of previous meetings surged to the front of my mind, the way Paul had punched me in the solar plexus brought back an involuntary tightening in my gut, Pauline lying on the ambulance stretcher gasping for air with an oxygen mask on. I had to move, now!

The groom spotted my camera, turned to speak to me.

'JD Images?' He asked. I couldn't say no. I knew if I bailed out after promising Angie, I'd be fired on the spot on Monday morning. I didn't want to be fired as that would mean no dole money for six months, I now had a lifestyle to maintain.

'Yeah,' I said, shaking his hand.

'I'm Boaby,' he said. 'Can I introduce you to Pauline, my bride?' He was holding hands with her as she yapped with her family.

'Not right now, pal, I have to do a recce to check out the best places for shots.'

He nodded. 'Beautiful, isn't she?'

Jeez, I thought to myself, *the only way I'd ever interlock fingers with that monster would be when I was lowering her over the edge of the Grand Canyon.*

I went upstairs to the toilet to try to figure things out. On my way back down I stopped on the floor above the registry room. There were offices and nobody was around. I checked some doors to see if I could get inspiration from somewhere. The third door was open. I walked in, closed it behind me, quietly.

The blinds were down and there was a hint of sunlight getting through, I saw that there were a couple of jackets hanging up on hooks behind the door. I searched the pockets of the jackets, came across a glasses case. I popped it open; a nice pair of heavy black glasses lay there. *Perfect*. I thought. I tried them on quickly, they fitted perfectly. I stuck them into my rucksack, headed downstairs. By the time I'd got there, most of the family had turned up. The only ones dressed up were the bride and groom, the rest of them looked like they'd come back from a Red-neck's Convention. I was praying that Andrews was not on the guest list, thankfully he didn't show. So far nobody had recognised me, but I still had the problem of standing in front of everyone, taking a lot of photos without being recognised. The groom peeled off from the rest of the party, cornered me. He'd turned pretty aggressive, made me think I'd been rumbled.

'Are you gonnae start takin the photies then, pal, or what?'

'Sorry, mate,' I said, trying to pacify him. 'I wasn't sure when you wanted me to start.'

'What the fuck are we payin you for if yer no gonnae take photos?' He said. 'Get it done.'

He stormed off into the registry room. The Red-necks piled into the office after him, sat on the mish mash of chairs, some sat on the tables that were scattered around the room. The registrar babbled on while I snapped away. After about ten minutes of this I realised that I'd forgotten to put a film into the camera.

Fuck! I thought, *I'll have to tell Angie a lie to get around that bit.* I went to the back of the room, hurriedly put in a film. I had put the heavy glasses on and pulled the peak of the baseball cap right over my face. Nobody would recognise me, I was sure. But I was also sure that I couldn't see a bloody thing. The glasses were not quite milk bottle jobs, but they weren't far off. When I looked through the viewfinder of the camera I could barely see anything. Thank Christ the fat cow was so big, because all I had to do was follow this big blue blurred shape around, point the camera in the general direction.

I hoped that the blurred image I was seeing was due to the glasses and not my focusing. The dodgy shutter problem? I was aware of it but hoped that at least some of the images would appear as full images.

Not one of the family approached me, never even asked my name, I was so glad about that. They seemed a real bunch of arseholes, time and wisdom had obviously failed to penetrate their brain's. They used that part of their anatomy as an internal pom-pom hat, keeping the inside of their skull toasty.

'Right, pal?' The groom walked towards me after the registry office shots had all been done. 'We're goin up to the Bonny Bridge for the reception. If you take, say, a dozen photos thair, you can huv the rest of the day off, a half-day. How does that sound?'

'Half day?' I felt like saying. *'I've been here for two and a half hours and you want me to keep going for another hour for thirty quid, ya tight fisted, trampy bastard.'*

'Aye that'll be fine mate,' I said. I thought about the poor guy in bed with that thing later on and felt sorry for him.

I knew where the pub was and frankly the choice did not surprise me one bit. If anything it was a bit too up-market for them.

'Oi, pal,' Boaby shouted over to me. 'Jump in the green car and the boy'll drop you off at the BB.'

'Nah, yer all right pal, I've got my own car here,' I lied. I'd rather have got into a car with an HIV positive leper with rabies and weeping sores than that lot. I jumped into a Joe, was prepared to lose some of the fee on that rather than get a lift. I'd contemplated jacking the gig in three times already, as we drove down Leith Walk I thought about it for a fourth time. The only thing that kept me on track was keeping my job.

When I walked into the pub an upside down face stared at me. The pole dancer winked at me as she removed her knickers, it was the first time I'd seen a lassie take her pants off up the way! Loud hypnotic music battered the glass bottles on the shelves and the beer glasses on the bar bounced in time. The clientele was so old I'd guarantee they spent more on Steradent than they did on deodorant. The pub was full of fag smoke, the old giffers were puffing away as if nicotine was oxygen. I thought about taking off there and then, I had no idea how much more of this utter joke I could take – I half expected Jeremy Beadle to pop out from the cake, shout something at me.

I wandered over to the corner, stood beside a table with a crudely folded A4 sheet of paper on it.

Reserved For Wedding Reception had been scrawled in two colours of ink, looked like the black pen had run out at the 'F' and somebody else with better handwriting had completed the job in blue ink. There was food on the table. I say 'food' in the loosest sense of the word. It was probably edible at some point in time. I looked at my watch for the tenth time in a few minutes. Where were they? I was hoping they'd given me the wrong pub name; I could go back to Angie with an honest reason for not getting the reception shots. 'Boaby told me to go to the Bonny Bridge, Angie, honest!' Deep down I knew this was the place, though. It was perfect for them.

I looked at the platter again, my stomach was getting angry at me. The triangular sandwiches were curling up at the edges like one of those magic fish that you got as a kid, a bit of red cellophane shaped like a goldfish that you put in the palm of your hand to tell your future. These sandwiches had similar fortune telling powers: 'Eat us and a trip to the hospital will be coming your way,' they said. They had a brown nicotine dusting on them as if they'd lain here all week. The sausage rolls looked like they'd pissed themselves, but on closer inspection they were sweating grease onto the paper napkins.

I'd noticed earlier that there was chippy next door, I nipped out and headed there for a chip roll. AJ's – Chippy of the Year Nominee 1975 – it said on the sign outside. *Must be pretty decent*, I thought.

I went through the door, a bell sprung into life. It looked a dump, but the commendation encouraged me to stick it out. A guy walked through with a bucket of peeled spuds. Never said a word to me.

'How long are the chips gonnae be, mate?' I said. He looked up; fag clinging to his bottom lip. He put his hand up, showed me his thumb and index finger, about three inches apart.

'Very good,' I said. 'Part time comedian, eh?'

He ignored the comment. I was so hungry that I had no option but to hold on until they were ready. I sat at the scruffy table in the corner, shoved the full ashtray and plates with fish and chip remnants onto the floor, flicked through a photography mag that I'd taken to the wedding with me, see if there were any tips I could pick up. A good twenty minutes later he was ready to serve me.

'Two chip rolls, plenty of brown sauce as well, please,' I said. He made them up, wrapped them in the traditional newspaper, handed them over.

'I'm no trying to be funny, pal, but I can see where you got your name from.'

'What are you talking about?' He said.

I threw the money at him. 'AJ's. Twenty minutes for a couple of chip rolls, yer having a laugh.'

'Fuck off then,' he said. I gave him the finger as I opened the door to leave the shop. He shouted, 'Fuck you,' as I went through the door.

'Nineteen seventy-five was a long time ago, pal,' I said. 'If I was you, I'd get some work done on my customer relations skills.'

A rolled up newspaper hit the door as I closed it. I could hear muffled obscenities.

I scoffed the rolls pretty quickly, went back to the bar, ordered an orange juice, straight from the bottle; I felt it was the safest option. The rolls did the trick, although I'd never admit it to the ignorant twat, they were delicious. As I was downing the orange juice, the door burst open, Boaby and Paul staggered in, pissed as a couple of farts.

I put the glasses and baseball cap back on, hid away at the back of the bar, kept out of sight until the rest of them got there. I couldn't wait to finish the job and bugger off, although the wait gave me time to think back to when we'd all lived in Pilton.

They were pretty well off compared to us, always had new clothes, the best toys and sports stuff. Their dad was pretty high up in Ferranti. Now he walked about on two walking sticks, had a permanent scowl, the old fucker looked like the chair he regularly sat on had a cattle prod built into it that zapped him every time he changed channels with his remote. He was always a bad old bastard, especially to me, I must admit, it was great to see karma paying him a visit. My mind wandered …

'Hey, Jimbo, how you doin, my man?'

'I'm fine, Karma, how are you?'

'Yeah, I'm doin real good, in fact you, my man, are about to see a whole lot more of me.'

'Yeah?'

'Yes, siree. I'm waiting on a whole big bag of payback bein delivered first class to Old Man Jackson,' he said, pointing up to the sky. 'As soon as it arrives I'll pop down, we'll go for a couple of jars and I'll get you a front row seat to let you watch the fucker suck it up. How does that sound?'

'Will it hurt?'

'Yeah, sure will. Your sides'll be aching,' he said, laughing. We high fived, he disappeared in a puff of something blue, smoke or dust or something.

I hid in the corner for a good fifteen minutes. By that time those two wankers had eaten most of the buffet, I could see a faint brown residue around their lips, almost boaked. They'd also consumed a good three quarters of the fizz that had been on the tray next to it. They'd been emptying the champagne flutes into pint glasses and glugging it down. There was no way that it was champagne.

They were too pissed to understand what was going on and grabbed at the leftovers, eyelids barely staying open.

It was obvious that something major had happened with the rest of the party. It'd been almost an hour and a half since they tied the knot, the pub was only fifteen minutes away from the registry office. I couldn't fathom what the problem could be.

Paul always loved Pauline. If you said even the slightest negative thing about her, he'd be on you like a ton of bricks, pummelling your head into the ground, I knew this from experience. Yet this guy must've insulted her horrendously for her not to turn up at her own wedding reception, yet here the two of them were. There was no point in wasting any more time thinking about it. I decided to leg it.

I got outside, had a good look around, making sure there was none of the wedding party about to come into the pub. I walked in the direction I came from so that I could at least tell Angie I went looking for them. Thankfully, no one appeared, I was on my way home.

'Well, how was the blushing bride?' Angie said to me excitedly when I'd been in the shop a nanosecond on Monday morning.

'Yeah,' I said.

'Did you take some great shots?' She wasn't even listening to me, she was too busy rattling through her own questions.

'Yeah, got some good ones.'

'It was a lovely sunny day, wasn't it?'

'Yeah, lovely,' I replied inanely.

'I can't wait to see the shots; have you got the spools there?' She said, holding her hand out to me. I dug around in my rucksack, pulled out four spools. I'd only taken one spool's worth of pics, but wanted to make it look as if I'd taken hundreds of shots.

I made a mental note to call Gazza to delay the delivery until Angie's day off. That way I could filter the results, pretend I'd selected and edited the best ones, which would explain the low number of shots.

I waited till Angie buggered off to Linda's room for the usual Monday morning soap catch up chat, then got straight on the phone.

'Hi, Gaz, Jim here. When you pick the delivery up from us this morning, any chance of delaying the delivery of my spools until Thursday?'

'Sure pal, no problemo. Any reason?'

'Yeah,' I whispered the story, keeping an eye out for movement from Linda's office. I heard him creasing himself on the other end. 'Seriously, Gaz, my tail'll be in the vice if this goes tits up, could be the end of the line. She is a seriously stroppy young Ermintrude when she doesn't get her own way.'

'I'll get it delivered straight into your mitts Thursday a.m.' He said.

'THEY WHAT?' Angie screamed at me next day.

'They lost the spools,' I said, holding my hands to my forehead, faking concern.

'Oh my absolute God!' She said, pacing about the front of the shop. 'Pauline'll go ballistic.'

I pretended to dial Gazza again.

'Nah, still engaged, Angie,' I said, my hidden finger sitting comfortably on the phone rocker, pressing on the buttons to ensure it stayed engaged. She rabbited on about something, I lifted my finger from the rocker. She was away to say something to me, but I put her gas at a peep with a raised finger. I spoke into the handset. 'Gazza? Yeah, uhu, mmhm …' Pretend conversation. 'What's that? You've found the spools?'

I gave her a thumbs up, she actually jumped up and down, stuffing her fists into her mouth.

'Excellent work, Gazza,' I said to a dead phone. 'Where were they? The boss's dog? Really? Wow, that was lucky then. Here's hoping the spools that you recovered were the good ones. Yeah, see you later.'

I hung up. Her face had sagged again, looked like her facial muscles had buggered off somewhere more interesting.

'Dog?' She said. 'What dog?'

'Gazza said that when he picked the bags up from me this morning, Mr Lindsay, his boss, asked if he'd take Jake in the van as he was looking after him while Mrs Boss was on holiday or something. It seems Jake had a chew at the bags while Gaz went into the different branches on his rounds. Jake must've bitten a hole into our bag, a few of the spools went missing. Mr. Lindsay's taking him to the vet this afternoon for an X-ray, see if he's swallowed any.'

'But the X-ray'll ruin the films,' she said, eyebrows creeping up to her hairline. I was glad she'd put two and two together.

'Nothing we can do about it,' I said. 'Got to hope it's not my films.'

The Lost Tornado

Thursday morning arrived, the door crashed open.

'Delivery for Mr D,' Gazza shouted through to the back office where I was standing with a hot teabag finely balanced on a very small teaspoon.

'Time for a Rosie Lee, Gaz?' I shouted.

'Nah, sorry pal, no rest for the wicked,' he said, as he dumped a big brown box onto the counter. I popped my head out of the door, waved to him as he disappeared, gulped my drink down, strode meaningfully over to the counter.

I opened the box, raked around a bit, took out my single packet of prints. There were another three packets addressed to me, but they were the blank spools that I'd stuck in for effect. I only got charged for the prints that actually came out, benefits of the job and all that. I removed the blanks, threw them straight in the bin, then quickly scanned through the main packet.

'FUCK!' I looked away, disgusted at the lack of quality. I lifted my hands, covered my face in a gesture of resignation. I was racking my brains for a way out of this exceptionally tight spot. I thought about trying to contact Harry Houdini in the afterlife, but he was on another call, even he'd be struggling to find a way out of this.

Angie would be back in tomorrow morning and if I couldn't find a good reason to explain to her why those photos were so shite, I'd have thirty quid to pay back and probably get my jotters.

That night I worried myself to sleep. Woke up next morning, wandered into the bathroom, put my face up to the mirror and took a look. I was a real mess, bags under both eyes, hair wouldn't stay down. I kept licking my hands and slapping the saliva up there, but it wasn't interested, I could virtually hear the boing! As the big chunk of hair popped up again. My mind wandered off again, must have been the stress …

'You've always had a coo's lick,' my Nana said to me, time and time again. To be honest I get pissed off at the state of my hair. A couple of years ago when Bowie was all the rage, I wanted his hairstyle, like all my mates had. I used three cans of hairspray within an hour on the little bastard and the nearest I got to looking like Bowie was the different coloured eyes, one red with rubbing the hairspray out of it, the other yellow with the pus from the stye I'd developed! My hair looked more like Jim Bowen than David Bowie. It took my mum months to get my pillow cleaned properly and the dandruff I got from it was horrendous. If I sat in class with my black jotter on the desk, I only had to lean over slightly and in no time it would tumble from my scalp resembling the opening scene from *Star Trek*!

The thinking didn't get me away from the dilemma, though. I couldn't think of a single, believable excuse to give to Angie. My brain hurt. I resigned myself to the fact that I'd be sacked. They'd find some reason to boot me out.

I knew I was eye candy for them at the start, but when they realised I had a brain with a fully charged battery pack, it kept them at bay, put a barrier up between us. Not a sophisticated gender or socio-political barrier, more of a TV barrier; they liked soaps, I didn't. It was all they talked about and the main reason for my boredom and desire to leave at a point of my choosing. At times, when the three of them were deep in conversation about Dirty Den, Ena Sharples or Benny from *Crossroads*, I honestly could have taken a Polaroid camera from the display cabinet, performed the world's first Instant Colonoscopy™ on them.

If I showed them the results they'd probably have thought they were stills from the shows, they were so used to looking at shite.

I got in exceptionally early Friday morning. Had the photos sitting on the top of the counter waiting for Angie to look at and go mental. Never bothered to unpack my rucksack as I knew I'd be on my way out of the door in no time.

Half nine, still no sign of her.

'Linda?' I shouted through to the back office. 'Is Angie in today?'

'No. She's taking the day off, one of her pals tried to commit hari kari last night.'

'Which pal?' I said, ears pricking up.

'Pauline. In fact, was that not the lassie whose wedding photos you were taking?'

'Fell on her harpoon, did she?' I said under my breath.

'What was that?' Linda said.

'Married too soon,' I said, amazed in general, at the power of women's hearing. 'And yeah, I did. Took them on Saturday. What happened?'

'Apparently, on the way to the reception, she found out her fiancé was sleeping with somebody else. Went mental, chucked him out of the car.'

'Jeez, I've got the prints here,' I said, seeing a glimmer of opportunity popping its head over the horizon. 'What should I do with them?'

'If it was me, I'd want to burn them.' Linda said.

'Do you think I should?' I said. 'Say yes, say yes,' I was whispering, trying to encourage her.

'Yeah,' she said. 'If she sees them, all it'll do is bring back bad memories and who knows where that'll lead.'

'I agree,' I said, 'and if they patch things up, they'll probably want to do the service and reception all over again to make amends. Think so?'

'Yeah, it's what I'd do,' she said, now walking through to the shop with a coffee for me. As she walked over I took the prints from the packet, ripped them in half. I put the negatives through the shredder, took my coffee, gulping a sweet, warm draught. It tasted like nectar, I knew victory was said to taste sweet, but this was relief-victory, a rare phenomenon for me.

'Will you explain to Angie?' I said.

'Being her boss and all?

Of course I will,' she said. 'You know something, you're a really thoughtful young man at times.' She looked at me, I wasn't sure what she was thinking but her eyes lingered long enough to get my undercarriage squeaking a bit. I took another gulp, felt magic.

Mr Karma was right, the delivery must've arrived and he'd delivered it to me big time.

'Thanks, Mr K,' I said, under my breath, looking upwards.

'Don't be too hasty now there, boy,' he said. 'You know how I work.'
'Cool,' I said.
'Just appreciating you.'

Linda walked into her office, then came back out as if she'd forgotten something.

'Oh, by the way Jimmy,' she said, 'I'm on holiday next week, for a fortnight, off to Mallorca with my mum, so my Dad'll be coming in to cover for me.'

I could hear the distant echo of Mr Karma laughing at me.

I spent that whole weekend wondering and worrying. There was no way I could avoid her dad at such close proximity. I thought about a disguise, but to keep it up for two weeks would be impossible. I didn't want to resign as the dole money would be out of my reach for too long a time. After a lot of deliberation I chose the route to my destiny.

I had a week to get myself laid off. There was a very fine line between the options of losing your job and being able to claim.

I'd had the Saturday off to go to watch the Hibbies. A great win over the Jambos ensued, but I didn't really enjoy it, the scent of future poverty threatened, I didn't like it one bit.

Monday morning and the first surprise of the day grabbed me by the bollocks. The front door of the shop was open, the place looked ready for business a good hour before it was meant to be. I walked in, Linda was pacing around in her office, I could see her silhouette behind the frosted glass, knew the way she walked. As I crossed the threshold, the bell at the front door alerted her; she came through, still with her overcoat on, a worried look on her face.

'What's up, Linda?' I said.

'Ah, good.' She said, 'I'm glad you came in early.'

'What's up?' I said again.

'Bad news,' she said.

I was hoping her auld man had popped his clogs, could Mr K Be looking after me again.

'Is it your dad?' I said, feigning concern.

'No. It's you,' she said.

This really threw me.

'Me?'

'Yes. Mrs Whitworth came in on Saturday afternoon.'

'Oh?'

'She said you'd given her some pictures.'

I put my hand to my chin, looked up as if trying to remember. 'Must have been an accident,' I said.

'JIMMY!' She said, 'you can stop there. I know for a fact that those photos were locked up, there is no way they could've been given out by accident.'

'Was she upset?'

'Of course she was. So much so that she had a policeman with her.'

'Shit!' I said, putting my forehead into my hands. Had I gone too far this time?

'It's OK,' she said. 'She's not going to press charges. I got her onside by offering her free spools and processing for a year. The policeman told me she'd sat in her chair for three hours in total shock after opening the packet you gave her. Her daughter found her shaking uncontrollably. It was her daughter that wanted to press charges, but you're lucky the police were on the side of common sense.'

At this point Linda began to laugh. I joined in.

'I'm really sorry, Linda, but she was doing my head in for weeks and weeks.'

I went to take my rucksack off and head to the changing room when she stopped me.

'There was another part to the deal,' she said. 'We have to terminate your contract.'

'Terminate? What does that mean?'

'Your job is gone, you can no longer work here,' she said, sticking out her bottom lip.

'How long do I have?' I asked.

'I spoke to the boss, he's happy to pay you for this week and give you a month's pay in lieu. You finish now. I'm really sorry. I've written you a great reference letter; might help you get another job, you've got a lot to offer.'

She handed me a white envelope, shook my hand and I was gone.

Was it a victory? I wasn't sure, but at least on Monday I could sign on. I was sure I could hear a faint chuckle somewhere in the background.

'Karma, you can be a real arse at times'. I whispered.

CHAPTER 27

On Stevie Maxwell's seventeenth birthday, two days after he'd passed his driving test, his uncle Guppy turned up with a gift. This heap of junk of a car that was held together with light blue Dulux paint that had been hastily applied to it by his shaky hand. It looked drivable-ish.

We were desperate to get out of Claremont Court, had ambitions to see the world. So in spite of the state of the thing, it looked like it could possibly function as a car. Our first driving adventure was going to be a trip to Lilliesleaf, a small village in Scotland's border country where we'd been a couple of times with the Boy's Brigade; most of the guys from the Court joined when we found out we could all play in the same football team and get a free strip.

The car was an absolute heap but it was either that or the bus, and four hours of bussing it and walking with heavy rucksacks on our backs was not an option.

We set off after everyone had finished work on the Friday evening, around five thirty, it took forty minutes of arguing before we agreed who should sit in the front passenger seat Alex wanted it but Higgy demanded it. This was going to be a long, painful weekend I was desperate to get moving as it was the beginning of the World Cup, the big match was on at eight. We packed my famous orange tent, which had been used by a few of the guys over the years, some pals and some pals of pals of pals. I hadn't looked at the tent in a long time, but I opened the carry bag, and sniffed, it smelled OK. We packed the boot with provisions, sleeping bags, a few beers and a cassette recorder.

Just because Stevie had passed his driving test, we soon realised, did not necessarily make him a good driver. After a few hairy moments down the A7 we got to our camp-site around half seven, the camp-site was actually a football field, which had previously been a ploughed field, it brought back great memories of the BBs vs the village football match for me, scoring that beauty of a header for the opening goal. The pitch had more undulations than a square metre of cheap jumbo cord carpet, wasn't ideal for lying on, even though we had sleeping bags and straw mats.

Alex had an airbed, he was posh compared to the rest of us, he only had one sibling; Suzanne while we had 22 between the three of us. He was going to be immune to undulations, as he reminded us time and time again, smirking.

The field was about half a mile from the main village, my one concern as we approached it was that there was a small narrow bridge spanning the river, I wasn't too confident that Stevie could make it. As we approached, he drove the car towards the bridge, he was moving slowly, losing control a bit, he braked suddenly. It had been raining the whole day, the car slid on the slimy wooden slats. Stevie fought the wheel for control and lost, ending up leaving two wheels over the edge. At one point we thought we were going to tumble over the edge, prepared for the impact, but thankfully something stopped us. Three of us got out, tried to lift the car back onto the bridge.

It was too heavy, we were slipping in the muddy stream. As we tried and tried to lift it, bits of the bodywork were coming away in our hands, blue paint was running between our fingers. It mustn't have dried properly from Guppy's hatchet paint job. Stevie tried a few times to get the car going again, but the result was a horrible grinding noise coming from the axle and exhaust pipe. We abandoned it on the bridge. It was now pretty dark, we hadn't even got into the field to set our tent up!

We removed everything from the boot, left the car sitting precariously on the bridge, trudged over to the field, feet sodden, began to set up the tent. We could hardly see, the obvious thing to me was to use the car headlights, they provided a superb floodlight system. As we couldn't move the car, we set the tent up directly where the headlights were pointing. Ingenious, job done. We got the tent pitched without any problems, the four of us working like a dedicated team. After the tent was up, our accommodation was looking hunky dory, we walked along to the pub in the rain but worth it, as the drinks were really cheap compared to Edinburgh. The World Cup was on in Argentina, although Ally's Tartan Army had long since surrendered.

The Cross Keys had no telly but good lager, while the Plough Inn had a telly but crap lager; good blackcurrant and Pernod though. Alex and I got absolutely hammered, Stevie was blootered and Higgy was miraculous. We had spent half as much as we would have on an ordinary Saturday night in town, yet here we were staggering up and down the village, looking for food and local talent. We kept going from the Cross Keys to the Plough Inn. Alex and I didn't think we were too bad – we could at least walk without the aid of support and could hold a decent conversation.

Higgy was beginning to sing the kind of songs that you'd expect his dad to sing; *Some Enchanted Evening, Blue Moon, The Street Where You Live*! We'd never even heard of these songs and we were older than him. He was so set in his ways that you knew he'd have his own bunnet and tartan slippers before his twenty-first birthday. He began to stagger all over the place, I think his brain was telling him that he was on the good ship Venus in a force twelve! He swayed all over the road from Haldane's grocery store to the Co-op and back again.

As we passed the swing park I could see he was going down. Alex and I ran over, grabbed him, held him up, just in time. We walked along the road for a while, Higgy was never the lightest of guys. After a few minutes his weight was beginning to take its toll. I stopped for a breather, shoved the bulk of the weight onto Alex. Unfortunately we both chose to do this at precisely the same time with the result that nobody was holding him up. I glanced around to see Higgy plummeting face down towards the pavement in slow motion. It was too late to stop him.

The local council had very recently laid tarmac which hadn't quite set; the cones, bollards and 'do not walk on tarmac' signs were obliterated in the crash. Alex and I looked at each other, feeling guilty. We untangled him from the crash site and I noticed there was something different about his mouth. SHIT!

His two front teeth were gone, they had sunk into the tarmac and snapped off. This brought Alex and I to our senses immediately. We searched in the dark for Higgy's teeth but could only come up with a few of those white stones that they put in new tarmac. The orange lampposts fizzed overhead as they were splattered by the rain. His teeth were gone, we handed two of the biggest white stones we could find to Higgy, he fumbled them into his back pocket, oblivious to any discomfort. We managed to drag him back to the field; getting him over the five bar fence was a struggle, only once catching his bollocks on the barbed wire.

The next morning I was first to get up. It was still raining, it sounded, judging by the pounding on the tent, like it wouldn't stop. The straw mats and groundsheets were soaking. I looked up, noticed about fifty small holes in the roof of the tent. They were all the same size. I was scoobied. The rain was pouring in through them.

'Higgy,' I said, 'wake up.'

He came to, rather groggily. He'd been lying on the plastic groundsheet the whole night and had been sick a few times. He sat up, his hair was standing up straight, completely flat and shiny on one side, dyed purple with the Pernod and blackcurrant, which had set rock hard as it had mixed with his vomit. He had blood all around his mouth. Reminded me of the lead singer from The Cure. He put his hands to his head as if trying to support its weight, then rubbed his eyes.

My beautiful tent was ruined, I was blazing. I'd saved up long and hard for it many years ago, it was our passport to free accommodation, and had been for a long time, now it was finished. I roared at him.

'You were the last one to borrow this tent, it was in perfect condition when I gave it to you. How did all these holes get here?'

There was no reaction from him. He was still coming to.

'Well?'

'Well what?'

'My tent. Who ruined it?'

'I gave a loan of it to Paul O'Neill a few munthththth ago,' he said.

As soon as he said this he put his hand to his mouth. 'What the fuck? What happened to my fuckin teef?'

'Why did you do that?' I said.

'Fuck your stupid tent, what about my teef?'

'Higgy,' I said, 'you better tell me who did this or I'll drag you out into that shitty rain and fucking drown you.'

'Paul told me that you said he could borrow it.' He said dabbing blood from his mouth onto his sleeve.

'And you believed him?'

'I didn't think,' said Higgy, examining the rest of his mouth.

'You fell flat on your face last night, ya fat drunken bastard, we had a look for your teeth but couldnae find them.' Said Alex, from under his duvet. He was laughing.

'Did Paul tell you he put holes in my tent?' I said.

' I forgot to tell you,' Higgy said, getting annoyed with me.

'He told me that one of his pals was getting really fed up with the flies buzzing around the tent, so he shot them with his air rifle. Where are my fuckin teef?'

'What?' I shouted in utter disbelief. 'How he shot flies in my tent with an air rifle? You better tell him to get me a new tent.'

'Tell him yourself,' said Higgy.

'You were the one that gave it to him.'

'I'm not tellin him, fuck off. Has anybody got a painkiller?'

'I think the shop opens in a while,' said Stevie. Who was sitting on his sleeping bag reading a joinery magazine. 'We can go up and get some rolls at the same time.'

'You better get me a new tent, Higgins.'

'Piss off.'

'Piss off yourself.'

'Fuck off'.

'You fuck off.'

There was a scream from the corner as Alex got up from his camp bed.

'What the fuck's happened to my new Ralph Lauren polo shirt?' Alex lifted up his white polo shirt and wrung the dripping orange rainwater from it. It was covered in orange streaks from the leaking tent.

'Right, Higgins, you're buying me a new fuckin polo shirt. I only bought this thing after work yesterday, forty fuckin quid down the fuckin drain.'

He threw the shirt at Higgy's face, Higgy threw it straight back at him, covering his head with the soggy mess. It now had blood from Higgy's face on it as well as purple sickness and orange dye.

'Fuck you, Higgins. I want a new shirt delivered to my door on Monday.'

'I'll be at the fuckin dentist on Monday ya daft prick' he screamed. 'And you can go and fuck yerself, it wasn't my fault you left your fuckin poof's T-shirt on the floor.'

'It's a polo shirt, you thick fucker, if you hadn't given the tent to that wee twat O'Neill it would've been alright.' Alex stormed out of the tent, tripped over one of the guy ropes on the outside. The ping sent a shower of orange rainwater down on top of us.

'Fuck off, you!' He shouted at the guy rope.

There was silence for a long time. Squeaks of hunger came from bellies. Breakfast time was leaking into lunchtime. We wandered into the village, bought a few rolls, some Dairy Lea triangles and some Askit powders from the shop. Big Haldane, the owner, eyed us suspiciously, followed us around, aware that we used to steal from his shop when we were younger. Nobody was in any mood to have this twat following us. We split up just to annoy him. Everyone of us stole something, not because we needed to, but because we wanted to prove we were still smarter than him.

After eating we were pretty bored; the swing park no longer held the thrill that it had a year or two earlier and the pub didn't open for another six hours. We spent half an hour looking at the white stones in the daylight, trying to spot Higgy's teeth.

The Lost Tornado

'Let's go to Hawick,' I said.

I had woken up that morning with a thumping headache. I'd mixed lager with Pernod, cider and blackcurrant, which tasted all right at the time. I wasn't sure if that is what caused the headache or if it was the undulations in the field, my spine felt like it had quick-setting concrete poured into it.

I'd nicked a packet of Askit Powders from the shop, but they proved difficult to take in a 'non-domestic' environment, so I stuck them in my pocket for later on, when we could get to a café in Hawick, I'd use a teaspoon and a glass of water to administer the medicine.

Before we headed for Hawick I had an ingenious idea after spotting some tattie sacks behind the pavilion. As the guys were heading to the car I put the sacks over the tent, in my imagination, what would happen would be this:

'OK God, that's the last of the rain due for Lilliesleaf today'.

'Cheers Genevieve doll', I'll just beam some intense sunlight down on those two tattie sacks on the top of that wee orange tent in the field there'.

'Think you could maybe add some of those special tent-repair drops in there as well, the boys could do with a wee break?'

'For you dear, anything'. Zap!

As I walked to the car, smiling at my ingenuity and thinking how pleased the guys would be on our return, I noticed the Askit powder packet was wet, my top must've still been wet from last night. I went into the supplies box in the tent, emptied the white powder into a bit of cling film, rolled it up, then stuck it in my clean shirt pocket. After a bit of effort we managed to get the car back onto the bridge. Things were looking up. Stevie turned the key in the ignition. Silence. Nothing. He had left the lights on from pitching the tent last night, now the battery was flat.

'Fuckin great,' said Alex. 'What are we supposed to do now? You're such a fuckin moron, Maxwell.'

'Don't blame me, ya fuckin stick insect. Keep yer bad mood to yourself. It wasn't my fault your T-shirt got ruined. I'll drive you to Hawick just because I want peace and quiet, but I'll chin you if you start any crap with me.'

Alex knew that Stevie was stronger than him so he shut up. We traipsed along to the garage in the village, managed to get the mechanic to sell us a second hand battery. Eventually after getting the heavy battery back to the field and fitting it we headed for Hawick. Stevie put the radio on it was Bill Withers singing *Lovely Day*. Ha!

We got into the Safeway car park in Hawick about ten. It was empty except for a group of decorative gypsy caravans and a couple of silver Mercedes cars. We went for a coffee at the supermarket. Bland, tasteless, like the people in the shop. My headache was getting worse, it seemed to thump with every beat of my heart. We gulped the coffee down, got a few supplies, headed back to the car. I got there first, jumped into the front seat, pulled the Askit powder from my top pocket, unsure how to swallow it because I'd completely forgotten about it in the café and I didn't have a teaspoon or any liquid. I unwrapped it.

'Where are we going now?' Stevie said.

'You're the driver,' Higgy said. 'Can we see if there's an emergency dentist here? My mooth's on fire.'

'I know I'm the driver, Higgy, but I can't think of anywhere to go. We're definitely not going to a dentist, though, this is meant to be a holiday. For fuck's sake.' He slammed both hands onto the steering wheel.

While these guys were getting more and more frustrated at each other, my head was pounding, I decided to down the powder in a oner without any kind of liquid accompaniment. I opened the cling film up, shaped it nicely to tip into my mouth when WHAM!! Stevie reversed the car straight into one of the gypsies' Mercs.

'Fuck!' He said, and drove forward – straight into the fence at the front of the car park, smashing both front and back bumpers within a few seconds. 'Fuck, fuck, fuck!' He said, thumping the steering

The Lost Tornado

wheel.

Alex was pissing himself laughing in the back seat. I was sitting there with white Askit powder all over my black Gary Numan shirt. Stevie regained control, did a three-sixty in order to make an escape, relieved that there was nobody in the caravans. There was a small boy playing with a skateboard under his arm. He stood there pointing at us. Stevie rolled the window down.

'What the fuck are you lookin at?'

'I saw you boys takin the drugs,' he said. 'I'm gonnae tell the polis. And you crashed the caur.' His eyes were popping out of his head.

Stevie turned the car around, headed straight for the guy.

'What do you think you saw?' He said.

'You smocked into that muckle caur, and that boy there was taking drugs' he said. Pointing to me.

Stevie got out of the car, grabbed him by the lapels of his denim jacket.

'If you tell anybody about this, I swear I'll come back here and give you a fuckin kickin, ye hear me?'

'I hear ye, mister,' he said.

Alex wound the window down.

'Oi, come here', he shouted at the boy.

'Here's a quid, if anybody asks what happened, you saw nothing. OK?'

'You got it mister'.

Stevie got back into the car, we headed back to Lilliesleaf.

The boy still stood there with his skateboard under his arm, mouth open, pointing at us.

Back at Lilliesleaf we went to the village shop, picked up a couple of family size tins of tomato soup and were again followed all around the shop and back to the counter by Haldane.

'Get a fuckin life Haldane.' Alex said.

'Right Chambers, you're banned, for two weeks'.

Alex gave him the finger.

We drove back to the field, smoothly over the bridge and out of the car.

'Where's the fuckin tent?' Higgy shouted.

Shit, my plan had not worked as well as it should have. There was no tent, only a pile of soggy tattie sacks in the place where we'd left the tent.

'What the fuck's happened?' Said Higgy.

I said nothing.

'Looks like somebody's sabotaged our camp,' Alex said, 'I bet it was that fuckin Speeder. Saw me bagging off with his sister last night.'

'Well, whatever happened, it looks like the tent's fucked, fit for the bucket now,' said Higgy.

'What about our clothes?' Said Alex. 'They'll be fucked.'

'Would you shut the fuck up about your clothes,' Stevie said. 'All we're doing is arguing. This is a fucking shite camp'.

We looked at each other; it had been crap, wet and painful for us. We had to make a decision: go home or stay. To be honest, the weather was clearing up a bit by then, there was a possibility that the sun would come out. We decided to give it a couple of hours, then make the decision.

I walked over to the sports pavilion, tried the door handle and window locks to see if we could get in, but it was no use. Stevie picked up a stone, put it through the window. He cleared the glass a bit and climbed through. There were some football benches, the long ones that we used to get in PE. It would make a nice steady surface to put the gas canister and the pot with the soup on. Alex was the cook for the day. The rest of us were bringing the soggy clothes from the tent into the pavilion. It took a bit of time as our only entrance and exit was through the broken window. This had given us a bit of solace, we played cards before lunch.

Thirty minutes later Alex was getting frustrated, we were all getting hungry, the soup was still not even lukewarm. Someone suggested that we have a kick about until the soup heated up. We played a couple of games of crossing and penalty kicks which helped to keep us from thinking about eating. After about another half hour Higgy went over to see if the soup was warm enough. He stepped through the window, onto one side of the bench, there was a huge crashing noise, Alex, Stevie and I ran over. There was tomato soup everywhere, except none where it really mattered, in the pot.

'You must be the fuckin clumsiest prick in the world,' shouted Alex. 'How the fuck did you not realise what would happen?'

'I forgot that the soup was there.'

'Remind me again why you were going into the pavilion?' Said Alex.

Higgy said a sheepish, 'Sorry, lads,' and went about cleaning up.

By teatime, we had to make a decision on whether we stayed or went home. By now it had turned into quite a pleasant evening. Everyone was still talking to each other, I think the football had acted like some binding tonic. Football was one of our main interests; we were all big Hibs fans.

After a few pints and a fantastic pub dinner it was getting pretty dark when we headed back to camp. As we walked from the Cross Keys to the camp field it dawned on me that we didn't actually have a camp. The only option was to put all the benches in the pavilion together to make a long bed. We unzipped all of our sleeping bags, joined two together, making a big duvet thing that would cover us all. This lasted about ten minutes, it was so uncomfortable, we kept falling off the benches. I sat up, asked if anyone fancied a hot drink, boiled some water for hot chocolate. We had discovered after the pub that there had been a working cooker in the pavilion the whole time. By midnight we were all getting tired and restless, Stevie figured that we could all sleep comfortably in his car. I'd figured that out, too, but given the result of my last thought I'd kept quiet.

All four of us got into the car, wrapped our sleeping bags around us, attempted to sleep. There was no chance, it was far too small for four guys with an average height of six foot. After an hour of fidgeting and moaning, Alex piped up.

'This is shite,' he said.

'Fuck it,' said Stevie, 'I'm going home.'

'You can't drive,' I said. 'You've had three pints and two Pernod and blackcurrants; what if you get caught?'

'I'll drive carefully.'

I knew that this really was the only solution, it would be great to end this hellish weekend at home, in a nice cosy bed. I knew that if he was caught driving he would be banned for years, but selfishly I encouraged him. Stevie took his time as he drove the car back over the bridge, faultlessly this time.

Higgy got out, closed the gate behind us.

'Thank Christ this is over,' he said.

As Stevie drove along the small dirt track that led to the main village road, there was a thump, sounded like it came from the bottom of the car; I presumed it was the exhaust pipe hitting the long grass. We continued over the ruts and bumps when there was an even bigger thump. Immediately the car sounded like a formula one racing car. The whole exhaust had been ripped from underneath. The accident at the bridge must have done so the damage.

Stevie got out of the car, booted the left wing a couple of times. 'This is a fuckin heap of crap,' he said. 'Why did I trust that fuckwit Guppy to get me a fucking car?'

He waited a few moments, then gave it another three sharp, fast kicks. It was now one fifteen on Sunday morning. We were cold and tired, my headache had returned. Alex got out of the car, still wrapped in the sleeping bags. He shone a torch along the path we'd just taken, walked back along, dragged the exhaust, dumped it next to the car.

'We need something to tie it back on with,' I said.

'The guy ropes from your tent?' Said Higgy. 'That's about all it's good for now.'

At times I really resented that guy. He did have a point though.

Stevie sat in the car, staring ahead, trying to sober up, while the three of us unpacked the boot, pulled out the soaking tent. I cut four of the guy ropes from it, threw the rest of the canvas into a field. Alex pulled a soggy coloured mass from his bag, threw it next to the discarded tent.

'No chance of ever getting that clean,' he said as he threw his polo shirt away.

"I'll take twenty quid Higgins, tomorrow morning.' He said.

'Two words. Second one off.' Higgy replied.

I managed to tie the exhaust up. I was crap at tying knots, that was the main reason I wore slip-on shoes, figured that if I created a massive bunch of them the exhaust might stay in place. It meant that we had to drive at max, fifteen miles an hour all the way home. We didn't want to draw attention to ourselves by roaring through the quiet border towns at such an ungodly hour, given that it still sounded like an F1 car. After all Stevie was still inebriated and under age!

A long, painstaking, silent journey followed, when we eventually got back to Edinburgh, my stomach was really playing up, I'd been through a failed attempt with the Askit powders in the car park, so I took another one a bit later, it made no difference, my head ached and my stomach was churning.

As we got closer to home my stomach was getting squelchier by the mile. In normal circumstances I would have taken a dump in the woods, but we were not confident that the car would restart. When we got to Claremont Court I searched hurriedly for my key, it was nowhere to be found, I figured I'd dropped it whilst under the car. I was desperate.

'Give me your key,' I said to Stevie. He gave me his front door key, I ran as fast as I could up three flights of stairs, opened his front door, ran upstairs to the toilet. I ripped open my jeans, the buttons went flying, I didn't care.

I was sitting there on the pan, squirming, sounded like I'd managed to swallow a roll of diarrhoea filled bubble wrap.

Every time I moved a muscle there was a loud pop or two followed by the sound of running liquid. I was glad that everybody was asleep.

After what must have been ten minutes of this Stevie's big brother got up from his bed, which was next door to the bathroom, grabbed me by the arm, I was dripping at my back-end as he threw me out of the house, trousers around my ankles.

I ended up spending the night in Higgy's bathroom, sleeping on the toilet pan! The next day my stomach was a bit better but my arse felt like it had been dabbed with chilli-infused bog roll.

The next day I invited the guys up to our house to watch the quarter finals of the World Cup. Argentina were looking amazing, Holland looked like they could do something this time. As usual we were going on about 'what if Scotland had done this or that'. It was always the same. We had never got out of the first round ever!

'Fuckin Peru?' Alex said.

'Fuck fuckin Peru, what about drawing wi Iran?' Higgy said.

We walked over to the tuck shop to get some supplies for the big game, then headed back to my house.

When I pushed the living room door, it only opened a fraction. I pushed again, but it would go no further. I got the guys to help me shove it open, as it opened newspapers were being shredded underneath the door by the force. We walked in, there in the middle of the floor was a car engine.

The guys pissed themselves at the sight. The auld man walked through from his room, wiping his hands on an oily rag. He'd obviously been drinking.

'Dad,' I said, 'why is there a car engine in the middle of the living room during the World Cup?'

'I'm looking for bats'. He said.

CHAPTER 28

After that shitty camping trip I'd decided that I'd get a decent job. I was sick of all my mates having dosh and me having hee-haw. I'd only been on the dole two weeks when I got a call to go and see a man called Eddie. Unfortunately it wasn't Mr Turnbull, it was Eddie the boss at Midas Exhaust Fitters; I was to see him about a job as an apprentice exhaust fitter. I turned up, pleasantly surprised at what I was looking at. The place was immaculate, Eddie seemed a really nice guy and the job looked like it had great prospects. He looked at the reference I'd handed over to him, the one from Linda.

'Very impressive, James,' he said.

'It's Jim,' I replied. I'd decided to change my name; Jimmy sounded way too immature for me.

'OK, very impressive CV, Jim. What happened at the last job in the photo processing place?'

'They decided to downscale due to the introduction of some new technology, I was last in so had to be first out.'

'That's a pity,' he said. 'Still, cracking reference from your old boss, did you give her one?' He nudged me. 'Only kidding pal.'

I smiled. 'She was a bit too old for me, maybe more your type,' I said.

'Nice one, pal,' he said. 'Give us her number, I'll be sure to swap references, see if we click. Get it? Camera shop?'

I looked skywards.

'Talking about giving somebody one,' he said, 'We've got Joanna Lumley coming in to officially open the place next week.'

'Seriously?'

'Yip, got a gold Roller picking her up from the airport, bringing her straight down Leith Walk to the shop. Sure to be a big crowd and a nice bit of coverage in the papers.'

'Wow! How did you manage that?' I said, still not sure whether to believe him or not.

'Our owner has megabucks,' he said rubbing his fingers together to demonstrate. 'Wanted to do a 'Midas, everything we touch turns to gold' type of marketing campaign. Thought Joanna represented the market we're after, paid her a fucking fortune and she agreed. She'll be wearing a gold leopardskin jumpsuit with nothing underneath, nae pants or bra. The boss wants to push the Midas link.'

'Midas link?' I said, confused.

'Midas was a king,' Eddie explained. 'Everything he touched turned to gold; never heard of him?'

'Nope,' I said. 'English?'

Eddie raised his eyebrows as if thinking about the answer then said, 'I'll demonstrate.' He leaned over the counter, touched my shoulder. 'That should work.'

I was lost.

'Fancy a job?'

I wasn't sure if he was kidding or not and said nothing.

'Well? Do you want the job or not? The Midas touch seems to have worked, you've only arrived and already the job's yours if you want it, you're head and shoulders above everybody else who's applied.'

'I'm not even that tall,' I said, having never heard the expression before, taking it literally.

'Nice one,' Eddie said, 'like your sense of humour. Well?'

'I'd love to work here,' I said, and jumped up onto the counter to shake his hand.

'Deal,' he said.

'Thanks, Eddie, you'll not regret this.'

'Cool, see you Tuesday morning, eight o'clock.'

Jeez, I bounced down the road home, it was the first time I'd had a feeling like it. The last job felt pretty good at the very start, but there was a real air, an atmosphere of hope in this place that I'd never experienced before. I felt it was offering me my first real opportunity to do something.

Two days after I started, we finished early in order to get the place ship shape for Joanna. We'd been open a few weeks, but not in an official capacity.

As soon as Joanna sliced through that yellow ribbon with the scissors that I'd polished specially, we would be official. There were cars and people everywhere, the Evening News and Scotsman had even turned up. She emerged from her car and was dressed in this wonderful leopard-skin outfit. After she'd signed a few autographs and shaken hands with all of the staff and customers, Eddie asked me to hand her the scissors. I was extremely nervous, I almost dropped them as I handed them over. She cut the ribbon, a glass of champagne in one hand, the scissors in the other, what a woman. Everybody was drooling over her fabulous figure.

Frank, the assistant manager, sneaked up behind her, pretended to hump her; she was oblivious as she climbed onto a table so that we could take some pictures. We were expecting a speech, but it never happened. She posed for about half an hour then the car whipped her off. What a buzz it gave everybody and what a way to start a job. I loved this place.

It didn't last long, though. Eddie left a couple of weeks after I joined and that arsehole Frank was given the manager's job. He was a weird guy. Had no idea what personal space was and his breath smelt like a dead badger's armpit. The combination was overwhelming. When he spoke in close proximity you felt cornered. I always looked for an escape route when I saw him coming. The Lumley effect had been massive for the first few weeks, but after that business dropped off, Frank wanted us to use underhand tactics to get people to come into the shop.

'Right, Jim, I want you to head down Easter Road, make sure nobody's watching you, when the coast is clear, stand on the exhaust pipes of cars, making sure you don't snap them but bend them beyond repair. We've got about thirty-two Fiat Panda exhausts in stock, so target them. If you can get about twenty, that should mean we'll get about half of them.'

'I can't do that, Frank, that's cheating,' I said.

'I'll do it, boss,' said Bob, who was Frank's best mate.

'Good lad,' Frank said. 'You know there's a promotion coming up pretty soon, I'm looking for some initiative. I'll be scoring and taking the actions of both of you into account.'

'Does that mean that if I don't cheat, I won't get the promotion?' I asked.

'No, not at all, young Jim lad,' he said. 'It's accumulative, the process has already begun, I'll decide when it concludes. I'll then inform the winner, simple as that.'

I knew I had no chance; Bob was sucking up his arse like a leech in a black pudding factory. This went on for months and months. I was going nowhere. Bob was like a favourite son and they had regular bonding sessions in which I was not included. It didn't bother me too much, though, as I had other plans for my life.

I was really enjoying drawing and painting again. Frank had began shagging a couple of single mums around Leith Walk and was away a lot of the time, which suited me perfectly.

I felt sorry for those lonely, sad lassies, letting a creep like that into their beds. He gave them exhausts as payment! He'd get me to drop off an exhaust pipe and accessories to their flats every now and again. None of them had cars, I'd no idea what they were doing with them.

'Frank, what's going on here?' I said one day.

'What do you mean?'

'The exhausts? Going to girls' flats?'

'They're old stock, I tell them they can sell them on for a good price and they believe me.'

'You'll be found out. What happens when they try to sell them and find out that they're no good?'

'I'll fuck off if they get too lippy, last thing I want is some hoor givin me a hard time. Plenty of fanny in the sea. I'm a fanny magnet, man, I've got a lassie in most of the streets around here.'

'I'd say they were the magnets the way they're accumulating metal,' I said.

'Ach, you're a jealous prick,' he said.

He was right. How he did it was way beyond my understanding. He was such an arrogant bastard. I'd met a few of the girls, they were all pretty decent, desperate for company, obviously.

It was summer, I was sick of being the gopher. I had to go to the shops for juice every day, do the menial jobs. Bob was Frank's pet lamb, always got to study and work on the good jobs. All I got was the shite, like removing old VW Beetle exhausts. Most of the time I had to use a blowtorch because the nuts and bolts were welded to the manifold; those exhausts lasted forever. Well forever until they had to be replaced. I burnt myself a hundred times using that equipment, which I'd had no training for; lucky the place didn't go up in flames.

'I've got an idea, guys,' I said to the two of them as we dug into our morning rolls. 'My mum's got a cash and carry card, I can get her to buy us a twenty-four pack of tins of juice, we'll get it really cheap.'

'Excellent idea,' Frank said. 'Initiative points may be coming your way.'

It worked a treat; for the price of four ordinary cans, we got eight cans, half price at the stroke of a kitten's belly button. We opted for Lilt, twenty-four cans divided by three, eight cans handed over to all parties and put in a safe place.

After only two days my cans were disappearing fast. I'd open one, sit it on the shelf or ramp as I was working, next thing I knew it was empty; some thieving bastard was at it, I thought I knew who it was, but had to prove it.

I went into work on the Wednesday, saw that there were only two of my cans left. I was extremely pissed off. They had plenty left. I nipped through next door to see my mate Jimmy, who worked at the garage adjacent to the exhaust centre.

'Can I borrow some liquid?' I said.

'What kind of liquid?' He asked. 'Anything specific?'

'Yellow liquid, I need something to fool somebody.'

He opened the door to a big room at the back of the garage, it looked like it hadn't been opened for years, there was dust everywhere. I spotted two Alfa Romeos in pristine condition, apart from the dust that covered them.

'Wow, why are these in here and not out there?' I said, pointing to the car sales room.

'We've been waiting for parts from Italy for four years; the owners gave up on them, piles of junk now,' Jimmy said. He switched on a whole bank of lights. 'Help yourself, give me a shout when you're finished, I'll turn these off, lock the door.'

'Perfect,' I said. I hunted around for a while, I was trying to find something that matched the colour of the Lilt. There were quite a few yellow liquids, some were too thick, others were too much on the green side. Eventually I found a jar of something that I thought would work. I gave him a shout, thanked him, headed back over to the exhaust centre. It was time to set my trap.

I opened my second-last remaining tin of Lilt, drank half of it and poured the yellow liquid into the half empty can. I then opened my last can, dribbled some of the contents around the lip of the other can to make it look natural. I laid the bait on the main ramp where most of the exhausts were examined; I then went into hiding.

Unfortunately it was a very slow day, none of the other two came anywhere near it. I forgot all about it and went out for lunch. When I came back the place was dead.

I looked around, searched the place; there was nobody around. The door was open, the till was unlocked and the alarm was not set. Frank burst in through the front door.

'Where have you been?' He said. 'I've been looking all over for you, Bob's been rushed to hospital.'

'What's up with him?' I said, forgetting about my trap.

'He's having vomiting cramps, foaming at the mouth, I had to rush him to hospital. I was looking for you to take over the shop while I was away.'

'Sorry, Frank,' I said, 'I had an emergency myself. Diarrhoea.' I then realised that whatever I'd put into the can had caused Bob's problem. I ran around to the ramp, spotted the can lying on the floor; the liquid had mostly spilled out and gone down the drainage hole, the part it had dripped down shone like new. I emptied the rest of it, trying to get rid of any evidence, then went through to the toilet and washed the can out with very hot water. I then took it, poured half of the remaining Lilt from my last can into the clean can. I put it back on the ramp and left it. I wandered through next door to see Jimmy, handed him the jar of stuff I'd borrowed.

'What's this stuff, Jimmy?' I said.

He unscrewed the lid, sniffed it, quickly recoiling at the smell.

'Fuckin hell, brake fluid,' he said.

I was none the wiser. 'What does that do?'

'Come here, I'll show you.'

We walked back through to the old room where I'd found the stuff. He put the lights on, waited until they were powered up fully, poured the liquid over the bonnet of one of the white Alfa Romeos. Within thirty seconds the paint began to bubble up. Within a few minutes we could almost see through to the metal. 'That answer your question?'

I put my hands to my mouth, trying to figure out the consequences and hide my shock at the same time. Nobody could find out what I did. Whether it was an accident or not, I could still end up in prison.

'That's perfect, Jimmy, thanks pal,' I said. 'Mind if I have another look around? This place is fascinating.'

'Feel free,' he said, and headed off.

I took the jar, headed to the back of the building, where I threw it into the rubbish skip, pummelled it with bricks to pulverise it and destroy all evidence.

I spent the rest of the day waiting on news about Bob's impending death. Every time the phone rang my sphincter hit my ribs. When I left work that night Frank was carrying on as normal, he didn't really care about people, I hoped he had no idea about what I'd done. I got home, prayed that Bob would be OK, even though I didn't really like him, I couldn't really justify killing somebody for drinking my juice.

I spent a very restless night in bed, tossing and turning, awaiting the knock at the door. Thankfully it never happened. Next morning I got into work and was surprised at how chirpy Frank was.

'Alright, boss?' I said.

'Couldn't be better he said. 'Got wee Caroline up the stair lined up for ten o'clock.'

'Wee Caroline? She's gorgeous,' I said. I was amazed at this guy, he was dirty and smelly, halitosis hung around him like a poltergeist, still he managed to get girls. I was still looking for my first experience and I was much more of a catch than him. I couldn't fathom it.

I ventured the dreaded question.

'Heard from Bob yet?'

'In actual fact, I have.'

I waited anxiously for his next words.

'He'll be in Monday. Looks like a really bad case of food poisoning.'

'Wow, that's a relief,' I said. 'I mean, great news.'

I'd almost given myself away. I walked off to start work, knowing I'd been let off. He must've taken enough to make him sick, thank god I hadn't poured as much of the fluid in as I initially intended.

My job as an exhaust fitter earned me nothing like the megabucks John was getting working on the roofs as a slater. Every week he could afford to buy a new outfit, shoes, trousers, jacket, whatever he fancied he could have. On the plus side, though, I was the same size as him and everything he bought fitted me perfectly.

The relief I felt from Bob being alright gave me a real high. I wanted to go out and celebrate. I got off early as Frank was pumping the lassie all day. I locked up, knowing he couldn't say anything as he'd been AWOL for hours. I got home, grabbed something to eat, opened our shared wardrobe, ignored my shabby clothes, went through John's collection. Picked out a nice checked shirt and a pair of dark blue jeans with a dark brown leather belt, laid them on the bed, nodded; these would work a treat. I used my own pants and socks as a means of balance.

I noticed a shoe-box hidden at the back, pulled it towards me. I opened it up, there was this pristine pair of beautiful blue suede shoes. The box had a big logo on it – PODS. 'Made in Rushden', it said proudly; it meant nothing to me. *Wow, these are incredible*, I thought.

The Lost Tornado

I picked one of them up, held it like a piece of art. It was so light, the design was stunning. Probably the best clothing article I'd ever seen. The shoes had blue tissue paper inside them, indicating that John hadn't worn them yet. I thought long and hard about breaking them in for him, eventually justified it to myself. I'd be doing him a favour, didn't want him getting blisters, I'd take the hit for him.

Saint Jim ... hero ... martyr for the cause ... Of course, I doubt he'd see it that way, but I'd made my mind up, didn't care about afterwards, that was way too far in the future.

I had a quick wash in the sink, dried my hair and got ready. I'd arranged to meet Alex and Higgy at half-six to go for a drink in the Blind Beggar before heading up town. As I was going out of the front door, about to shut it behind me, I heard John's voice echoing in the stairwell below; he was with Tam Townsley.

'Fuck,' I said to myself. I bolted back upstairs to the room, ripped the clothes off, jumped into my Hibs tracky. I put his clothes back into the wardrobe, packed the shoes into the box, making sure I'd put the tissue paper back in. I wandered down to the kitchen for a cup of tea.

I could see John and Tam behind the frosted wire glass of the front door. 'Come on,' I said under my breath, 'get a move on.' I looked at my watch, there was still plenty of time before we were meeting. If John was staying in I'd have to revert to my shitty clothes and have no chance of bagging off with a bird.

After I'd finished my tea they were still nattering. I had to force the issue. I opened the door, popped my head out.

'Fancy a cuppa?' I said, knowing that Tam only drank Coke and beer.

'I'll take one,' John said.

Shit, I thought. I was hoping he'd be too busy to have one. Still, at least it moved things on.

'Are you going to tell him or will I?' Tam said.

'We've bought a mobile disco,' John said.

'Eh?' I said.

'We bought it this afternoon from the disco supplier in Rodney Street,' John said.

'Chas and Dave's place?'

'Yip,' said Tam. He tried to high five John, but John had no idea what he was up to, just looked at him.

'We are now officially Phoenix Mobile Disco,' he said, grabbing John by the shoulders from behind. John moved forward a bit, unsettled by Tam's close proximity.

'What made you do that?' I said.

'It was an opportunity we couldn't refuse,' John said.

'Guaranteed income,' Tam interjected. 'Fanny galore, here we come.' He rubbed his hands together.

I laughed. 'Aye, right, Tam, you? Fanny?'

He ignored me, walked along the landing towards his house.

'OK, Johnny, my man, see you in half an hour,' he said, pointing his index finger like a gun.

'What are you up to in half an hour?' I said.

'We've got our first gig in Corstorphine at eight,' John said.

'Tonight?' I asked.

'Yip, a wedding, two hundred people.'

'How did you get that so quickly?'

'Chas and Dave had a cancellation. Tam and I have been thinking about this for ages, we've even saved up enough to put half the money down.'

'How come you never said anything to me?' I said, a bit upset. 'I could've been in on it as well.'

'No chance,' John said, 'you've got no money. It's going to cost us three grand for the equipment and another three for records. Plus we'll have to spend about a hundred quid a week on the latest records, it's never ending.'

'I suppose you're right.' I said. There was no way I could afford to be part of this.

'You can still be a DJ with us if you want,' John said. 'We'll pay you for it.'

'Sounds great.'

'Not tonight, though. We need to get up and running with all the stuff first.'

Wow, that was exciting news. My brother in a business venture. I wasn't sure how long he'd put up with Tam, though, because ever since he'd come out of his shell, usually after a few drinks, he was an absolute pain in the arse. Always tried to act like an American TV star. I couldn't figure out where his confidence came from because on the outside he looked like a fat, ginger arsehole.

I could take him in very small doses but as soon as he had a drink on him personal space turned into a vacuum. I was sure he was a bufty, but never really had any evidence to prove it. I knew he was about three times more of a virgin than me, but we never spoke about it.

I hung around the bedroom playing my new OMD album on the record player, waiting for John to decide what he was wearing, trying to hurry him up in the subtlest way. I actually picked some clothes out of his wardrobe, trying to convince him this shirt or that pair of trousers would look good on a DJ at a wedding, obviously steering him away from the stuff I wanted to wear.

It worked. I convinced him to wear a more formal look.

'Do you know how to work all of the equipment?' I said, genuinely concerned, hoping that Chas and Dave hadn't ripped him off.

'We've been going down to the shop every Saturday for the past few months, looking at the decks and lighting systems, Chas has been brilliant.'

'So how did this gig come about?'

'It was a call off one of the MDs, couldn't make it.'

'MDs?' I said.

'Mobile Discos.'

'Oh. Right, of course,' I said.

'Chas called the wedding party up to say Phoenix Mobile Disco would be there tonight. We get a hundred and fifty quid for doing it.'

'Shit!' I said, 'a hundred and fifty for one night? That's more than I get for two week's work.' I was well impressed and could see my future ahead. No more of this shitty exhaust fitting crap. 'What about your logo and light box designs and stuff?' I said, seeing an opportunity.

'If you fancy having a go, we'll pay you,' John said, as he was tying the laces on his black leather brogues.

This was music to my ears. My first real design job and I'd be paid for it.

'Definitely,' I said. 'I'll get onto it tonight.'

'No rush,' he said. 'We're using temporary stuff tonight; our actual equipment won't be here for another few weeks, so we're using borrowed stuff to start off.'

'Deal,' I said offering him my hand. We shook as he headed out the door. 'Hope it goes brilliantly.'

'As long as Tam keeps his mouth shut it should be great,' he said. 'See you in the morning.'

I was wired. The Bob let-off and now my first design job. I was so excited, couldn't wait to tell Alex and Higgy. I got all of the stuff I'd previously worn back out from John's cupboard and put it all back on, including the blue Pods. I'd never felt more happy about myself or my future prospects, reckoned tonight could be an adventure. I caught up with the boys at the BB. Had a couple of Pernod and black currants, followed by the usual two pints of cider and black. The Human League, Ultravox and OMD blasting out from the jukebox, who could ask for more?

We then headed to a disco, Oliver's on Rose Street. Perfect, great music and the birds are cracking. Alex has a look about him that gets him a foot in the door with the girls, I'm next in line as Higgy's dress sense and chat are second rate at best. I've got good chat but can never find the words to turn it into anything that'll lead to sex or anything in that vicinity. The best I've ever got is a phone number to meet for a coffee in BHS but that's it.

Tonight, despite my big hopes and great outfit, it's more of the same; a beautiful lassie called Caroline wants to mother me.

'Yeah, call me, I'll meet you for a coffee, I'll give you the latest gossip and stuff, here's my number.'

Jeez, I'm not interested in that. I want some real action.

'Listen, Caroline. Is there any chance we can go back to your place, remove our clothes and jump into the sack, I'll give you the best seeing to you've ever had?'

I think about this and shit myself at the prospect of having those massive boobs as a responsibility. I wouldn't have a clue where to start or what to do with them. I say nothing.

Higgy and I end up walking along Princes Street as usual, aimless. Alex has scored again, gone back to a girl's flat, left us with a bit of consolation.

'Here, lads, here's some cash to buy yourselves a couple of drinks, I feel guilty as fuck about leaving you, but you know how it is. Enjoy the rest of the night.' With that, he winked at us and headed off.

I felt shit, even with a great outfit on I still couldn't get any lassie to give me a second look. I was on the doorstep of resigning myself to virginhood for life. I wasn't sure if Higgy was still a virgin, we never talked about it, the difference was, he seemed content. He'd got his bookies and bakeries to satisfy his desires. I had deeper feelings than that.

Johnny Craddock's ancient comment came to mind for some reason.

'I hope your doughnuts turn out like Fanny's.'

I ask myself if I'd risk getting sugar and jam on my knob.

Yes.

We decided that as it was getting on we couldn't be bothered with any more pubs or discos. Robert Halpern, the hypnotist, was on at midnight. That gave us a good forty minutes to get along to the Playhouse. We'd been before, it was a great laugh watching morons making complete arses of themselves. At the door, before we bought the tickets, we got chatting to some girls who were going in to see him, so we tagged along with them.

The lights went down and the music started. There was a real buzz about the place, a sense that something special was going to take place. People were looking around at each other wondering if it had been a good idea to come or not. I could see that some people were terrified, nobody that I knew understood hypnosis. Most people thought the guys were acting hypnotised. I'd always been there to watch, but that night I felt like joining in. I looked around, there were some great looking lassies around, I could imagine getting to snog them on stage or bagging off with them after the show.

As the music built to a crescendo, a man dressed in a black suit, cape and top hat appeared in the middle of the stage. A puff of smoke evaporated, he was standing there. Wee black moustache, beard and cane. All very dramatic. I was feeling the vibes. I wasn't sure if it was stupidity or curiosity but I found myself clasping my hands together, as Halpern was saying the words, 'Tighter and tighter and tighter,' my hands were obeying him. I was desperately trying to unclasp them, but it was no good. I tried and tried to pull them apart but he had control. Higgy was laughing at me, pointing to my shaking hands.

Eventually Halpern said, 'If your hands are sticking together and you cannot separate them, come up to the stage.'

I sat there frantically trying to unclasp my hands, they wouldn't budge an inch, if anything they were getting tighter! I panicked as they were starting to hurt. The only course of action was to go up on stage.

I followed the long trail of people making their way up to the stage. He had helpers in place to get us up as we couldn't climb the steps with joined hands. I realised how embarrassed I was, how did I let myself get into this? I tried to convince myself that I could control it, closed my eyes trying to break his spell. It was no use. The lights went up, he carefully examined his catch.

There were about fifty of us, all ages, all social classes. Halpern walked up and down along the three long lines of people, lifting heads up with his hand, examining eyes and how strong the grip of people's hands was. He pulled about a third of the people's hands apart easily and sent them back to their seats. Unfortunately my hands remained solid, bonded to each other. He positioned the remaining folk in two long straight lines along the front of the stage.

'Tonight, ladies and gentlemen,' he said, in his posh Edinburgh accent. I was surprised when I heard him lisp, it had never been obvious before; *how come he can't cure his lisp if he's such a great hypnotist*? I thought to myself.

He waved his hand in a long drawn-out gesture, walking along, pointing to every one of us.

'Ladies and gentlemen, here is your evening's entertainment; some will be great, some will be embarrassed and some will be … SLEEP!' He said to one girl.

She dropped like a stone, he caught her, lowered her gently to the stage floor. Sleeping.

The audience erupted with laughter and amazement. He knelt down, put his microphone to her mouth, snoring echoed all around the auditorium; more laughter ensued. I'd been to watch this show many times, one of his tricks was to get a 'hypnotee' to eat an onion, believing that it was a juicy, scrumptious, golden delicious apple. Onions were my number one most hated thing on the planet. I even despised the look of them. I was dreading the thought that he would pick me. I tried to avoid eye contact with him and instead concentrated on freeing my hands. By then the lights had been dimmed a bit, the music of pulsing synthesizers was growing. I looked around the crowd. My eyes ventured up to the back of the theatre, I tried to locate Higgy. I couldn't see him, I seemed to have lost my bearings. As I looked around I saw some people waving behind the front row. I looked harder and couldn't believe what I was seeing.

FUCK! John and Tam were sitting there! They must have got away from the disco early and decided on some hypnotic entertainment.

Shit, fuck, shit, I thought to myself.

What was I to do? I decided that if I took a step back and manoeuvred myself into row two I'd be able to hide behind all of the other people on the stage, there'd be no chance of John seeing my footwear and clothing. I was hoping he hadn't spotted the shirt and trousers. He was laughing and pointing at me, mouthing the word 'onion'. I heard Tam shouting out, 'Gie Jimmy an onion, Halpern.'

'Fuck off, Townsley,' I mouthed back. I didn't want to swear as I'd seen what Halpern did to people who used bad language on his stage.

It was 'SLEEP' and the next thing you knew you'd be naked in the arms of another guy. I looked along the lines of people who had come up, there to my utter amazement was my mate Jimmy Maxwell. He must have come in with John and Tam, got caught up in the scenario, the same as me. As Halpern paced slowly up and down the lines, looking for victims to star in his show, I began to feel sick, I could feel sweat running down my back, the lights above us were roasting. I was still wrestling with my disobedient hands, they seemed to have a will of their own. It was getting to the point where they were really hurting. The lights went down further, Vangelis' music began to play. The big red curtain at the front of the stage closed slowly as the words 'Sleep, sleep, relax, relax,' soothed us all. The curtain opened again, as the applause died down, the hypnotic music got louder. It reached a crescendo, then … utter silence. I heard Halpern walking behind my line. He tapped people on the head, on the shoulder and arms, seemingly at random. I heard him close to me and turned around.

'Sleep,' he said as he tapped me on the shoulder. I immediately slumped to the floor, totally relaxed. I was surprised at how awake, yet unable to think I was. I was very conscious of what was going on, but seemed to have no power to resist. I lay there for a while. The show seemed to be going well. There was a lot of laughter and applause. Two guys sat in an empty bath with only their pants on, they were cuddling each other.

Halpern went on to his next round of entertainment, telling people that they'd won the lottery and, when he counted to three, they would realise that they'd blown it all on a horse that had come in second. He was getting into this when all of a sudden he stopped dead in his tracks.

He sniffed the air, sniff, sniff sniff. He exaggerated for dramatic impact.

'Do I smell shit?' He said. The audience laughed uproariously. Sniff, sniff, sniff, along the back row. Sniff, sniff, sniff, along the front row. Sniff, sniff, sniff, along the back row again. He stopped near me.

'I'm sure I can smell shit somewhere nearby.

'Listen everyone,' he said, to all of us hypnotees, 'when I count to three, you will all lift your legs into the air while I sniff out and identify the shit merchant. One, two, three.'

About a hundred legs went up in unison, mine included. He walked quickly along the rows, looking at the soles of people's feet. I heard him getting close to me. He stopped.

'Aha!' He said. 'I think I've found the shit squelcher, the man with the smelly brown soles.'

As he walked around the stage he said, 'When you feel me tapping your leg you can put it down, back onto the floor.' I heard the thumps as people let their legs drop back onto the stage carpet. He was getting closer. He walked right behind where I was lying, getting closer and closer. He knelt down, tapped me on the right leg. I put both my legs down.

'Oh no, you don't,' he said. 'I did not tap your left leg; put it back up.'

I looked around and of the hundred or so legs that were up in the air there was now only one. Mine.

'OK, shit boy, are you proud of yourself dragging that foul mess into my lovely show? We'll have to teach you a lesson, won't we?'

The audience was howling at him. Inadvertently, it seemed I'd stepped into a big shite, it must have been a Great Dane or a pony judging by the size, it was all over the bottom and sides of John's left Pod. I looked down, I was surprised that I hadn't noticed it before, it was humongous! I couldn't even think about John's reaction to it as I was sooooo relaxed, I didn't care one iota, besides, it was dark out there, chances were he'd never know that it was me that was being picked on. To my horror, the cameraman walked behind Halpern, focussed on my left foot; the big screen flashed up a giant squishy turd, the consistency of Nutella, firmly attached to a blue Pod. The audience all showed their disgust. Halpern held his nose, waving away the smell with his gloved hand. I twisted my foot a couple of times and found that the image on screen copied my movements. He said, 'When I count to three, I want you to take off that shitty, blue shoe and throw it as far away from me as you can.'

If John hadn't twigged before, there was no chance of him missing it now,

'And while you're at it, you can throw away the other one as well; don't you know Elvis went out of fashion years ago?'

The audience laughed, they were lapping it up.

'Blue suede shoes, in this day and age? I don't know,' he said, shaking his head. 'One, two, three.'

I reached down and without untying the laces, I tore off the shitty shoe and launched it as hard as I could behind me, right onto the big cinema screen. The shoe hit the screen and slid down slowly, leaving a brown trail behind it. There was a roar of disgust from the crowd. The other shoe went straight into the crowd. I could hear the audience laughing. I put my legs down, hoping that my stint was finished.

'Now, Mr Brown Stuff,' Halpern said, 'we're going to have to teach you a lesson, aren't we? When I say UP, your left leg will rise of its own accord, reach as high as it can go and will stop. It will then be stuck there until I say otherwise. UP.'

True enough, I couldn't help but watch in awe as my left leg rose up into the air. I was flat on my back with my foot in the air. Halpern walked away from me, carried on making people think they were sitting on electric chairs or meeting old girlfriends in funny situations.

After a long time, the 'don't give a shit' attitude that I'd had began to wear off. I'd suddenly become awake. I tried to lower my leg but it was stuck. I was getting cramp. As if that wasn't bad enough, I noticed that the cute blonde girl with the backless dress who was lying next to me on stage was about to roll onto a dod of shite. It must have fallen off my shoe when I threw it onto the screen. I tried to kick her with my other foot, but she was still away with it.

I watched as she slowly rolled on top of it. I expected the coldness or softness of it against her skin would wake her, but no. The rest faded out for me. I'd gone into some kind of unconscious state. Next thing I knew, I was watching people get up and walk towards the back of the stage. It looked like the show had finished as the crowd had dispersed, there were only a few dozen people left. I watched the cute girl as she sat up, the shit was on her back, as she stood up it slid down the back of her dress. She still seemed not to have noticed.

I got up and by then I'd got a dead leg. I had to virtually drag it off the stage. Another attractive girl stood up from the stage, it looked like she was with cutie. Nobody had noticed the shite; how could that be? I was confused but relieved.

I got to the edge of the stage after a long hobble, shook hands with Halpern.

'Sorry about that, sir,' he said, pointing to my dead leg. 'It'll wear off in an hour or two.' He handed me two free tickets for the next week's show.

As I walked off I rubbed my eyes, trying to shake myself awake. Felt like I'd been asleep for a long time. I was about to walk down the steps from the stage when I realised I was in my stocking soles. I went looking for the shoes. I vaguely remembered throwing one towards the screen and headed towards it. I found it directly below the brown line on the screen, it was lying in the orchestra pit. I picked it up and used a couple of used ice cream tub wooden spoons that were lying about in the pit to scrape off the remaining shit, hoping that John had disappeared, unaware of what had happened, but I doubted it. The shit had stained the lower edges of the blue shoe, it looked a real mess. 'Fucking hell!' I shouted, I knew I was in deep. I'd never get that off and there was no way I could afford to buy John another pair, they cost twenty-five quid! That was a couple of weeks' wages to me. I knew he'd go mental.

I got as much of the shit off as I could, realised the other shoe was nowhere to be seen. I then remembered throwing it into the crowd. *Fuck! What if it landed near John?*

Shit, I really was in for a kicking. I put the shoe on and climbed back up from the orchestra pit with great difficulty, due to my dead leg, scrambled onto the stage and went looking for the shoe I threw into the crowd. By now the place was virtually empty. Higgy walked down the vast row of stairs towards me, smiling. In the corner of my eye I spotted John walking over to me, slowly and deliberately. He was holding up a very scraped blue Pod with no lace. He walked right up to my face, I could feel his nose touching mine.

'You LIT-TLE BAS-TARD,' he said, through clenched teeth. 'I'll fucking see you about this later.'

He stared at me not blinking, pulled at my shirt and trousers. 'And these? You'll pay for them, one way or another.'

Tam was standing behind him making cut throat gestures.

'Fuck off, Tam,' I said, trying to get John back onside. They both turned and walked away.

'John,' I shouted, 'I'm sorry.'

He kept walking, gave me the finger without turning around.

'Can I have the other shoe?' I shouted desperately.

He tucked it under his arm, walked out of the theatre.

Higgy and I got outside, it was chucking it down. I took a few painful steps and began my long hobble home, but after a couple of seconds I had to stop, my leg was cramping again.

I heard a scream and turned round to see the blonde girl in the foyer, her hand covered in shite. Her pal was desperately trying to rub it off with a tissue, the look on their faces said it all, they were both scoobied. Higgy and I picked up the pace, hobbling towards Claremont Court.

'Can I stay at yours tonight, Higgy?' I said, wincing.

'I think that would be a wise idea pal,' he said, laughing.

CHAPTER 29

By this time, I was one of the last ones in the house, there was only me, Gordon, Catherine and Debbie left. Mum was a bit more relaxed, the auld man had moved out, somewhere near Joppa I'd heard. I didn't really keep up with him as his drinking had pissed me off so much the last few years that I could have, and should have swung for him but that's another story. We rattled around the big empty house and didn't really gel as a smaller unit, I think it was the shock of the constant mass and volume of the family abruptly being turned off like a tap. Within three years we'd gone from a population of eleven to five people. I felt like I was living in a half-way house. I continued at Midas for a while. I was virtually the boss as Frank, the actual boss was shagging his way through Leith, mostly mid-morning to mid-afternoon when most of the husbands or boyfriends of the gullible were out working or drinking their sorrows away. Frank would appear at the shop around the back of two most days, looking knackered.

It got to the point where he stopped boasting about who he was shagging. He looked like he was hooked on it, a sex junkie. His eyes had bags under them, his skin was grey; at least his appearance matched his breath. There was definitely no enjoyment in his chat. He'd come in, ask how business had been that day and head off to the back room where he'd curl up in the sleeping bag on the folding bed that he'd brought in a month or two earlier, to catch up on his sleep. He didn't want his girlfriend, Rachel, to suss what he was up to so took work-time to recover his energy. It pissed me off something awful, but I had nowhere to go; he was the boss so I couldn't complain to anyone.

We had been deadly quiet for six weeks. The one great thing about the situation was that I somehow got hooked on painting and design again. I'd no idea where the urge came from. One day I was browsing in an art shop with Gordon and was gripped by the need to buy some paints and a pad. I went home and found I'd somehow improved since the last time I drew. I thought back to the day I'd ripped up my portfolio and found I was over it. I was a new kind of artist now, and I was loving it, the stuff I was designing felt great. Over the past month I'd built up a brand new portfolio of very different stuff, I was chuffed with it.

Business was shit, though. There was no way Midas could carry on without some kind of financial or marketing input. I sensed the place dying a bit more every time I went in, the dust was settling thickly on the stock.

Our year's marketing budget had been blown on Joanna Lumley popping into the shop for a small part of a day, the rewards from that had all dried up. Hoping that people would get lost and drive into our cul-de-sac was as good a marketing plan as we had.

Frank kept asking me to go around breaking more and more exhausts. I pretended I was doing it, but I wasn't going to heap misery on people for that twat. If I got caught he'd deny all responsibility, like the time I caught him stealing from our safe about a week earlier.

I was in the pit putting an exhaust on a Lada for the garage next door when I heard a noise from our security room. It should've been empty. Frank was away swapping lengths of exhaust for lengths of something else, Bob was at the hospital for his weekly check-up, which I felt incredibly guilty about, but I said nothing.

I cocked my head, trying to make sure I had indeed heard something, there was another crash. I got hold of a mash hammer, headed to the room. The light bulb had been smashed a week or two earlier, Frank didn't want me to replace it, said we'd get round to it sometime, which I thought was strange as the bulbs were in a box a footstep away.

My grip on the hammer was tight; I'd battered the shit out of a particularly stubborn exhaust so I was pumped for action. I stopped outside the half-closed door, stood still, listening.

Silence. Another period of quiet then I heard what sounded like the safe door being dragged open. I kicked the door open. There was a guy kneeling down at the safe, dressed in black, I could see from the light streaming from the big open garage door that he had a balaclava on. He looked round, stood up, rushed past me; the surprise disabled me for a few seconds, as he pushed past, I fell onto my arse, the hammer falling to the floor. There was something about him I recognised, but I couldn't put my finger on it. I scrabbled around on the floor, eventually found the hammer, got up and ran after the guy. He'd headed out of the front door, which was weird as the big open garage roller doors were the obvious escape route.

I ran straight out onto Leith Walk, it was busy as usual. As I looked around the recognition I had sensed earlier hit me, it was Frank's BO. No question. I sniffed the air, there was no mistaking that stink. He'd broken into our safe. 'Why?' I said out loud, looking at my palms for some reason. At that moment Frank walked around the corner, he was fixing his hair, ruffling it up, sweating, he was also wearing black rather than his normal blue jeans; the only thing missing was the balaclava.

'What the fuck are you doin out here?' He shouted angrily. People stopped in the street to look. 'You're supposed to be mindin the fuckin shop, we could be gettin broken into.'

Awareness smacked me in the forehead, he was expecting me to run after the intruder and I'd fallen for it. I was lost for words, had no idea what to say. I had no proof that it was him, even if I had, what could I do?

'Get back to the fuckin shop NOW,' he screamed, shoving me in the chest.

I turned tail, ran back to the shop. I was embarrassed as quite a few people were now looking at us. I went into the hallway, got a bulb from the leccy cupboard, got the stepladders, removed the remnants of the smashed bulb from the security room with a tea towel, then replaced it. I was now able to see everything.

The safe lay wide open, the only thing that was left in it was Frank's broken watch and some papers. I lifted the hidden square of carpet at the base of the safe, where I knew we kept the takings; everything had gone. My watch and wallet had also been nicked. I always put them in there every morning, on Frank's advice.

When I first started there he told me that a lot of exhaust fitters broke their watches with all the hammering and squeezing their hands into tight, awkward spaces.

'It'll be secure in the safe,' he said, so I did that from day one. Same with my wallet.

'Remember that we leave the big roller doors up all the time, so last thing you want to do is leave your wallet in your jacket where it could be nicked.'

Bastard! I thought, *he must have planned this all along*. I sat on the chair in the room, pulled the remaining contents from the safe; as I did this he walked in.

'What the fuck's happened here?' He said. 'Did somebody break in? If they did I'll go fuckin ape.'

There was no surprise on his face; I knew he'd done it.

'They got my watch and wallet,' I said, gutted.

'Get the fuck out of the way.' He grabbed me by the shoulder, shoved me aside.

'We'll have to call the cops,' I said.

'No plod,' he said immediately.

'We'll have to,' I said. 'The week's taking have gone, and my wallet and watch.'

'No cops,' he repeated. 'Get me a coffee.'

'No,' I shouted back at him, 'my wallet and watch have been nicked, I want them back.'

'OK,' he said, 'call the cops, tell them there's been a break-in.'

I went through to call, but when I picked up the handset the line was dead. I tried a few times from the three different phones around the shop, but they were all dead.

'Forget it,' he shouted.

I walked back through to the security room, Frank was standing there with my wallet in his hand, the takings bag lying on the small table.

'You're fuckin useless at looking for things, Divine,' he said, laughing, shaking his head. 'Look,' he pointed to the items on the table, 'they were there all along.'

'They were not there,' I said adamantly. 'They were definitely gone.'

'How could they be? Here they are.'

'Is my watch there?'

'I'll have a look,' he said, bending down to the safe.

I could clearly see him take something out of his pocket. He held my watch up, one of the straps was snapped.

'Here you are, useless bastard,' he said, throwing the watch for me to catch.

'It's broken.'

'You must have broken it when you put it in this morning.'

'Fuck you!' I shouted at him, knowing fine well I was powerless to do anything about this.

He rushed over, grabbed me by the throat, he was pretty strong after years of manual labour. 'What the fuck did you say, you little prick?'

I squirmed away from him, headed to our changing room, ripped my hated yellow overalls off and changed into my jeans. On my way out I took the notion to look at the main phone line boxes, my suspicion was bang on, he had unplugged the lines at the main junction box. It was all part of his elaborate plan. I left him to his mess and went home.

I stayed off for a couple of days, long enough for me not to need a sick note. When I got in on the Wednesday Frank was standing at the counter in the front shop. He was fuming with me, I could sense it when I saw his ugly red puss, but he never said a word. There was a big blue vein on his forehead that grew as thick as a lug worm when he was worked up. It was almost writhing.

Bob popped his smiling face round the kitchen door.

'Fancy a coffee, Jim?'

'Yeah, great Bob, thanks.'

Bob and I sat and chewed the fat while Frank stood at the counter pretending to do some work. There was still fifteen minutes before we were due to start so I was pretty relaxed. Frank came through a couple of times, looked at his watch, saw that he still couldn't shout at us and walked back. By the time eight-thirty arrived he walked through but the two of us were already at the ramp in our overalls, examining the Blue Fiat that was sitting there. He was pissed off, but tried not to show it.

I smiled to myself.

'What's so funny?' Bob said.

'Nothing,' I said, 'you had to be there.'

Two days later Frank called me into his office. 'We're letting you go,' he said.

'What?' I said in complete disbelief.

'You heard,' he said, a smug look on his fucking uglier than ever coupon.

'Why?' I said.

'Not enough work to go around.'

'But Bob was last in.'

'Doesn't matter, it's up to me, I want Bob to stay.'

'Is that because he's your mate?' I shouted at him.

'Officially? No. Unofficially? Maybe. Between you and I? Definitely.' He laughed.

'You're an ignorant fucking bastard,' I said, keeping my voice low.

'And you're an unemployed wee cunt,' he said, 'and if you keep that fuckin cheek up I'll jump over this counter and punch yer fuckin lights out.'

I walked closer to the door in case I had to run. 'I hope you catch something from your wee tarts and scratch your way to a painful, gooey death.'

'That's a bit over the top,' he said, 'but do I look like I give a fuck?'

I was still pissed off that he'd broken my watch.

'I'll grass you to the cops,' I said, bringing up the break-in.

'About what?' He said, playing the fool.

'The break-in. I know you did it,' I said, pointing my finger at him.

'You got any proof of that rather serious accusation?'

I had kept the plastic envelope that had the receipts and bank statements in it from the safe.

'I do.'

'Show me.'

'No chance. I'll show it to the cops, then we'll see how smart you are.'

'Tell you what,' he said, 'fuck off now, never let me see your fucking ugly pus near this place again and I'll throw in a week's wages. How does that sound?'

I let go of the door handle, went to my locker, cleared the bits and pieces from it, headed out.

I showed the plastic bag to Frank on the way out.

'Is that it?' He laughed. 'That's your evidence?'

'It's got your fingerprints on it,' I said accusingly, holding the bag up, shaking it at him.

'I'm the fucking manager of the shop, you thick little bastard, whose fingerprints do you think should be on the bank stuff?'

I hadn't thought of that, felt a real arsehole, I threw the bag at him, slunk out of the place without saying a word to Bob, who stood at the back of the door pretending to wipe an exhaust with an oily rag. He knew he'd taken my job and I hated him for not having the balls to say anything. In a way I was glad I'd almost killed him.

On the dole again. Being let go served in my favour. It gave me time to find my next vocation, Graphic design was still tugging away, but I still had exactly the same non-qualifications I had when I left school. Midas had given me a great platform to work on my ideas, as Frank spent a lot of time out shagging, I spent most of my time drawing and painting. Unbeknown to him and Bob, I'd set up a studio type thing in one of the unused rooms at the back of the shop, I was able to paint there, perfecting my skies and landscapes, mixing colours to my heart's content. It was bliss, there were bugger all customers, I'd definitely gain more by using that brush than the one Frank had in mind for me. I used spray paints from Halford's to get the subtle skies and spheres, there was no ventilation in the room and I didn't realise it at the time but I must have been as high as many of Leith's other artists - the piss type. I remember when I coughed or blew my nose, the hankie would have marbling on it.

When he threw me out I spent my last week's wages on painting materials. I felt wired by the new potential that had gotten into me, that and the aerosol chemicals that were coursing through me. I had a sense of purpose that was eating away at me; it was as strong as my Hibs dream had been. That particular dream had died a death long ago, Turnbull's Tornadoes were gone, Willie Ormond had come to manage the team after good old Eddie.

John and Tam had left me in charge of a disco in Musselburgh, it was in Mr. Ormond's pub, a special night, Mods vs. Rockers. This was the first time Phoenix Mobile Disco had hired a place purely to make money. It was an absolute disaster, the mods turned up in all their paraphernalia, they looked pretty cool, in all honesty, except for the cardboard cut-outs of Vespas that some of them carried around under their arms; I'd never seen that before. The rockers, on the other hand, almost made me wet myself when they came into the pub with different cardboard cut-outs, air guitars they called them.

I put the first rocker song on, something like Status Quo *Rocking all Over the World*, I burst out laughing, a dozen of these guys were actually up on the floor pretending to play the cardboard guitars. I was tempted to put another record on straight away for a laugh. I had been playing one mod record, then a rocker one and so on. Eventually the mods wanted more, they were pretending to drive their cardboard Vespas into the rockers and threatened to take over the disco. When one of them hit a rocker with his Vespa, the rocker grabbed it from him, ripped it in two, the whole place erupted. The cops were called, Willie Ormond was not a happy chappie.

I didn't tell him about my ambition to play for Hibs as I knew exactly where he'd tell me to go. I'd really lost the desire to play football by that time anyway and spent most of my time running.

Seven a.m. There was a knock at the door.

I was in the deepest most pleasant sleep that I'd had for a long time. I was having this recurring dream, one I'd been having for a long time. I was about to go to bed with a couple of the most sexy girls I'd ever seen. They were both besotted with me, couldn't wait to get me into the sack. They'd wooed and trapped me in their bedroom; they had on short tartan mini-skirts, white blouses, no underwear that I could detect, their hair was in pigtails, their eyes were targeting me, no blinking, tongues licking full, red lips. They were walking, stumbling towards me on a big water bed, removing their clothes as they approached. By the time they got to me on the bed they only had their skirts on. I played hard to get for a short while, then allowed them to attack me. They were about to remove their skirts when I was hauled unceremoniously into the other cold, hard woman-free world that was my reality. I was lying there in my scratcher feeling really annoyed and cheated. I quickly closed my eyes, tried to find the memory of them, hoping it'd propel me back to the moment.

The door was hammered on again, this time more firmly. There was no chance of me returning to that moment, at least until tonight. I admitted defeat, thumped my pillow in frustration.

My bed was in a room directly above the front door of our house. This was not the A1 position in the house, especially with eight kids, two adults and two cats occupying the other rooms. The hinges and lock on that door must have come from Krypton, they'd been abused for years, showed no sign of weakness! I lay there thinking about the hinges, decided to do the maths; twelve people and two cats coming in and out of the front door an average of ten times per day, five times out five times in, perhaps the cats were a bit less as they sometimes used the kitchen window, but let's not worry too much about the mechanics. So here we are, how many? 14 x 10 = 140 per day x7 =980, approximately 1000 times per week, 52 weeks in a year, that's the hinges being called into action approximately 52,000 times in one year. I had been in that room for ten years! So that was approximately half a million door openings and closings, some loud, some quiet, some unexpected, some unwanted, some in amazement, some in disbelief, but ALL directly below my room, and not once had any of those knocks found me in bed with a girl, unless you counted the type I was just with! So there I lay, one, two, three more knocks, then an extra big pummelling knock. The foundations shuddered, still I heard no movement from any of the other rooms.

I knew exactly who it was: Jimmy Maxwell.

Jimmy's brother-in-law, Kenny, who owned the garage next door to Midas, felt sorry for me. He hated the way Frank treated me, said that I could come in, work with them for a fortnight. It was a trial, I agreed to work for nothing because I was absolutely sure that I could clinch a deal. They had the major contract in the city for Lada. Some people called them skips with engines, but I didn't have a clue about cars despite nearly a year fixing exhausts.

I was clattered back into reality by a major shout through the letterbox.

'Oi! Anybody in?'

I jumped out of bed, shivering as my feet touched the freezing lino on the floor. I went halfway down the stairs where I could see his shape at the door through the wired frosted glass. He stood up when he saw me. I put my hand up.

'Be there in five,' I said. I got dressed, grabbed a couple of slices of bread from the fridge, ran downstairs to where he was sitting smoking in his green and white Triumph Herald. He was wearing black leather driving gloves, how could he think that was cool? He did a lot of weird things that really pissed me off.

'Pop the hood,' he shouted, rolling down the window. A cloud of stinking horseshit flavoured smoke bellowed out, I waved it away, coughing to let him see my disgust. He didn't even acknowledge it.

'What?'

'Pop the hood.'

I deliberately ignored him, he was always trying to be an American, it bugged the shite out of me, he knew this.

Jimmy got the car from his uncle Guppy. It was a bigger pile of crap than his brother Stevie's blue one. After a bit it started up, I jumped in, we headed to the garage.

I'd seen Frank and Bob a couple of times as the garage was directly opposite Midas. They'd both ignored me, which suited me fine. I knew how they worked, or didn't, as the case may be, I nipped in a few times when they were sleeping or skiving off, stole some expensive exhausts. I put them in Kenny's garage store without any of the parties realising I'd done it. I reckoned Midas would shut down soon, hopefully the stuff I'd nicked would get Kenny some nice spare exhaust parts that he could sell on. After a week there I'd learned nothing about cars. I wasn't interested. Jimmy tried to walk me through how an engine worked, but by the time he'd got to the spark plugs I was yawning.

In truth there was no way I could work there, the only satisfaction I got was sticking the sausage rolls and biscuits into my gob at ten every morning. In the first week I managed to set one of the engines on fire. I was meant to be loosening the mainframe bolt with a blowtorch, but lost concentration. We managed to save the car, but it cost Kenny in spare parts.

The second week I was kicking a ball about in the garage courtyard as there was nothing happening, somehow I managed to trip myself up and pull a hair in my right leg. I felt pain right away, within a few minutes it had turned poisonous. I had to sit in the customer waiting room with my leg in the air for two hours until the swelling went down.

When it looked OK I wandered back through to the garage, not watching where I was going, banged into a fire extinguisher on the wall. It fell off, hit me right on the same spot where the poison had gathered. The leg of my dungarees swelled up so quickly, Jimmy rushed me to hospital to get it lanced on the spot. I had to take three days off, so there was no point in going back. That was the end of my apprenticeship.

I was job free again and pretty relieved the mechanic thing was not going to go ahead, I hated most of it. I still needed money, though and the dole were pressing me to get a job as I'd been on and off with them for years. As I was walking to the park for a kick-about on my own, I had a great idea. John and Tam were working full time as roofers, still making a fortune, but they also had a mobile disco that needed to be marketed and branded. I could do that. I couldn't wait till John got home from work for me to ask him. He'd mentioned it a while back, but nothing had come of it. I could also do the discos for him. I was flying again. When I felt this way my footy skills really took off, I could run all day and the control I had over the ball was mesmerising, even if there was only me, a ball and a patch of grass to witness it. Even though I no longer wanted to play for Hibs, I still loved the feeling of the ball at my feet. Every time I looked at a ball it set fireworks off in my heart, it's still the same to this day.

I heard them talking as they walked up the stairs. As usual they stopped outside the front door, gassed for a bit. As soon as John's key hit the lock, I was downstairs.

'How was work today, then?' I said.

John looked a bit surprised, probably because I'd never asked before.

'What are you after?' He said. He'd only recently forgiven me for the Halpern incident, I was glad that it was over with.

'Nothing. I've got an idea, that's all,' I said.

'What kind of idea?' He said, suspicious, raising an eyebrow.

'I reckon I could help Phoenix take off,' I said, smiling.

'It's already taken off, we've got over three grands worth of records, probably the best collection in Edinburgh, a great sound system and a light show to die for.'

'But I could help it take off more, let more people hear about it. Book more functions. Make more money.'

'Sounds good. How?'

'Like this,' I said, pulling my sketchbook from behind my back, showing him the ideas I'd scribbled up.

'Looks great,' he said. 'Tam and I are going to the pub later on, bring your ideas along, we can go over them.'

'Yes!' I said.

Tam was up for it as well, when they gave me a bundle of ten-pound notes for materials I was almost jumping. I got the logo and business cards designed and printed, got the van a nice big Phoenix Mobile Disco sticker with a matching one for the main light box. It looked great. We took an ad in Yellow Pages and the phone was buzzing off the hook. It was great for a while....

One night Dave Flucker, who also had a mobile disco with various gigs in and around the city, had double booked, needed a DJ to take over at one of his venues.

'You'll have to take your own record collection and light show,' he said to John over the phone.

'Are you sure you can work his decks and the lights?' John said to me.

'Of course, it'll be the same as yours or at least similar; if not, I'll figure it out,' I said confidently.

'Well, if you're sure,' he said.

'I am. One hundred per cent,' I said.

'Hi Dave,' he said, putting the phone back to his mouth, 'Jimmy will do it.'

'Great.' I heard Dave's voice leap out from the phone. 'Can we say usual fee?'

'How about a tenner extra,' John said, 'since it's at such short notice?'

'Deal,' Dave said.

Wow, this would be the first time I'd actually be in charge of a disco, it wasn't the usual mobile disco set up, this was an actual discotheque, Uptowns Disco. I was pumped.

John drove the van up to the venue in the city centre, helped me unload all of their records. We hauled them into this big disco hall, it looked amazing. It was early so the only people hanging around were bar staff and management.

John waved as he drove off. 'Have a good night,' he shouted. I waved back, quickly realising that I hadn't practised with John and Tam's equipment, never mind trying to work out something way more complex. I was capable of doing the mobile disco stuff with them taking over for a few hours and so on, but this was on a totally different level. I'd moved up three divisions. I tried to forget about the technicalities, got to work setting up the light show. I nipped to the bar, got a beer, everything fell into place, after the third drink it was a breeze.

Around half-eight, the punters began to arrive. It was easy, I put on a compilation record, a Jive Bunny twelve inch or something like it, a few folk got up, started dancing. I continued with the comps, the floor was filling up, they seemed to like my taste in music. I thought I'd throw in a few unconventional ones from the Phoenix magic boxes, stuck on a bit of Human League, Being Boiled, then Empire State Human. They were loving it, I was in my element. Ultravox, Quiet Men, OMD, Electricity. They went wild. I had found my new job. I was a DJ! The place was stowed, there were lassies all over the place, some crackers, I was up on that plinth, they loved me. A few girls came up to the decks, brought me drinks. I had never felt so important before, I was a God! The power went to my head, I tried mixing a few things on the decks; Blondie mixed with the Dooleys, Jilted John v The Buggles and Boney M v Shakin' Stevens was an absolute disaster. I quickly shifted back to what I knew.

The night flew in way too quickly. By the end of it I had a choice of two girls to go home with. Before I left, I plucked half a dozen smoochy records from the 'slow' box, headed out with Joelle. She was blonde, quite tall, she had these incredibly big boobs.

The nearest I'd got to touching a lassie before was a good year or two earlier when I'd bagged off with a girl in Tiffany's. It was the week before Christmas, we'd spent the night snogging in a corner. She looked amazing, almost let me touch her boobs, but pulled my hand away at the last minute.

'You can go there next time,' she said.

'Next time?

'You can take me to the Christmas Ball here next week, I may have a little surprise for you.'

I was as excited about that as I'd ever been about anything. I was pretty smashed, if the truth be told, but still remembered what she'd said.

The following week I went to meet her at St Andrew's Square bus station, she was coming in from Fife. I turned up half an hour early, went for a beer first. I couldn't really remember exactly what she looked like, searched my memory banks for clues, but there was not a lot there.

I hid behind the pillar at the stop where the Fife bus pulled in, making sure nobody would see me unless I wanted them to. A couple of buses pulled in but nobody that came off registered in my head. About ten past seven another Kingdom of Fife bus pulled in, as the passengers disembarked, I got a horrible jolt in my gut. This was definitely her.

I was horrified, how could I bag off with a munter like that? She was everything I did not like in a girl. Fat, frumpy, too much make up, shit dress sense, if my mates saw me walk into Tiffany's with her I'd be laughed at for years; there was no way this was going to happen. I decided to leg it.

I walked quietly around the back of the pillar, making sure she wouldn't spot, me, but unfortunately as I was crossing the gangway I slipped in some spilt diesel from a bus, fell onto my arse. She spotted me as I let out a pained cry. *FUCK*! I thought to myself, *how the hell am I going to get out of this one*? More to the point, how would I get diesel out of John's new jeans?

'Jimmy? Jimmy?'

She was walking over to me, waving and smiling. I had no chance of escaping.

'Hi, Alison,' I said, smiling. I think it was believable. She helped me up, getting some diesel onto her dress.

'Sorry,' I said. 'I slipped in the diesel, I was heading over to the flower stall to get you some flowers, but my shoes haven't got great grip.'

'That's so sweet,' she said, smiling through her brown teeth.

How the fuck could I have been so close to that dental graveyard and not have noticed? I thought. The bottom row of her teeth looked like the New York skyline after a nuclear strike. I wanted to hit myself for being so drunk that night, I was raging at my stupidity.

I retched a bit as I distinctly remembered putting my tongue into her mouth last week, surprised I didn't cut my tongue.

As we were walking towards Tiffany's she pulled a packet of Drum tobacco and some cigarette papers from her bag, proceeded to make a roll up with one hand. She flicked it into her mouth and pulled a cheap lighter out of her blouse pocket.

'Fag?' She said. Offering it to me. It reminded me of a witchety grub, ready to burst open, spilling it's disgusting innards in my direction.

I let go of her hand immediately, tried to rub my hand clean on my jeans.

'It's tempting,' I said sarcastically. Of all the things I hated about her this was by far the worst, women smoking turned me off so much that I could not even stand being near them. She lit up, screwing her eyes up with the blanket of smoke that engulfed her. We walked in silence for a minute or two.

I had to dump her, NOW.

'How about a drink before we get to Tiffany's?' I said. 'It's still early.'

'Aye. Sure pal.'

I hadn't noticed how bad her accent was last week, it was pure schemie. I thought back, realised that we hadn't talked much, necked our way through the night. I could almost feel my guts bubbling up at the memory, wanted to steep my soiled lips in bleach, get rid of the mental brown coating on them.

We walked down past the Conan Doyle, I guided her along York Place to the Wally Dug, a basement pub that had been there for hundreds of years. I was hoping it would offer me a way out of this nightmare; surely there must have been tons of guys in my position within its walls during its existence?

I went up to the bar, ordered a beer for me and a Cinzano and Coke for her. I kept taking glances to see if she was really as bad as I thought, every time I looked, there was no improvement. I waited on the drinks, looking around for inspiration to escape. As the barman was getting some lime for her drink, a guy opened the toilet door, I looked inside and was sure I could see a half opened window at the back of it. My heart beat a bit faster. I paid for the drinks walked back to her and began some incredibly small talk.

'Hold on a minute,' I said putting my hand to my stomach. 'I don't feel too good.'

'Is the beer off?'

'Might be.' I turned the pained expression up a notch. 'I'll have to go to the loo,' I said, almost keeling over. I made sure that nobody was watching me as I didn't want to make an arse of myself. 'Hold that,' I said, giving her the half-finished beer.

I went to the loo, saw that the window was big enough to get out of. There were a couple of guys at the urinals so I waited for them to go before climbing onto the window ledge.

There was a constraining bolt on the window, but I reckoned I was thin enough to squeeze through the gap. I moved the net curtain out of the way, stuck my legs out. As I did this an old man came in, I was a bit embarrassed, I smiled at him and continued to struggle out of the window.

'If yer brekkin in, pal, ye'll have to come back in a few hours.'

'Nah, I'm alright, pal,' I said. 'Just getting some fresh air.'

'You'd be better using your lungs rather than your legs for that?' He said. Laughing.

As I got my arse out of the window the back pocket of John's jeans caught in the restraining bolt, I was stuck fast. How would I explain this, not just to Alison but to anyone else in the pub? The old boy looked round at me shaking his head as he pissed into the urinal.

I forced myself down, the only way to get free was to rip the back pocket off. I landed in a heap in the basement. I hadn't really looked out of the window and found that it was enclosed. It was covered in wire and had a metal gate that looked locked. I couldn't believe the mess I was in. I'd been in many of these basements before, we used to go in and steal the juice bottles and soda syphons, then sell them on. I looked up to the loo window, it was too high to climb back up to. I was stuck. How embarrassed was I going to be? How could I possibly explain this to her?

I got to the top of the stairs and was incredibly relieved to feel the gate open as I turned the rusty handle. I ran from the pub as fast as my legs would carry me. I didn't bother going to Tiffany's that night, ended up in the Caves disco instead, the main reason being that John's jeans were ripped at the back pocket and had a big streak of diesel on them. I never wore pants and could feel the cold whipping my arse cheek. The Caves was a nice dark place to hide this. I knew a few of my mates would be there as this was a regular haunt.

I made my way there via Princes Street, went down past Waverley Bridge and headed along King's Stables Road.

When I got there I bumped into Alex, who was there with a couple of his mates from work. I joined them, we had a good laugh. I told him about how I'd dumped Alison.

'She was fuckin bowfin,' he said.

'You could've told me how bad she was.'

'I did tell ye, but ye wouldnae listen.'

I remembered him telling me, but had thought he was jealous. 'Oh, shit. So you did,' I conceded, remembering how he'd tried to drag me up to the dance-floor away from her.

'Right boys,' he said rubbing his hands together, 'let's get talkin to some women.'

It was great venue, much better than Tiffany's. It had a load of coves all around the building, it used to be caverns where they put the victims of the plague and left them to die, looked like some of them had come back to life, the state of some of the punters in here.

They'd sanitised it since those days, there were a load of guys and girls snogging in the hidden cubby holes. I got bagging off with a lassie in no time. She was pretty chubby but had a nice face and good dress sense. As I was snogging her Alex walked past with a tall blonde.

He gave me a thumb's up; I was hoping it was acknowledgment that this one was better than the last.

At the end of the night I asked her if she wanted me to walk her home.

'That would be nice,' she said. 'There may even be a present in the park for you.'

'Present?' I said.

'Well, it is Christmas Eve,' she said, moving her hands to my back pockets, slipping her hand into the hole at the back of my jeans; she stopped, raised her eyebrows as she hit pure skin. 'I want to find out what's in Santa's sack,' she said, putting her coat over her shoulder, heading to the door.

I shit myself at this. I was still a virgin. I'd had a few drinks, the Dutch courage had given me a boost, I reckoned I was ready, but I guessed time would tell.

We walked a long way, my arse was freezing by this time. We got down to Inverleith Park where it was cold and pitch black.

'Come over here,' she said, walking towards the small swing park. We sat on a bench under a flickering lamppost, she grabbed me, we began snogging again. I was liking it, so was the wee felly.

'Let's have a look at you then,' she said.

I was embarrassed. 'Can we just do it?' I said. 'It's cold, I don't want to be naked too long.'

'Naked? What are you on about?' She said. 'I was only going to give you a hand job.'

'OK,' I said, gulping. This was the first time anybody other than me had been near my knob. I unzipped my fly, she stuck her eager hand in.

'How does that feel?' She said, not even looking at me.

'Freezin,' I said.

'Don't worry, I'll soon warm him up.' She pulled harder and harder, it was getting painful. I didn't know how it should feel, so I let her continue, almost whimpering with every pull. Her tongue was working away at the side of her mouth, she was looking away, whistling. Looked like she was trying to unblock a sink with a plunger.

After a good few minutes of pure agony I pulled her hand away.

'What are you doing?' She said.

'Can you do it more gently? It's meant to be soft and sensual.'

'That is gentle. Sorry I didn't bring Italian hand cream.'

She went to put her hand back into my jeans again, I stopped her.

'If that's the best you can do, forget it.'

'Forget it? Are you gay or something?'

'Piss off,' I said, annoyed at her mechanic's hands. 'Where did you learn to wank people off like that? Pulling a fucking Spacehopper's horns through a cat flap?' I said, examining my aching knob. 'It was meant to be pleasurable, now it looks like I'll need first aid.' I knew I had nothing to lose so I went for it. 'Any chance you could get your lipstick around my dipstick? At least your mouth'll be warm and soft.'

'Fuck you, ya ungrateful bastard,' she said, stormed off into the darkness. She came back a few minutes later looking sheepish.

'Gonnae walk me to the gate? It's dark, I might get attacked or something.'

'I wouldn't worry about that.'

'What do you mean?'

'If anybody threatens you, wank them off, that'll soon have them running.'

'Fuck you,' she said, and stormed off again, that was the last time I ever saw her.

I carefully zipped myself up, swore that I'd had enough of lassies for a long time.

A long time later... The night at Uptowns. After I'd made sure the records were safe and packed back in their cases, I walked with Joelle towards her house at Porty, kissing and cuddling in the alleyways. It felt great. I was aware that the records I was carrying were getting a bit awkward. I had brought three twelve-inch singles and three Commodores classics on six inch coloured vinyl. She had nice soft lips and was a good kisser, at least I thought so having so little experience to pull upon for comparison. We were going along beautifully introducing our nice soft lips and soft skin to each other when she ruined it.

We were lying on the warm soft grass in the middle of a big roundabout in the middle of Porty, I was on top of her.

'Gonnae geez a beardy?' She said.

'What's a beardy?' I said, really confused, I thought it was some kind of sexual thing.

'Ye rub yer stubble on my body.'

I was thrown, completely. 'Are you serious?'

'Aye? How no?'

'Feel my chin,' I said, guiding her hand to it. It was as smooth as a baby monkey's shaved arse.

'Oh, aye. Yer smooth. It's just that my brother geez me them sometimes.'

'Your brother?' I wanted away immediately.

'Aye. But he disnae go anywhere dodgy,' she said, as if that would make a difference. I had been carrying these records about, hoping to take them to her bedroom, play the smoochiest music, hopefully end up under her covers. By this time my arm was getting sore, I didn't want to go anywhere her brother had been, that was for sure.

'Listen, Joelle,' I said, 'I'm knackered, I'll get a taxi home, it's past three o'clock now, I have to be up early to pick the disco stuff up.'

'OK,' she said. 'See ya.'

That was it.

She wandered along by the promenade, shoes in her hands, dangling over her shoulders, I headed back to the Court. I didn't have enough money for a taxi so ended up waking all the way home. My arm and feet were aching as I'd been wearing John's newest leather shoes. It was way too long a walk, it took me a good two hours, I ungratefully felt anger at him for not breaking the shoes in first.

I got home absolutely pooped. It had been a good, long night, John was out for the count in the bed next to mine. I made sure I was quiet as I took his shoes off, untied a particularly tight knot in one of the laces, put them back in his cupboard. I hoped he hadn't noticed they were missing. I took my clothes off, jumped into my warm bed. As soon as my head hit horizontal I was out cold. We had no curtains on our windows, so as soon as dawn broke we'd be hit by the bright light as the sun made its way past the school's big bell tower at the front of the Court, this could be really early some mornings.

I was deep in sleep when I felt the heat and light hit me. I Knew I hadn't had enough sleep. It felt like there were congealed breadcrumbs in my eyes. I rubbed them, trying to clear them away, summon up some energy.

I looked to my left, John was sitting up in his bed with a cup of tea, listening to the radio. As soon as he saw I was awake he turned the music down a tad.

'How'd it go last night then?' He said, sipping his tea, biting on a digestive.

'Great, it was an amazing night if I'm honest. They loved the music, the lights were brilliant, I almost got a bag off…'

As I was yabbering on, the Radio Forth news caught John's attention. He'd stopped listening to me and was concentrating on the words from the newsreader; he turned the volume up another few notches. I caught on very quickly as the radio announcer said the words:

'Last night there was a major fire in central Edinburgh. Uptowns Discotheque was completely gutted, the police are investigating the cause, it's said to be under suspicious circumstances. The roads have been closed since two o'clock this morning, there will be continue to be road closures for the rest of the week …'

As he said this I found myself being instantly endowed with super hero qualities. I somehow bounded out of bed, got my Hibs tracky on, got to the other side of the door before John even had time to put

The Lost Tornado

his tea down and get out of bed to grab me. I pulled the door shut and held the handle as if my life depended on it. I assure you, it did.

'Did you bring the records home last night?' He screamed. I could feel the power and rumbling raw energy of his anger as I held onto that handle; I was praying that the quality of the door handles would hold out. 'Did you bring the records home last night?'

It felt like the Incredible Hulk was on the other side of the door. I was sweating, it was making the plastic handle slippery. I got the sleeve of my tracky, pulled it over my sweaty hand to give me more purchase.

'Did you bring …?'

'NO!' I shouted. 'I was going to go and get them this afternoon.'

'AAAARRGGHHHH!' He shouted. There was a flurry of energy as the handle twisted to and fro. I was intent on not letting the handle go past the thirty degree mark; if it did, the door would pop open. He was getting even more furious at not being able to get out, the fact that I was able to keep him at bay made him even more annoyed, his aggression ramped up to level 99. I was fighting for my life here, I had to think fast.

I was weakening and knew that if I let go of the handle he'd be on top of me in an instant, pummelling my head with all of his pent up fury and whatever weapon lay to hand.

'Four thousand records?' He was shouting. 'Where are they?'

I was as shocked as him, but could only think of my survival. 'I'll get you your records back,' I said, trying to pacify him but only adding to his anger.

'Fuck off!' He shouted. 'Open this fucking door now or I'll kill you.'

'You'll kill me anyway.'

'Too right I will, ya wee bastard, open the fucking door.'

He booted the door. I looked around for escape routes.

Our room was at the top of the stairs, there were fourteen steps to the bottom of the stairs and a further stride or two to the front door. I was trying to figure out in my head how much time I'd need to get down the stairs.

'Open the door, sprint along the landing,' I said to myself. I knew that if I got a clear run of fifty or sixty metres I could outrun him. The problem was that by now most of the kids and Mum had got up from their beds and were loitering around me and the top of the stairs.

'What's happened?' Mum said, looking alarmed. John and I never fell out; well, I never fell out with him, at least.

I had no time to explain. John was getting stronger, I was getting weaker, I could definitely sense the power shift, the handle began to give, I was fast running out of time, sweat was now dripping from my head and arms, I could feel it work its way to the low point.

'Get out of the road,' I said to four of the kids who were now sitting on top of the steps watching, eating toast. 'Move out of the way.'

'Billy, Robert?' John shouted. 'Stop him, I'll give you money.'

The two of them made a move for me, but were way too small to stop me. I kicked them away with my left leg, making sure I did not let the handle go.

'Sorry, Mum,' I said.

I counted down inside my head, *three, two, one,* let go of the handle, pushed the door inwards. As I let go I could feel the pressure release, John had been putting so much effort into pulling the door open that he fell back into the room, flat on his back. 'AAARGH ya bastard.' I heard him almost cry with anger as he fell onto something. He wasn't down for long, though.

I took three huge steps and found myself at the bottom of the stairs, grabbed my trainers from the pile of shoes behind the front door, tucked them under my arm. I could hear John scatter the kids at the top of the stairs. I ran to the front door, my sweaty hands and panic kept me from gripping the lock properly. As John hit the bottom of the steps the door opened just in time, I bolted along the landing.

He was shouting at the top of his voice, 'Come back here, ya wee bastard. You owe me.'

I ran, and ran as fast as I could. I ran down to the front of the Court, that way it offered me a good half dozen escape routes. I knew I'd be able to get away from him. This gave me time to take stock of the situation and put my trainers on. What had happened? How could this disco have gone up in smoke in only a few hours? As John made his way towards me, anger written all over his face I tried to reason with him.

'I'm sorry, pal,' I said.

'Don't 'pal' me,' he said. His eyes were boring right into me, not blinking, teeth being ground against each other, his jaw set with pure hatred. I had seen him angry many times recently, mainly because of me, but nothing like this. This kind of anger could only be resolved with blood. Mine!

'Listen, John, could we at least check the facts before you kill me?' I said, semi-serious. 'It could be only hearsay.' I certainly hoped so.

'I'm going to kill you,' he said. He was walking slowly towards me, hoping that he could get close enough to pounce. I was way too aware of his moves after years of chasing him and vice versa. I ran a couple of steps back. As I passed the old garage next to Clapperton's I heard the bang, bang, bang again. I'd heard it a lot recently, made a mental note to investigate it. He ran after me and I ran until I got to St Mark's Park. As I ran down the road, I heard a stream of abuse, a couple of objects flew past my head, a traffic cone, a telephone directory and something else. I kept going, running and running until I was out of breath. I was delirious, my head was buzzing but it was all confusion, I could make no sense of any of it.

I'd lost him ages ago, but had to find somewhere to go to figure this out.

I was devastated, I really felt for John and Tam, they had invested all of their money, saving for a long time before buying the records and disco stuff. I also felt sorry for myself, my new life as a DJ had crashed and burned through no fault of my own. I sat on the grass next to the water of Leith down at Powderhall and wept through, fear, anger and frustration. I must have dozed off.

When I came to, I was famished, I hadn't had anything to eat since the night before I started the disco. My stomach rumbled, I got up, walked. I had no money with me, the trainers I'd picked up were a duff old pair with no laces, I must have looked like a tramp, my hair was still greasy, I smelled of sweat. I knew going home was not an option. John and Tam would be out looking for me in the van, although if Tam tried to come it, I'd fucking kill him.

He thought he was tough, but I knew he was softer than ginger shite. It was John I had to worry about. I knew Mum would be at her wits' end and hoped John had explained the situation to her.

I climbed over the walls around the greyhound stadium, making sure nobody saw me. I knew that it would be easy to grab a dozen rolls from the trays at Redbrae's Bakery, Gordon the baker left the new batches outside to cool at least six times a day. When I got over the wall opposite the bakery, he was putting the trays out. *Perfect timing*, I thought. I waited in the long grass. When he went back in, I knew I'd have plenty of time to nab some as this would be a tea break for him and the bakers. I made a quick assault on the closest tray, almost burnt my fingers. The rolls tasted like heaven.

I noticed there were a couple of bottles of milk inside the bakery door, so I grabbed one of those as well. It was simple food, but I could think of nothing better. I was still a bit weepy, when I welled up it was quite hard to get the chunks of dough down my throat; a good slug of milk did the trick, though.

I sat for ages. The food and drink had given me solace and the energy flooded back. I'd decided that the best bet was to investigate the fire myself. The first stopping point would be the guy who started the ball rolling in the first place, Davie Flucker. He stayed over the water at the park. I wandered over planning what I'd ask him.

'Naw, Davie's not in son,' his dad said, as he spoke to me from his window. 'He went out a few hours ago an he's no been back since.'

'Any idea when he'll be back?'

'Naw, son.'

'Thanks, Mr Flucker, Ah'll see if I can find him up town,' I said.

I headed down past the river, towards Pudicky pool, then made my way up Rodney Street, Broughton Street, headed for South Bridge, where Uptowns was, or used to be. When I arrived, there was a huge crowd gathered around the still smoking building. With me looking like a tramp, I blended in with the down and outs there. It was an unexpected bonus, the jakeys and skag boys were all hanging around the place, to see what they could blag, no doubt.

I made sure I kept in the background. The place had been cordoned off, there were fire engines and Pandas all over the shop.

I spotted Davie Flucker talking to John and Tam. There was a cop beside them, they were deep in conversation. I could see Tam looking around, he looked like he was enjoying centre stage. I stepped back behind a couple of auld pissheads in case he saw me; they were stinking, made me feel manky, felt like my clothes were having a gravitational pull on their dirtiness. I put my hands in my pockets, hunched my shoulders a bit. I'd gone from stud to dud in less than twelve hours.

I defo didn't want to be caught up there by John, I could never run away in those trainers.

I saw the proof with my own eyes; it wasn't hearsay, the place was gone. Phoenix Mobile Disco would never rise out of those ashes, that was definite. There was nothing I could do. I decided that since John was up here, I could go home, quickly grab a bag with some clothes, stay away for a while, at least until he had calmed down a bit.

When I got home, Mum was waiting behind the front door, worried. She opened it as soon as she saw my shadow on the glass.

'I'm sorry, Mum,' I said. 'Somebody burnt down the disco I was working in last night, I never had time to get John's records out.'

I could see she was hurting. 'Are the records insured?' She asked.

I hadn't even thought of that. 'I don't know,' I said, hope leapt up, re-energised me. If they were insured, I would be let off, Scot-free.

'If they're insured it usually takes a couple of weeks to sort out,' she said. I could sense the hope in her voice. The hope for John and I talking again, there could be nothing worse for her than John and I not talking. We'd grown up together our whole lives, been fostered out three or four times, developed the best brotherly love and bond through the adversity of those cold, sad places they called foster homes.

How I could find out if the insurance was going to save me, I wasn't sure.

'I'm going to grab a bag, stay with one of my pals for a few days, to get out of John's hair.'

'That's probably a good idea,' she said. 'You know what he can be like at times.'

I ran upstairs, packed my Hibs training bag, grabbed my best trainers, got a couple of pounds from my cupboard and headed out. As I opened the front door, Mum appeared at the kitchen doorway.

'If I hear anything about the insurance I'll send somebody to let you know. Where will you be?'

'I don't know, Mum. I'll be in touch, cheerio.'

I knew that none of my pals would be able to put me up, none of them had their own places, there was only one point of sanctuary I could go to without being found out. The cages.

I looked around, made sure nobody was following me and waded into the cold, dirty water, opened the door and disappeared for a few days. I wasn't sure how long I could last in that horrible, fungus-strewn basement, but I had no choice. The only good thing about it was that it was easy to get to different parts of the Court through its maze of tunnels. It also somehow amplified sounds from outside. I hoped I would be able to hear what was going on, the dream scenario would be if I heard somebody saying that John and Tam were insured. I opened the gate at the very back of the cages, dumped my bag on the old sofa, pulled a tea chest over, folded my arms, curled up and fell asleep. I was under the covers dozing when I heard people speaking, whispering.

I knew straight away that it was McCowan. He was not from the Court but came over here to muck about with some of the guys. It sounded like he had a lassie with him. McCowan with a lassie? I'd heard he'd been mucking about with a lassie that had run away from approved school, they were here in the cages; from the broken words I could hear, it sounded like they were going to shag!

I heard them walk right past me as I burrowed deeper into the sofa. They disappeared into the far away parts, I heard nothing more, until maybe ten minutes later. I sneaked up on them, could see they were cuddling, his chest was puffed out like a pigeon. That was the only interference of note the whole time I was down there.

Every night I woke at least a dozen times, shitting myself from the noises that I thought I heard. Scenes from films haunted me, zombies, dead children, aliens ready to abduct me.

I was getting more knackered than I thought possible. On the third morning, I'd had it. I had to go, take my punishment, if John knocked me out at least I'd be asleep. I stretched a bit to loosen my aches and pains, got all of the bits and pieces together, headed out into the early morning sunlight. The warmth was totally unexpected, it was glorious. I stood at the door of the cages like a lizard, absorbing that warmth. I headed up the ramp and was instantly thumped in the solar plexus by some writing on the main wall where we played football. In big, black, spray painted letters were the words:

JIMMY DIVINE IS STILL A VIRGEN

I had never been anybody's graffiti target before, I cannot explain how much it crushed me. The fact that the thick shit had spelt virgin incorrectly would probably mean my public virginity would be even more laughable.

There it was. My humiliation. Wide open for anybody, everybody, to see, my secret had been exposed, not that I ever said I wasn't a virgin. If I met John right now I didn't care, he could kill me, at least the ridicule of this exposure would stop.

I dropped my bag, ran to the wall. I'd hoped it would be fresh enough for me to remove, but the paint had solidified, there was no way that I could clean it off. I knew that my mum, dad, brothers, sisters and all my friends would without doubt have passed this wall in the days I'd been hiding and seen what was written.

I went upstairs to my room, ready to face John. As I put my key in the door, Mum was coming downstairs.

'What are you doing up so early?' I asked.

'Couldn't sleep,' she said. 'Are you OK?'

'Yeah, I'm fine, any news about the fire?'

'They weren't insured,' she said, looking upset.

'Ach well, I guess John and I will have to find a way around it.'

'He's away for a week.'

'Away? Where to?'

'Him and Tam got the opportunity to work in Manchester for a week, they said they'd get triple time and it looks like they still want to go ahead building the disco.'

'Oh,' I said, taken aback at the chance to get myself sorted out. 'I'm going for a bath, Mum, then I'll maybe have a sleep, but first I've got to do something.'

'OK,' she said. 'Fancy a cuppa?'

'That would be great.' I said. 'Maybe a bit of toast as well?'

I went upstairs to the cupboard filled with lots of junk and bric a brac, dug out a big tin of white paint and a brush, headed downstairs. When I got there I began painting the wall. The paint was far too thin, it would require at least three coats.

Jimmy Henderson, one of the guys who'd moved from The Fort to The Court, was heading over as I was finishing the first coat.

'McCowan did that,' he said. 'It's no use painting over, it everybody's seen it.'

'What do you mean?' I said, horrified.

'It's been there a couple of nights. McCowan lost his virginity with that curly burd, he's now a stud, or so he thinks.'

'Bastard, fucking thick bastard,' I said. 'Thanks for the info. I'll get that twat back.'

'Shouldn't be too difficult,' he said, and wandered off.

I painted over it three times that day, but it still showed through. I could not figure out why he'd do such a thing, I'd only ever been nice to him. That was it, though, a dose of revenge would be coming his way.

The banging in the garages had started up again. It really piqued my interest. I climbed onto the garage roofs, worked my way through the wooden beams, I opened the hatch that led to the garage.

There were three people standing below, a woman and two men, hitting a punch ball attached to the wall. They were dressed in tracksuits, towels around their necks, sweat pouring from them. They looked pretty fit. I'd never seen this type of training before I sat and watched them for a while, it was mesmerising, the thump, thump, thump of the punch ball.

One of them, the biggest guy, looked up, caught me watching. As soon as he moved towards the door I was out of there. It was easy to get away from him as I had a good two minutes to escape and an intricate knowledge of the rabbit warren we lived in. Getting away from him would present no problems.

CHAPTER 30

When John and Tam got back from Manchester, I was waiting for them at the train station. I wanted to face them, I felt really bad about losing their records, I had to stand up for my actions. This was my new idea, to take responsibility for my life, I'd done it with my health and fitness for a long time, this seemed a natural progression. When they got off the train they spotted me straight away, waved at me, there were no histrionics or accusations.

I was shocked and delighted.

'Fancy a pint?' Tam said to me as they walked through the barrier.

I shook hands with them both, apologised profusely for the records.

'It wasn't your fault,' John said, taking a big deep breath.

'What do you mean?'

'How could you have brought the records back with you when you had no van or car? Flucker told us that he'd promised to pick everything up.'

'Yeah, that's right,' I said, rubbing my chin. 'I'd forgotten about that.'

My heavy burden had shattered into a million pieces and floated away, I was deliriously happy. All within a few minutes.

We went to the Balmoral Hotel where we knew we'd be frowned upon, especially these two with their roofers' overalls and boots, covered in all kinds of dust and dirt. As we walked in the doorman went to stop us but we strolled right past the stuck up twat, into the bar. We had a couple of beers and got a cab down the road. I told John about the McCowan graffiti, we agreed to come up with a plan to get him back.

Two weeks later John moved into a flat in Bernard Street. This was the first time since he'd been born that he did not share a room with me. The house was leaking siblings, as Karen and Susan had also moved out in the past year.

It felt so strange having a room to myself for the first time at the age of twenty-one. It was quite liberating, gave me space to think. For the first time in my life I felt in control. I'd decided that I really wanted to be a graphic designer, all the negativity and cursing that I did after the funeral director interview had gone. It was replaced by a bridling, energetic enthusiasm.

I was still aware of my naivety in the subject, but I was more than willing to learn. I began to sell my futuristic paintings to one of the games arcades in Rodney Street. It was great for my confidence, all of my mates were quite proud of my work, which was a strange feeling, having tough guys appreciate art.

I became so confident that one day I walked into the dole office and asked about courses in art. Thankfully I was assigned a girl who gave me a whole lot of information, I must have timed it perfectly because within two weeks I was at college.

I did not have the qualifications for even the most basic art course as I left school with nothing but my name. I sat O' levels, then some highers, from there I got onto a diploma in graphic design and illustration course. I was jumping for joy when the letter came through. At the same time I'd had a hankering for music, after listening to the electronic bands that were in the charts. I saved my grant money for a deposit on a synthesizer in my neighbour's catalogue. I was also getting very fit.

I was having a kick-about with my mates at Warriston. There was a group of athletes training on the running track that was marked out in summer, they looked pretty good. Then some of my mates shouted at their coach, 'He could beat your guys anytime.'

I was really uncomfortable with them doing this, asked them to shut up. The coach came over to us when they were on a break.

'Right, if you think you're fit enough to train with these guys, come along to St Mark's Park a week on Thursday at six, we'll see how fit you are.'

'I didn't say anything, mister,' I said.

'Well, the offer's there.' He went back over to his squad and we got on with our game.

It got me thinking, though. Allan Wells had won the Olympic gold for the one hundred metres and the silver for the two hundred in Moscow. I couldn't believe my eyes when I saw him on the podium, it was the guy who'd chased me from the garage.

I could see how well built he was, it looked like the punch ball they'd been working on had worked a treat. I got home and set to work on getting myself even fitter than I was. I decided that I needed some starting blocks. I looked at the price of a real pair, a hundred and fifty pounds was about a hundred and forty seven pounds out of my budget.

I had a look at some in a sports shop, realised that they'd be pretty straightforward to make. All I needed was an old door-frame and some blocks of wood. There were always plenty of skips around East Claremont Street, people doing renovations in the old flats. I picked up a couple of nice old door-frames, sawed them to around three feet in length. I then got a couple of blocks of wood from the same skip, sawed them to the angle I thought my feet should be in on the starting line. I hammered the contraption together with some big nails that I borrowed from my mate's tool-kit and headed over to the park to practice.

It was awkward taking all of that weight, plus a hammer. I was knackered by the time I got there. I measured out a hundred metres and set the starting blocks down. I used six-inch nails to secure the blocks into the grass. I had a hand-held stopwatch with me, did a quick warm up before attempting the world record.

I got down on all fours, not really knowing what to do in the blocks. Counted down: *three, two, one, go.*

I flew out of the blocks and the blocks flew away from me in the opposite direction. They disintegrated, I ended up face down in the dirt. I tried to patch them up, but the wood had split all down the middle. I threw them into the bushes, making sure I bent the nails first so that no animals or kids would get injured. I stretched again and decided to carry on. I ran the first hundred metres, then looked at the watch.

Eleven seconds dead. Allan Wells had run 10.2 to win gold at the Moscow Olympics so I was not far behind him. I got my breath back and ran again, this time 10.5. I knew I was fast, but this surprised me. I eventually got it down to 10.2, the same as the Moscow Olympics winning time.

I was buzzing. In my first session at really trying to sprint I'd equalled Allan Wells' Olympic time, that was me wearing some cheap baseball boots that Uncle Richard had brought up in one of his black bin liners. I began to think they were special boots. There was a comic about a kid who had these magic football boots, 'Billy's Boots', it was called, I truly thought I'd found the running equivalent.

I went home that night and could hardly sleep for the excitement. I couldn't wait to race these professional guys, show them how special I was!

I told Mum and a couple of my pals about it, but there was no real interest.

'That's good son,' Mum said, while peeling spuds. 'Remember to bring your washing down.'

I bumped into one of the Court's real good guys Rab Robertson, told him about my time, I knew he'd be interested as he was a pro runner years ago.

'Pop intae the hoose next time yer headin over tae the park an I'll gie ye an auld pair ay spikes, great time by the way pal'. He said giving me a double thumbs up.

The next day I popped into his house and the spikes were waiting for me in a blue training shoe bag. I opened it up as I walked along the landing, they must have been thirty or forty years old, the leather was harder than concrete and the spikes were actually three inch nails hammered through from the inside. It was a lovely gesture but I'd have ripped my feet to bits if I'd tried to run in them. I took them back to my room, stuck them under the bed. I jogged the park and ran around a bit, I'd probably knackered myself in the warm up, I was so eager to prove myself. I never mentioned my times to the guys I was training with. I wanted to blow their minds.

'Right, pal, what's your name?' The coach said.

'Jim Divine.'

'I'm Fred. Right, Jim Divine, are you ready to work hard?'

'Yip, sure am,' I said. Nervous, not really sure what to expect. He introduced me to the squad; Adam, Steve, Tracy, Valerie, I shook hands with them all.

'We'll be running ten by two hundred metres, with a minute recovery'. Said Fred.

'What does that mean?' I said. 'I've never done a session before.'

'It means that you run two hundred metres, you get one minute's rest, then you go again, ten times.'

'Ten times?' I said, failing to believe it.

'Yip. Ten times, then a run to warm down.'

'What? Ten times, then a run? Are you serious?'

He ignored me, walked to where the guys were warming up.

After the first run I was floored. I'd gone at it one hundred per cent and left the others behind. They smiled at me, knowing that I'd tire soon. What surprised all of them was that I didn't, I kept ahead of them all on every run.

'Great running, pal,' Fred said to me after the session. 'You're a natural talent. Do you fancy running for our club?'

'I'd love to. What distance should I do?'

'I think you might be pretty good at eight hundred or fifteen hundred metres.'

'I'm a sprinter, though,' I said, a bit confused.

'You're not a sprinter, pal,' he said. 'You're quite fast, but I don't think you can sprint.'

'But I did the same time as Allan Wells for the one hundred metres,' I said.

'Is that right, pal?' He said, raising his eyebrows.

I could see he thought I was loony toons, the rest of the group looked a bit embarrassed.

'Right, I'll prove it,' I said. 'I'll get my breath back and do a hundred metres, OK?'

'Fine.'

After a painful stretch, I got down into the sprint position.

'Say go,' I said to him, holding the stopwatch in my hand.

'Three, two, one, go!' He shouted.

I bolted, I felt I was running like the wind. I finished, clicked the watch and headed back to the group.

It showed 10.4 which, given all of the training I'd done, I was happy with. As I walked back I watched for the looks of incredulity on their faces.

'Told you you weren't a sprinter,' Fred said.

'What do you mean?' Would I have to break ten seconds to impress this guy? I showed him the watch. 'Look, 10.4,' I said.

'Sorry, pal, your watch must be wrong, I got you at 12.5.'

'Eh?' I said, grabbing the watch from his hand. He had a digital stopwatch, right enough it said 12.53.

'Let me see your watch,' he said.

I handed it over with the 10.4 still registering. He held it up to his ear.

'This is a mechanical watch. Run again, but this time use my digital stopwatch.'

I took a short rest and did the hundred metres again. At the end I looked at the watch, it showed 12.9 seconds. I was devastated. 'What happened?' I asked.

He showed me my mechanical watch which he held, it registered at 13.1 seconds.

'Sorry, pal, believe me, you are not a sprinter. What happens with a mechanical stopwatch is that when you run with it, the force of gravity as you're swinging your arms back and forth slows it down dramatically.'

'So all that time I've been running two or three seconds slower than I thought?'

'That's right. You're a middle distance runner.'

I'd no idea what he meant.

'Why don't you come down to Meadowbank next week? There's a

meeting on, we'll get you entered for a race. How does that sound?'

'What distance will I run?'

'There's a fifteen hundred metres or a three thousand metres; I'll enter you for the fifteen hundred metres if that's OK?'

'Great,' I said.

He gave me his phone number, I set off back to the house, upset and slightly red faced about my sprinting, but incredibly confident that I could do some serious running in the race at Meadowbank. The Commonwealth Games had been held there fairly recently, it looked amazing on TV, I couldn't wait to set foot on a real track for the first time.

Fred called me later, gave me the details, from that moment all I could think about was the fifteen hundred metres. I was nervous but exceptionally confident. I had no idea what time I'd run but was pretty sure it would be close to the world record. I had no idea what that was, but I knew I was fitter than anybody I knew, therefore if I really tried, I could probably get close to or break it.

I was thinking about what to wear to the track and what I'd say to the press after the race. I thought about the headlines that would appear. I thought it would be worthwhile writing a small speech about my new record, how I'd come from nowhere. I went to the sports shop in Leith Walk, ironically enough, next door to Midas Exhaust. I was tempted to go in and let that arsehole Frank know that I was about to become a legend, but in the end I couldn't be bothered.

I bought some blue running shorts and a nice white vest with a red and blue stripe. I felt awesome and unbeatable. From there I walked down to Meadowbank, it was only a twenty minute walk. When I got there, a few people were buzzing around. I got to reception and told them I was racing tonight. They sent me downstairs; I could hardly get down as my legs were like jelly.

A big queue of men and women were signing forms and warming up all over the place, they were the fittest bunch of people I'd ever seen. I looked for Fred and the gang but there was no sign of them. I knew I was running at 7.15, it was now 6.45. I looked around, spotted the queue for the men's fifteen hundred metres. As soon as I saw this my stomach went to bits.

The butterflies were going mental. I looked at the list, saw that there were four heats, with about twelve people in each. I'd never raced before and in truth only done one proper training session and that was only a few days ago. As I got to the front of the queue to sign in a man approached me.

'You must be Jim,' he said, extending his hand.

'Yes, I am,' I said.

'Hi, I'm Ken,' he said, 'I'm in charge of Edinburgh Southern Harriers.'

I stood back a bit. ESH was Allan Wells' club, how did this guy know who I was?

'Fred said you'd be down to try the fifteen hundred metres. You're going in heat four, so make sure you warm up and are ready to go around 7.40.'

'Thanks,' I said. 'Where do I warm up?'

'Go into the concourse, behind the track. Good luck,' he said. 'I hope we'll be seeing more of you.'

Had he heard something about me? I wasn't sure. I popped my head into the concourse, had a look at the track, it looked massive. I scanned the stands and the stadium, the big orange track looked incredible, I stepped onto it, the sponginess of it felt great. It was a beautiful summer's night, the sun was heating me up nicely. There were no TV cameras about. *Why not*? I wondered, *they'll miss a world record.*

I spent a lot of time burning nervous energy. I watched the other three heats, these guys were seriously fast. I was in the last heat; did that mean it was the fastest guys I was running against? I had no idea. I got out, looked at the eleven guys I'd be running against trying to weigh them up. We waited on the line, the starter guy got the gun at the ready.

'On your marks …' he shouted.

I got down into the sprint position, on all fours. The other guys looked at me as if I was mental. *I wonder why they haven't done this?*

I thought, *surely I'll get the best start.*

'…. Go!'

The guy with the gun fired. They were off, I fell over trying to get to my feet from my knees. I blasted after them, caught them, ran to the front of the group, lasted for about six or seven hundred metres. I was knackered and was overtaken. Everybody was running past me. How could this be? I lost more and more power, by the time I got to the third lap I was done in, I could see the second last guy way up ahead of me, but I had nothing left. I never realised that the bouncy surface would take so much out of my legs.

My lungs were burning, my arms and legs seized up, I was gasping and lumbering like an asthmatic gibbon who'd climbed the stairs of the Empire State building.

I swore I'd finish, though I had to dig in so hard to get over the line. A few people in the crowd gave me the sympathetic hand-clap. I fell over the line, snot and sweat dripping all over the place, I lay there trying to get my breath back. I was mortified.

Still lying on the ground, I reached into the small pocket on my shorts, took out the bit of paper with the speech on it, blew my nose on it and ripped it into a thousand bits.

'Fucking loser,' I shouted.

I could hardly move, cramp was setting in everywhere.

'Come on son'. The starter said. 'The next race is starting soon'.

It took all of my energy to get onto all fours and scrape myself off the track. I lay on the sidelines for ages, feeling completely worthless. Cursing myself for my stupidity. As I lay there I sensed somebody above, a big shadow covered me, they were blocking my sun.

'Nice start, pal,' someone said.

I looked up, squinting as the sun hit my eyes, shielded them to see who was speaking. I didn't recognise the bloke, he was tall, looked a bit familiar, but I couldn't place him.

'I mean it,' he said. 'You really did get a good start.' He reached down offered me a hand up, I took it gratefully, stood up.

'I'm Willie,' he said, 'Willie Wells.'

I realised immediately that he must be Allan's brother, they looked like each other. I took his hand, shook it.

'I'm Jim.'

'I know, Ken told me. Fancy a jog to loosen off?'

'I'm not sure if I've got the energy,' I said, bending over trying to get some air into my lungs.

'You have, I can tell.'

As we jogged around the track my energy slowly returned. Willie gave me some good advice and by the end of the night we were training partners. He invited me down to Fettes to train with Edinburgh Southern Harriers. From then on I trained five days a week. My nights were being filled up, as I split them between this, my band and college.

I got a couple of guys to come along to the BB hall, the idea was that we would jam, me with my synth, them with their instruments. It went pretty well, I'd been writing some lyrics and music now that I had my own room, my own space. Eventually we hired a practice room, it was in the old Regal cinema in Abbeyhill. Stevie Ross and I had bumped into each other, first time since school and he'd mentioned that he too had started a band, they practised there.

It was amazing, the cinema had literally closed and shut down overnight. Everything was still there, the seats, stage, ticket booths, it was like practising in a haunted cinema, some great inspiration.

My life felt amazing, like this was how it should be. It was as if I'd had some kind of epiphany. Not long ago I had nothing, no hopes or dreams, no energy or ambition, but now I had too much of everything except time.

I loved my new design course. I'd leap out of bed in the morning with renewed energy every day, look at what I was going to learn and bound up to Telford college. The learning was great and the girls were spectacular.

There were all types and most to my liking, except for the smokers, of course. There was one guy who was very confident, he looked like Ted Danson, always came around looking at everybody's work. I thought he was an arrogant, judgemental arse and did not like him one bit. One day we got talking, surprisingly it grew into a great friendship.

His name was Rab, but we called him Billy Beak. He was a great artist, totally different from me, he was more into classical art whereas my bag was graphic art – state of the art, art. We hung out a lot, it turned out he stayed in a rented room at the end of my street.

We used to go to galleries and museums, discuss all kinds of things. The one thing he didn't have that I did was virginity. He grew up in the Borders, they say if you're still a virgin at fourteen there, your mum and dad would take you to a specialist to get it removed. He had all these stories of the girls he'd been with and what he'd done to, and with, them. I wanted to learn from the master.

Billy Beak was now really late for the pre-event drinks we'd arranged, I was getting pretty hacked off. In fact, I was getting to the stage where I wasn't going to be talking to him, seriously. It was ten past six, there was still no sign of him. He was meant to be there at half five so we could have a few beers before the college fancy dress. He was going to help me get ready, put on my make-up, show me how to put on sussies and that. There was a pause as the Tainted Love single on my deck set itself up to play another time, probably worn the needle out as I'd had it on all night.

As the song was about to start again I heard laughing coming from the street. I opened the big awkward windows making sure I didn't get my dressing gown covered in condensation from the damp on the glass and frame. I looked out, saw this big, lanky, ugly lookin woman laughing her head off. She looked up, shouted at me.

'Aw right, Jimbo boy?'

I realised it was Billy Beak, dressed as a hoor, he could hardly walk for laughing.

'What are you doing?' I shouted.

He looked up, collapsed onto the ground, he couldn't move for laughing. I thought he was pished.

'Come on, ya mongol,' I shouted. 'Get up here, we're meant to be going to the disco in a while.'

He got himself up from the ground, made his way to the front door. Robert looked through the letterbox, unsure of what was on the other side of it. It took him a few minutes to figure it was Billy Beak, but he opened the door, let him in.

He headed for the stairs, made his way up to my room, no directions required. When he got up he fell all over me, laughing like a loony.

'What is it?' I said, all serious.

He couldn't talk for laughing, he was waving all these tenners in his hand at me. I noticed his stockings were all mud around the knees and automatically assumed he'd been up Calton Hill giving blow-jobs to sailors. Again.

I tried to be serious again and pointed to his knees. That brought about another collapse of hilarity, even though I was trying to be serious, I began to laugh as well, in no time I was on the floor, we were both pishin ourselves laughing.

After a long time he told me his story.

Mrs McDonald, his aging landlady (who fed toast crusts to her dead goldfish via her toilet pan) burst into his room crying her eyes out.

'Billy Beak's dead, Billy Beak's dead,' she was saying. She didn't even acknowledge that he was dressed in a long floral dress, applying bright red lipstick in the mirror. She grabbed his arm, dragged him though to her bedroom, then pointed to the brass birdcage next to her bed.

'He's in there,' she said, hands shaking, hoping Billy Beak could perform one single miracle.

Billy opened the cage up, saw the wee yelly felly lying there. Dead. She was right on that score.

I called Rab Billy Beak because when I first met him he used to stutter and mumble a lot, one day he was talking about something and mentioned 'B B Billy B B B Beak'. I thought that was his name. Turned out he was talking about his landlady's canary.

The name stuck, so now everybody that knew him called him Billy Beak.

Mrs. Mack pointed to the cage. Billy picked up the wee felly gently, took him over to the bed and laid him on the old woman's pillow.

'What d'ye want me to do with him, Mrs Mack?' He said.

'Oh, Bob,' she said, 'can you try mouth to mouth?' She was sobbing her old heart out.

Billy pretended to try it by blowing into his fist.

'It's no good, Mrs Mack, he's gone.'

She burst into uncontrollable weeping.

'Can we cremate him? It's what he wanted, he always talked about this moment.'

At this point, Billy fell back on my bed, began to piss himself again, thinking about it.

'No, Mrs Mack,' he said, 'I think maybe he should go to meet wee Herbert, via the toilet pan?'

'No.' She insisted, 'it's got to be cremation. He told me a few weeks ago, insisted in fact. We could do it in the oven,' she said, pointing to the kitchen, her old hand shaking with the loss of what would definitely be her last pet and companion.

'I really don't think that's such a good idea,' said Billy. 'We might set off the smoke alarm. Don't want the fire brigade coming up here thinking we're cooking canaries, do we?'

'Yes, I suppose you have a point,' she said, tears running down all the crevasses in her auld face, turning to a kind of pink sludge with all the foundation she'd got on.

Her hankie looked like an artist's rag.

'Can we bury him, then?' She said, hopefully.

'I'm sure we could do that, Mrs Mack. You put the kettle on, make yerself a nice cup of tea, I'll nip down into the back garden and dig a grave for him, then we can put him to rest with a wee prayer.'

'OK,' she said. As she headed to the kitchen he nipped down to the back garden. When he got down there he realised how cold it was, it was freezing and him with only a dress and some long socks on.

He'd got the canary in one hand and a soup spoon in the other, ready to dig a grave. As he plunged the spoon into the solid ground it was so hard that he twisted his wrist. He tried again, he was putting so much pressure on his fists that he accidentally squeezed Billy in his other hand. Billy was practically liquidised. Thankfully most of the feathers kept the goo in one piece. He tried again, this time putting the remains on the ground first.

No chance. The earth was way too hard to penetrate, he then had a brainwave.

He went back up the stair, got the kettle that'd boiled, took it down to the garden to melt the cold, hard ground, no problem this time, he laughed at the daftness of the situation. He piled up the bit of mud ready to fill in the tiny grave after the funeral and looked around for Billy.

As he was kneeling down, scratching his head, a ginger cat dashed out from a corner, with yellow bits in its mouth, mostly feathers.

'Fuck,' Billy said as he puts his hands to his face getting mud all over it.

'Come here, ya wee shite,' he shouted. The cat was kind of cornered but determined not to let go of its prize. Billy'd got the spoon, ready to throw at it when he heard shouting from up the stair.

'Bob, Bob? Are we ready for the service yet?'

He looked right up to the top landing, saw that Mrs Mack had got herself all dolled up for the send off.

'Fuck,' he shouted. 'Just preparing the final bits, Mrs Mack, not be long now.'

He knew it'd take her about ten minutes to get down the stair. Spotting an opportunity, the cat bolted out of the corner and disappeared down the road. Billy chased it for a couple of seconds, but there was no chance of catching it.

'Fuck!

He walked back to the stair, checked the progress of the auld yin; still plenty of time to do something, but what?

He went to the cupboard at the bottom of the stair, raked through the bins. There was a cardboard box and some tissue paper. 'That'll do nicely,' he said to himself. He took the spoon, wrapped it up in the tissue paper, put it in the box and wrapped it up, the first time being an art student has EVER come in handy. He felt the weight of it and was surprised that it was pretty convincing, not too far off the weight of a heavy canary, so he didn't think the auld yin'd notice.

She arrived at the bottom of the stairs.

'Where is my poor wee chap?' She said, still wiping tears away.

'I've dug a plot and got his coffin sorted for you, Mrs Mack,' Billy said. He showed her the box.

'Bob,' she said, 'it's wonderful, what he'd always talked about having when his time came.'

He handed her the box, she took it with both hands, looked like she was going for a final peek when Billy stopped her.

'Sorry, Mrs Mack, it's bad luck to look at a canary when it's been laid to rest. Remember, your father was a miner?'

'Oh, of course, sorry, I wanted to see him for one last …'

And with that she broke down again. Billy gratefully took the box out of her hands, laid it into the hole in the ground.

'Do you want to say somethin, Mrs Mack?' He said.

She shut her eyes, said a prayer. Billy kicked the dirt that was lying at the side onto the box while she had her eyes shut. When she opened them it was covered.

'Can we get a little cross for him, Bob?'

'Of course we can, Mrs Mack, I'll see to it tomorrow. It'll cost though.'

'I know, I know. Let's not worry about the money now.'

Billy took her hand, walked her incredibly slowly back up to the top of the stairs, cursing as every step was making him a step later. As they were going up there was a ginger cat sitting next to a mat licking its lips, Billy made sure he gave it a sly boot as he was passing.

When everything had gone back to normal, he got himself ready to come along to my house. As he was leaving the flat, Mrs Mack handed him a bundle of notes, said to him, 'Here's the money for the gravestone.'

As he went downstairs he counted the money, laughed, he was still laughing when he got to my house.

After all the hilarity, laughing and the realisation that we'd got enough money for the next month of nights out, we got down to getting ready for the disco.

'Two hundred quid Jim, and do you know the worst thing?' He said as he was doing my make-up.

'I killed the wee felly.'

'What?' I said, 'How?'

'I was lookin after him last week when she was away at her sister's place. I gave him half a banana as a treat, thought he would peck away at it a bit at a time. I ended up staying over at a lassie's house for a couple of nights. When I got back, the banana was gone and he was about twice the size, looked like a feather-covered tennis ball. He wasn't dead, he was looking up at me unable to move, his beak was glued together in a big brown sticky mess with the dried-up banana. I tried to loosen the mess with hankies and hot water, but it wouldn't budge, he was getting bits of hankie stuck on his beak. Eventually I had to get one of the craft knives I use to sharpen my pencils and scrape it off. As I was doing that, he panicked, keeled over.

That was it.

I thought to myself, well she's not back till Sunday, I'll clear him up in the morning after the party. That was an hour ago, when I was getting ready, in she came.

'Billy Beak's dead.' And the funniest thing is,' he said, as he started pissing himself again, 'she thought he'd committed suicide! Found the craft knife at the bottom of his cage.'

The two of us were poorless for ages after that. We were drinking some Woodpecker cider, and Pernod and black currants as we were getting ready for the college fancy dress disco. Hall and Oates, *Abandoned Luncheonette* was giving it big licks on the record player. I'd decided to go as a female vampire an Billy was going as a hoor. I borrowed my wee sister's mini skirt, and I'd got a wee cape thing that covered my shoulders, long fishnet stockings and a pair of my big sister's high heels.

Once Billy had helped me to put my make-up on, I looked

pretty hot, actually,

'I'd sleep with me if I was a lassie,' I said.

Billy agreed. 'Aye, yer no bad pal, you better hope I get laid the night or you could be in for a surprise.'

After listening to Hall and Oates, Ultravox, John Foxx and Human League for hours, we decided to hit the road. The two of us were feeling barry, ready to take on the world and get laid.

Billy Beak had picked up more women than I'd picked head lice, so it wasn't a problem for him. He could always pull, I didn't know how he did it. After cruising down Princes Street in Lothian's finest carriages, we jumped off at Shandwick Place, made our way to the disco in Lothian Road.

Jeezus. It was jumpin in there. More lassies than St Trinian's, they all looked as tasty, but in a non-pervy way.

We got right onto the floor, began boogying. We really had landed on planet get your end away.

I was dancing with all kinds of girls, with togas on, nurse's uniforms, and one with only a top and sussies. The lassie with the toga, Denise, really fancied me. She'd had her hands all over my backside, even encouraged me to put my hand into her toga.

I liked what I felt, but even though I was desperate to lose my virginity I thought I could do a bit better. There was a lassie, Bernie, who really was top class totty. I thought I'd got a chance, but she was getting a bit pissed, I was sure she'd pass out before long and I'd never want to sleep with a sleeping lassie.

I looked around for other options. Eventually a pal from college, Violet, came up to me.

'Ma pal fancies you and says if you dance with her there might be something a bit special for you later on.' She pointed her pal out to me, from what I could see under the bobbly green suit, she was better lookin than I thought she'd be, considering that Violet looked like something that you'd find Bagpuss dragging into his shop.

The lassie smiled at me, I was straight over to her. I could tell that she'd been around the back of a few bike sheds in her time, and with the mouth on her the boys wouldn't need a bicycle pump!

'Hullo, Mr Dracula, or should that be Miss?' She said.

'Call me Dra.K.O.O.L.' I said, spelling it out to her so as she got the 'kool' bit. 'And what have you come dressed as?'

'Well,' she said, 'the theme was films so I've come as James Bond's director.'

'OK,' I said, not really having a clue what she was on about.

'So, DraKool,' she said, 'can you turn into a bat?'

'No,' I said, 'but I can make hell of a racket in bed with my balls.'

She laughed for a long time at that, raised her eyebrows a couple of times, took a slug of her Stella. By this time it was about an hour from closing time, the DJ was experimenting with the slow dances.

'Fancy a boogie?' I said to her.

'Sure, why not, as long as you dinnae bite me. At least not yet,' she said, laughing.

I could feel my knob thinking about this girl, he was curious. He was trying to get out for a peek, I found it hard to control him with the silk pants and the mini skirt. I hobbled to the dance floor dodging in and out of tables trying to hide the wee felly's excitement. We danced, she grabbed my arse, there was no doubt, the wee man was gonnae get his first ever introduction to the soft fleshy thing that women have, and guys like me haven't.

Her tongue was all over my mouth, I felt like I'd driven into a car wash. I really had to control myself. This was something I'd been trying to do since god knew when. I'd failed miserably so often I thought it'd never happen.

We left the Citrus Club, headed to hers. Violet was hanging back a bit and her pal, Rhoda, her name was, said, 'Come on, Vi, yer holdin us up. I want to get hame, gie this sucker a taste of my blood.'

Violet looked at her all coy, for some reason, that scared the shit out of me. I'd read about weird lassies, mostly lesbians in America, taking guys home and chopping them up because they hated men. I got a bit of that vibe, but in reality I never had any choice, the wee felly was pulling me to her house.

We got up to Tollcross and she decided she was hungry. 'Fancy a chippy?'

'I could eat something.'

'Violet?'

'Nah, not my type.'

She killed herself laughing at that, Violet took the hump. 'I'll get hame for Toby,' she said. 'He's not been fed since the sefty.'

'Awright,' Rhoda said, 'I'll see you the morn.'

Violet didn't even wave to us, went off towards the meadows in a cream puff. I'd always suspected her lonely brain cell was recruiting for a flatmate, but hadn't realised she was a nutjob as well.

We wandered over to a kebab shop cum chippy. There was a guy there, looked Turkish. I could see that all the freshly cooked stuff was gone, all that was left were lukewarm remnants.

'I'll have a fish supper, pal,' I said.

'Sorry, mate, no feesh left. Meence pie?'

'Nah. What else have you got?'

'Steak sandweech supper?'

I'd never even heard of a steak sandwich, I really wanted to get back to her place. 'Aye, pal, that'll do. Can I get plenty tomato sauce on it please?'

'No problem, Mr Vampire,' he said, laughing at my outfit. He plonked about half a bottle on the thing, wrapped it up and left a couple of mouthfuls of the sandwich sticking out so's I could get immediate access.

'Can I have a single smoked sausage, pal?' Rhoda said.

'No problem, doll. Salt and sauce?'

'Nah, bung in two pickled onions, pal.'

She looked at me and smiled as I was busily chomping into my meat. She'd gone past the normal length of time for eye contact, I was thinking, *have I missed something here*? We got out of the shop, started walking.

'Over there,' she said, pointing to a side street next to a snooker club.

I was still getting stuck into my steak sandwich, getting tomato sauce all over my mouth. It was better that I'd expected, I hadn't realise how hungry I was. She unwrapped her sausage and pickled onions, positioned them so's it looked like a massive cock and two balls.

Fear suddenly hit me. That's what she was smiling at back at the chippy. She picked the sausage up, began to lick it. I was absolutely cacking myself and the wee felly had decided he wasn't sure if he was up to her expectations.

Fuck me, I thought, *if that's what she's after, she's picked up the wrong kinda kool.*

I was now thinking, *how can I get out of this?* My appetite had gone.

As we headed up to her gaff, up a small dark lane, we passed an auld jakey lying in the doorway of a carpet shop. There were empty cans Elnett hairspray scattered around him with holes in the bottom, looked like he'd been drinking the stuff. *Cannae be good hairspray coz his hair's in a shite state,* I thought to myself.

'Awright, doll?' He said to me. 'Any chance of a bite?'

I wasn't sure if he was talking about my chippy or the fact

that I was dressed like a vampire. I gave him the rest of my supper and followed Rhoda. She was in a real rush.

'Not eating yer sausage?' I said to her.

'Nah, only got it for a laugh. I'm hungry but I dinnae want food.'

She looked at me as if she'd devour me. Literally!

By this time I could feel the wee felly shaking in the sister's pants, he did not want to come out.

We got to a blue door with patterned glass in the top half, frosted at the bottom. Looked like it hadn't been painted in years. She put the key in quietly. As we were heading into the pokey flat, she headed to the kitchen, dumped her chippy. She whispered to me, 'Be quiet. My big brother's sleeping along the landing, he hates me bringing men back.'

Fuck, I thought, *this is a mistake, she wants a man, a big man at that, if the sausage is anything to go by. All she's got is a fluffy wee virgin and I know if I get close to her undercarriage I'll explode on impact, and she'll not be happy.*

The wee man was desperate for his education, carnal knowledge at Narnal College and all that, but he'd have preferred to have gone to school rather than straight to college!

Jeez, straight to the big time.

We tiptoed to her room, there was art stuff all over the place, paintings and drawings and stuff. It was all shite, her best stuff would struggle to reach 'passable' in my book. She pulled her big green broccoli fancy dress suit off, got under the rainbow duvet.

I'd seen my first real 'touchable' naked woman. I followed her, sat on top of the bed, wondering what to do next. The smell coming from the bed was honking, the smell of dope and yoghurt mixed together, but it was warm. She grabbed my mini skirt, yanked it off, ripping it a bit.

'Careful,' I said. 'My sister'll kill me if you rip it.'

'Sorry, Drakool,' she said, 'I want you inside me.'

I was doing everything I could to keep from creaming my undies. Jeez, I hoped I'd be able to do a bit of exploring, but there was no chance of that. I tried to think of things that'd prolong my pre-squirt time, all I could think of was how funny the big green broccoli outfit lying on the floor looked.

She was grasping at me, getting all desperate. I got the sister's pants off and slipped under the duvet. We cuddled. She was so warm and soft, it felt lovely, but wrong somehow.

She sat up, tucked her hair behind her left ear. 'Gonnae bite me?'

I went all gaga looking at her real tits. I could feel the slavers running from my gob, I stared and stared.

I realised then that I'd still got my rubber fangs in and dived on to her boobs, the rubber sank in, I chewed away like a gummy pensioner trying to eat a giant marshmallow. As I was about to pop her nipple into my gob she turned round, jumped on top of me, I thought I was in heaven. She was a bit porkier than the girls I'd been with before, but much softer to the touch than a magazine.

I'd still got the cape on, I tried to take it off but she stopped me.

'Leave it on, there's something sexy about it.'

'Can I at least take my fangs out?'

She shook her head, put her finger in between my rubber fangs and dived back under the duvet.

What the fuck's going on here? I thought.

'Do me now,' she whispered, 'I'm gaggin for it.'

She threw the duvet aside, she was lying on her back, her legs were wide open. I felt incredibly stupid with the cape on, but didn't want to lose the moment. I looked at her lying there, *how the hell is my wee thing even going to touch the sides of that?* I thought to myself.

I felt like a chipolata entering the channel tunnel hoping to cause a traffic jam! The wee felly was on a hair trigger, I think he must've touched a hair as he passed the border, I exploded before I'd even touched any part of her. I couldn't feel the sides of her, it was like a big gooey cave in there. I collapsed on top of her.

'What have you stopped for?' She said.

'Ehm, I've…'

'You've no come, have ye? You better no huv, if you've done anything stupid …'

'I think it's brewer's droop,' I said, trying to give myself a bit of time to regroup.

'Hold on a minute,' she said and got out the bed.

I heard her going to the kitchen, rustling and rattling about. The tap ran for a few seconds then she came back in.

'Here, do something wi this.'

It was dark, I was wondering what she was doing. There was a tiny bit of light coming in through the net curtain, I saw the smoked sausage, glistening in the orange glow from the street light. The silly cow must've taken it out of the bucket and washed it.

'Here, use it,' she said.

I was kneeling on her bed wearing a black plastic cape with my rubber fangs in one hand, a bit of smoked sausage in the other, and the other half of the sausage was missing.

I stopped, sat up with half the sausage in my hand and looked at her, she opened her eyes, I pointed to the half sausage.

'AAAARGHH, fuckkkk,' she said in a whisper. 'You're fuckin useless.'

God knows what she did but the remainder of the sausage flew out of her and skittered over the yellow nylon sheet, onto the floor.

'Are you getting hard yet?' She said in utter desperation.

I was thinking to myself, *I've got to get out of here, now.*

'Eh, I'm not getting hard yet twenty minutes maybe?'

'Fuck that.' She grabbed me again.

'Ouch!' I whispered. 'That's sore.'

She let go, tried to use her mouth on me, but I'd turned off ages ago. 'Fuck it. Looks like we'll have to wait, give me a shout when you feel something.' She turned over, thumped the pillow a couple of times.

'I'll nip to the loo,' I said. 'Where is it?'

'Up at the top of the landin, far end. My brother's in the room next to the bog, so keep very quiet.' I could tell she was utterly pissed off, I actually thought there was a chance she'd start hitting me.

She stuck her head back under the duvet. I was thinking, *this is my chance to escape.* As her head was under the covers I very quietly picked up the mini skirt, handbag and the shoes. My black shirt was still on the pillow, I couldn't risk taking it, arousing her suspicions. I found the toilet, had a look at myself in the mirror, thought, *what a fucking state.* My hair was all over the place with the gel that I'd used to flatten it down like a vampire, the dark make up on my coupon had been wiped to the four corners, I looked like a manic depressive. I decided to give myself a wash before I got out of the nut house.

I ran the hot tap, used the remnants of a bar of Imperial Leather soap to wash my hair and face.

'Fuck.' It dawned on me that I'd nothing to wear home bar the clothes that I'd got with me. I looked out of the bathroom window, the sun was coming up, there was a nice warm orange tint coming into the bathroom through the cracked window, but it was still freezing outside. I decided that I couldn't face going back into that bedroom.

'Right,' I said, looking in the mirror, 'Let's get out of this asylum pal.'

I dried myself, put the mini skirt, tights and cape back on. I quietly opened the bathroom door and headed for the front door. I was sneaking down the hall, trying to move away from all the squeaky floorboards. I was managing nicely, was just about at the front door, when I heard her whispering loudly, 'Where are you goin?'

'I'm gonnae go,' I said in a similar loud whisper. I made a quick move to the snib.

'Get back here. Now!'

I ignored her, continued trying to open the front door. I twisted the Yale lock and pulled; it didn't budge.

I tried again, same result. I could see that there was a mortise lock with no key in it. I looked down the hall, she was standing with it. Arms folded, leaning against the door frame, everything on show, I was sort of tempted. Looking at that soft nakedness, all the lovely parts in the right places, exactly what I'd wanted an hour ago, but I wasn't really big on the hassle again.

'Is this what you're lookin for?' She whispered. 'Come an get it.'

It was certainly a dilemma. I wanted sex but I also wanted it on my terms, this was mental. I knew there was no going through the front door, so looked for options. I ran to the kitchen, saw there was a big window in front of the sink.

I removed the chippy wrappers and a couple of dishes from the plastic basin in the sink. The window looked like it'd open fairly easily. I climbed onto the bunker, shoved the blind to one side and unlocked the snib on the top of the window. I pulled it up and I could see that there was a drop of about eight feet. I was about to go for it when I realised I'd left my handbag in the bog. It'd got my wallet in it with all my ID and things.

I scrambled down from the bunker, made my way quickly to the bog. I could hear her running down the hall, both desperate in our own way. There was a big quiet scramble as I got my bag and ran back to the kitchen.

She grabbed onto my leg and wouldn't let go. 'Get back to the fuckin bed,' she said.

This time it wasn't a whisper, though. She was going mental. She ripped at my tights, made a couple of ladders in them.

The hall was bright all of a sudden, I realised the silly cow had woken her big brother up.

'No,' she screamed, 'he'll go fuckin ballistic.'

The distraction gave me a couple of seconds to make my escape. I kicked her in the head, dived through the window. I lost my breath as I crashed on top of a bin.

The pain I was expecting didn't arrive as I realised that I'd landed on a bucket of offcuts from the carpet shop. In different circumstances it would have been quite a nice place for a kip, I'd been up for about twenty-two hours.

There was all hell breaking out in the kitchen. Her brother was up and he wasn't happy.

'What the fuck's goin on?' He was shouting at her. 'If it's you fucking guys again, ah'll fuckin kill ye.'

I heard her pleading. 'No, Archie, he's a pal.'

I was lying on the soft carpets, legs in the air, no pants on, a mini skirt wrapped around my head.

I looked up from the mattress of bin liners, there was this big massive curly head of brown hair and a lumberjack shirt lookin out of the window. He spotted me.

'You, ya fuckin cunt, get back here now,' he shouted.

A wine bottle whizzed past my head, smashed into the wall behind me. I ran like the clappers. Difficult in women's shoes but I wasn't waiting around.

I could hear him desperately trying to open the mortise lock, shouting, 'Where's the fuckin key?'

I took the shoes off and ran. I had to stop for a breath and spotted the auld jakey still sitting on the step.

He was about to pierce another can of hairspray, he looked at me, raised the can.

'Hair o the dug, pal,' he said.

I pointed to his head and said, 'Looks like it's working.'

He laughed as if he got the joke, took a slug from the tin.

I pointed to the sun coming up and said, 'Got to get back to my coffin, pal.'

He lifted the hairspray tin in salutation. I looked down the road, I could see Grizzly Adams looking about for me. I'd caught my breath again and ran until I found myself in Princes Street.

I walked home through all the back streets and back gardens, making sure that nobody saw me dressed like that. It took me an hour to walk a mile and a half, my feet were screaming at me. After what seemed like the longest night of my life I eventually arrived at the top of Claremont Court. *At long last*, I thought, finally breathing a sigh of relief. Bed, sweet bed, to sleep, to dream, no alarm clock for a few weeks.

I was walking past the buckets, almost home, when I heard two people talking, whispering.

I climbed into the big communal bucket as they were coming towards me. It was Sandy Thomson and Mikey Corrie. Looked like they were coming home from the town.

If they saw me dressed like that I'd be as well staying in the bucket until bucket day, ending it all at the tip.

Thankfully somebody shouted from a window, sounded like Gary Preston, they both about turned and headed to his house.

I climbed out of the bucket, the old food that'd stuck to me didn't bother me. I made my way up the stairs to the house, dug out my key from the handbag, ducked along the landing, in case anybody in their kitchen spotted me.

I was virtually on my last legs as I turned the key in the door. As I pushed it open, Tigger squeezed out. I clapped him as he passed me.

'Hope you have a better night out than I did pal,' I said to him.

I closed the door quietly, turned around.

The auld man was standing there, a cup of tea in one hand, a bacon roll in the other.

He didn't bite the roll or say anything.

He stood there looking at me, dressed as a manically depressed vampire lady-man.

He put the roll down on top of the electricity box, reached for his glasses. As he struggled to get focus I was way past him and up the stairs.

I dragged myself into my bed, collapsed in a big smelly, sore, tired heap. I didn't even bother removing my clothes, pulled the covers over me.

I lay there, eyelids seeming to weigh more than the rest of my body, I was breathing heavily, dazed, knackered, trying to figure out what I'd just lost; my virginity, dignity or sanity.

CHAPTER 31

That fuckin bastard, fuckin peg leg bastard, I'm gonnae kill him. John was beeling. He was back staying at our house while his flat was being renovated, as the dust from Leith was constantly getting in, leaving grey-black piles all over the place. Every couple of days he'd have to Hoover up a bagful, it was really getting on his tits.

'I'm scared tae sleep in', he said to me one day, 'Ah'll end up like thae boys fae Pompeii. You'll come in for me and I'll be under a pile ay black sand, like this'. He made a face that looked more like Frankenstein to me than a Pompeii .

He'd returned from another stint down south with his roofing company. He was fair raking the baubees in, him and Tam would go down for a week or two, return with hundreds of pounds, paid in cash. I was so jealous. I had absolutely no clue how to make money.

'When did it happen?' He said.

'Two nights ago,' I told him.

Alex Pugwash, the peg leg junkie bastard, had been holed up in the cages for weeks now. The pigs were after him for dealing drugs and assaulting somebody with a knife. Two mornings ago he must have woken up in a mood or junkie haze. Tigger, being his nonchalant carefree self was always after a clap, must have wandered up to him; he feared nobody as long as there was a clap in it for him, he was a cat that craved attention.

'The fuckin arsehole booted your ginger cat right in the jaw with his wooden leg,' Sandy Thomson had said.

He was right up to the house after witnessing it, turned up at the door with Tigger wrapped in a towel, mouth bleeding badly.

'Jimmy, ye'd better get the vet,' he said to me as I opened

the door. He was shaking as he held the cat. I took the bloody towel with Tigger wrapped in, swaddled tightly to keep his face together. I had a look. Poor wee thing was unconscious. I could feel his heart beating fast so I knew he was still alive. I peeled the bloody fur and blanket from his face. I was horrified. His bottom jaw was split in two, right down the middle, his tongue was caught in the bone at the side, looked like it had split in two as well, like a serpent's tongue. There were a few teeth missing. I was bubbling like a big lassie, so did Sandy.

'What happened?' I said. 'Who booted him?'

'It was Pugwash. Booted him right in the face, knocked him right across the landing.'

All I could think about was the impact of that bastard's fucking heavy plastic leg hitting Tigger's wee ginger face.

'Bastard,' I said. The thought of the kick brought more tears from me. 'D'ye think yer dad would gie me a lift up to the vet?'

'Aye, sure,' he said, 'I'll go and get him now.'

I remembered the conversation word for word as I relayed it to John...

'I went to the kitchen, wiped Tigger's mouth with a damp towel, making sure I didn't hurt him any more. After a minute a horn beeped outside, I looked out of the kitchen window. Spud and Sandy were waiting for me in their car. I wrapped him in a clean towel, headed out. Gordon and Catherine were hanging about, wondering what was going on. I hid Tigger from their eyes.'

'Good call,' John interjected. 'And ...?'

'The vet patched the wee felly up pretty well. He sewed his tongue up with some blue nylon thread, then took a long time to fix his jaw, he used wire. Tigger was in and out of consciousness for a while but the vet said he was one of the toughest cats he'd ever seen. That made me proud. He said the poor chap's had massive trauma, but he'll survive, you can pick him up tomorrow.'

'I gave the vet a fiver, Spud gave me some money to put into the volunteer's fund.'

John took his wallet out, handed me a twenty pound note. 'Here, give this to Spud.'

I took the money, put it in my pocket.

'So was the fiver enough for the vet?'

'Yeah,' I said. 'I felt guilty as hell, but I told him 'That's all I've got', he said it was fine.'

'Really?'

I nodded.

'So where's Pugwash now?' John said, anger escaping through his clenched teeth.

'I think he's still in the cages. Are you sure you should be doing this?' I was concerned that he was getting into something he'd regret.

Pugwash was a complete basket case. His whole life had been about him taking what he wanted. He'd lost his leg when a gravestone he was playing on fell on top of him, he was ten years old, had gone off the rails since. An elderly aunt had brought him up, there was no discipline in his life, he did what he wanted to do. He was a tough nut because he didn't care about anything, that made him reckless and dangerous.

When I was around him I could feel the danger emanating from him like an electricity sub-station. I always kept my distance, never getting within arm's length of him, but more importantly, within a leg's length. He had a big peg leg that could reach further than you expected, I'd found this out a few times, had the bruises to show for it. I didn't trust him but some of my mates were his mates so I had to tolerate his company occasionally.

It was late evening, when we got into the house. John went straight upstairs to Tigger's basket in our room. Tigger lifted his head from the tartan rug, tried to meow as we put the light on. The small pillow where he'd been sleeping was covered in a gooey blood. I could see a tear form in John's eye, he'd been the one that had looked after Tigger since he came to our house.

He lifted him gently, clapped him as if he was a newly born bairn, Tigger looked up at him, began to purr, it was magic. It was the first time I'd heard him purr since the accident – I'd decided to call it an accident because if I kept thinking about it as an attack I'd be tempted to kill that bastard, I had no idea what I'd do given the chance.

As I looked at Tigger purring it made me happy.

'Go an get him a saucer of milk,' John said.

He hadn't even taken his coat off yet. I nipped downstairs, there was a carton of cream in the fridge, which was a big surprise. I took the carton out, dropped a fair bit of it onto Tigger's saucer. After he'd polished it off, we put him back into his basket, turned the light off, then we had a quick bite and a cuppa.

'Right, let's go,' John said.

We headed down to the cages, being as quiet as possible. I'd picked up a torch from the electricity cupboard as we'd left the house, we'd both changed into dark clothes so as we could be as stealthy as possible.

It was easy locating Pugwash, there was a heavy snoring in the distance, although it was dark we could see a flickering glow, maybe a candle or fire.

As we approached the cage where he was sleeping, crawling on hands and knees through the gunge, the snoring got louder. We turned the last corner, saw him lying on a chair, head lolled right back, out for the count. There was a syringe lying discarded next to him and a pile of empty Cally Special cans. He was gone. John left my side, ran up to him, punched him straight in the face. It sounded awful, Pugwash hardly moved.

John smacked him again and again, drawing blood from his nose and mouth.

There was no sign of life in him. John shouted every time he punched him, he was really going to town on him.

'Kick-my-wee-fuckin-cat-would-ye,-ya-junkie-bastard?' He said, smacking his fists into him like he was a butcher's carcass.

A minute or two and he'd sorted himself out, the tension seeped away from him. I stood there, wincing with every punch, loving John for doing this but also realising that I was feeling the satisfaction too. I didn't have that sort of revenge or aggression within me. I had planning and subversiveness.

When John stood back he was sweating.

'Better?' I said.

He nodded.

'Right, now my turn,' I said.

John looked surprised. I walked up to Pugwash, grabbed the foot of his false leg, yanked it from the socket. John laughed. 'Brilliant' he said. 'Why didn't I think of that?'

I then sat on the other manky chair, undid the shoe on the leg. He was wearing a nice pair of Italian black leather pointy shoes, nicked no doubt.

'Can you take his other shoe off?' I said.

When we had both shoes off, I said, 'Swap.'

John handed me the right shoe.

'Here,' I said, 'put this one on his good leg.'

John looked confused, but he did it.

'Now do it up.'

He tied the lace, I put the right shoe on his false left leg.

'What are you up to?'

'You'll see'.

Before we left the cages, I raked through Pugwash's pockets, pulled out a set of keys. As we left I found the right key on the set, locked the padlock on the cage door. This would really piss him off when he woke up to discover he'd only got one leg with the wrong shoe on and he would be locked in, it would be priceless.

'Where are you going now?' John said.

'Just follow,' I said. 'You'll love it.'

He followed me into the school next to the Court, there were clubs and diet classes on so I knew getting past the Janny would be easy. John followed me all the way, along the dark passages, up the spiral staircase to the bell tower at the top of the building.

'Right, now give me a hand.'

We got the small hatch at the tower open and both climbed in, the big copper bell sat there, motionless. It took a lot of effort, but we managed to attach the plastic leg onto the bell clapper.

'Brilliant,' John said. 'That's inspired thinking.'

I felt really smug, the only downside was that we'd have to wait until the morning before the Janny rang the bell.

'One more thing,' I said. I headed from the school over to the phone box, John followed. I dialled 999.

'Police,' I said. I got through to emergency services.

'There's an escaped felon in the cages at Claremont Court,' I said, in a whiny, nasally Weegie voice, making sure I wouldn't be traced. 'It's Alex Pugwash, the peg leg.'

I put the phone down sharpish, wiped the receiver in case they got fingerprints.

John patted my back, smiling. As we headed back into the Court we bumped into Sandy.

'How's the wee man?' He said.

'He's actually doing really well, all things considered,' I said, handing him the twenty from my back pocket. 'Give this to your dad.'

'Very generous,' he said.

A couple of sirens sounded in the distance. Bang on cue two panda cars appeared at the top of the road. John and I smiled at each other.

'Wait till you see what we've done to that peg leg bastard, though,' John said.

We told him what we'd done, he burst out laughing.

'I'll have tae get a posse around in the mornin at bell-time.'

Everyone passing or going to the school the next morning looked up as the bell thudded out a horrible flat sound, fingers pointed at a leg with a fancy Italian shoe hanging from underneath the bell, the Janny scratched his head looking up.

'Eh?' He said, almost knocking his hat off. 'How in fuck's name …?'

A crowd of us lay opposite, on the bowling green club roof, laughing. I'd really wanted to set McCowan up, make Pugwash think that it was him that had taken his leg and put it up the tower. I still hated him for writing about me on the wall. I was seeking revenge but realised this would be a step too far.

If Pugwash thought it was McCowan he'd literally kill him. I decided to enjoy this, I'd get McCowan back some other day.

Chapter 32

My life had changed, I was getting incredibly fit, felt great. College was going really well, I'd decided that graphic design was my career, I'd also discovered that eight hundred metres was my running distance. Two laps of the track, or a half a mile in old money.

I'd run quite a few races now and was loving it, I liked challenging people. One evening I was going to do some screen-printing at college. I'd nipped home for tea, headed back about seven. It was a twenty-minute jog from the house to Telford.

As I walked up the long, dark, tree-lined road that led to college I was admiring the architecture of Fettes College. It was stunning.

Out of the blue two guys dropped out of the trees, landed either side of me. I was shocked initially, but my adrenaline shot kicked in, I was ready to deal with it.

'Awright, pal?' The big guy dressed in a once-white shell-suit said.

'Yeah, fine. Lovely evening for a stroll in such fine garments,' I said, tucking my portfolio a bit tighter under my arm. The insult went over his head.

'Got any fags?' The wee one said. He had a cream and light blue pin stripe suit on, piss marks all down the legs, well past its best. They were both scrawny, scruffy louts, reeked of stale cigarettes. That was something that really irked me. I hated the way the smell could encroach on my lungs and nasal passages without asking me for permission.

'Nah, dinnae smoke,' I said. Trying to sound tough, dropped the voice an octave lower than normal. 'Smokin's for losers.'

'Do you mind if we search ye?' The big one said. 'Just tae

make sure yer no hidin any roll-ups or stuff.'

'Fuck off,' I said. I was annoyed at these thick pricks, trying to dominate me, the effort I'd put in to my life so far. No way was I going to have it compromised by these lazy bastards.

I picked the pace up a bit and was at a brisk walking pace, I could hear skinny thicko start to wheeze a bit.

'What did you say to us?' The big one said.

'You heard, or are you deaf as well as stupid?'

He turned to pin stripe. 'Did you hear what he said to us?'

By this time I was really walking fast, they could hardly keep up. They were still either side of me, but I was a few steps ahead, feeling supremely confident. I stopped dead. They did too. We stood there facing each other, I could see big yin's fists were balled ready to throw a punch or two in my direction.

'Listen, lads,' I said. Holding my palms, downwards, towards them. 'I don't smoke because I think it's an incredibly stupid thing to do.' I emphasised the word stupid to really get on their tits. 'I'm really fit. I'm also really fast, you have absolutely no chance of catching me, so can I suggest that you turn around and go looking for somebody a bit fatter and smellier?'

They looked at each other.

'CHARGE!' They shouted in unison, as if they'd practised the routine, it was so funny.

I jogged eighty, ninety metres, easily doubled the distance between us. I looked around, they were out of breath, jogging slowly. I stopped again, they stood bent over, hands on their thighs, trying to claw some breath back into their wasted lungs.

'What did I tell you?' I said, more smugly than I'd ever felt. 'I told you not to waste your time.'

They half attempted a run, but gave up quickly.

'We'll fucking get ye, ya smart bastard. Just you wait,' the big one said, pointing his finger at me like a gun.

'You know what, guys?' I said, holding my hands up in the

air Rocky style, pretending to shadow box, punching fresh air. 'FUCK YOU. You pair of trampy bastards, if I ever see you again I'll kick yer arses back to Gyppoland or wherever you came from.'

They were absolutely raging, the big one was almost crying with pent up frustration at not being able to get me. I was as cocky as I'd ever been, it was like I had a superpower over these tramps, I loved it. They jogged towards me again, but were clearly knackered.

'Come on then, guys,' I said. I put my portfolio on the ground, did a couple of sets of twenty press-ups on it. They walked slowly towards me, trying to catch me out by quickly running at me. I was like a cat playing with a couple of mice, I was well in control. They wanted to hurt me with anything they could lay their hands on. The only things lying around were big branches that had fallen from the trees overhead, they made a few futile attempts at lobbing them towards me, but they were too big to throw any decent distance. I could feel their frustration and fed on it. I was loving this power.

'Sorry, boys, but I'm going to have to go now, people to see, things to do. Tata.'

I walked away wiggling my arse at them. I was high, untouchable.

'Say goodbye to this, cos it's all you'll see,' I said pointing to my tush. Man, that was such a high. I loved humiliating those fools.

I got to the class, and got on with my work. The euphoria subsided, turned to fear, in actual fact, as I realised that I had to take my big, heavy, framed painting home with me that night or lose it. I'd spent way too much time on the artwork, it was going to be used for my main exam. I wandered over to the window, looked out. The hair on the back of my neck stood up;, those two arseholes were making their way into the building. The maintenance team was refurbing the screen-printing facility, it was chaos, I hoped security was still good enough to keep them out. It was also the last night of the current art room set up. If I did not get my painting out that night it was going to be binned. I began to worry. Did those guys see me coming into college? I couldn't concentrate on the class, all I could think about was keeping out of sight as I knew they'd be scanning all of the rooms to find me. I spotted them wandering into the room next-door and bolted out of the room I was in.

My nerves were shredded. I made sure they didn't see me leaving, ran downstairs, massive picture and frame under my arm, headed for home.

It was now very dark, I decided to take the long, but presumably safer dark road, shitting it at every corner, arms tiring by the second. I cursed myself for doing those stupid press-ups, I was paying for it now.

I thought I spotted them on a couple of occasions and took bigger detours, eventually making my way through the graveyard. I couldn't see a thing, but heard enough noises to make me leave remnants of my last meal on my underpants.

I managed to get back safely, couldn't move my arms for three days after, though.

Chapter 33

The sunshine of my happiness blew everything away, there was nothing left to cast any shadows, those dark recesses of my past were illuminated by it. Joy filled me like never before, it was like everything in my life, my hard, difficult choices had all converged at the right point and come up trumps. In the space of ten days everything changed, I mean everything.

I'd had a particularly good training session with Willie.

Ken, the team manager approached us both at the end of the session.

'Good work out there boys,' he said. 'Now for the good news, you've both been chosen for the British League Division One match in London.' He shook our hands, we were delighted.

'What event, boss?' Willie said.

'I'm afraid the eight hundred slots have gone, I've pencilled you both in for the four by four hundred; how does that sound?'

'Fine,' we chorused.

This was my first ever away match, the fact that it was in London in the top UK division was amazing. Allan Wells was also in the team, he lived in London, so Willie was going to introduce me to him when the team got together. I was ecstatic, I thought back only a couple of years, remembered my efforts to make starting blocks from an old door-frame, laughed out loud.

'What are you laughing at?' Willie said.

I told him about the blocks, how I used to jump over park benches for hurdle practice. We laughed as we warmed down. We were both delighted that our training was paying off.

Two days later, on the Thursday, John called me up, asked

me to get the band together. He'd met up with Cliff, our new manager, who'd arranged a very nice gig for us. I called the guys, Wee Chris McArthur, Scotty, Billy D, Brian, Gary and Malcolm. Arranged to meet in the Velvet Coat, at Seven. We met John and Tam there.

'Where's Cliff?' I said to John as I stood at the bar getting the drinks in.

'He's up at the Nightclub, arranging our gig for Saturday week,' he said, smiling.

'What?' I said. '*THE* Nightclub?'

'Yip, *THE* Nightclub.'

'Ya beauty. How did he manage that?'

'No idea,' John said. 'He said he had contacts, it looks like he really does.'

'Wait till the lads hear,' I said. 'Malcolm will shit himself.'

We'd picked Cliff up as a manager about a month earlier. We'd been doing some small gigs around town, people seemed to like the stuff we were playing, we had a following of a couple of hundred fans, it felt great. The smaller venues were always sold out, that made us look like we had a bigger fan base. Cliff had been at a few of our gigs, liked what he heard. He introduced himself to us after a particularly good gig in a hugely New Romantic crowd at Valentino's.

'So, who's the boss-man?' He said, in a Jamaican or Caribbean drawl.

John pointed to me.

'See Jim, he's the band leader.'

'Nah,' I said, 'I'm too busy with other things to get into any contract talks. Can you take it on, John?'

'OK.'

John had chatted with Cliff for a good forty minutes, by that time we'd packed all of the gear into the van. John came back over after we'd finished, told us we might have a manager, everyone was neither up nor down with the news. I'd been doing most of the writing and arranging and getting gigs was something that just happened.

'How'd it go then?' I said.

'He wants us to sign a contract.'

'When?' I said.

'He's going to draw it up next week, let us see it before we sign.'

'That's good of him,' I said.

In the Velvet Coat we went upstairs with the drinks, the guys were sitting there, wondering what the hell was going on.

'Listen to this, guys,' I said putting the beers down, pointing to John.

'Well? What is it?' Billy said.

'We've got a big gig a week on Saturday.'

'Where?' Chris said.

'The Nightclub.'

Everyone looked around at each other.

'*THE* Nightclub?'

'Yes, we've been through this.' John said. 'But the even better news is that Depeche Mode are playing there the night before, we've got front row tickets.'

Everyone sat there, eyes wide in disbelief, this was by far our biggest opportunity.

'SHIT,' Brian said. 'We'd better get rehearsing.'

'Relax,' I said. 'We know the stuff off by heart, it'll be a breeze.'

Chris and Billy were high fiving each other, Gary sat with his hand on his chin, thinking about the possibilities.

I really couldn't take it all in.

As I sat there sipping my beer I pinched myself, things were going too right.

A shadow floated by me, with my Catholic upbringing I still had the fear lurking around me. With all of this good stuff happening to me it was inevitable that the bad would follow. I expected it would be waiting around the corner for me. I wanted to believe so much that all of my hard work had at last paid off, but couldn't.

I met the Edinburgh Southern Team outside St James' Centre. I recognised a few of them from Meadowbank, there were all shapes and sizes. Long jumpers, high jumpers, hammer throwers, javelin, long distance runners, sprinters. So many shapes for one team. Willie got out of a taxi, headed over to me.

'Ready?' He said.

'Guess so,' I replied. 'I'm a bit nervous, to be honest.'

'Don't worry,' he said, you'll be fine. Your four hundred splits are really good, and you were running much better that me last week, so I'm the one that should be nervous.'

'Ach, let's enjoy it,' I said.

Ken arrived with a big fancy air-conditioned bus.

'I thought we were getting the train down?' I whispered to Willie.

'So did I.'

The door opened, Ken popped his head out. 'Sorry, guys,' he shouted, 'change of plan. We're getting the bus down to Newcastle, picking up the Borders guys on the way. The good news is that we're going first class to London from there.'

There was a cheer, everyone piled onto the bus. I got talking to Tom, a guy I'd been on nodding terms with at the track. He looked a good prospect, a really good middle distance runner.

Tom and I ended up sharing a room as Willie opted to stay with Allan in London. It was a great event, we came second overall, after the first competition we were sitting second in the league. It felt great mixing it with all kinds of top class athletes, I recognised a lot of them from TV.

Our two main sprinters, Elliot and Jamie, had been injured in their warm up. They were meant to be doing the two hundred metres but couldn't, they pulled out with not a lot of time until the race. Ken approached Willie and I as we were eating lunch. There were still a couple of hours until our event, so we had time to eat.

'Hi lads.' He said. 'Nice lunch?'

'It's OK,' I said, 'fancy a sandwich?'

'No, thanks.' He looked a bit nervous. 'Can I ask you both a favour?'

Willie and I looked at each other.

'Guess so,' I said pausing my chewing on the sanny.

'How do you fancy doing the two hundred?'

I almost spat my lunch out.

'What? The two hundred? We'll be annihilated!'

'Yeah,' Willie said, 'Linford's doing the two hundred.'

'I know,' Ken said, 'but if we don't put somebody in, we lose the points; if you two do it then the worst we'll get is a point each from you.'

'For finishing last?' I said.

'I guess so.'

I was up for it, Willie was nervous.

'Come on, Willie,' I said, 'at least it'll be a good warm up for the four hundred.'

'Yeah, that's true,' he said, nodding.

'Great,' Ken said, patting me on the back.

'When is the two hundred?' I asked him.

'Half an hour, get your numbers from Stuart. Thanks, boys.'

He winked, headed off with his clipboard under his arm.

Half an hour later, I found myself on the starting line of the two hundred metres at Crystal Palace. I was two lanes away from Linford Christie. I was in lane one, which was way too tight for my long lanky legs, I could see him going through his routine in lane three. Willie and I had tossed a coin to see who would be A string and B string. Willie got A string but looked too nervous, so I said I'd do it. I was enjoying myself, had nothing to lose. The starter called us all up to the line. I got down on my hunkers, shaking my head, laughing. Again, I thought about that night at St Mark's Park with those door-frame starting blocks and the six-inch nails.

One of the officials had brought a set of real fancy blocks over for me.

'Here you are, sir,' he said.

'No thanks, pal,' I said. 'I won't be needing them.'

'Sure?'

'Yeah, definitely, I wouldn't even know where to put the batteries,' I joked.

'They don't have batteries, sir,' he said, not getting it.

'Only kidding.'

I settled down, and was really mimicking the sprinters doing their strange drills. I turned a couple of times to Willie, as I was completely lost; he was still nervous, but smiled at my antics.

The starter blew his whistle, we all got stripped. I knew I was putting nothing on the line. If I finished the race I'd put my first ever point on the board for Edinburgh Southern Harriers, simple as that. If I beat Linford, then headiness would be mine. I toyed with the idea of winning, but was snapped out of it by another whistle.

I got into position. I wanted only one thing. I'd give Linford a fright, I'd get to the first bend, make him notice me, then I knew I'd fade away into the back of the pack, I didn't have the speed endurance that these guys had been working on for years.

On paper I was only two or three seconds slower than them.

'On your marks ...' Silence in the stadium, all eyes on Linford. The sprinters were twitching in their blocks.

'Get set ...'

Tension built; I felt none of it.

'GO.'

I was off, sprinting as fast and hard as I could from the white line. The tartan track felt smooth as my spikes ripped through the surface, the rubber crumbs flew in all directions as I thrust my accelerator to the floor. I looked up, was already ten metres down on these guys, I pumped my arms, legs, everything.

I demanded speed from my body, but even though I was going as fast as I could, all I could see was sprinters' afterburners. I seemed to be going in slow motion by comparison. I was so aware of how far two seconds difference was, it was a mile! I finished the race in last place. Not the first time I'd been there.

I wasn't embarrassed, I reckoned I'd do the same thing to Linford, in fact I was sure I'd finish at least ten seconds ahead of him if he ran an eight hundred metres.

Willie finished last in his race as well. We warmed down, had a laugh, got ready for our event later on, feeling much more relaxed.

We got home late Sunday night, I was a changed man.

Turnbull's Tornadoes was a distant memory, I had a renewed confidence. It permeated through me, my whole being was more complete after that weekend, I felt like I had something to offer, the fact that I was about to play in a great venue with my band helped. I'd told a few of the Southern Harriers about the gig, they said they'd come along. I was getting respect from these top athletes, they were sure I'd be a pop star soon.

'You're wasted running for ESH.' Some of them said.

Depeche Mode were brilliant, they'd released their first album, I remember the cover was a swan wrapped in cling film, I thought it was a bit strange but the music was incredible. I wanted to write stuff like that.

We were right at the front of the stage, amazing. Cliff tried to get us into the backstage party, but failed.

Saturday came, we were all up for a great night. As we walked up to the venue there was a big queue forming,

'Is that for us?' I said to John.

'Looks like it.'

'There's more people here than the Depeche Mode concert.'

'I know, how good is that?'

We walked through the crowd, the doorman let us in as John flashed the pass that Cliff had given him. We walked in, chests puffed up like mating pigeons.

'Look at the burds,' Chris said. 'We're aw gonnae get our holes the night.'

We did a quick sound check, we were first on, being the headline act, it felt great. We sounded so slick, the mixing desks were top notch, not quite as big and electronic looking as last night's gig, but they had more money than us. Still, it was the best we'd ever sounded. I was positioned way up high on a podium, two keyboards sat in front of me, we could hear the loud murmuring of the crowd behind the curtains. Nerves jangled in anticipation.

As the noise died down, we looked around at each other, thumbs up all around.

The curtains drew open, there was a roar, we kicked into action with a massive bass line from Brian, Chris waited, then thumped his bass drum, hit on the snare in perfect time. The crowd knew the song, the roar almost knocked us off the stage. As I played the keyboards, I made the mistake of looking down at my fingers, they were jumping all over the place. I'd played these songs for ages and only realised now, how complex they looked, I stood there mesmerised at the speed and agility of my fingers.

I tried to calm myself down, I was aware that I had to forget what I was looking at, concentrate on letting my hands do what they wanted. As I hit the high notes a big red light blasted onto my shoulder. It hurt. Burned like sunburn. I winced but had to keep playing. I hit the high notes again, as the song required, got burned again. I realised that the lighting guys had wired the sound-to-light boxes up to respond to my high notes. The next song used the top end of the keyboard, by this time I could feel my shoulder burning beneath my shirt. I tried to manoeuvre myself around in order to avoid the lights, but it kept flashing, on and on, burning me with every pulse. I was almost crying with the pain, but I couldn't let the guys down.

We were awesome, the crowd was indeed much bigger than the previous night, it felt amazing.

I got down off the platform, went straight to the loo, I took my shirt off, ran the cold tap over my shoulder for a good ten to fifteen minutes, it took ages to heal.

A few days later my shoulder was still burning when I went to meet the boss of one of Scotland's top ad agencies. I was going to be interviewed for a job as an art director. I'd been writing letters to all of the ad agencies, graphic design studios and art houses in Edinburgh. I was into the last few weeks of my diploma, had no idea what I was going to do after it was finished.

About two weeks before I was due to leave I heard about a group of my fellow students who'd been invited up to all of these agencies to try out with some briefs and ideas. It was called the creative workshop. I'd been so busy at band practice and training that I had no time for after college activities. I asked if I could join them and was told I'd have to be invited.

I found out how to make this happen, got the invite just in time as they were having their penultimate meeting. I went along to Marr Associates, in George Street. They were stunning offices, fourth floor, nice big boardroom, all done out like a Gary Numan video, black and red all over.

I'd never been tested like this before. A group of top art directors, graphic designers and copywriters sat around drinking beer, briefing us on their expectations. I got nervous. They gave everyone an A3 pad and a couple of felt pens. We all sat around this huge round black table, waited on the sheets of paper being passed around with the details of the job. We had half an hour to complete the task. The brief told us that we had to create a billboard poster for Black Heart Rum. It had to appeal to a certain category of people, had to be big, bright and bold. I sat there scribbling. All of those times I'd spent asking the kids to tell me something to draw were paying off. I got a good half-dozen ideas down and was really getting into it when one of the designers came in, said stop.

All of us let out a huge sigh of relief.

'Right, guys, I'll collect your ideas, take them through to the main office, we can discuss the ones that work and the ones that don't,' said a tall man with a white panama hat. We had to show our ideas in front of about fifteen professional people. I was gobsmacked, they'd selected one of my ideas as the ad of the night. I was so chuffed on a lot of different levels, it gave my confidence a massive injection. Three life-changing confidence boosts in a very short space of time.

I was so different inside.

I had arrived. I knew who I was and what I was good at.

Before we headed out we were given a brief to complete by the following Tuesday, something much more complex. As I was heading out of the office the big guy in the panama hat called me back.

'I like your style,' he said.

'Thanks, I appreciate the compliment, Mr. Marr,' I said.

'Colin. Call me Colin. In fact why don't you come and see me next week? I got your letter a few weeks ago, it's on my desk in a short-list. My secretary will call you tomorrow, arrange a date and time if that's OK?'

My Adam's apple plunged and rose so quickly that I squeaked, 'Yeah, that would be brilliant.' I shook his hand vigorously, skipped out of the door.

I sat in the black leather swivel chair in the slick office before the interview, looking at the massive wall in front of me. It was covered in framed awards, looked like they were for all kinds of things, but the words that kept cropping up were best creative, best art direction, best design … The boardroom looked like it was a set-up, how could a small company like this win all of these international awards? It shouldn't be possible.

I sat in the chair, swinging from side to side. The room overlooked the George Hotel. I wondered if I still had any residual pain from my time there, but all I felt was relief. Colin came in, he had a cowboy hat on this time and a white canvas suit. He cut an impressive figure.

At his back was a small fat guy with a comb-over. He reached over to me, hand out.

'Tarquin,' he said.

I reached out, shook hands with him.

'Tarquin is our top copywriter,' Colin said. 'Do you mind if he sits in?'

'No, not at all.'

Colin had a black case in his hand, it was a portfolio. He opened it up, he and Tarquin talked me through their ads, most of which had won awards all over the world. I was so impressed. But in all honesty most of the ideas went over my head.

'We think you've got what it takes,' Colin said to me.

'Thanks,' I said, 'but I could never do anything as clever as any of that stuff, it's way too sophisticated for me.'

'That's true,' Tarquin chipped in, 'but we're not after the finished article, we want a diamond in the rough. Colin showed me your Black Heart ideas, I think they're great.'

'But I don't have any ideas left,' I said. 'Well, not many.'

They both laughed for a long time. Colin held his hand out while laughing, indicating to me that they were not laughing at me.

'I'm laughing because I was exactly the same,' he said.

'How do I get more ideas then?'

'I bet you think your brain is like a reservoir of ideas,' Tarquin said.

'Yes,' I said.

'Isn't it?'

'Nope.'

He said, 'The more ideas you work with, the more ideas you generate. It's like a momentum thing, once you start it takes over. If that's your biggest worry, then you're a lucky fellow.'

We sat and chinwagged for another hour, then Tarquin left, shaking my hand. 'Hope to see you again,' he said, winking as he went out of the door.

My heart beat really fast at this gesture, did he know something I didn't? Colin and I sat drinking coffee, talking for another three hours. My stomach rumbled as we spoke, I'd come straight from a session at Meadowbank without having anything to eat.

'Is that your stomach?'

'Yes, sorry. I came straight from a training session.'

'You should've said,' he said, getting up from the chair. He went to the door, shouted on Carol, his secretary.

'Call Bar Napoli, Carol, get a couple of pizzas delivered.'

She shouted back, 'What kind?'

Colin popped his head back towards me. 'What do you fancy?'

'Cheese and tomato, please.'

'Nine or twelve inch?'

'Twelve, please, I'm starving.'

'Perfect,' he said. 'Usual for me, Carol. Fancy a beer?'

'Yeah that'd be great.' I said.

'Follow me, then.'

We went through to Colin's spacious modern office, there were ads of all kinds all over the desk, ideas, drawings, some finished artwork, lots of pads and pens. There was a trolley that sat next to his chair full of coloured Pantone pens; I'd bought a couple of these during my college time, they cost a fortune, there must have been a hundred different colours here. It smelled and felt like opulence, everything in the office did, everyone had a glow about them. This was where I wanted to work, this was the only place I ever wanted to work, all the other jobs had been forced upon me through circumstance and lack of skills.

He opened up a big American style fridge, it was packed with every kind of beer, lager and wine imaginable.

'Wow,' I said.

'Courtesy of our clients. Whitbread and Stella give us a delivery every fortnight. Take your pick.'

I picked up an ice-cold bottle of Grolsch, Colin followed suit.

We went back to the boardroom, sat drinking our beer, enjoying the late evening sunshine streaming in through the blinds. I laughed to myself, he caught me.

'What is it?'

'I was thinking, not that long ago I was working over there,' I said, pointing to the George Hotel. 'Getting my hair pulled and my arse kicked by this big galoot from Glasgow.'

'Really?' He said.

'Yeah, I hated it.'

'The job or the kicking?' He said, laughing.

'The job,' I said. 'The kicking was quite therapeutic.'

He laughed hard at that.

Carol came in with the pizzas, mine was lukewarm but it didn't matter. I scoffed it, Colin did the same. No standing on ceremony here, he'd grown up in Bathgate but was now one of the UK's top art directors.

'Anything's possible,' he told me. 'Your history is your history, the only way you can change it is by changing your future.'

It went right over my head. I nodded as I tucked into another slice. We talked about my route to exactly where I was sitting now, it was a long, funny complicated story, Colin laughed at it all.

It was half-past nine at night when I left the building.

As each second passed, I was hoping Colin would tell me I had the job. This had been the easiest, most rewarding interview I'd ever had, it was so natural. I wanted that job so badly. I could see myself in there no problem. Working on great accounts, doing real creative work, winning awards! I couldn't grasp that what they did here was even work. It was fun, exciting, cutting edge, everything you'd do as a hobby, never mind getting paid for it.

I thought about one of the first interviews I'd had as a designer, the one at the funeral director's place. I thought about how far I'd come since that day when I'd ripped my portfolio to ribbons, kicked it down some stairs. I felt something inside that I'd never felt before; this job was meant for me, if it was taken away from me I would be devastated, I felt like I belonged, the sense of loss would be more than I could bear.

A couple of guys at college had got jobs in the past few weeks, but they were going to be working in the Council graphics department or in the University. I'd spent two weeks in Edinburgh Uni's graphics department, almost fell asleep the moment I walked in. Beards, pipes, slippers and hot chocolate was not my idea of cutting edge design. The only time I'd ever raised my heart rate at that place was one Friday evening, they gave me keys to the ancient building in Buccleuch Street. I stayed on after everyone had gone home to do some illustration work, they had an amazing airbrush and compressor that I was allowed to use.

It was in the basement. I got everything set up, ready to begin. It was dark down there, and eerily quiet. As I switched the noisy compressor on I felt a chill down the back of my neck. I turned it off, walked over to the door, to make sure it was shut. It was. I went back, as I was about to switch it back on a figure passed right in front of me. Hair stood up all over my body. I saw a man dressed in an old leather smock, he looked like a blacksmith. I did a double take, to see if there was a door I hadn't noticed before. There was no door. I shit myself, I'm not sure if I screamed but I ran up those stairs quicker than ever.

I left the doors open, ran a mile, literally. I phoned my brother Gordon up, only when he arrived would I go back down to switch the lights off.

I didn't want to be like them, all preparing themselves for a life of sleepy contentment. I didn't want a job, I wanted the Marr job, the job that wasn't a job.

I'd written letters to everyone in the phone book that interested me, had hardly any replies to date. I thought, for some reason, of one of the guys from college – Dougie.

One day, towards the end of our time at college, Miss Lindsay decided to have a show and tell day.

I brought in a tape of some of the band's songs, it was a bit scratchy but it did the trick.

Dougie came in, sat two empty looking specimen jars on Miss Lindsay's desk.

Most people wandered up to them. I saw there was a sticker, on each, roughly drawn in blue biro. One said; 'Mexico – June 1970', the other 'Berlin – April 1945'. That one had a couple of black hairs caught in the lid.

'What the fuck are these meant to be?' Bobby Nimmo, the class's cool guy, said to him.

Dougie slapped a ruler off the desk, making sure he had everyone's attention. He stood behind the desk, lifted the Mexico one up.

'This, my friends, is the air from the ball used in the 1970 World Cup final.'

'Fuck off,' Bobby said.

'I swear it,' Dougie said. 'I bought it from a guy in Edinburgh. He knows Pele.'

He then held up the other one, then passed it to Nimmo. 'Whatever you do, don't open it.'

'What the fuck's in here?' Nimmo said, looking disgustedly at the hair caught in the lid.

'Hitler's last breath,' Dougie said.

'Don't tell me,' Nimmo said, 'You bought it from a guy in Edinburgh.'

I thought of Dougie and guys like him who'd wasted their time in college, basically skiving until their next course, serial educational institute screen savers.

I was really no better off. I was, on the verge of nothing and everything. I wanted to get into Colin's head space, tried to send out telepathic positive thoughts.

Give Jim the job, give Jim the job.

He walked me to the door. As I was heading out I popped my head into Carol's office to say thanks for the pizza. I hadn't set eyes on her yet, only heard her voice. She was good looking, glasses, nice figure, very secretarial.

'Thanks for the pizza, Carol,' I said.

'You're welcome, good night,' she said.

Colin shook my hand firmly.

'I really enjoyed our chat,' he said, 'you've got something.'

'A job?' I said, half joking.

'A good grasp on life and a really creative brain. I'll have to go through all of the candidates' CVs and get back to you. I've still got a couple of people to see, but you never know.'

He waited with me until the lift came. 'Well, cheerio then,' he said. 'All the best.'

My heart sank as he said this; had I fallen flat again after all that hope and my desperation to work there? I got to the ground floor, walked out into a warm George Street. Headed home thinking that I'd lost out again. As I walked down the hill into the New Town the sun caught my shoulder, making me wince. I'd completely forgotten about the pain for all those hours. Of the three amazing things that had happened to me, this was the one I wanted most. The band was great, but it was only fun, we had earned nothing the whole time we'd been playing together, in fact it was costing us money to keep going, money that I no longer had access to.

Athletics was brilliant as well, but again, there was no money in it. If I was to ever earn money from the sport I'd be classed as a professional, never be allowed to compete again in any Scottish Athletics Association events. I'd end up in the Borders running against people on grass tracks, probably be handicapped out of the winnings.

My head was down as I slunk back home. I still had another fifteen to twenty companies that I'd yet to hear from. Things could still be good.

The next day I walked into the house after a long run.

'There was a man on the phone for you,' Mum said.

'Who was it?'

'I don't know, he never said.'

'Did he leave a number?'

'Yeah, here it is.' She leaned over to the coffee table, handed me a scrap of paper with an Edinburgh number on it.

'Thanks, Mum.' I said. 'Did the guy sound hopeful?'

'What do you mean, hopeful?'

'You know, if it was a job interview, did it sound like he was going to offer me it?'

'What are you on about?' She said, really confused by the question.

'Och, it doesn't matter.'

I took the paper, ran upstairs. I pulled the plastic folder out from under my bed; it had copies of all the letters I'd sent and a whole pile of papers with contact details for all of the companies I'd written to. I frantically dug out the Marr Associates letter, looked at the phone number, desperately hoping it would be the same. It wasn't, it was a Leith number. I was flat again.

Jeez, my emotions had been up and down like a hoor's knickers, I didn't know how much more I could stand. If I didn't get a job soon I'd be on the dole again and after all that I'd been through that was the last thing I wanted. I had a week to go at college, all of my friends were getting jobs, some in design some as illustrators, some wanted nothing to do with the subject they'd spent years studying. I went for a wash, got changed had a cuppa and some toast, sat in my room listening to OMD's new album. It was quite moody, suited me perfectly.

I looked at the scrap of paper that I'd brought up with me. I called the number, it rang a couple of times, then a young girl's voice answered.

'Hello,' she said.

'Hi. My mum got a call earlier on, but I wasn't in.'

'Uhuh?' She said. 'Who are you?'

'Who are you?' I said.

'Melissa.'

'Melissa who?'

'Marr.'

Butterflies jumped all round my stomach, then into my

mouth, I couldn't speak.

'Are you still there?' She said.

'Yeah, sorry,' I said. 'Can I speak to your dad?'

'Hold on,' she said. I heard her shouting on Colin but wasn't sure if I wanted to hear what he had to say, I couldn't bear it if it was rejection, it would end me. I heard a lot of noise, extension phones being lifted and clicked, eventually there was one clear line.

'Hello?'

It was Colin, his voice clear and strong.

'Hi, it's Jim Divine.' Voice shaking with utter fear.

'Hi, Jim, how's it going?'

'OK. I think.'

'I've been trying to get you all night. Out and about, were you?'

'Yeah, had a long run to do.'

'Good stuff,' he said. I could tell he was shaping up to announce something that would one way or another be life changing for me.

I held my breath …

'When can you start?' He said.

CHAPTER 34

That phone call changed everything. Before it my life was on the same trajectory, stumbling upon jobs and situations I'd no real control over, accepting them as part and parcel of my lot, going nowhere.

Now I'd earned the first real reward in my life. I'd gone in search of a dream, and for most of that time it seemed it was a dream too far.

Not only had I made that dream real, I'd topped it by securing a unique position in one of the most sought after companies in the country. I was ecstatic. I couldn't get my head around this, I was about to do something I loved and be paid a handsome salary in return.

Chapter 35

As I closed the door behind me at 54 Claremont Court on the first morning of my new life, I felt like I was a different person. The shackles, problems and old skin of Jimmy Divine were evaporating with every step I took towards George Street. I could feel the love and warmth emanating from the soft golden sandstone of those ancient buildings that I'd passed most days in my life. In the past they'd felt like huge constricting slabs of cold, hard stone, scowling down on me, forcing me gauntlet-like to school, my workplace or the dole office. Now they resembled a bright, shining New York cityscape. I imagined a crowd cheering, a ticker-tape parade with beautiful women blowing kisses to me, acknowledging my tenacity and endurance.

The sun beat down on me that early summer morning, life had never felt sweeter, my possibilities were boundless.

I was dressed in my very own suit and shoes, portfolio in hand, head held high. I smiled all the way to work. I opened the main door, passed the little smoked glass coffee table with the day's papers, fresh coffee and croissants laid out, their aromas wafting sweetly into the air. I walked back, picked up a warm croissant, took a deep satisfying breath and headed to the elevator.

Hope, fear and excitement roared inside me like a furnace.

I took a few deep breaths, stepped into the elevator and pressed the button for the top floor.

The Lost Tornado

Jim Divine is (at last:) an Award Winning
Graphic Designer and Photographer.
He lives in the old Mining Village of Newtongrange
with his Wife Trish.

For more information visit: www.TheLostTornado.com
or Email: Jim@TheLostTornado.com

If you enjoyed **The Lost Tornado** please
give it a review on
Amazon.co.uk
Thank you. This means a lot to me.

:) Jim

48362857R00237

Made in the USA
Charleston, SC
01 November 2015